The Hyperlinked Society

Joseph Turow
SERIES EDITOR

Broadcasting, Voice, and Accountability: A Public Interest
Approach to Policy, Law, and Regulation
*Steve Buckley, Kreszentia Duer, Toby Mendel, and Seán Ó Siochrú,
with Monroe E. Price and Marc Raboy*

Owning the Olympics: Narratives of the New China
Monroe E. Price and Daniel Dayan, editors

The Hyperlinked Society: Questioning Connections in the Digital Age
Joseph Turow and Lokman Tsui, editors

DIGITALCULTUreBOOKS
is a collaborative imprint of the University of Michigan Press and
the University of Michigan Library.

The Hyperlinked Society: Questioning Connections in the Digital Age

Joseph Turow and Lokman Tsui, Editors

THE UNIVERSITY OF MICHIGAN PRESS &
THE UNIVERSITY OF MICHIGAN LIBRARY
ANN ARBOR

Copyright © by Joseph Turow and Lokman Tsui 2008
All rights reserved
Published in the United States of America by
The University of Michigan Press
Manufactured in the United States of America
♾ Printed on acid-free paper

2011   2010   2009   2008   4   3   2   1

A CIP catalog record for this book is available from the British Library.

Library of Congress Cataloging-in-Publication Data

Turow, Joseph.
   The hyperlinked society : questioning connections in the digital
age / edited by Joseph Turow and Lokman Tsui.
      p.   cm.
   Includes bibliographical references and index.
   ISBN-13: 978-0-472-07043-5 (cloth : alk. paper)
   ISBN-10: 0-472-07043-6 (cloth : alk. paper)
   ISBN-13: 978-0-472-05043-7 (pbk. : alk. paper)
   ISBN-10: 0-472-05043-5 (pbk. : alk. paper)
   1. Internet—Social aspects.   2. Digital media—Social aspects.
I. Tsui, Lokman. II. Title.

HM851.T87   2008
303.48'33—dc22   2008002885

Contents

PART 3. Hyperlinks, the Individual and the Social

JOSEPH TUROW

Introduction: On Not Taking the Hyperlink for Granted

At the end of the first decade of the twenty-first century, a computer user searching on the Web is unlikely to consider the enormous achievement represented by the highlighted links that beckon from the screen. In 1945, by contrast, Vannevar Bush was excited just to imagine the possibility of a hyperlink. He saw it as opening new gates to human understanding.

An MIT-trained electrical engineer who cofounded Raytheon in the 1920s, Bush headed the Office of Scientific Research and Development during World War II, the office that oversaw the development of radar, the proximity fuse, and the atomic bomb. Afterward, as the main force behind the establishment of the National Science Foundation, he pushed the federal government to fund what he called "The Endless Frontier." What was needed, he said, was a scientific establishment that would contribute to the public good by devoting itself to questions of the utmost national and international importance. For Bush, figuring out how to create an instant intertextual link was one of those world-historical questions.[1]

In the July 1945 *Atlantic Monthly* magazine, Bush asked what sorts of problems would most challenge physicists after the war. His answer: the need to keep track of the growing mass of specialized publications that were, in his opinion, making it impossible for scientists to learn about studies in other fields that might help them solve society's problems. He asserted that "our methods of transmitting and reviewing the results of research are generations old and by now totally inadequate." He complained that indexes, the dominant method of pointing people to information, were too limited in their categorization of knowledge and too far from the texts they were citing to be useful as creative sparks. He added that the human mind "operates by association." The best way to build knowledge, then, would be to create links between recorded ideas that could be retrieved and passed on.

This basic idea was not unprecedented. For centuries, the publishers of the Talmud have, for example, linked individual phrases in the text with the opinions of select commentators about those phrases. They have placed the commentators' works in a frame around the Talmudic text, making it easy for readers to go back and forth between one and the other set of writings. Bush's idea, however, was to link all types of textual knowledge in a continual, unfolding manner, and he saw science—a major cause of the knowledge "problem"—as the source of solutions. He himself conceived of a *memex*—a desk that combined a microfilm reader, screen, special electronic tubes, and a keyboard—that would allow the user to insert code to link any point in a microfilmed document to any other point. The reader could retrieve those connections at will, pass it along to anyone else with a memex, and buy knowledge with prerecorded linkages. It would, he asserted, open a new world of understanding:

> Wholly new forms of encyclopedias will appear, ready made with a mesh of associative trails running through them, ready to be dropped into the memex and there amplified. The lawyer has at his touch the associated opinions and decisions of his whole experience, and of the experience of friends and authorities. The patent attorney has on call the millions of issued patents, with familiar trails to every point of his client's interest. The physician, puzzled by a patient's reactions, strikes the trail established in studying an earlier similar case, and runs rapidly through analogous case histories, with side references to the classics for the pertinent anatomy and histology. The chemist, struggling with the synthesis of an organic compound, has all the chemical literature before him in his laboratory, with trails following the analogies of compounds, and side trails to their physical and chemical behavior.
>
> The historian, with a vast chronological account of a people, parallels it with a skip trail which stops only on the salient items, and can follow at any time contemporary trails which lead him all over civilization at a particular epoch. There is a new profession of trail blazers, those who find delight in the task of establishing useful trails through the enormous mass of the common record. The inheritance from the master becomes, not only his additions to the world's record, but for his disciples the entire scaffolding by which they were erected.

One can easily sense the excitement that Bush experienced when thinking about the implications of these retrievable associative trails.

Other technologists eventually began to share his enthusiasm for these new modes of connection as well, and in the mid-1960s, the writer and technology philosopher Ted Nelson coined the term *hyperlinks* to describe them. Nelson also began to sketch ideas about how the rather crude model of the memex that Bush laid out could work on contemporary computer systems. In particular, Nelson conceptualized the link in relation to specific text strings rather than whole pages and emphasized the value of a worldwide computer network through which to share the linked materials. Working independently around the same time, a Stanford Research Institute team led by Douglas Engelbart (with Jeff Rulifson as chief programmer) brought the hyperlink concept to fruition, first (in 1966) by connecting items on a single page and then (in 1968) by implementing a way to jump between paragraphs in separate documents.[2]

Those foundational activities paved the way for the links that most Internet users know today—the highlighted words on a Web page that take them to certain other places on the Web. But these "embedded" links are only the tip of an iceberg of types of instant connections. Links have morphed beyond their initial look to function as hot areas (where a picture or graphic are turned into a link), in-line links (where thumbnail photos or other elements are connected from one site to another automatically), tags (that allow people to categorize links), API (application programming interface) mapping "mashups" (where people use data from open-source cartography programs to make maps with links that suit their purposes), and RSS data feeds (that enable users to connect to changing information from sites without going to them directly). And we also see the creation of links that are based not on individual nomination but on the aggregation of opinions. A hyperlink on Google, for example, is the product of a complex computer-driven formula that calculates the popularity of a Web site by noting, among other things, how many sites link to it. The Google example also, of course, points to yet another development: the "industrialization" of the link. The past decade has witnessed the growth of an entirely new business that measures an advertisement's success by an audience member's click on a commercial link. The idea is to entice the user to the advertiser's site, opening a raft of marketing possibilities. And there's more. The growing convergence of digital media means that instant linking is no longer just the province of the Web on the desktop. Already we see interaction among desktop computers, cell phones, PDAs, MP3 players, store payment systems, television sets, digital video recorders, and even billboards.

These sorts of activities validate Bush's intuition about the utility of "associative trails"—though they don't always match his utopian vision of their august intellectual purpose. In 2006, a *New York Times Magazine* article suggested that the link may be one of the most important inventions of the last fifty years. For links are not only ubiquitous; they are the basic forces that relate creative works to one another for fun, fame, or fortune. Through links, individuals and organizations nominate what ideas and actors should be heard and with what priority. They also indicate to audiences which associations among topics are worthwhile and which are not. Various stakeholders in society recognize the political and economic value of these connections. Corporations, governments, nonprofits and individual media users often work to privilege certain ideas over others by creating and highlighting certain links and not others. The fact that the Federal Trade Commission's Web site, for example, highlights links to reports with certain approaches to privacy protection and not to others not only reflects the commission's political views' but may also bolster those views by pointing the public toward certain ideas at the expense of others. Through these sorts of activities, linking affects the overall size and shape of the public sphere.

Any discussion of how to promote a healthy society offline as well as online must therefore pay close attention to links. The aim should be to facilitate the widest possible sharing of varied, reliably sourced information in order to encourage specialized groups and society as a whole to confront their past and present in relation to the future. With a cornucopia of new media technologies and millions of Web sites and blogs, it would be easy to assume this goal is imminent. Yet a wide range of critics has lamented that this is not in fact the case. Some claim that both mainstream and nonestablishment sectors of the digital media target people who already agree with them, by producing content that reinforces, rather than challenges, their shared points of view. Other critics claim that media users themselves show little inclination toward diverse ideas. On the contrary, they tend to use the Web to confirm their own worldviews—for example, by going to political blogs with which they sympathize politically or even by ignoring news on the Web and on TV altogether.

How should we understand these claims that linking is not living up to its possibilities? What evidence do we have for them? What are the political, economic, and social factors that guide linking in mainstream media firms and among individual actors such as bloggers and wikipedians? What should we expect audiences to know about links? What *do* they know, and what do they want? And, finally, what new research approaches are needed to (1) track the various considerations that drive the creation of particular links and not others, (2) map the various vectors of knowledge and power that digital connections establish, and (3) understand how people interact with the connection possibilities that call out to them in various media?

The essays in this collection engage these questions and others in their attempts to understand the social meaning of the hyperlink. The project started as a conference called "The Hyperlinked Society" that I convened at the University of Pennsylvania's Annenberg School for Communication on Friday, June 9, 2006. With the support of the John D. and Catherine T. MacArthur Foundation and the Annenberg Public Policy Center, about two hundred people from around the United States as well as Canada, China, the Netherlands, Israel, Australia, Germany, and England came together to address the social implications of instant digital linking. The guiding assumption of the meeting was that we need cross-disciplinary thinking to do justice to this multifaceted subject. Our panelists therefore included renowned news, entertainment, and marketing executives; information architects; bloggers; cartographers; audience analysts; and communication researchers. The audience, also quite accomplished, participated enthusiastically.

We did not intend to solve any particular problem at the meeting. Instead, the goal was to shed light on a remarkable social phenomenon that people in business and the academy usually take for granted. Just as important, the conference made clear that although research exists on other aspects of hyperlinking (most notably the mapping of Web interconnections), key aspects of the linked world have yet to be explored systematically. In keeping with this, many of the participants commented on the need to promote greater awareness of and discussion about the world of fascinating issues surrounding the instant digital link.

By bringing together essays from several of the conference panelists, all of which were commissioned and written in the months after the event, this collection aims to begin/catalyze/jump-start this larger discussion. When Alison Mackeen at the University of Michigan Press, who attended the conference, suggested that we consider a related book project, Lokman Tsui and I checked again to find that there are indeed very few writings about the economic, cultural, political, or general social implications of instantaneous digital linking. We thus asked our contributors to write essays that would encourage thinking and research on an aspect of contemporary life that is so central that it is often taken for granted. The aim was not to drill deeply into particular research projects. It was, rather, to write expansively, provocatively—even controversially—about the extent to which and ways in which hyperlinks are changing our worlds and why. In short, we hope that this book will function as a platform from which others—professors, graduate students, lawmakers, corporate executives—will launch their own research projects and policy analyses.

We thank the contributors for rising magnificently to this challenge. Each essay contains enough ideas to spark a multitude of other writings and research projects. Moreover, various implicit conversational threads wind their way through the material, as each of the seventeen authors references issues discussed elsewhere in the book. Reading through the essays several times, I was struck by a Vannevar-Bush-like desire to place "associative trails" onto pages so that the reader could jump to other places in the book that question or confirm or rethink the ideas just expressed. We've actually begun to do that in the online version of this book, and we've opened the site up for others to join in as well. So please check it out.

One challenge posed by these interrelated essays was how to organize them. Lokman Tsui and I considered a number of organizing principles, as we moved chapters into different relationships with one another, before deciding on the following three parts: "Hyperlinks and the Organization of Attention," "Hyperlinks and the Business of Media," and "Hyperlinks, the Individual and the Social." The first of these three, "Hyperlinks and the Organization of Attention," focuses on the fundamental nature of hyperlinks and the purposes for which various actors—companies, governments, individuals—create certain links and not others for different/certain types of users. The second part drills down specifically to the considerations that motivate businesses, particularly the news and advertising industries, to use hyperlinks in particular ways. The final section of the book, "Hyperlinks, the Individual and the Social," asks what we know and need to find out about hyperlinks' roles in encouraging individuals to think about themselves and their society in certain ways and not others.

As I noted earlier, though, the broad themes of the essays overlap in significant ways, even across the three parts. So, for example, James Webster's piece, "Structuring a Marketplace of Attention," not only introduces the central theme of the first section—how entities organize links and, in turn, command users' attention—but suggests how that theme relates to the business of media as well as the individual and the social. Webster recommends that the reader "think about the hyperlinked environment as a marketplace of attention." Drawing from Anthony Giddens's theory of structuration, he argues that while an examination of the political economy of links indicates that organizational interests shape the array of links that Internet users confront, a step back suggests that users have more power over the system than might first appear. Webster explains that search and recommendation systems, as well as many other collaborative features of the hyperlinked environment, present findings that are not based on the edict of a few dominant organizations but, rather, built "by amassing people's preferences and behaviors." Webster maintains: "No one opinion leader or vested interest is able to dictate the output of these systems; hence they have a compelling air of objectivity. . . . Yet, they create, perpetuate, and/or modify structures that direct the attention of others."

Arguing that "this duality of structure is an essential and increasingly pervasive dynamic of the marketplace," Webster then turns to ask about the "patterns of attention" that the marketplace produces and their possible social consequences. In so doing, he introduces issues that thread through other parts of the book, including (perhaps especially) that of social polarization. Webster notes that some observers are concerned that the structure of linking might lead people to see and follow only those connections that match their own narrow interests and political opinions. But he doesn't take a definitive stand on how realistic this worry is. Instead, he ties the concern back to his main theme: that the aggregated "actions of agents" through links are profoundly influencing "the structures and offerings of the media environment." Webster's piece is a nice setup for the various voices that follow—voices that agree with him, disagree with him, or take some of his points in new directions.

Alex Halavais does a bit of all three of these things. One way he moves the discussion forward is to provide a historical perspective on linking's so-called curse of the second order. That is the idea that once people considered measures of hyperlink popularity important, they worked to game the results in their favor. One sensational result is "Google bombing," a technique used by angry groups to associate a keyword search with a Web site. So, for example, an organized campaign led to Google's association of the word *failure* with a biography of George W. Bush. More mundane but also more long-lasting is another result: namely, that "an entire industry has grown up around the manipulation of search engine results." In emphasizing this development, Halavais is pointing out that the aggregated "actions of agents" that Jim Webster foregrounds are not necessarily as innocent or democratically created as they sometimes appear. In so doing, he identifies a tension that threads through many of the essays in this collection, between the recognition that link patterns might sometimes be the uncoordinated results of various desires and the awareness that they might also reflect a struggle for power by corporate, government, or advocacy interests to lead people toward certain sites—and certain worldviews—and not others.

The essays by Philip Napoli, Lokman Tsui, Eszter Hargittai, and Seth Finkelstein focus in different ways on the manipulation of links in the service of power. Napoli brings a political economy perspective to bear on the broad claim that links are among the primary tools that big media firms use in their attempts to gain the kind of power in the Internet world that they enjoyed before its ascent. He makes a case generally that "the technological forces compelling a new medium such as the Internet to defy the confines of traditional media are counteracted to some degree by a number of countervailing social and institutional forces that clearly are influencing both the structure of the online realm and the ways that consumers navigate the online space." Turning specifically to hyperlinks, he argues that emerging research supports the political economy logic that "the imbalances in content accessibility and prominence that characterize the traditional mass media world are being replicated in the online world."

Along the way to this conclusion, Napoli offers several provocative assertions about the workings of power in the online world. He cites, for example, Jonathan Zittrain's remark that in the online world, "the dynamics of the gatekeeping process have changed significantly, perhaps becoming a bit more covert." In a related vein, he notes that hyperlinking "serves as a primary mechanism via which an online provider exerts control over its audience and . . . manages 'audience flow.'" An examination of these issues is crucial to understanding the relationship between linking and social power; and while Napoli provides an introductory framework for examining them, Tsui, Hargittai, and Finkelstein engage and extend them more deeply. Lokman Tsui presents a comparative examination of the manner in which newspapers and blogs control their links. Eszter Hargittai sketches both various ways entities try to use links to exploit individuals online and research on the knowledge people need to have in order to resist such exploitation. And Seth Finkelstein focuses on the assumptions that guide what Web users see as important when they explore the Web through contemporary search engines.

All three writers reveal a world behind the links people see—a world that is complex and not easily accessible to most Web users. Lokman Tsui's research deals with the decisions that different sorts of Web publishers make as they point their readers through links to certain worldviews as opposed to others. Tsui finds that the *New York Times* and *Washington Post* point almost exclusively to their own articles, while major blogs link much more frequently beyond themselves—especially to other blogs. His piece raises fascinating questions about the commercial and professional imperatives that might be causing those differences.

Hargittai discusses the commercial and ideological reasons behind splogs—that is, Web sites that include nothing but links. She points out that while search engines are continually involved in a "cat-and-mouse game" with spammers over these sites, Internet users "are caught in the middle, having to deal with the resulting confusion." Noting that "links are at the forefront of how user attention is allocated to content on the Web," Hargittai goes on to point out that researchers have only begun to investigate how users interpret and approach links. Hargittai's own formative work in this area reveals a wide range of expertise among Internet users and suggests that the high degrees of link literacy may be correlated with higher socioeconomic status. One takeaway of her research is, thus, that link literacy may be a key intervening variable for predicting people's ability to navigate online in ways that protect their money and sensitive personal information. Another takeaway is the need for researchers to study the often complex world of links in greater detail.

As Seth Finkelstein sees it, though, the kind of link literacy that Eszter Hargittai rightly would like all Internet users to have is still not enough to correct for basic structural problems in the reasons people confront certain links and not others. Finkelstein's topic is the arcane world of search engine algorithms. Using a number of provocative case studies as illustrations, he worries that Internet users misread Google rankings as indications of authority—and authoritativeness—rather than as simply the indications of popularity that they really are. He notes that the common search assumptions push minority views downward in the rankings, and he suggests that links play a primarily conservative role: "Rather than subvert hierarchy, it's much more likely that hyperlinks (and associated popularity algorithms) reflect existing hierarchies." Thus, he cautions that society must realize that "businesses that mine data for popularity," such as the major search engines, "are not a model for civil society."

In view of the commercial nature of so much of the Web, the business considerations that drive linking are clearly a crucial subject. Part 2 presents essays on hyperlinks and the business of media, by executives who are deeply involved in exploring this relationship. Although they don't answer the questions Tsui's study raises, they nevertheless reveal much of the current and future direction of the Internet and other digital media. The first essay, by Martin Nisenholtz, who leads the *New York Times*'s digital business, provides insight into the profound rethinking that links are forcing on traditional newspaper organizations. The *Times* was in the forefront of newspapers' experimentation with the Web with links as early as 1996. The newspaper's management did not, however, really begin to retool for the new world until after around 2000. *Times* executives recognized that "Web content is part of a huge, swirling 'conversation' taking place across the Internet twenty-four hours a day, seven days a week, in every corner of the earth." Nisenholtz sketches some of the pressures that flow from this basic circumstance, including the realization that up to 40 percent of the online newspaper's readership comes in through links that point to the paper's articles but are unrelated to the *Times*. How to think about those "side-door" readers, how to maximize the time spent on the site by them and (more important) by the 60 percent who go directly to the *Times* site, how to make money from all of this when people don't seem inclined to pay for most of their online news material—these are key issues that speak directly to the challenges faced (often with far more desperation than in the case of the *New York Times*) by newspapers around the world.

With people wandering to so many virtual places, including areas— such as Craigslist—that take profitable classified advertising from traditional papers, management has reason to be deeply concerned. So do executives from the entire spectrum of traditional media—from television, radio, and magazines through yellow pages and billboards—who worry that in coming years, marketers will transfer much of their money to Google, Yahoo, AOL, MySpace, MSN, and a handful of other Web powerhouses that can locate and communicate directly to consumers who fit the exact profile they want. But executives across the media spectrum are not sitting idle. On the contrary, they are acting on their understanding of threats to and opportunities for revenue in the new digital age. Old-style media companies, including the largest conglomerates, are reshaping themselves with new divisions, alliances, and business models.[3]

A large part of their challenge involves persuading marketers to advertise on their sites. Simply attracting consumers may not be enough. As MySpace and YouTube found in 2006 and 2007, many national marketers are wary about placing their ads next to user-generated content of poor quality or taste, which might embarrass the brands. Media executives, then, must develop their plans for the digital environment with the perspectives of advertisers and their agency advisors firmly in mind. As influential actors in this arena, Tom Hespos, Stacey Lynn Schulman, and Eric Picard point to important directions in marketers' approaches to communicating with consumers, with a particular emphasis on links.

Their different suggestions regarding the roads marketers ought to take are complementary rather than conflicting. Tom Hespos asserts that pushing ads toward consumers "becomes less effective year after year," and he applauds companies that are spending the resources to understand how to use "the fundamental shift in the dynamic of human communication brought about by hyperlinking" to have a "conversation" with their target customers. "There are," he states, "millions of conversations taking place right now on the Internet—on blogs, social networks, bulletin boards, and other Internet communities (including virtual worlds like Second Life)—that have something to do with unaddressed needs." Hespos adds that all of these conversations are connected through "the building block we call the hyperlink," and he points out that firms such as Nielsen, Cymfony, and Technorati have built ways for marketers to "listen to these conversations" about their brands. In keeping with this, he exhorts marketers to find more and more ways to have potential customers come to them through links, instead of continuing to try to push old ad formats at them.

Stacey Lynn Schulman would likely endorse Hespos's position wholeheartedly. For her, the challenges that industry strategists face in attempting to understand and persuade consumers are not confined to the declining value of the push commercials that Hespos mentions. They also relate, she states, to the pitfalls of traditional syndicated research about consumers, which "is battling dwindling cooperation rates each year, while fragmented consumer segments demand bigger and better respondent samples." Her alternative goes beyond the auditing of consumer discussion that Hespos urges, into exploration of hyperlink clicks as "a map of actual behavior that expresses not only what purchases we make but what passions and concerns we have." She points out: "Media preferences, brand preferences, attitudinal disposition, and consumption habits are still primarily measured in separate studies by separate research vendors. By following and segmenting the patterns of hyperlinking, they can now be rolled into a single-source, behavioral composite of core consumer segments."

Eric Picard and Marc Smith would probably concur with both Tom Hespos and Stacey Lynn Schulman. Their objectives here are nevertheless different. Picard's aim is to suggest ways to turn the traditional television set into an arm of the digital marketplace, while Smith sees the future mobile phone from that standpoint. Picard sees Americans' relationship with the domestic box changing dramatically in the coming years. The spread of the digital video recorder (DVR) will allow people to record programs; "next-generation cable solutions, such as IPTV, will make almost all content available on demand through a simple set-top box, over a broadband connection"; and "video delivered to mobile devices over wireless broadband and downloaded to handheld media players will flourish, enabling place shifting as well as time shifting of content." To the consumer, this may seem like a cornucopia; but for marketers, it could spell a disastrous difficulty, since the presence of a DVR and digital audiovisual material will make it easier than ever for viewers to skip commercials.

For Picard, though, hyperlinks offer a means of solving this potential problem. First, they make it possible to extend the demographic and behavioral profiling that is conducted on the Web to all media, including digital television, "in completely anonymous and privacy-appropriate ways." Second, they make it possible to serve different commercials to different viewers based on their interests, with the expectation that the matchup will lead the viewer to pay attention. Third, they create interactive formats for those targeted commercials, "giving the audience the ability to hyperlink from a short version of the ad into a longer version of the ad" or letting them connect to lots more information about the product.

If Eric Picard somewhat futuristically sees cross-media information about individuals coming to bear on the ways marketers use digital television to reach them, Marc Smith goes even farther into the future. He conceives of a new form of hyperlink emerging. He calls it a *hypertie* and describes it as a technology, in a smart phone or other mobile device, that allows people to quietly relate their background, interests, and prior encounters with others (people or companies) via inaudible digital communication. Smith points out that collected hypertie data would be a gold mine to academics and marketers, especially because it allows "for the unnoticed and unreflected consumption of content." This is precisely the value that Stacey Lynn Schulman sees in tracing hyperlinks on the Web. But Smith and Picard are extending this same logic to other media domains.

One theme that runs through all the essays of part 2 is that of privacy. Marc Smith's comment about the unobtrusive data-collecting capabilities of futuristic handheld devices brings the issue into stark relief. With such capacities, he states, "privacy issues are sharpened." He concludes, "The

walls have ears and eyes, and others' eyes and ears are now high-fidelity
and archival." In fact, Hespos, Picard, and Schulman also realize that
there is a marked tension between their desire to learn huge amounts
about individuals in the interest of persuading them and the individuals'
desire not to have certain information about themselves shared. In keeping with the latter worry, the authors express a desire for openness about
the data-collection process or for anonymity in using the data. Such comments are, however, made only in passing and with no details. While it
may be comforting to believe that the kind of surveillance of consumers
that these marketers foresee can be carried out with genuine transparency
and anonymity and without controversy, it is not at all clear how such
protections can be implemented or guaranteed.[4] The technologies of privacy as they relate to hyperlinking deserve a lot of attention from executives, policy makers, and academic researchers.

One of the six writers in the final part of the book—Stefaan Verhulst—
does take up the privacy gauntlet. But all the essayists in part 3 deal centrally with another crucial issue of hyperlinking: the nature of the connections that links encourage. David Weinberger starts it off with a
simple statement: "Links are good." In explaining his equating of links
and morality, he presents an elegant disquisition on how to think of
things in terms of goodness, badness, prototypical uses, and moral behavior. He concludes: "The goodness of links comes not from the quality of
the pages they point to or the semantic contexts in which they're embedded. The goodness of links operates at a level below that." That structural
level fulfills a fundamental function of the link, which to Weinberger is
sharing. Weinberger notes, "We send people to another site (assuming
we aren't the sort of narcissists who link only to themselves) where they
can see a bit of the world as it appears to another. . . . Our site probably
explains why we think it will matter to them and how it matters to us,
even if that explanation is 'Here's a trashy site I hate.' Pointing people to
a shared world, letting how it matters to others matter to us—that's the
essence of morality and of linking."

Weinberger's perspective may seem utopian, but he is quick to point
out that while linking provides a potentially invaluable structure for understanding how the world matters to others, the actual implementation
of those connections can, in fact, be positive or negative: "The linked
structure of the Web . . . is a giant affordance that we may do good or bad
with." Although none of the other authors in part 3 puts the issue in such
stark terms, they all grapple with the extent to which hyperlinking, as it is
evolving now, is facilitating or hindering the creation of a pluralistic,

democratic, and caring society. To Stefaan Verhulst and Jeremy Cramp-ton, evaluating the relationship between hyperlinking, individuals, and society comes down to understanding that the patterns of links can be seen as maps of the world that help determine our sense of reality. Be-cause, as Verhulst notes, all maps "contain the biases of their creators," it is important to bear in mind that citizens have historically received their ideas of the world through maps drawn by the authority of rulers. The rise of new mapping technologies, such as Google Earth, provides for the real possibility that members of the public can generate data that they can link to the mapmaking software in order to create alternative versions of the world that highlight the presence of poverty, pollution, and other is-sues that challenge those in power.

Verhulst notes both positive and negative aspects of the new mapping age that hyperlinking to databases has brought. "New maps," he says, "can widen our horizons, build new social and political affiliations, im-prove policy and industry decisions, and democratize perceptions of the world." At the same time, he recognizes that the new technology of the "linked age" can also lead individuals, governments, and corporations to exercise power for such problematic purposes as auditing of people's ac-tivities without their knowing it and presenting useful links selectively, by making them available to some types of people and not others, so as to create "a balkanized landscape of censored information." Thomas Crampton places more emphasis than Verhulst on the favorable impact of the increased democratic control over links. He writes of "a new, populist cartography in which, through new forms of linking, the public is gaining access to the means of producing maps." He presents examples of ways that advocacy groups have linked the free Google Earth and Yahoo Maps to free or inexpensive GIS (geographic information systems) software in the service of causes relating to the environment, disease, and electoral politics. Such activities, he states, are part of "a larger movement of coun-terknowledges that are occurring in the face of ever-increasing corpora-tization of information, such as the consolidation of the news media into the hands of a few global multinationals and their dominance by fairly narrow interests." Unlike Verhulst, Crampton does not emphasize the ability of these global interests to turn link technology against the pop-ulists. The problems he notes involve knowledge barriers: how can poor people with little IT support ever learn to use links to blogs and maps to advance their own interests, and how can those who have the relevant skills be persuaded to promote such learning?

While Crampton and Verhulst point to the possibilities that politically engaged uses of links offer to forces concerned with the equalization of social power, Lada Adamic, Markus Prior, and Matthew Hindman ask what people's everyday activities online suggest about the Web's contribution to pluralism and understanding across socioeconomic classes. Adamic describes her realization that examining vectors of online links made it possible to see "what had been hidden before, the social relationship." Her essay is a personal reflection on her research efforts to understand the link patterns that emerge among people when they engage in different spheres of life—social, commercial, and political. But her overarching theme is that "the hyperlink frequently reveals very real underlying communities" and that some interests, such as cooking or knitting, "have the ability to span cities, if not continents." She stresses, too, that bloggers' approach to the use of links in online interactions is often quite self-reflective, sardonic, and lighthearted. Echoing Weinberger a bit, she muses that "this [self-]awareness and the basic human inclination to take in and share information will continue to shape the hyperlinked landscape of online spaces."

Adamic's association of linking patterns with information sharing also begs a basic question: sharing with whom? Markus Prior poses the question this way: "Can hyperlinks, by connecting people who would otherwise go their separate ways in the sprawling new media landscape, prevent the kind of fragmentation that observers see looming large?" Research by Lada Adamic and Natalie Glance does shed light on this subject. They asked whether conservative blogs link to liberal blogs and vice versa, and they found a quite divided blogosphere. Liberals clearly preferred to link to other liberals, conservatives to other conservatives; only about 10 percent of the links were across the ideological divide. Prior moves the topic forward by asking two questions: "Can anything be done to keep media users from exclusively exposing themselves to ideologically extreme media outlets that offer little information to challenge their existing opinions?" and "Can anything be done to keep media users from ignoring political information altogether?"

Drawing on data from cable television and some early studies of Internet use, Prior's answer, in capsule, is that the problem implied by the first question has been exaggerated, while the difficulty implied by the second question is quite real. He concludes: "In a world where media content of many different genres and subgenres is abundantly available around the clock, tuning out of politics is easy. Hyperlinks could make their greatest contribution to democracy in encouraging the politically uninterested." Marshaling data from Adamic and Glance and others, however, he argues that "this is the function they are least likely to serve."

It is a gloomy assessment that might become still gloomier as a result of the marketing trajectories that Stacey Lynn Schulman, Eric Picard, Tom Hespos, and Marc Smith outline in part 2. Each of these four contributors expects that the future of marketing communication will be about finding out what people are like and what they like and then surrounding them directly and through links with advertising and editorial content based on those calculations. That strategy may well result in people being exposed (rather than exposing themselves) to certain views of the world that reinforce their existing images of themselves and offer little information to challenge their existing opinions. The processes through which this sort of personalization will take place are in their infancy, and it will take decades to learn the ways in which and the extent to which people receive very different views of the world that stifle pluralistic perspectives and conversations.

In the meantime, Matthew Hindman gives us yet another concern to consider regarding sharing and the public sphere. While Prior is centrally concerned with the ideological pluralism of the new media environment, Hindman focuses on source diversity by asking about the number of people who get a chance to be heard in the public sphere. He grants that the Internet is strengthening some democratic values, such as encouraging collective action and public oversight over institutions. Yet, he proposes, the public's ability to make an impression online is vastly overrated. "Many continue to celebrate the Internet for its inclusiveness," he says, but that inclusiveness is "precisely what the online public sphere lacks," and "part of the problem is the extraordinary concentration of links and patterns in online traffic." As Hindman notes, observers of the Web have often suggested that A-list political bloggers attract disproportionate attention. He goes farther, however. Using data from Hitwise, a company that audits Web traffic, he argues that "even the emergence of a blogging A-list barely scratches the surface of online inequality."

This brief summary of Hindman's core point only skims the surface of his piece. The contribution is rich with ideas that echo, extend, and grapple with many of the thoughts about the social impact of hyperlinking that appear elsewhere in this book and beyond. Despite being the final essay in this book, it does not sum up the meaning of instant digital connections; nor does it intend to do so. We are only at the beginning of an age where these sorts of ties are becoming part of everyday life. The great possibilities of information sharing that so excited Vannevar Bush about links are still exciting today, and many of them are becoming reality. But it will be decades before the most interesting and provocative implications can be assessed or even identified. In fact, despite these writers' wide-ranging knowledge and imagination, they focus primarily on the Internet and do not discuss the other areas in which companies are beginning to make instant linking a crucial part of life.

Retailing is a hotbed of this emerging activity. Many supermarkets already link customers' purchases (as audited by frequent shopper cards) to customized discount coupons at checkout. A few large chains are now testing small computers attached to carts and activated by customers' frequent shopper cards. The computers can link to a history of shoppers' purchases and, with help from a tracking device that tells where each customer is in the store, continually offer individualized discounts and alert shoppers to specials that history (or statistical analyses) says they would want. The customer's mobile handset is becoming part of this linked-in shopping experience, too. For customers who "opt in," mobile phone companies are starting to use their ability to locate customers continually in time and space to offer them advertisements for restaurants or other establishments based on where they are or where they are likely to go and when. Phone manufacturers are working with credit card companies to implement near field communication (NFC) chips that allow people to use their phones to pay for things. These are fascinating developments, the tip of an iceberg of changes in consumers' relationships with stores and goods. They raise important questions about people's understanding of how information collected about them is stored, moved across different media, and used. They also bring up some of the nonspecifically political issues about linking and power: Who gets connected to the best discounts and why? Do customers have control over the ways retailers, phone companies, and credit card firms categorize them—in essence, over the ways companies tell stories about and evaluate them? To what extent and how do the digital labels firms place on customers as a result of their handset habits become part of the profiles that marketers and governments use about them when they go on the Internet, watch television, or even walk down the street?

Although these questions don't relate directly to the overt political concerns that so many of the contributors to this volume discuss, their relevance to the broader issues of social power that run through the essays is clear. How can we maximize citizens' ability to use links to better themselves, recognize the existence of other points of view, and learn about alternatives that can give them power? How can we encourage people to understand the maps that companies and governments make about them and to make new ones that give them greater ability to understand themselves and others and to advocate for change? As the essays, taken together, suggest, it is crucial for all of us to keep asking these questions about the nature of our connections in the digital age.

NOTES

1. V. Bush, "As We May Think," *Atlantic Monthly*, July 1945, http://www.theatlantic.com/doc/194507/bush. Michael K. Buckland has pointed out that Bush's idea of quickly linking knowledge derived from his attempt to improve upon a microfilm retrieval system pioneered by Emanuel Goldberg, the Russian-Jewish head of Zeiss Ikon in the 1920s, whose career and celebrity in Europe was cut short by the Nazis. See Michael K. Buckland, "Emanuel Goldberg, Electronic Document Retrieval and Vannevar Bush's Memex," *Information Science* 43, no. 4 (May 1992): 284–94.

2. "Hyperlink," Wikipedia, http://en.wikipedia.org/wiki/Hyperlink.

3. See, for example, J. Turow, *Niche Envy: Marketing Discrimination in the Digital Age* (Cambridge, MA: MIT Press, 2006).

4. See, for example, J. Turow et al., "The FTC and Consumer Privacy in the Coming Decade" (paper presented at the Federal Trade Commission meeting "Protecting Consumers in the Next Tech-ade," Washington, DC, November 8, 2006); J. Turow, *Open to Exploitation: American Shoppers Online and Offline* (Philadelphia: Annenberg Public Policy Center, [2005]); J. Turow, *Americans and Online Privacy: The System Is Broken* (Philadelphia: Annenberg Public Policy Center, 2003). All can be accessed at the Annenberg Public Policy Center Web site: http://www.annenbergpublicpolicycenter.org/AreaDetails.aspx?myId=2.

Part 1: Hyperlinks and the Organization of Attention

Preface to Part 1

In a digital era where information is seemingly in abundance, the hyperlink organizes our attention by suggesting which ideas are worth being heard and which are not. Hyperlinks do not exist in a vacuum, however. They are created and situated in a political-social context. Despite their ubiquity, we know little about the social and political factors that drive the production of hyperlinks. The essays in this section cross a variety of disciplines to explore the forces that guide and constrain the creation of hyperlinks and the way they organize our attention.

James Webster draws from economics, sociology, and communication to develop a conceptual model he calls the "marketplace of attention." He argues that the hyperlink can be seen as a form of currency in a marketplace where different producers of online content vie for the attention of the public. After describing the conditions under which this market operates, he focuses on the often expressed concern that linking might lead to social polarization such that people are no longer exposed to a diversity of views but instead retreat into "information enclaves." Webster argues that the best way to understand the extent to which social polarization will come to pass is to realize that neither the actors nor the structure of the marketplace will be all-determining. Instead, he says, what happens at the individual level will influence how the marketplace responds, and vice versa. He states that how people will be guided toward information will influence the extent to which social enclaves will come to pass. In the digital world, he contends, search engines give audiences new ways to determine what society will share as important, because their results involve amassing people's preferences.

Whereas Webster highlights the importance of understanding how the hyperlink structures the marketplace of attention, Alex Halavais takes a step back and helps us ground our understanding of the hyperlink from a historical perspective. He explains the original function of the hyperlink as a citation mechanism and shows how it evolved over the years to involve full-fledged networks. He also argues, however, that we can no longer afford to treat the hyperlink simply as a request for a Web document, since an entire industry has now grown up around the manipulation of links connected to search engine results. To grasp the social meaning of the hyperlink, then, requires exploring the struggles between various entities to come out on top of the rankings.

Philip Napoli looks at ways that mainstream media firms try to come up on top of the rankings. While acknowledging that some elements of the Internet are indeed challenging mainstream media, he insists that we should not lose sight of the fact that many others are undeniably becoming highly commercialized and targeting mass audiences. In his view, big media exert substantial institutional and economic power over the shape of the emerging digital environment.

Lokman Tsui's essay explores one facet of mainstream media's relation to this new world. He compares the ways prestigious newspapers and major political blogs are using the hyperlink and finds stark differences. Whereas blogs link heavily to external Web sites, some newspapers hardly link, and others link only to themselves. Considering that online versions of major newspapers are used as a primary means of directing the public's attention to what is deemed valuable information, Tsui's findings have important implications with regard to how the public learns about the world.

Eszter Hargittai is also interested in what the public learns from links, but she takes a different tack. She looks critically at the potential for abusing users via hyperlinks and at the extent to which the users themselves are likely to know that abuse is happening or be aware of this potential risk. She shows that certain users are better positioned than others to note which links are advertisements or online scams and which ones are not. Finally, Hargittai insists that we need to understand the processes that contribute to people's online literacy if we are to avoid exacerbating the current divide whereby the savvy are able to use the Internet to their advantage while the less knowledgeable remain vulnerable to misleading or sometimes even malicious content.

Seth Finkelstein sheds a somewhat different light on the problem of link manipulation. He argues that people think search results imply a Web site's authority on a topic, whereas they are in fact simply popularity measures. Using a number of case studies involving Google, he demonstrates the social dilemmas that confusing popularity with authority can cause. At a time when search engines play a pivotal role in shaping our experience online, Finkelstein's essay reminds us that it is critical to understand the processes that create the messages we see.

JAMES G. WEBSTER

Structuring a Marketplace of Attention

At the conference "The Hyperlinked Society" at the Annenberg School for Communication, Eric Picard of Microsoft asserted that with the exception of maintaining personal networks, people blogged for one of two reasons: fame or fortune. It seems to me that those motives propel most media makers, old and new. And the recipe for achieving either objective begins with attracting people's attention. Patterns of attention, in turn, establish the boundaries within which the economic and social consequences of the new media environment are realized. This essay invites the reader to think about the hyperlinked environment as a marketplace of attention. I begin with a brief description of market conditions, outline a theoretical framework for thinking about the marketplace, and then use that framework to explore two socially consequential patterns of public attention: fragmentation and polarization. The former addresses the overall dispersion of cultural consumption. The latter addresses the tendency of people to retreat into comfortable "enclaves" of information and entertainment. Finally, I'll suggest questions and concerns about a hyperlinked society that I believe deserve our attention.

Market Conditions

The hyperlinked environment can be thought of as a virtual marketplace in which the purveyors of content compete with one another for the attention of the public. Three realities set the conditions for the marketplace. I take these to be axiomatic.

Convergence. A popular term that means different things to different people,[1] *convergence* here describes the move toward fully integrated media delivery systems. While the conference focused on media that have emerged in the hyperlinked environment, like blogs, social networking sites, and other forms of user-generated content (e.g., Wikipedia,

YouTube), all content is increasingly being distributed on the same high-speed networks. Traditional media, including newspapers, radio, television, and movies, are moving into the hyperlinked space. Consumers, in turn, function in an environment where they can move fluidly among what were once discrete media outlets. In the long term, it makes sense to think about a common media environment where all manner of content is readily available to consumers.

Abundance. The sheer volume of content is vast and increasing at an explosive rate. Exact numbers are hard to come by, in part because they change so quickly. At this writing, Technorati is tracking some sixty million blogs, MySpace has over one hundred million accounts, and the number of podcasts and video clips in circulation seem without end. A great many of their authors undoubtedly seek public attention. Once the delivery of more traditional broadcast content becomes ubiquitous, it will add perhaps one hundred million hours a year of new programming to the mix.[2] All this will be in addition to whatever repositories of movies, music, and news are available on demand. Media are, if nothing else, abundant.

Scarcity. While the supply of content seems endless, the supply of human attention to consume that content is not. There are a limited number of Internet users in the world and a limited number of waking hours. The problem of too much content and too little time is not new. In the early 1970s, Herbert Simon famously noted that "a wealth of information creates a poverty of attention, and a need to allocate that attention efficiently among the overabundance of information sources that might consume it."[3] Obviously, the problem is more acute today and getting worse.

As a result, public attention is spread thin. A relatively small handful of items will achieve widespread notice, but most will not. Those that do will have the potential to produce the fame and/or fortune that their authors desire. Richard Lanham recently wrote: "Assume that, in an information economy, the real scarce commodity will always be human attention and that attracting that attention will be the necessary precondition of social change. And the real source of wealth."[4] What is less understood is how public attention actually takes shape in the new media environment. The following sections outline a theoretical framework for structuring the marketplace of attention and the patterns of consumption that emerge as a result.

Toward a Theory of the Marketplace

Adopting a marketplace metaphor may suggest that the operative theory is grounded exclusively in the rational choice model of neoclassical economics. I have in mind a somewhat more flexible framework borrowed from sociology, drawing especially on Giddens's theory of structuration.[5] While structuration has been adapted to explain the use of information technology within organizations,[6] it hasn't been used for a more wide-ranging consideration of media consumption. The principle components of this framework are agents, structures, and the interaction between them that is characterized either as "duality of structure"[7] or "dualism."[8] These provide the conceptual tools needed to imagine a marketplace of attention.

Agents. In this context, agents are the people who consume media. Their use of media is purposeful and done at a time and place of their choosing, though in practice, it is often embedded in the routines of day-to-day life. Media consumption is rational in the sense that it satisfies various needs and preferences. Agents know a good deal about the media environments within which they operate, reflect on how best to use those environments, and can be expected to give a reasoned account of their choices. It doesn't follow, however, that they know all there is to know about the environment or the causes and consequences of their own behaviors. In fact, they are complicit in many unintended consequences of which they are probably ignorant.

The marketplace has far too many offerings for any one person to be perfectly aware of his or her options. It is for this reason that actions can deviate from the rational, utility-maximizing viewer behavior assumed by traditional economic models of program choice.[9] Rather, agents operate with "bounded rationality."[10] In part, they deal with the impossibility of knowing everything by using habits and routines. Television viewers confine themselves to idiosyncratic "channel repertoires."[11] These are manageable subsets of ten to fifteen familiar channels. Repertoires tend to level off even as the total number of available channels skyrockets. The hyperlinked analog is bookmarks that guide users to previously helpful or interesting sites. Invoking these time-saving habits minimizes "search costs," but they may cause people to miss content or services that might better gratify their needs and desires. In Simon's term, consumers "satisfice" rather than maximize.[12] The world of hyperlinking, of course, offers users more powerful tools for finding content, which I address below as an example of duality of structure.

Structures. Structures—or, in some bodies of literature, "institutions"—cover a multitude of macrolevel constructs, including social conventions, language, legal systems, and organizations. Giddens described these as "rules and resources."[13] They can be internalized by an agent or stand apart as external constraints. Either way, they are more durable than agents to the extent that they exist before and after individual actors appear on the scene. I see structures primarily as the resources that people use to enact their media preferences. This includes the technologies that power the hyperlinked environment, as well as the organizations and producers that animate those systems with content and services. For the most part, governments and media industries provide the necessary structures. Of course, they have their own motives for doing so and attempt to manage patterns of attention toward those ends.

The case of user-generated content, so often the topic of conversation at the conference, presents an interesting wrinkle in the neat division between agents and structures. While "distributed construction" is hardly new,[14] the hyperlinked environment enables it as never before. Benkler has argued that we are witnessing the dawn of a "networked information economy," in which decentralized peer production will shift the balance of power away from established media industries.[15] An important motivation for this form of production is what he calls the "Joe Einstein" phenomenon, in which people "give away information for free in return for status, benefits to reputation," and so on.[16] Surely, contributors to this volume will recognize the syndrome. It's hard to know what sort of equilibrium will eventually emerge between industrialized and consumer-generated production. But for the purposes of this discussion, the question seems moot.

Whether the producer seeks fame or fortune, the operative strategy is to attract attention by catering to people's preferences and/or to direct attention by exploiting the structures of the environment. To do this, purveyors constantly monitor the marketplace, judging failures and successes and otherwise looking for opportunities to gain advantage. Suffering from their own form of bounded rationality, they can only respond to what they "see." The sophistication of their surveillance depends largely on the size and sophistication of the institutions. Typically, the actions of agents are most salient when they are aggregated to form markets, or publics, or audiences. These are what Ettema and Whitney have referred to as "institutionally effective audiences."[17] It is this manifestation of agency that most effectively fuels the duality of structure.

Duality of Structure. There is a tendency in many quarters of academe to attribute social behavior almost entirely to purposeful, reasoning agents or, conversely, to macrolevel social structures. This schism is also evident in the literature on media consumption.[18] Duality of structure suggests that the two are mutually constituted;[19] that is, people use structures as vehicles to exercise their agency and, in doing so, reproduce those very structures. This notion can be adapted to explain how the marketplace of attention actually takes shape. In the short term, the structure of the marketplace is relatively "hard" and may limit or direct attention. In the long term, however, it is heavily dependent on the choices of individual media consumers for its very architecture.

The hyperlinked environment is particularly well suited to accomplish this reciprocal act of creation, because of its ability to easily aggregate and make visible the behaviors of many discrete individuals. It creates institutionally effective audiences with a vengeance. Nowhere is this more evident than in the operation of search and recommendation systems, both of which are indispensable tools with which agents address their problems of bounded rationality.

Using a search system is an exercise in finding what you're looking for. The idea of consulting a guide to find content is nothing new, as the fortune that endowed our hosts at the Annenberg School will attest. What is new is the way in which modern search engines construct the guide. While algorithms vary, the basic strategy is to sort items in terms of their popularity. Google, for example, ranks Web sites that possess the requisite search terms according to the number and importance of their inbound links.[20] Hence, the linking architecture of the Internet, which is itself the product of thousands of more or less independent decision makers, provides the principle guide for navigating hyperlinked space.

Recommendation systems alert us to things we aren't affirmatively looking for. Here again, the basic function is nothing new. Advertising is an old, if transparently self-serving, variation on this genre. The outbound links on Web sites, which are the input for search engines, constitute a decentralized network of recommendations. The tagging, bookmarking, and rating features of social networking programs serve similar functions. The most elaborate recommendation systems, based on collaborative filtering software, aggregate the behaviors of large numbers of anonymous individuals to divine what a person "like you" might prefer. Those of us who use Amazon.com to buy obscure academic books are all too familiar with the seductive power of those systems.

Search and recommendation systems, as well as many other collaborative features of the hyperlinked environment, share a number of noteworthy characteristics. The most elaborate systems are built by amassing people's preferences and behaviors. No one opinion leader or vested interest is able to dictate the output of these systems; hence they have a compelling air of objectivity. In effect, we trust the "wisdom of crowds."[21] It is unlikely that individuals in the crowd fully understand how their actions produce a given output, if they are aware of having made any contribution at all. Yet they create, perpetuate, and/or modify structures that direct the attention of others. This duality of structure is an essential and increasingly pervasive dynamic of the marketplace. But what patterns of attention does the marketplace actually produce?

Fragmentation

Certainly, from the perspective of old media, the most consequential and widely noted feature of the new media environment is fragmentation, the tendency of audiences to be widely distributed over the many outlets or items of content competing for their attention. Its conceptual opposite is audience concentration. In the days of old media, public attention was inevitably concentrated on the few stations or newspapers available in local market areas. Since the 1970s, the increased penetration and capacities of cable and satellite systems have caused steady "erosion" in the size of broadcast television audiences.[22] The Internet added even more capacity and global reach, seemingly overnight. With huge national and international markets available, media makers could sustain themselves with niche offerings. The expansive structure of the new environment, populated by institutions desperately seeking attention, provided the necessary conditions for fragmentation.

Setting aside the economic woes it causes old media, the trend toward ever greater fragmentation (and the consequent demise of "lowest common denominator" programming) has generally been greeted with approval. While the cultural landscape has undoubtedly changed (for reasons I develop shortly), the demise of mass appeal content is, in the words of Mark Twain, "greatly exaggerated." In his popular book *The Long Tail*, Chris Anderson notes, "The era of one-size-fits-all is ending, and in its place is something new, a market of multitudes."[23] Consumers, empowered by "infinite choice"[24] and equipped with the tools of search and recommendation, can find whatever suits their preferences, no matter how obscure. For Anderson, this shift manifests itself in a migration from "hits," which have concentrated attention on the "short head" of a distribution, to niches, which inhabit the increasingly long tail of consumption. Other pundits, noting how the new environment enables various forms of consumer-generated expression, have adopted a similarly celebratory tone.[25] All of these developments apparently lead to greater diversity of choice in the media environment and, so it would seem, promote a more perfect cultural democracy.

Even if we take these trends at face value, they are not without their worries. Elihu Katz, wistfully recalling the days when one broadcast network served the entire State of Israel, has suggested that the proliferation of new media runs the risk of denying societies a common forum with which to promote national identity and a shared sense of purpose. He has warned:

> Throughout the Western world, the newspaper was the first medium of national integration. It was followed by radio. When television came, it displaced radio as the medium of national integration, and radio became the medium of segmentation. Now, following radio again, television has become a medium of segmentation, pushed by both technology and society. Unlike the moment when television assumed radio's role as the medium of national integration, there is nothing in sight to replace television, not even media events or the Internet.[26]

Indeed, it's plausible that fragmentation will make it harder for issues to reach the "threshold of public attention" necessary for agenda setting.[27] Even more troubling is the prospect of the common public sphere breaking into many tiny "sphericules"[28] that fail to interact with one another. The possibility that people will effectively retreat into comfortable little enclaves of like-minded news and entertainment is a topic I address below as the polarization of attention.

Before accepting fragmentation as a fait accompli, however, I think it's worth considering a number of countervailing forces that pull public attention in the opposite direction. While it's fascinating to contemplate the cultural and business implications of long tails, what is even more noteworthy is the persistence of the short head in the distribution. Despite the availability of infinite choice, a relative handful of outlets continue to dominate public attention. Ironically, as we look across media that offer consumers progressively more options, audiences become more, not less, concentrated. Using various measures, researchers consistently find that the most abundant media produce the most concentrated markets. Radio and television, it turns out, are more egalitarian media than the World Wide Web.[29]

The persistence of short heads undoubtedly has much to do with the operation of "power laws," which accounts for the success that physicists have had modeling the architecture of the Web.[30] Such models need not make assumptions about the quality of offerings to produce an expectation of short heads. But quality and social desirability do enter into the allocation of public attention. One possibility is that the most popular items are, in fact, worthy of that attention. A number of arguments I note shortly suggest just that. Rather than moving consumption in the direction of obscure niches, many new technologies let people spend even more time with what's popular. Early indications on DVR usage, for example, suggest that people typically record top-rated TV programs.[31] As panelist Jack Wakshlag noted, people use TiVos as "hit machines." Similarly, many of the most frequently viewed clips on YouTube are the professionally produced work of networks and marketers.[32] In a world of limited attention, such media use necessarily displaces watching less popular fare. Another irony of moving to an on-demand media environment, then, is that good old-fashioned linear media may have enforced a measure of exposure to things that weren't hits. Even Anderson noted how the move from CDs to iTunes has allowed listeners, "with the help of personalized recommendations," to cherry-pick the "best individual songs" from albums and skip the "crap" in between.[33] The best, it would seem, are the most recommended. And the most recommended will inevitably be the most popular.

An accounting of fragmentation is usually made by measuring the attention paid to relatively discrete outlets or items of content. Such numbers are often readily available in the form of audience ratings or paid attendance. Another phenomenon, less easily documented, may further mitigate the fragmentation of public attention. Suppose the many nodes across which attention was distributed offered essentially the same thing. There are a number of reasons why the environment might move in that direction. Several observers have noted that consumer-generated production makes liberal use of the most popular (often copyrighted) output of culture industries.[34] If new outlets are simply repurposing existing content and if petty producers are simply playing with the culture's most salient themes and products, fragmentation may be more apparent than real. Phil Napoli, another contributor to this volume, noted at the conference, "I could put ten more water faucets at different places in my home, but ultimately that water is still coming from the same reservoir."

More specific mechanisms seem to be at work in the world of news and opinion. Recent studies in the production of online newspapers suggest that the Internet, coupled with competitive journalistic practices, actually contributes to the homogenization of news content. It appears that journalists use the online environment to continuously monitor their competition. Not wanting to be scooped and relying heavily on commonly available wire services and electronic media, newspapers increasingly replicate the same stories.[35] One can imagine a similar dynamic operating in the blogosphere. In fact, Benkler's analysis of how meritorious news and opinion percolate to the A-list blogs seems to be a related phenomenon. For him, this is the mechanism that overcomes the "Babel objection" about the democratizing effects of the Internet.[36] It does suggest, however, that public attention is not as fragmented as it might at first seem.

Polarization

What is sometimes harder to see is the extent to which attention is being polarized. Unlike our view of fragmentation, which comes in the form of a snapshot showing the distribution of attendance across sources, polarization requires a consideration of which media people consume over time. Fragmentation provides evidence that public attention is, in the aggregate, spread across many more sources than was the case a decade ago. This is what Napoli has called "horizontal exposure diversity."[37] It does not follow, however, that each individual's diet of media content is also more diverse. It might be that people avail themselves of the abundance by sampling a little bit of everything. That would be evidence of a "vertical diversity" of exposure and would, by most accounts, be a socially desirable pattern.[38] Alternatively, it could be that people use the environment to binge on a few favorites. Either pattern could lie beneath the veneer of fragmentation.[39] The latter, however, has potentially chilling social implications, since it suggests that people withdraw into various "cocoons."[40] Two factors will determine the outcome: the psychological predispositions of agents and the structures of the environment.

There is certainly reason to believe that rational, utility-maximizing consumers will selectively choose media materials that conform to their preferences. Traditional economic models of program choice assumed fixed preferences that were systematically related to viewer-defined program types.[41] While it seems likely that preferences are, in the long term, cultivated by the environment, people do have relatively stable likes and dislikes. These operate along many dimensions, including (1) an appetite for specific program genres, perhaps as broadly defined as information versus entertainment;[42] (2) the utility of information;[43] (3) language or cultural proximity;[44] (4) conservative versus liberal political ideologies;[45] and (5) various manifestations of fandom.[46] In short, much of what we know about the psychology of media choice suggests that people will consume relatively restricted diets to suit their tastes. With virtually every type of content available in limitless supply, it remains to be seen when or if people become sated.

The media environment does more than simply offer an abundance of choice, however. It structures and filters what is available and, in so doing, privileges some things over others. While search and recommendation systems are apparently objective aggregations of many independent decisions, they may exacerbate the tendency of people to retreat into comfortable enclaves of like-minded speech. Cass Sunstein, among others, fears that these filtering technologies encourage people to seek out what is agreeable and to avoid anything that challenges their predispositions. Over the long haul, he writes, this is likely to promote "group polarization."[47] But even if one assumes that search engines simply do our bidding, not all structural features of the hyperlinked environment are so benign. The media institutions that, in large part, create the environment will attempt to manage and concentrate our attention with all the means at their disposal. Joseph Turow asks:

> Who will create opportunities for various social groups to talk across divisions and share experiences when major marketing and media firms solidify social division by separating people into data-driven niches with news and entertainment aimed primarily at reinforcing their sense of selves?[48]

Of course, not all writers have concluded that countless niches are a bad thing. With his characteristic enthusiasm for infinite choice, Anderson has imagined a "massively parallel culture" formed into "millions of microcultures" or "tribal eddies."[49] Good or bad, it's worth developing a better understanding of how, if at all, public attention is being polarized.

As best I can tell, the jury is still out. The clearest evidence so far is that the new marketplace allows a substantial segment of the population to avoid news and information altogether. Increasingly, we are becoming a nation of people who do or do not know about world events. While the old world of linear media succeeded in enforcing almost universal exposure to TV news, the new world of choice does not. Markus Prior has argued convincingly that changes in the structure of television have enabled differential patterns of news viewing, which effectively polarize the public into those with and those without political knowledge.[50] While a case can be made that people who avoid hard news are "rationally ignorant,"[51] I find Prior's results a troubling prospect for democracy. What is less clear, though, is the extent to which consumers of news and information limit their diets largely to one ideological point of view. Iyengar and Morin's study of online news readership[52] and Adamic and Glance's analysis of the linking structures among political blogs[53] suggest systematic "blue/red" biases in people's patterns of consumption across time. Conversely, Hargittai, Gallo and Kane's study of political blogs[54] and a Pew study of Internet use[55] emphasize the tendencies of people to reference and/or know opposing points of view. Prior himself has noted that viewers of the Fox News Channel see other sources of TV news, which suggests a vertical diversity of exposure consistent with broader findings on TV viewing.[56]

Questions about the Marketplace

The shape of public attention is important because it suggests how the marketplace of ideas will operate in an age of on-demand digital media. Two questions are, to me, particularly salient. The first is whether our society's cultural center will hold in the wake of all these changes. This is and should be subject to ongoing empirical investigation. The second normative question addresses the wisdom of the data-aggregating systems that increasingly define the character of the nonlinear media environment.

Will the Center Hold? In his zeal for the long tail, Anderson has asserted that "infinite choice equals ultimate fragmentation."[57] It's hard to imagine a common culture—let alone a vibrant democracy—whose patterns of attention are evenly spread across an infinite number of choices. Nor do I think that's likely to happen. I suspect the forces that concentrate attention, as already outlined, will save us from flying off in every conceivable direction. That said, it's clear that many more things are competing for our attention. These inevitably come at the expense of the older forms of media that once commanded center stage. They were sometimes derided as offering only the lowest common denominator, but by their very commercial nature, they steered a course through the heart of culture. And for all practical purposes, attendance was mandatory.

Now attendance is up to us. A veneer of fragmentation does not mandate social polarization if individual media consumers do the work necessary to "connect the dots." They might spend time moving from the obscure to the popular or simply from niche to niche and still manage to construct a fully featured marketplace of ideas. But the very concept of a niche suggests a degree of stickiness. Every niche maker, commercial or not, wants repeat customers. Most would be happy if those customers settled exclusively on what they had to offer. Many will, undoubtedly, do what they can to make that happen. If customers are happy with their niches, they'll stay put. It's only rational.

For all those reasons, public attention is likely to be reorganized along dimensions of taste and structure. For now, we should do our best to monitor the social and cultural divisions that emerge. That will be a daunting task for two reasons. First, a complete view of how people navigate the marketplace will require following them across time and across media. The world of media research is still largely balkanized by medium.[58] Today, it's virtually impossible to know with any precision what a person reads, watches on television, hears on the radio, and consumes on the Internet. Yet all those sources are competing for attention and, in turn, shape that person's environment. As media converge on a common distribution system, it will become easier to paint a complete picture of consumption. Second, assessing exposure alone will not fully answer the question. We must also have a nuanced understanding of the content that's being consumed (e.g., how links are referenced, how issues are framed) and what sense people make of those representations. Only then will we see what fault lines are forming within the culture.

Are Crowds Wise or Stupid? While hyperlinking is, on one level, about technology, the hyperlinked spaces that we use are given life by ordinary human beings. Sometimes it is the work of individual agents, but often it happens through the instant and ever-changing aggregation of choices made by others. This is true of the most powerful tools we use to navigate the environment, and it goes to the heart of what many commentators find so revolutionary about the technology.[59] It is hard to imagine an arena of human activity that is more heavily dependent on the wisdom or stupidity of crowds. And it is on this point that many social commentators strike me as a bit schizophrenic.

The phrase "wisdom of crowds" was popularized by James Surowiecki.[60] In his eponymous best seller, Surowiecki argued that averaging input from many ordinary, diverse, and independent decision makers often produces better results than the judgments of experts. A marketplace offers one example of such a mechanism. Anderson frequently repeats the "wisdom of crowds" mantra, pointing to any number of apparently successful collaborative endeavors, from Wikipedia to various forms of recommendation.[61] Benkler and many others also put stock in the ability of the blogosphere to sort though and collaboratively produce the most accurate news or meritorious ideas.[62]

When I first read the conditions that Surowiecki suggested will unleash the wisdom of crowds, I was reminded of Blumer's classic definition of a "mass" in social theory and of its adaptation to audiences.[63] A mass audience is a heterogeneous collection of many anonymous, independent decision makers.[64] The wisdom of such crowds is routinely measured in audience ratings. Recently, the top-rated program on TV was *Dancing with the Stars*. I suspect you could find similarly reassuring gems if you checked the most viewed clips on YouTube. Anderson tries to finesse such uninspiring measures of public taste by insisting that "what matters is the rankings *within* a genre (or subgenre), not *across* genres."[65] Apparently, it's only when we dig deeply into our niches that crowds become wise. To me, this reads like an invitation to cultural polarization. If we want to encourage sampling the best across genres, why is it that crowds should no longer be our guide? At what point do they become stupid? At the very least, we need to develop a more discriminating stance on the wisdom of crowds.

But, like it or not, crowds increasingly shape our world. The actions of agents are instantly aggregated and made available for all to see. These, in turn, affect the structures and offerings of the media environment. Online newspapers are discovering that it's "soft news" (e.g., stories about celebrities, sex, and animals) that attracts readers' attention. A recent piece in the *American Journalism Review* warned print journalists, "Television news veterans predict papers will face huge challenges maintaining their editorial independence while seeking to grab the attention of Web readers."[66] In matters of taste, no empirical test will tell us whether the decisions of crowds are wise or not. More realistically, it will be for each of us to judge whether the results of the process offer a path to enlightenment or the road to perdition.

NOTES

1. H. Jenkins, *Convergence Culture: Where Old and New Media Collide* (New York: New York University Press, 2006).

2. P. Lyman and H. R. Varian, "How Much Information?" http://www.sims .berkeley.edu/how-much-info-2003 (accessed September 14, 2006).

3. H. A. Simon, "Designing Organizations for an Information-Rich World," in *Computers, Communications, and the Public Interest*, ed. M. Greenberger (Baltimore: Johns Hopkins University Press, 1971), 41.

4. R. Lanham, *The Economics of Attention: Style and Substance in the Age of Information* (Chicago: University of Chicago Press, 2006), 46.

5. A. Giddens, *The Constitution of Society: Outline of the Theory of Structuration* (Berkeley: University of California Press, 1984).

6. G. DeSanctis and M. S. Poole, "Capturing the Complexity in Advanced Technology Use: Adaptive Structuration Theory," *Organization Science* 5, no. 2 (1994): 121–47; W. J. Orlikowski, "The Duality of Technology: Rethinking the Concept of Technology in Organizations," *Organization Science* 3, no. 3 (1992): 398–427.

7. Giddens, *Constitution of Society.*

8. N. Mouzelis, "The Subjectivist-Objectivist Divide: Against Transcendence," *Sociology* 34, no. 4 (2000): 741–62.

9. E.g., B. M. Owen and S. S. Wildman, *Video Economics* (Cambridge, MA: Harvard University Press, 1992).

10. H. A. Simon, *Administrative Behavior: A Study of Decision-Making Processes in Administrative Organizations* (New York: Free Press, 1997).

11. K. A. Neuendorf, D. J. Atkin, and L. W. Jeffres, "Reconceptualizing Channel Repertoire in the Urban Cable Environment," *Journal of Broadcasting and Electronic Media* 45, no. 3 (2001): 464–82; E. J. Yuan and J. G. Webster, "Channel Repertoires: Using Peoplemeter Data in Beijing," *Journal of Broadcasting and Electronic Media* 50, no. 3 (2006): 524–36.

12. Simon, *Administrative Behavior.*

13. Giddens, *Constitution of Society.*

14. P. J. Boczkowski, *Digitizing the News: Innovation in Online Newspapers* (Cambridge, MA: MIT Press, 2004).

15. Y. Benkler, *The Wealth of Networks* (New Haven, CT: Yale University Press, 2006).

16. Ibid., 43.

17. J. S. Ettema and D. C. Whitney, "The Money Arrow: An Introduction to Audiencemaking," in *Audiencemaking: How the Media Create the Audience* (Thousand Oaks, CA: Sage, 1994), 5.

18. J. G. Webster, "The Role of Structure in Media Choice" (forthcoming); J. G. Webster and P. F. Phalen, *The Mass Audience: Rediscovering the Dominant Model* (Mahwah, NJ: Erlbaum, 1997).

19. Giddens, *Constitution of Society.*

20. J. Battelle, *The Search: How Google and Its Rivals Rewrote the Rules of Business and Transformed Our Culture* (New York: Portfolio, 2005).

21. J. Surowiecki, *The Wisdom of Crowds: Why the Many Are Smarter than the Few and How Collective Wisdom Shapes Business, Economies, Societies, and Nations* (New York: Doubleday, 2004).

22. J. G. Webster, "Beneath the Veneer of Fragmentation: Television Audience Polarization in a Multichannel World," *Journal of Communication* 55, no. 2 (2005): 366–82.

23. C. Anderson, *The Long Tail: Why the Future of Business Is Selling Less of More* (New York: Hyperion, 2006), 5.

24. Ibid., 12.

25. E.g., Benkler, *Wealth of Networks;* Jenkins, *Convergence Culture.*

26. E. Katz, "And Deliver Us from Segmentation," *Annals of the American Academy of Political and Social Science* 546, no. 1 (1996): 33.

27. W. R. Neuman, "The Threshold of Public Attention," *Public Opinion Quarterly* 54, no. 2 (1990): 159–76.

28. T. Gitlin, "Public Sphere or Public Sphericules?" in *Media, Ritual, and Identity,* ed. T. Liebes and J. Curran (London: Routledge, 1998), 175–202.

29. E.g., M. Hindman, "A Mile Wide and an Inch Deep: Measuring Media Diversity Online and Offline," and J. G. Webster, "Diversity of Exposure," in *Media Diversity and Localism: Meaning and Metrics,* ed. P. Napoli (Mahwah, NJ: Erlbaum, 2006), 327–47, 309–25; J. Yim, "Audience Concentration in the Media: Cross-Media Comparisons and the Introduction of the Uncertainty Measure," *Communication Monographs* 70, no. 2 (2003): 114–28.

30. E.g., A.-L. Barabási, "The Physics of the Web," *Physics World,* July 2001, http://physicsweb.org/articles/world/14/7/9 (accessed July 10, 2006); B. A. Huberman, *The Laws of the Web: Patterns in the Ecology of Information* (Cambridge, MA: MIT Press, 2001).

31. F. Aherns, "Fears over TiVo on Pause," *Los Angeles Times,* August 29, 2006, http://www.latimes.com/entertainment/news/homeentertainment/la-et-tivo29 aug29 ,1,7984227.story?coll=la-entnews-homeent (accessed September 27, 2006).

32. W. Friedman, "CBS Scores Viewers with YouTube Alliance," *Media Post,* November 27, 2006, http://publications.mediapost.com/index.cfm?fuseaction=Articles.san&s=51543&Nid=25374&p=263743 (accessed November 27, 2006).

33. Anderson, *Long Tail,* 22.

34. Benkler, *Wealth of Networks;* Jenkins, *Convergence Culture;* L. Lessig, *Free Culture: How Big Media Uses Technology and the Law to Lock Down Culture and Control Creativity* (New York: Penguin, 2004).

35. P. J. Boczkowski and M. de Santos, "When More Media Equals Less News: Patterns of Content Homogenization in Argentina's Leading Print and Online Newspapers," *Political Communication* 24, no. 2 (April 2007): 167–80.

36. Benkler, *Wealth of Networks,* 233.

37. P. M. Napoli, "Deconstructing the Diversity Principle," *Journal of Communication* 49, no. 4 (1999): 7–34.

38. Webster, "Diversity of Exposure," 309–25.

39. Webster, "Beneath the Veneer of Fragmentation," 366–82.

40. C. R. Sunstein, *Infotopia* (Oxford: Oxford University Press, 2006).

41. Owen and Wildman, *Video Economics.*

42. E.g., M. Prior, *Post-Broadcast Democracy: How Media Choice Increases Inequality in Political Involvement and Polarizes Elections* (New York: Cambridge University Press, 2007); R. T. Rust, W. A. Kamakura, and M. I. Alpert, "Viewer Preference Segmentation and Viewing Choice Models for Network Television," *Journal of Advertising* 21, no. 1 (1992): 1–18.

43. E.g., M. S. Y. Chwe, *Rational Ritual: Culture, Coordination, and Common Knowledge* (Princeton, NJ: Princeton University Press, 2001); J. T. Hamilton, *All*

the News That's Fit to Sell: How the Market Transforms Information into News (Princeton, NJ: Princeton University Press, 2004).

44. E.g., J. Straubhaar, "Choosing National TV: Cultural Capital, Language, and Cultural Proximity in Brazil," in *The Impact of International Television: A Paradigm Shift*, ed. M. G. Elasmar (Mahwah, NJ: Erlbaum, 2003), 77–110.

45. E.g., S. Iyengar and R. Morin, "Red Media, Blue Media: Evidence for a Political Litmus Test in Online News Readership," *Washington Post*, May 3, 2006, http://www.washingtonpost.com/wp-dyn/content/article/2006/05/03/AR200605 0300865.html (accessed November 30, 2006); C. R. Sunstein, *Republic.com* (Princeton, NJ: Princeton University Press, 2001).

46. E.g., Jenkins, *Convergence Culture.*

47. Sunstein, *Republic.com*

48. J. Turow, *Niche Envy: Marketing Discrimination in the Digital Age* (Cambridge, MA: MIT Press, 2006), 33.

49. Anderson, *Long Tail*, 182.

50. Prior, *Post-Broadcast Democracy.*

51. Hamilton, *All the News That's Fit to Sell.*

52. Iyengar and Morin, "Red Media, Blue Media."

53. L. A. Adamic and N. Glance, "The Political Blogosphere and the 2004 U.S. Election: Divided They Blog," in *Proceedings of the 3rd International Workshop on Link Discovery* (New York: ACM, 2005), 36–43.

54. E. Hargittai, J. Gallo, and M. Y. Kane, "Cross-Ideological Discussions among a Group of Conservative and Liberal Bloggers," unpublished ms.

55. J. Horrigan, K. Garrett, and P. Resnick, *The Internet and Democratic Debate* (Washington, DC: Pew Internet and American Life Project, 2004).

56. Webster, "Diversity of Exposure," 309–25.

57. Anderson, *Long Tail*, 181.

58. J. G. Webster, P. F. Phalen, and L. W. Lichty, *Ratings Analysis: The Theory and Practice of Audience Research*, 3rd ed. (Mahwah, NJ: Erlbaum, 2006).

59. E.g., Benkler, *Wealth of Networks;* Sunstein, *Infotopia.*

60. Surowiecki, *Wisdom of Crowds.*

61. Anderson, *Long Tail.*

62. Benkler, *Wealth of Networks.*

63. H. Blumer, "The Field of Collective Behavior," in *New Outlines of the Principles of Sociology*, ed. A. M. Lee (New York: Barnes and Noble, 1946), 167–222.

64. Webster and Phalen, *Mass Audience.*

65. Anderson, *Long Tail*, 114.

66. R. Shiver, "By the Numbers," *American Journalism Review*, June–July 2006, http://www.ajr.org/article_printable.asp?id=4121 (accessed November 11, 2006).

ALEXANDER HALAVAIS

The Hyperlink as Organizing Principle

The Hyperlink

What does a hyperlink mean? The question itself is problematical. We might be satisfied with the simpler and related question of what a hyperlink is and what a hyperlink does. But in trying to understand what the larger social effects of hyperlink networks are, it is not enough to be able to define a hyperlink, we need to understand its nature, its use, and its social effects.

This meaning is neither unitary nor stable. There are a number of ways the hyperlink could be theorized, at different levels and toward different ends. This essay will argue that with the explosion of the World Wide Web, we are beginning to see increasing awareness of hyperlink networks as meaningful, malleable, and powerful. This is in contrast to initial views of hyperlinks, which only barely glimpsed the degree to which they are able to express meaning at a conscious and intentional level. With the ability to see hyperlinks within a larger networked structure, we have already begun to understand that, en masse, they reflect deep social and cultural structures—a kind of collective unconscious. That understanding has in turn changed the ways in which hyperlinks are used and exploited. As hyperlink networks become more easily manipulated and reach farther into our social and physical lives, we will have a continuing need to understand the hyperlink as more than a way of automatically requesting documents from a Web server. As these networks increasingly represent the structures of knowledge and social interaction, they acquire the ability to influence themselves and attain some form of self-awareness.

Hyperlinks as Citations

The idea of a hyperlink—a reference that automatically brings the user to a particular point in a cited work—is deceptively simple. Those who first implemented hyperlinks were sometimes blind to their wider implications. There is, however, a relationship between the traditional uses of citation and the development of the hyperlink. If we wish to understand what individuals mean when they use a hyperlink, it is worthwhile to understand what they mean when they cite.

Identifying the first use of a hyperlink is difficult in part because the concept of a hyperlink is simple enough to be applicable to a wide range of technologies. If it is merely an automatic citation device and not limited to any particular medium, we might suggest a number of precursors to what we traditionally think of as a hyperlink. Indeed, it could be argued that the hyperlink is in a continual process of reinvention, or what Neville Holmes refers to as "cumulative innovation."[1] Any claim to be the inventor of the hyperlink, as in the case of British Telecom's short-lived attempt to assert a patent on the concept, quickly becomes mired in a long history of scholarly citation and other forms of linking.

So where does the history of hyperlinking begin? If we do not stipulate that the document be digital in format, quotation and citation do certainly appear to be forms of textual links. Commentaries on religious texts, especially within Talmudic scholarship, are often seen as the earliest exemplars of citation, in part because the commentators could generally rely on standardized copies of the texts in question. Even when deviating from standard copies could have dire effects, hand-copying virtually guaranteed that fidelity would be difficult to maintain. The emergence of the printing press—and with it, standardized, distributed libraries—provided a fertile platform for the practice of citation. As Elizabeth Eisenstein has argued, this standardization allowed for new forms of cataloging and indexing, which led to increased citation, which in turn allowed for the distribution of scholarship and eventually the Enlightenment.[2]

But the function of citation is not as obvious as it may appear. The most obvious function is as a way of presenting others' ideas as support for the author's own argument—that is, it allows the use of "sources." In some ways, this might be seen as a way of allowing the author, as Eisenstein suggests, to assume access to a generalized pool of authoritative texts and avoid recapitulating the development of an entire field. In this way, the reference might also serve a pedagogical role, pointing the reader to helpful resources. Because teaching and persuasion go hand in hand, the pedagogical function bleeds easily into a persuasive one, as Gilbert suggests.[3]

However, as Collingwood argues, the ability to interrogate previous authors—presenting their ideas in part rather than as a whole—by "dissecting a tradition" also allows for the undermining of authoritative sources, even as it reinscribes them.[4] The motivation for linking to previous work is often to criticize, analyze, or refute that work, as well as to build on it. Polanyi argues that the development of modern scholarship, in contrast to the motto of the Royal Society (*Nullius in verba*), is not original thought alone but engaging in a distributed conversation facilitated through the use of technologies of indexing and referencing.[5] Without effective citation, scholarly thought would have remained a relatively solitary endeavor rather than a textual conversation.

To be sure, it is a strange sort of conversation. Early citation was more likely to feel like a chat with the dead, and links to authors no longer among the living were predictably unlikely to be reciprocated. More recent journal publication may engage in something more interactive, though generally only linking backward in time. As a conversation, it is thus a strangely disjointed and asynchronous one. Taking a cue from Walther's "hyperpersonal" relationships, we might consider citation to be a sort of "hyperconversation," in that it occurs across contexts and across time.[6]

At the very least, a reference may be a nod of thanks that acknowledges the efforts of others or a more direct demonstration of gratitude. But the social affinity may also be stronger than just a thank-you. Indeed, in an essay subtitled "Scholarly Citation Practices as Courtship Rituals," Rose explicitly emphasizes the sociable nature of citation and indicates that creating a citation is as much about entering a discourse community as it is about establishing an authoritative basis for an author's argument.[7]

None of these possible motivations is obviously dominant. As critics of citation analysis have suggested, citations are created for a wide variety of reasons. Brooks identifies a set of motivations—persuasiveness, positive credit, currency, reader alert, operational information, social consensus, and negative credit—and others have created similar taxonomies.[8] Many agree that citation varies by time, by culture, and by personal style.[9] The relative dearth of empirical data and the variability of motivations and practices that characterize citation make it difficult to ascribe a simple, precise meaning to citation practices, though it seems clear that they have played an important role in the development of social knowledge.[10]

Vannevar Bush was aware of the importance of citation and the need for automating it, when he wrote his prescient "As We May Think" in 1945.[11] While it is possible to identify precursors to hyperlinks as automated citations in the use of punch cards or tabs, the visionary potential of hyperlinking is nowhere as clear as it is in Bush's imagined personal file system, the *memex*. Bush suggested that since the mind was organized as an associative network, a similar organizational structure would be an effective way of creating personal files and libraries as well. Moreover, the "associative trails" produced by a researcher as he or she examined the literature would provide pathways that others could follow. In this way, the scientific enterprise could be accelerated, and collaborative knowledge could be improved.

Bush's ideas helped to inspire the work of Ted Nelson and Douglas Engelbart, who provided the earliest versions of what we recognize as the familiar hyperlink. Nelson's Project Xanadu set out to create a new, broadly associative way of organizing knowledge, and in so doing, he coined the terms *hyperlink* and *hypertext*. The first working computer-based hyperlink system was demonstrated as part of the oNLine System (NLS) by Engelbart in 1968.[12] Nelson has expressed his disappointment in the limits of the hyperlink as it ended up being used: it is generally unidirectional, for example, and unable to reflect the richness of associative thought.[13] Nonetheless, the demonstration of the utility of a hyperlink led to a number of hypertext systems, culminating in the popular Hyper-Card application by the 1980s.

Throughout these early implementations, there was a clear conceptual relationship to previous uses of citation. As hypertext systems advanced however, differences became clear. Although hyperlinks may perform the functions of a scholarly reference, they often function in ways that references cannot, and they are often used for different reasons. For example, because electronic documents are more easily updated, it is possible to have two documents with hyperlinks pointing to each other, something that generally does not occur in printed literature.[14] Because of the instantaneous nature of hyperlinks, it was also clear that they could do much more than static references. Unlike a traditional citation, which requires an investment of time to locate and read the target document, hyperlinks allow for the instant "jump" to other texts. This immediacy allowed hyperlinks to be used to more directly structure documents, collections of documents, and—as the World Wide Web rapidly expanded—recorded media more broadly.

The emergence and popularity of the World Wide Web moved hyperlinks farther from citation, and the terminology changed to reflect that of the memex. Reading became "browsing" or "surfing," and the user was transported along the pathways generated by large collections of hyperlinks. Those hyperlinks were created not by a single designer but by millions of authors linking to one another's work. As database systems and programmatic interfaces became the norm, not only were a greater number of people able to create hyperlinks (e.g., with the increasing popularity of wikis), but the hyperlinks were often created on the fly by the servers themselves.

As a result of the increasing popularity of the hyperlink, their uses and significance have expanded and changed. Even within the world of academic linking, the role of the link has gone beyond citation to focus more on navigational issues.[15] Indeed, online scholarship tends to retain the traditional text-based citation, even on pages that are replete with hyperlinks.

Outside of the scholarly world, hyperlinks have taken on an even greater role. Clicking a hyperlink may lead to a camera changing its orientation, to a book being ordered and sent through the mail, to an e-mail in-box being reorganized, or to a closer view of a satellite image. These potential uses were not outside of the expectations of some of the originators of the hyperlink. In 1968, Engelbart was already integrating e-mail functions with hyperlinks, and in 1965, Nelson wrote that the "ramifications of this approach extend well beyond its original concerns, into such places as information retrieval and library science, motion pictures and the programming craft; for it is almost everywhere necessary to deal with deep structural changes in the arrangement of ideas and things."[16]

The universal nature of hyperlinking makes it a very difficult sort of artifact to understand. The question of what someone means when they create a hyperlink or when they activate one is entirely determined by the context of the hyperlink's use. While there have been some initial attempts, at least within scholarly sections of the Web, to discover the conditions under which hyperlinks come into being, these remain at an early stage. It seems that hyperlinks clearly hold some social meaning, but beyond this broad implication, it is difficult to characterize a single hyperlink in any rigorous way.[17]

Hyperlink Networks

Why should we be interested in the nature of individual hyperlinks? If hypertext is structured by hyperlinks, understanding the psychology behind those connections is valuable. With that understanding, we would be better able to comprehend what individual hyperlinks indicate. Even more important, those hyperlinks seem to provide an opportunity to understand social behavior when taken in the aggregate.

Focusing on the structural properties of hyperlinks has been particularly important for Web search technologies, especially for Google. By measuring which pages are most central to the network of hyperlinks on the Web at large, Google is able to rank its search results according to some indication of salience.[18] Other systems have followed suit, collating links to provide a guide to the most popular sites. Technorati, for example focuses on the network of blogs, providing indications of which blogs garner the largest number of inbound hyperlinks from their peers.

In some ways, the effectiveness of these approaches is sufficient justification of their use. While using measures of network prestige is certainly not the only reason for Google's success, there can be little doubt that it has been effective. The reason for this effectiveness does not, at the surface, appear to be surprising. Measures of prestige within social networks have a long history, and the conceptual relationship between the structure of these networks and their behavior has been well considered.[19] When such measures were used, it was often based on information gathered directly from individuals regarding their behaviors or their attitudes. While there is certainly room for systematic error in such a process, there was generally a clear connection between the data collected and the inferences made.

Likewise, the measurement and tracking of citation networks in order to map a field and its development has a long and successful history. The relationship between citation networks and hyperlink networks is clearer: citations, like hyperlinks, represent a latent, unobtrusive measure. An advantage is that respondents are not shaping answers to fit the preconceptions of the researchers. However, researchers are left with interpreting the nature of the citations themselves. In most cases, the citations are taken as a whole and considered to be links—either present or not. As suggested earlier, references may be made for a wide range of reasons, including to signal that a work is faulty or lacking in some way. Given the range of meanings that might attach to any citation, can we make sense of measures taken from the network of those citations?

The question becomes even more pressing when it comes to the interpretation of hyperlink networks. Park and Thelwall detail the increasing use of hyperlink network analysis to help understand the structure of everything from debate over public policy to e-commerce.[20] While researchers have engaged the question of interpretation of hyperlinks to varying degrees, such investigations have remained tentative and generally have investigated linking within scholarly domains. This has not slowed the use of hyperlink analysis, however. In its most extreme form—studying only the hyperlinks themselves—such analysis approaches the purely theoretical.[21] When combined with the text of the target pages, their geographical location, or other data, hyperlink analyses provide what appears to be useful information about structural relationships.

As an example, if we measure the hyperlinks stretching between cities, does this tell us something valuable? I measured links between sampled Web sites in eight world cities to determine the degree to which they interlinked.[22] The resulting network of hyperlinks (fig. 1) provided interesting insights. When the first study was conducted, New York was considered a bit of a latecomer to the information revolution, with attention focused heavily on California. Instead, it was by far the most central of the global cities studied, while Tokyo remained relatively isolated, neither linking to nor linked from other global cities. Lin, Zhang, and I took a similar approach to measure the links among blogs in various U.S. cities (fig. 2).[23] Tracing the links among several hundred thousand blogs, we found clusters among cities that had similar characteristics, and we found that New York was once again at the core of the network.

While structure is revealed, what do these links really mean? Why are these blogs linked at all? Individuals linking between blogs were in some cases expressing a social connection (i.e., they knew the person in "real life") and in others pointing to a blog that contained an interesting idea. But both within the world of blogging and more generally on the Web, links can serve a very wide range of social and technical functions. A link may represent an advertisement determined by a third party and intended to entice a customer (e.g., Google AdWords), a source of further discussions on the same topic in other blogs, a path for connecting via e-mail or voice, a way of demonstrating ownership, a link to other sites authored by the same individual, a link to a group (blog ring, church group, collective) to demonstrate membership, or any number of other things. These myriad meanings are all tied up in the code of a hyperlink, and it may not be immediately obvious how these are related—except, of course, that they represent a pathway between pages. Are the results, which suggest affinities or proximities between cities, to be believed? What do these characteristics mean in terms of "real" social structure?

The question is a vexing one, since the reason for performing such an analysis is to reveal latent structures that are not already obvious to an observer. In the case of the observations here, the network was similar to other geographically distributed communications networks, from telephones to package deliveries. These similarities and other similarities suggest that something structural is happening and provides a way forward. I have elsewhere suggested that the process is like inferring social

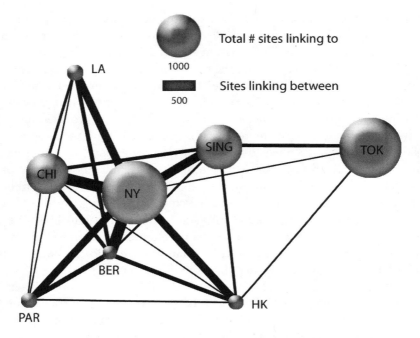

Fig. 1. Links among eight world cities: Berlin (BER), Chicago (CHI), Hong Kong (HK), Los Angeles (LA), New York (NY), Paris (PAR), Singapore (SING), and Tokyo (TOK). (From Halavais 1999.)

relationships from road maps, or Bush's "associative trails," even when it may not be entirely clear why any individual has followed a given path.[24] I drew on a history of the telephone by Casson, who suggests that "wherever there is interdependence, there is bound to be telephony."[25] Likewise, interdependence now breeds hyperlinking. The precise mechanism by which a particular path is cut, or a hyperlink formed, is not important. What is important is that some connection must have existed in order for that connection to be cemented hypertextually; hyperlinks are not random.

The Durkheimian tradition in sociology, like the cybernetic tradition, suggests not only that we can understand social behavior separately from the individual but that knowledge of individual motives is not required to understand "emergent properties" of society. Some have argued that despite the uncertainty surrounding individual citations, the observation of patterns at the network level can still provide valid and useful information.[26] Naturally, the ultimate aim is to integrate the microlevel and

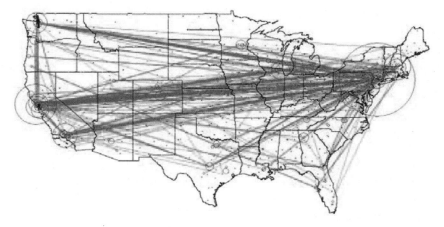

FIG. 2. Links among blogs in the United States. (From Lin, Halavais, and Zhang 2006.)

macrolevel understanding of hyperlinking behaviors, but it is not clear that the microlevel understanding must come first.

Understanding the structure of hyperlinked networks is not sufficient, nor is it intended to be. Whether geographical or not, examining the structural components of a network produces interesting questions. It insists that we ask why two documents, two organizations, or two people are linked together. It makes us wonder how certain parts of the Web come to be well regarded and others do not. There is something satisfyingly analytical about reducing mass impulses and hyperlinked networks to their constituent parts, and there continues to be value in doing so. But understanding the nature of the network can be an effective antecedent to understanding the nature of the individual hyperlink. It may be that the meaning of a hyperlink is best understood within the context of a hyperlinked network.

Curse of the Second Order?

For a short time, the field of cybernetics thrived in the United States. It was thought that the behaviors of complex systems were more telling than their constituent parts. Human systems are difficult to observe, in part because the observers are themselves necessarily a part of the system.

Second-order cybernetics attempted to incorporate the observer in the observations; that is, it insisted that a degree of reflexivity is required in studying social systems.[27] The trick with human systems is that they evolve and adapt not only to their environments but also to the observers who study them. When hyperlink analysis is present on the Web, especially when it is presented in real time, the same sorts of second-order effects begin to arise.

As noted, there are certain advantages to understanding the structure and dynamics of hyperlink networks. Indeed, even if we do not accept this hypothesis, a significant proportion of society has. The popular press is rife with advice about how to thrive in a newly networked society. Companies are throwing aside traditional hierarchies in favor of more agile, networked organizations. The network is becoming an organizing social principle, and in recognizing this, we are condemned to try to understand it from within.

Hyperlinks are not causing this shift alone, but the networks that are built up of hyperlinks allow for it. The hyperlink provides a basic building block through which complex, multidimensional, and easily changed documentation and communication systems may be constructed. The structural skeleton of an organization is the system by which it stores and transmits its accumulated knowledge. The move from the hierarchical, bureaucratic taxonomies of the traditional corporation—required, at least in part, by the nature of their records systems—to the more dynamic networked organization favored by terrorists and revolutionaries is the leitmotif of current business and political magazines and journals.[28] Manuel Castells remains the most identifiable proponent of the idea that networks are an organizing principle of modern society. He argues:

> As a historical trend, dominant functions and processes in the information age are increasingly organized around networks. Networks constitute the new social morphology of our societies, and the diffusion of networking logic substantially modifies the operations and outcomes in processes of production, experience, power, and culture.[29]

Of course, these networks do not require hyperlinks, but, notwithstanding Castells's own dismissal of hyperlinks, their ability to bind together and restructure media means that they are becoming the currency and connective tissue of the networked society.[30]

As a result, there is new attention being paid to network measures. Not only social scientists but their subjects are increasingly interested in where individuals are placed in the network. Google is built on the assumption that hyperlinks somehow transmit power or credibility. On the basis of that assumption, the search engine sends more traffic to the heavily linked sites, reinforcing that position of authority and leading to even more links. This occurs, arguably, to an even greater extent in the blogosphere, where some bloggers closely watch their ratings on Technorati and seek to rise in the rankings to the coveted A-list. Those who reach the most linked positions are likely to attract not only fame but fortune.[31]

There has always been some interest in uncovering, for example, the informal network of communication within an organization, but it has never been as easy as it is now to see who links to whom. As automatically gathered network measures become increasingly available, it is likely that behaviors will continue to change in an effort to affect these metrics. The result will be similar to what is already seen in academic circles, as tenure committees have adopted impact factors as an important way of measuring the performance of scholars. Once measures are visible, it is possible to play to the measures and to game the system.

Perhaps the most obvious example of this is a practice called "Google bombing," an attempt to associate a keyword search with a particular Web site. This manipulation is accomplished by encouraging a large number of Web authors to create a hyperlink to a Web site with anchor text containing a specific word or phrase. For example, by 2007 it was still the case that if someone queried one of the popular search engines for "failure" or "miserable failure," the biography of George W. Bush would be the first result; likewise a search for "liar" produced the biography of Tony Blair. Naturally, these phrases do not appear in the biographies of these two leaders, but because large numbers of individual links leading to the sites contained these key phrases, the Google search engine came to associate these pages with the phrases, as did several other search engines. Once it became clear that Google was susceptible to this form of manipulation, there were calls for Google to change its algorithms to reduce Google bombing. While Google initially refused to make changes, subsequent adjustments appear to have reduced the efficacy of this particular form of manipulation.

An entire industry has grown up around the manipulation of search engine results. Even those who do not consult an expert in "search engine optimization" remain interested in how best to improve their search rankings. In the blogging world, they may adjust their writing to attract a larger number of hyperlinks, just as a young academic might publish a literature review, rather than original work, knowing that a review is more likely to be cited. Young people come to attach as much value to the number of "friends" they have on MySpace as they do to other markers of social capital.

The effect on network measures is twofold. First, they are no longer as unobtrusive as they might once have been. As people within the network become more network conscious, their behaviors change in an attempt to affect who links to them and why. Second, at least in the case of commercial systems like Google and Technorati, the algorithms are changed to make gaming the system more difficult. This game of cat and mouse really means that those measuring the system have become a significant part of it. This may not affect social researchers as directly as it does search engines, but the conscious attempt to achieve favorable positions within the network structure means that network measures become as complicated by self-interest as are surveys and other obtrusive measures.

This is disappointing for those who would hope to be able to use hyperlinks as an unobtrusive way of mapping the structure of the collective unconscious, but it also suggests new, more "network-aware" uses of hyperlinks by those who create them. On the one hand, attempts to manipulate the network structure among bloggers are often seen in a negative light; the terms "link whoring" and "link doping" have emerged to describe behaviors directed specifically at shaping a blog's position in the network. On the other hand, that kind of conscious awareness of the importance of deep hypertext structures by those who make use of the structures suggests a kind of maturation of collective consciousness, a striving for self-awareness, and a collaborative move toward more effective manipulation of those network structures.

The idea that the hyperlink network is becoming self-aware may sound a bit like science fiction—and with good reason. While Vannevar Bush is often credited with forming the concept of hypertext, his hypertext was intended for the scientific community, not for a broader global population.[32] H. G. Wells had recently suggested the emergence of a "world brain," which sounded, in substance, much like Bush's "associative trails."[33] Wells's book on the topic addressed the creation of an encyclopedia that could (through microfilm, as with the memex) be accessed and modified by anyone in the world. Many have seen the World Wide Web as a reflection of Wells's vision, and some have taken this a step further and suggested that the Web is moving us toward a thinking superorganism.[34] While the particulars may differ, Wells clearly considered a global, hyperlinked encyclopedia to be a necessary part of a new form of global self-governance.[35]

The possibility for self-governance arises not just from an increase in global communication but from the emergence of a particular kind of communication. Deutsch suggests that self-government, or "steering" of society, is accomplished through a special set of control channels. Not all communication is used for self-government, but those channels that allow for the organization and action of a society are particularly important and constitute the "nerves of government."[36] Hyperlinks are, essentially, text. They differ from other content only in that they may be interpreted as a kind of control language: a code that provides for organization, coordination, and structure. Hyperlinks form the basis for this learning, adaptive, self-aware social system.

The Changing Nature of the Link

I want now to return to this essay's initial question—what is the meaning of a hyperlink, or, as I have refigured it, what is the meaning of a hyperlink network? It seems that the answer depends in part on when the question is asked and by whom. The citation and hyperlink have a long history, and in the last decade, the role and meaning of a hyperlink seem already to have changed considerably. The future of linking is likely to be even more convoluted as hyperlinks carry more semantic value and reach even further into our everyday lives. It seems that such networks are growing more complex and adaptive and that their use is becoming more introspective. Futurists and science fiction authors have long held the idea that the network is becoming self-aware. If such self-awareness is to come to pass, hyperlink networks are likely to be central to that process.

If we are to take a long view of the hyperlink, we see it appropriating an ever-increasing role in our interactions. Its initial function mirrors that of citations and annotations, shaping text into structures that are more useful than linear arrangements. Citing the works of others, like any other form of communication, is essentially a social act, and as the norms of citation evolve, citation practices continue to have social influences. With the initial extension of the Web, hyperlinks took on an increasing role as tools for navigation, transporting attention from place to place. Especially with the rise of user-created media online, the social and navigational functions have come to predominate.

Even into the late 1990s, the Web was just one of many applications available on the Internet. Increasingly, the terms *Internet* and *World Wide Web* are used interchangeably. While not strictly correct, this conflation speaks to the degree to which the Web and hypertext have become organizing structures for communications online. Much of what people do on a computer these days, from e-mail to word processing, happens from within a Web browser. Hyperlinks have become the default user interface for the Internet.

The penetration of hyperlinks is likely to become even more ubiquitous as our computing devices do. The idea that clicking can only occur with a mouse on a computer monitor is already fading as touch screens on portable devices are seen more frequently and other switches become programmable. The border between hyperlinks and other forms of actuators is already dissolving to a certain degree. While the start button on some cars may not feel like a hyperlink, the functions of the stereo or navigation computer probably do. The ultimate trajectory of hyperlinks may indeed be invisibility, the blue-underlined text merging with light switches and voice commands to become one of a superset of links.

As the hyperlink becomes more ubiquitous, it is also layered with more meaning. The long-predicted Semantic Web, a Web that provides both content and information about how that content is related, has been slow in coming. In part, this is because it has been difficult to encourage people to create metadata, explicit descriptions of what content is and how it relates to other content on the Web. In the last few years, as the value of such data has become clearer, users have slowly started creating explicit metadata that can be read and manipulated. There is a press toward adding tags to hyperlinks to make them more meaningful. Certainly, the OpenURL has gained some ground within library circles. Google's support of the nofollow tag came, in part, as a response to spammers commenting on blogs, as well as to a general interest (also largely among bloggers) in being able to link to something without appearing to endorse it. There is an incipient effort to tag certain hyperlinks "not safe for work."[37] Some of this metadata is created automatically by content management and blogging systems. Such uses of semantic markup in hyperlinks are only at their earliest stages, but the practice of what might be called "reflexive hyperlinking" is already widespread, leading to a new awareness about what it means to make a link.

While tagging and folksonomies have largely been conceptualized independently of their influence on hyperlink networks, several of the systems that allow for tagging are annotating particular pages on the Web and, by extension, the links that lead there.[38] Given the long-standing difficulty in producing metadata for electronic content, this "bottom-up" approach provides a great deal more context for Web links. As noted earlier, much of the research power in hyperlink networks comes not from the networks themselves but from their combination of structural information with other sources of data about the pages and links. This human-generated metadata, along with other sources of metadata about content on the Web and how it is linked, will make analyses of hyperlinked networks richer and more revealing.

The increased reach of hyperlinks and the richness of information that may be associated with those links demands the continued study of hyperlinked networks and the links that make them up. There are some obvious targets for further research. While several studies have attempted to measure the motivations, gratifications, and cognitive processes surrounding the creation of hyperlinks, as well as similar contexts for choosing to follow a hyperlink, the majority of these studies have concentrated on portions of the Web with a scholarly or academic function.[39] Understanding the contexts in which links are created and used represents an interesting challenge for the researcher, one that is likely to be rewarding.

This essay has suggested that the study of macrolevel hyperlink networks has been complicated by users becoming more aware of hyperlink structures. While this makes the interpretation more elaborate, it in no way obviates the interest or need to study hyperlink networks. In fact, the wider interest in such studies encourages public scholarship that provides data to the communities we study. Moreover, as the need for tools to understand the structure of hyperlink networks extends beyond the world of researchers, new tools are created that are useful in analyzing, visualizing, and making sense of these complex networks. Ideally, programs of research will allow for the macrolevel analysis to be integrated with a better understanding of why and how people contribute to the creation of these structures. Moreover, as such understanding is advanced, it is likely to alter the ways in which people create and use hyperlinks. Awareness of hyperlink networks is in some ways only an intermediary step toward networks that are able to understand and interpret themselves to an increasing degree.

In understanding what a hyperlink means, we need to look at what a hyperlink does. Over time, it has come to do more and more. At present, it stands as the basic element of organization for the Web, and as more and more of our lives are conducted through the Web, it becomes increasingly important that we understand how hyperlinked structures are formed and change.

NOTES

1. N. Holmes, "The KWIC and the Dead: A Lesson in Computing History," *Computer* 34, no. 1 (2001): 144.

2. E. L. Eisenstein, *The Printing Press as an Agent of Change: Communications and Cultural Transformations in Early-Modern Europe*, vol. 1. (Cambridge: Cambridge University Press, 1979).

3. G. N. Gilbert, "Referencing as Persuasion," *Social Studies of Science* 7, no. 1 (1977), 113–22.

4. R. G. Collingwood, *The Idea of History*, rev. ed. (Oxford: Oxford University Press, 1994), 62.

5. M. Polanyi and H. Prosch, *Meaning* (Chicago: University of Chicago Press, 1975), 184.

6. J. B. Walther, "Computer-Mediated Communication: Impersonal, Interpersonal, and Hyperpersonal Interaction," *Communication Research* 23, no. 1 (1996): 3–43.

7. S. Rose, "What's Love Got to Do with It? Scholarly Citation Practices as Courtship Rituals," *Language and Learning across the Disciplines* 1, no. 3 (1996): 34–48.

8. T. A. Brooks, "Private Acts and Public Objects: An Investigation of Citer Motivations," *Journal of the American Society for Information Science* 36, no. 4 (1985): 223–29.

9. A. Grafton, *The Footnote: A Curious History* (Cambridge, MA: Harvard University Press, 1999), 93.

10. E. Garfield, "Citation Behavior: An Aid or a Hindrance to Information Retrieval?" *Current Contents* 18 (1989): 3–8.

11. V. Bush, "As We May Think," *Atlantic Monthly*, July 1945, http://www.the atlantic.com/doc/194507/bush.

12. D. Engelbart, "The Click Heard Round the World," *Wired* 12, no. 1, http://www.wired.com/wired/archive/12.01/mouse.html.

13. T. H. Nelson, *Remarks on Xanadu* (Maastricht: Internet Research 3.0, 2004).

14. L. Egghe, "New Informetric Aspects of the Internet: Some Reflections—Many Problems," *Journal of Information Science* 26, no. 5 (2000): 329–35.

15. A. Scharnhorst and M. Thelwall, "Citation and Hyperlink Networks," *Current Science* 89, no. 9 (2005): 1518–23; M. Thelwall, "What Is This Link Doing Here? Beginning a Fine- Grained Process of Identifying Reasons for Academic Hyperlink Creation," *Information Research* 8, no. 3 (2003), http://informationr.net/ir/8-3/paper151.html.

16. T. H. Nelson, "Complex Information Processing: A File Structure for the Complex, the Changing, and the Indeterminate," in *Proceedings of the 1965 20th National Conference*, ed. Lewis Winner (New York: ACM, 1965), 84–100.

17. T. Ciszek and X. Fu, "An Annotation Paradigm: The Social Hyperlink," in *Proceedings of the American Society for Information Science and Technology* 42, no. 1 (2005), http://www3.interscience.wiley.com/journal/112785658; T. Bardini, "Bridging the Gulfs: From Hypertext to Cyberspace," *Journal of Computer-Mediated Communication* 3, no. 2 (1997), http://jcmc.indiana.edu/vol3/issue2/bardini.html; M. H. Jackson, "Assessing the Structure of Communication on the World Wide Web," *Journal of Computer-Mediated Communication* 3, no. 1 (1997), http://jcmc.indiana.edu/vol3/issue1/jackson.html.

18. S. Brin and L. Page, "The Anatomy of a Large-Scale Hypertextual Web Search Engine," *WWW7 / Computer Networks* 30, nos. 1–7 (1998): 107–17.

19. L. C. Freeman, "Centrality in Social Networks: Conceptual Clarification," *Social Networks* 1, no. 3 (1979): 215–39.

20. H. W. Park and M. Thelwall, "Hyperlink Analyses of the World Wide Web: A Review," *Journal of Computer-Mediated Communication* 8, no. 4 (2003), http://www.jcmc.indiana.edu/vol8/issue4/park.html.

21. A.-L. Barabási, *Linked: The New Science of Networks* (Cambridge, MA: Perseus, 2002).

22. A. Halavais, "Informational City Limits: Cities and the Infostructure of the WWW" (paper presented at the workshop "Cities in the Global Information Society: An International Perspective," Newcastle upon Tyne, November 1999).

23. J. Lin, A. Halavais, and B. Zhang, "The Blog Network in America: Blogs as Indicators of Relationships among US Cities," *Connections* 27, no. 2 (2006): 15–23.

24. A. Halavais, "National Borders on the World Wide Web," *New Media and Society* 2, no. 1 (2000): 7.

25. H. N. Casson, *The History of the Telephone* (Chicago: A. C. McClurg and Company, 1910), 97.

26. B. Van der Veer Martens, "Do Citation Systems Represent Theories of Truth," *Information Research* 6, no. 2 (2001), http://informationr.net/ir/6-2/paper92.html.

27. H. Von Foerster, *Understanding Understanding: Essays on Cybernetics and Cognition* (New York: Springer-Verlag, 2006), chap. 13.

28. J. Arquilla and D. F. Ronfeldt, *Networks and Netwars: The Future of Terror, Crime, and Militancy* (Santa Monica, CA: Rand Corporation, 2001).

29. M. Castells, *The Rise of the Network Society* (Oxford: Blackwell, 1996), 469.

30. M. Castells, *The Internet Galaxy: Reflections on the Internet, Business, and Society* (Oxford: Oxford University Press, 2001), 201–3.

31. C. Thompson, "Blogs to Riches: The Haves and Have-Nots of the Blogging Boom," *New York Magazine* 20 (February 2006), http://nymag.com/news/media/15967.

32. J. M. Nyce and P. Kahn, *From Memex to Hypertext: Vannevar Bush and the Mind's Machine* (San Diego: Academic Press, 1991), 50–51.

33. H. G. Wells, *World Brain* (London: Methuen and Company, 1938).

34. F. Heylighten and J. Bollen, "The World-Wide Web as a Super-Brain: From Metaphor to Model," in *Cybernetics and Systems '96*, ed. R. Trappl (Vienna: Austrian Society for Cybernetics, 1996), 917–22.

35. W. B. Rayward, "H. G. Wells's Idea of a World Brain: A Critical Reassessment," *Journal of the American Society for Information Science* 50, no. 7 (1999): 557–73.

36. K. Deutsch, *The Nerves of Government* (New York: Free Press, 1966).

37. P. J. Doland, "Genius Grant Please, or The NSFW HTML Attribute," *Frosty Mug Revolution*, December 28, 2006, http://pj.doland.org/archives/041571.php.

38. C. Marlow et al., "HT06, Tagging Paper, Taxonomy, Flickr, Academic Article, to Read," in *Proceedings of the Seventeenth Conference on Hypertext and Hypermedia* (New York: ACM, 2006), 31–40.

39. C. Hine, "Web Pages, Authors, and Audiences: The Meaning of a Mouse Click," *Information, Communication, and Society* 4, no. 2 (2001): 182–98.

PHILIP M. NAPOLI

Hyperlinking and the Forces of "Massification"

The role of hyperlinking in the development of the Internet warrants investigation for a number of reasons. First, along with the Internet's inherently global reach and its virtually unlimited content capacity, hyperlinking is one of the key factors that distinguishes the Internet from traditional media. Second, the dynamics of hyperlinking have evolved in a number of interesting and unexpected ways, particularly as a result of the mechanisms by which search engines choose to generate and display links. Finally, the underlying choices and dynamics of hyperlinking are, of course, central to the distribution of audience attention (and, consequently, dollars) online and can therefore exert considerable influence over how the Internet evolves as a medium.

An important component of the study of new media involves the investigation of the relationship between old and new media. Exploring how new media can either disrupt or become integrated into the existing media system offers valuable insights that can guide policy makers, industry decision makers, and scholars seeking to understand the organizational ecology of media, the evolution of media systems and media technologies, and the dynamics of media usage. Scholars from a wide range of disciplines have sought to understand the push and pull between the Internet's undeniable revolutionary potential as demonstrated by links and the various influences and constraints imposed by the existing media system that it has entered. In my own efforts to address this issue in the Internet's early stages of development, I focused on the then unclear question of the extent to which the Internet would ultimately demonstrate the characteristics of more traditional mass media and on the reasons the Internet might be likely to adopt many of the characteristics of traditional mass media rather than evolve as the entirely unique and revolutionary medium that many were hoping for and anticipating in those heady early days.[1] I dubbed the pressures compelling the Internet down more traditional media evolutionary paths the forces of "massification"—a term that referenced the then-common argument that the Internet represented the end (or at least the beginning of the end) of traditional mass media. Developed when the medium essentially was in its infancy, this analysis of the Internet and the predictive propositions it entailed managed to hold some water in the ensuing decade. The Internet has indeed come to serve many of the functions, feature many of the same institutions, exhibit many of the same audience behavior patterns, and provide much of the same content as many of the mass media that preceded it.

The present essay revisits some of these claims in light of the current status of the Internet and enlarges the analytical frame with an eye toward teasing out exactly how the process of linking online may or may not factor into the massification of the Internet. The first section of this essay provides an overview of the forces of massification that have traditionally influenced all new media (including the Internet); this section also considers recent developments online through this analytical lens. The next section looks specifically at the act of hyperlinking, asking whether it reinforces or undermines these forces of massification; this section draws on the growing body of literature analyzing the patterns of hyperlinking online as well as recent developments involving the process of hyperlink selection and generation. The concluding section assesses the implications of the dynamics of hyperlinking for the evolution of the Internet, considers policy implications, and offers suggestions for future research.

New Media and the Forces of Massification

New media technologies do not exist in a vacuum. Rather, they enter into a diverse, complex, and dynamic mix of established and emerging media. Consequently, understanding any new medium requires an understanding of its interaction with the existing media environment, both from the standpoint of consumer adoption and usage and from the standpoint of institutional responses.[2] Such an approach makes it necessary to focus not only on the interactions between old and new media but also on the key institutional and economic forces that act on any new medium as it begins to carve out its place within the established media system. Many of these forces (often the ones neglected by those providing the earliest assessments of new media technologies) in fact compel new media technologies along evolutionary lines established by traditional media. It is these that I have labeled the forces of "massification."[3] These forces fall into three broad categories: audience behavior, media economics, and institutional forces. Each of these will be reviewed briefly here.

Before examining each of these forces, however, it is important to outline the basic criteria that we associate with traditional mass media. Detailed discussions of this issue can be found elsewhere.[4] To briefly summarize, the common characteristics of traditional mass media include a one-to-many orientation (and an associated lack of interactivity); the prominence of "institutional communicators"; a strong commercial orientation; and an associated emphasis on audience maximization and, consequently, mass appeal content.[5]

Audience Behavior

Certain well-established aspects of audience behavior—across many media—can compel new media technologies to function along the lines of traditional media, particularly by encouraging audiences to maintain strong connections with one-to-many and noninteractive communicative forms, as well as connections to content with traditional mass appeal (as opposed to highly targeted and specialized niche content). There is, for instance, the well-documented tendency toward passivity in audience behavior.[6] There is a limit to the extent to which audiences want their media consumption to involve substantial interactivity or substantial search activities, although this limit may (or does?) vary across media, as well as across usage categories and demographic groups.

From an audience behavior standpoint, it is also important to recognize that there is a well-documented tendency across media for audiences to prefer content with higher production budgets and to interpret production budgets as some sort of (imperfect) manifestation of quality.[7] Of course, higher production budgets require the presumption of a satisfactory return; therefore, higher-budget content typically is geared toward having greater mass appeal. Thus the distribution of audience attention in most media contexts tends to cluster around high-budget, mass appeal content, which of course also tends to be the content produced by the traditional institutional communicators (with the resources to expend on big-budget content).[8]

Media Economics

The preceding discussion of audience behavior leads naturally into some of the basics of media economics. Perhaps the first key principle involves the powerful economies of scale that exist in the production of media content. Media content is defined in economic terms as a "public good."[9] Some key characteristics of public goods are high fixed costs, very low variable costs, and nondepletability. It is very expensive to produce and sell the "first copy" of a public good (e.g., a television program or Web site). But to sell additional copies to additional consumers requires very little additional cost, particularly given the fact that one consumer's consumption of the media product does not prevent another consumer from consuming the same media product (i.e., only one Web page needs to be created whether a thousand or a million people visit the site). There are enormous economies of scale to be achieved with such products, as production costs can be distributed over large audiences over long periods of time (consider the fact that *I Love Lucy* episodes are still collecting revenues).

This has a few implications for the massification of any medium. First, it creates a tremendous incentive for any new medium to function—if not primarily, at least significantly—as an ancillary distribution mechanism for content produced in older media. Second, it creates a powerful incentive for producers of content for the new medium to try to appeal to and thereby distribute production costs across as large an audience as possible. Third, the tremendous risk naturally associated with any product with very high fixed costs creates powerful incentives to employ traditional media industry strategies of risk reduction, such as derivations or recyclings of content already proven to be successful in other media or reliance on proven strategic approaches most likely to attract a large audience.[10]

Institutional Forces

Finally, we come to what are termed "institutional forces," those institutional characteristics of the media system that compel new technologies to adopt the characteristics of traditional media. First and perhaps most obvious, there is the well-documented historical pattern for existing media organizations to (somewhat belatedly, as it usually turns out) migrate into new media and, in so doing, transplant existing content (as already discussed), strategic approaches, and business models.[11] A second significant institutional force involves the process of audience measurement. Audience attention data is a vital commodity across all ad-supported media. It has proven to be particularly important to the establishment of any new technology as a viable advertising medium.[12] Unfortunately, one unavoidable by-product of most established audience measurement methodologies is that, given the nature of sampling, the larger the size of the audience, the more accurate and reliable are the audience data.[13] This creates an inherent bias in the audience marketplace, favoring content providers that attract large audiences.

The Massification of the Internet

When we consider these forces in relation to the Internet, it is important to acknowledge that the Internet has undoubtedly confounded traditional notions of a mass medium. Its interactive capacity is tremendous, and it facilitates not only one-to-many but also one-to-one and many-to-many forms of communication. Institutional communicators remain tremendously prominent, but opportunities for other types of actors to achieve prominence exist to an extent that cannot be found in other media. And while substantial portions of the Internet are highly commercialized and certainly devoted to pursuing large audiences, other components of the online realm are not. In these ways, the Internet has both adopted and expanded well beyond the characteristics of traditional media. But certainly, the traditional characteristics of mass media have become integral to the institutional structure and orientation of the Internet and to how consumers use it as an information and entertainment resource.[14]

From an audience behavior standpoint, it is somewhat telling that the typical television viewer, in an environment of channel abundance, regularly consumes only about thirteen of the available channels—and that this is roughly the same as the number of Web sites that the typical person visits on a regular basis.[15] It is not surprising, either, that the typical Web search seldom involves looking beyond the first page of links returned by the search engine or that a user looks beyond the first three pages of links less than 10 percent of the time.[16] The search-and-retrieve dynamic, perhaps the most basic attribute of an interactive medium, is one that extracts costs from the audience member. Consequently, we see audience behavior patterns, such as these, that illustrate important limitations in the extent to which the Internet's full potential to dramatically reconfigure the nature of audiences' interaction with their media can be realized.

Consider also the rise to prominence of content aggregation sites such as YouTube and MySpace. While these sites have received tremendous attention for empowering individuals to serve as content producers, facilitating a many-to-many communication dynamic and thereby "deinstitutionalizing" the media (all things, it should be noted, that the Internet was already facilitating without such sites), what has been largely ignored to date is the extent to which these sites function largely to confine the vastness and complexity of the Web into a simpler and more manageable framework. The days of scouring the Web for individual home pages or video clips are now being replaced by individual repositories/destinations that are subject to centralized editorial control. It is as if the large-scale gatekeeper bottlenecks characteristic of old media are being re-created in an environment in which they are not technologically necessary (or, presumably, desirable). Suddenly, many of the chaotic and independent features of the Web are being voluntarily placed under the control of a single institutional communicator (i.e., News Corp. in the case of MySpace and Google in the case of YouTube). This is a kind of downsizing or consolidation of the Web itself. Such patterns are a reaction to what has been inarguably described as "an enormous oversupply of web offerings that no human being can navigate without aides that give some structure to this ever-growing universe."[17] To the extent that this kind of aggregation of Web content is proving highly desirable or even necessary to users (in the same way that Amazon and eBay have consolidated online shopping), a potentially successful business strategy for going forward would simply be to identify other broad content categories currently scattered about the Web that are in need of aggregation and then develop the appropriate aggregation, search, and display mechanisms.

Related to this phenomenon, we also see a strong tendency for online audiences to cluster around relatively few content options, in a behavioral pattern that has been well established among the traditional mass media. Audience behavior research frequently has documented a "power law" distribution of audience attention and/or dollars, with 20 percent of the available content attracting 80 percent of the audience.[18] Recent research examining the distribution of audience attention across different media has found that the concentration of audience attention around relatively few sources in the traditional media realm has been largely reproduced in the online realm.[19] Some comparative studies have found an even greater concentration of audience attention online than is found in traditional media, such as newspapers, radio, and television.[20] Equally important is the fact that this audience attention is clustering around many of the institutional communicators that characterize the traditional media realm, as powerful media entities—ranging from News Corp. (particularly with its purchase of MySpace), to Time Warner (which, contrary to expectations, absorbed AOL rather than vice versa), to Disney—all have established prominent positions online.[21] Among the top ten "parent companies" online for the month of November 2006 were Time Warner, News Corp., the New York Times Company, and Disney (Nielsen//NetRatings, 2007).

Of course, given this institutional migration and the "public good" characteristics of media content, it is not surprising that the Web has developed as a key mechanism for accessing and distributing "old media" products, such as recorded music, television programs, motion pictures, and magazines. The Internet has been well described as "swallow[ing] up most, if not all, of the other media in an orgy of digital convergence."[22] To the extent that this is the case, the Internet's ability to exhibit fundamentally different characteristics from the media that preceded it seems limited.

This clustering of audiences also continues to be associated with patterns in advertiser behavior that are consistent with the massification effects of audience measurement. Established audience measurement systems naturally favor sites that attract large audiences (in the perceptions of advertisers) over sites that attract smaller audiences, even if the latter, niche sites might be attracting audiences that are more desirable (from the advertisers' standpoint). Advertisers have shown themselves to be willing to pay a premium for accuracy in audience measurement, which can help explain why, even today, the most popular Web sites attract a share of online advertising dollars that exceeds their share of the online audience.[23] This creates important economic disincentives for serving narrower, more specialized audiences online.

Hyperlinking and the Forces of Massification

As the preceding section illustrated, the technological forces compelling a new medium such as the Internet to defy the confines of traditional media are to some degree offset by a number of countervailing social and institutional forces that are clearly influencing both the structure of the online realm and the ways that consumers navigate the online space. The questions that this section seeks to answer is whether and how the practice of hyperlinking—a practice that, to a large degree, distinguishes the realm of online media—factors into the push and pull between old and new media that is at the core of the Internet's evolutionary process.[24]

Hyperlinks have been described as "the heart of the World Wide Web."[25] In thinking broadly about the process of linking online, it is important not to think only in terms of the links to text and video that can be embedded in discrete Web pages (thereby creating the distinctive "intertextuality" of the Web and Web navigation). We also need to consider the processes of link generation and display associated with the functioning of search engines (given the centrality of search engines to online navigation). And we need to note the processes of link generation that ac-company—and are meant to assist or manipulate—consumer choices on-line (i.e., the recommendations about other potentially interesting con-tent that now frequently accompany Web users' content selections). These represent perhaps the most fundamental contexts for exploring the potential significance of linking to the process of massification online.

A potentially useful conceptual lens for examining these various con-texts involves the concept of gatekeeping. Despite early proclamations to the contrary, it has become very clear by this point that the Internet has not, by any stretch of the imagination, eliminated gatekeeping or made it obsolete. Rather, the dynamics of the gatekeeping process have changed significantly, perhaps becoming a bit more covert.[26] Much gatekeeping can now be handled via technological means, though the human factor remains prominent.[27] Hyperlinking is perhaps the most significant mech-anism of online gatekeeping.[28] Through their decisions about when and where to hyperlink and, most important, what to link to, content providers exert substantial editorial control.[29] As Park has noted, Web sites can very usefully be perceived as "actors," and "through a hyperlink, an individual website plays the role of an actor who could influence other website's trust, prestige, authority, or credibility."[30] Hyperlinking thus serves as a primary mechanism via which an online content provider ex-erts control over its audience and, to use terminology drawn from tradi-tional media (specifically television), manages "audience flow."[31]

The concept of the "walled garden" arose primarily to describe AOL's early efforts to keep its subscribers within AOL-generated content and away from the true World Wide Web.[32] But it continues to have rele-vance in the context of contemporary linking activities. Research shows that online news sites overwhelmingly hyperlink only to internal Web pages and seldom link to outside sources.[33] Other research suggests that search engines produce results that suppress links to controversial infor-mation or news stories.[34] Recent efforts at mapping the distribution of links online (in terms of who links to who, how often, etc.) document a clear and coherent "information politics" that suggests that very deliber-ate editorial decisions are being made with an effort toward guiding audi-ence attention down certain preferred paths as opposed to others.[35]

When these types of traditional editorial dimensions of hyperlinking are coupled with the technical dimensions of link generation by search engines (in which the quantity of inbound links is a key driver of a link's placement in the search results), the question frequently has arisen whether the dynamics of linking are such that the imbalances in content accessibility and prominence that characterize the traditional mass media world are being replicated in the online world.[36] Research suggests that this may very well be the case.[37] Koopmans and Zimmerman, for instance, find that in terms of political news coverage, the same institutional actors and information sources achieve virtually identical levels of prominence (as measured, in part, by link quantity) in both the online and print media realms.[38]

The persistence of such patterns is in some ways surprising given the dramatic technological differences in how content is stored, exhibited, and accessed in online versus offline contexts. These important differences and their potentially dramatic implications are explored perhaps most extensively in Anderson's "long tail" analysis.[39] The essence of the long tail argument is that the combination of the greatly expanded content storage capacity of a digitized space such as the Internet (versus, say, a traditional book or record store) and the enhanced, highly interactive search tools that such a space can provide (e.g., peer recommendations; site-generated recommendations; and robust, multidimensional search features) contribute to a media environment in which the traditional power law distribution of audience attention can be altered or at least can become more lucrative than was possible in the offline world.[40] A consumption dynamic in which 20 percent of the content generates 80 percent of the revenue (and in which nobody knows what that 20 percent is going to be)[41] can be more profitable in an environment in which "shelf space" is much less scarce (and less expensive) and in which the consumer's ability to effectively and satisfactorily navigate this expansive shelf space is enhanced via a wide range of search tools and linking systems.

In such an environment, the content provider can make all of the relevant content available and not have to make editorial judgments about which content to include or exclude based on (often wrong) predictions regarding consumer tastes. The content provider can also be reasonably sure that all of the content will generate at least some revenue, even if the bulk of the revenues continue to be generated by only 20 percent of the content. Under this model, the chances of success are increased because (a) the content provider never has to worry about not having any of the 20 percent of content options that prove to be enormously successful and (b) the remaining content (the long tail) can be stored and exhibited cheaply enough and located and accessed easily enough by the consumer to become a meaningful contributor to profits.

This description of the long tail model has tried to emphasize an issue that has received surprisingly little attention: the extent to which these radical changes in content distribution, access, and exhibition do anything to alter the well-established dynamics of how audiences distribute their attention across various content options. The long tail phenomenon (i.e., the 80/20 rule) that characterized traditional media remains a defining characteristic of the new media space, as the research already cited suggests, though other recent research suggests that some very modest shifts toward a broader allocation of audience attention can result from the migration to online distribution and exhibition.[42] It seems safe to say that the online environment simply provides a potentially more profitable context in which to navigate the traditional constraints under which content providers have operated. But the fact that this dramatically changed technological environment can apparently do relatively little to alter the fundamental distribution patterns of audience attention is, in many ways, as remarkable, if not more remarkable, than the ways in which this changed technological environment can alter the economics of content distribution and exhibition. The persistence of such patterns in the distribution of audience attention may be a reflection of the fact that the exact same power law patterns can be found in the distribution of inbound and outbound links on the Web.[43] Thus the ecology of hyperlinks may itself represent a set of paths that is compelling a distribution of audience attention that bears a striking resemblance to the distribution of audience attention in the traditional mass media.

Conclusion

As this essay has illustrated, even the process of hyperlinking, which is representative of the distinctive, boundary-defying, and interactive character of the Internet, in many ways complies with or is influenced by a set of forces that help compel the medium to function (from both a content producer and a content consumer's standpoint) along lines established by traditional media. This is not to say that the innovative potential of the Internet has gone completely unrealized. But it does suggest that the evolutional trajectory of any new medium—even one as dramatically different as the Internet—is significantly constrained by a set of stable and influential social and institutional forces.[44]

There are also some important policy implications to be drawn from the patterns reviewed in this essay. Perhaps the most important of these is to question the argument increasingly heard in policymaking circles that regulation of traditional media's ownership and market structure is no longer necessary because the Internet provides a robust and viable alternative to them. Clearly, the more the Web exhibits the characteristics of traditional media, the less relevant this argument becomes.[45]

From a research standpoint, however, we still have much to learn about the processes of linking and how they impact the dynamics of content production, distribution, and access. As Wellman has illustrated, early Internet research focused primarily on prognostications.[46] The second stage involved the basic mapping of user behavior, and only now have we entered the stage where the dynamics of Internet usage are being subject to robust empirical analysis. However, not all aspects of Internet research are at the same evolutionary stage. While we are developing a sophisticated understanding of the dynamics of Internet usage, our understanding of the production side is not as far along. Today, we are still very much embedded in Wellman's second stage of analysis as it relates to the production and presentation of Web content.[47] This "mapping" of the online space is well developed. We are developing a strong sense of the distribution of links—of who links to whom and how often.[48] However, we do not yet understand very well the dynamics of the linking decision-making process. What factors determine whether or not a site is linked to another site? Why do certain sites become important nodes in Web space while others languish in relative obscurity? Inquiries in this vein have been infrequent up to this point.[49]

Moving forward, it seems important that researchers make further efforts to move beyond the consumption side of the Internet (i.e., how users navigate the online space and distribute their attention) and delve deeper into the processes surrounding the generation of content and how these content sources interact with one another (e.g., via linking). For instance, in light of the tremendous amount of attention that blogging is receiving as an alternative to traditional news media, we need to ask to what extent the links provided by bloggers are pointing readers to traditional news media sources? Similarly, we should investigate the extent to which the content populating sites such as YouTube is really "user-generated" content or simply content "ripped" from traditional media (e.g., TV and movie clips). Equally important, how is audience attention distributed across these different content types? Is traditional media content being consumed in proportion to its availability on such platforms? Or is it being consumed in greater or lesser proportion to its availability?

In some ways, this pattern in our understanding of the Web as a medium mirrors the evolution of the field of communications research, where the initial empirical focus was directed at the receivers of the information (their usage patterns, effects, etc.). Only after this line of in-quiry matured did we see researchers turn their attention to the organi-zations involved in the production and distribution of content. However, focusing greater attention on questions such as these is essential for de-veloping a clearer portrait of the interaction between old and new media and the extent to which a new medium is really performing new func-tions, instituting new communications dynamics, and providing new con-tent.

NOTES

1. P. M. Napoli, "The Internet and the Forces of 'Massification,'" *Electronic Journal of Communication* 8, no. 2 (1998), http://www.cios.org/www/ejc/v8n298.htm.

2. S. Lehman-Wilzig and N. Cohen-Avigdor, "The Natural Life Cycle of New Media Evolution: Inter-Media Struggle for Survival in the Internet Age," *New Media and Society* 6, no. 6 (2004): 707–30; P. M. Napoli, "Evolutionary Theories of Media Institutions and Their Responses to New Technologies," in *Communication Theory: A Reader*, ed. L. Lederman (Dubuque, IA: Kendall/Hunt, 1998), 315–29.

3. Napoli, "The Internet and the Forces of 'Massification.'"

4. Ibid.; W. R. Neuman, *The Future of the Mass Audience* (New York: Cambridge University Press, 1991); J. Turow, *Media Systems in Society: Understanding Industries, Strategies, and Power* (White Plains, NY: Longman, 1992); J. G. Webster and P. F. Phalen, *The Mass Audience: Rediscovering the Dominant Model* (Mahwah, NJ: LEA, 1997).

5. J. Turow, "The Critical Importance of Mass Communication as a Concept," in *Mediation, Information, and Communication: Information and Behavior*, ed. B. D. Ruben and L. Lievrouw, vol. 3 (New Brunswick, NJ: Transaction Publishers, 1990), 9–20; Napoli, "The Internet and the Forces of 'Massification.'"

6. Webster and Phalen, *Mass Audience*.

7. B. M. Owen and S. S. Wildman, *Video Economics* (Cambridge, MA: Harvard University Press, 1992).

8. Ibid.

9. Ibid.

10. Media products, in particular, have proven to be a very risky business across a wide range of technologies; see P. M. Napoli, *Audience Economics: Media Institutions and the Audience Marketplace* (New York: Columbia University Press, 2003).

11. Napoli, "The Internet and the Forces of 'Massification'"; Napoli, "Evolutionary Theories of Media Institutions."

12. Napoli, *Audience Economics*.

13. Ibid.

14. L. D. Introna, "Shaping the Web: Why the Politics of Search Engines Matters," *Information Society* 16, no. 3 (2000): 169–85; J. G. Webster and S. F. Lin, "The Internet Audience: Web Use as Mass Behavior," *Journal of Broadcasting and Electronic Media* 46, no. 1 (2002): 1–12.

15. D. A. Ferguson and E. M. Perse, "The World Wide Web as a Functional Alternative to Television," *Journal of Broadcasting and Electronic Media* 44, no. 2 (2000): 155–74.

16. iProspect, "Search Engine User Behavior Study," http://www.iprospect .com/premiumPDFs/WhitePaper_2006_SearchEngineUserBehavior.pdf (accessed January 9, 2007).

17. R. Koopmans and A. Zimmerman, "Visibility and Communication Networks on the Internet: The Role of Search Engines and Hyperlinks" (paper presented at the CONNEX workshop "A European Public Sphere: How Much of It Do We Have and How Much Do We Need?" Amsterdam, November 2–3, 2005).

18. A.-L. Barabási and R. Albert, "Emergence of Scaling in Random Networks," *Science* 286, no. 5439 (1999): 509–12; Webster and Lin, "The Internet Audience"; M. Hindman, "A Mile Wide and an Inch Deep: Measuring Media Diversity Online and Offline," in *Media Diversity and Localism: Meaning and Metrics*, ed. P. M. Napoli (Mahwah, NJ: Erlbaum, 2007), 327–48.

19. Webster and Lin, "The Internet Audience"; Webster and Phalen, *Mass Audience*; J. Yim, "Audience Concentration in the Media: Cross-Media Comparisons and the Introduction of the Uncertainty Measure," *Communication Monographs* 70, no. 2 (2003): 114–28.

20. Hindman, "A Mile Wide and an Inch Deep."

21. L. Dahlberg, "The Corporate Colonization of Online Attention and the Marginalization of Critical Communication?" *Journal of Communication Inquiry* 29, no. 2 (2005): 160–80; Koopmans and Zimmerman, "Visibility and Communication Networks."

22. Lehman-Wilzig and Cohen-Avigdor, "The Natural Life Cycle of New Media Evolution," 707.

23. Webster and Phalen, *Mass Audience*; Napoli, *Audience Economics*; A. Klaassen, "The Short Tail: How the 'Democratized' Medium Ended Up in the Hands of the Few—at Least in Terms of Ad Dollars," *Advertising Age*, November 27, 2007, 1.

24. R. Cover, "Audience inter/active: Interactive Media, Narrative Control, and Reconceiving Audience History," *New Media and Society* 8, no. 1 (2006): 139–58.

25. J. Giuffo, "The Web: Unlock Those Links," *Columbia Journalism Review*, September–October 2002, 9.

26. J. Zittrain, "A History of Online Gatekeeping," *Harvard Journal of Law and Technology* 19, no. 2 (2006): 253–98.

27. Introna, "Shaping the Web."

28. Ibid.; F. Menczer et al., "Googlearchy or Googlocracy?" *IEEE Spectrum* 43, no. 2, http://spectrum.ieee.org/print/2787.

29. S. L. Gerhart, "Do Web Search Engines Suppress Controversy?" *First Monday* 9, no. 1 (2004), http://firstmonday.org/issues/issue9_1/gerhart/index.html.

30. H. W. Park, "Hyperlink Network Analysis: A New Method for the Study of Social Structure on the Web," *Connections* 25, no. 1 (2003): 53.

31. Webster and Phalen, *Mass Audience*; M. McAdams and S. Berger, "Hypertext," *Journal of Electronic Publishing* 6 (2001), http://www.press.umich.edu:80/ jep/06-03/McAdams/pages/.

32. P. Aufderheide, "Competition and Commons: The Public Interest in and after the AOL–Time Warner Merger," *Journal of Broadcasting and Electronic Media* 46, no. 4 (2002): 515–32.

33. D. V. Dimitrova, C. Connolly-Ahern, and A. Reid, "Hyperlinking as Gatekeeping: Online Newspaper Coverage of the Execution of an American Terrorist," *Journalism Studies* 4, no. 3 (2003): 401–14.

34. Gerhart, "Do Web Search Engines Suppress Controversy?"

35. R. Rogers, *Information Politics on the Web* (Cambridge, MA: MIT Press, 2004).

36. Introna, "Shaping the Web"; Koopmans and Zimmerman, "Visibility and Communication Networks."

37. Hindman, "A Mile Wide and an Inch Deep"; Yim, "Audience Concentration in the Media."

38. Koopmans and Zimmerman, "Visibility and Communication Networks."

39. C. Anderson, *The Long Tail: Why the Future of Business Is Selling Less of More* (New York: Hyperion, 2006).

40. Ibid.

41. Napoli, *Audience Economics.*

42. A. Elberse and F. Oberholzer-Gee, "Superstars and Underdogs: An Examination of the Long Tail Phenomenon in Video Sales" (working paper no. 07-015, Division of Research, Harvard Business School, 2007); D. M. Pennock et al., "Winners Don't Take All: Characterizing the Competition for Links on the Web," *Proceedings of the National Academy of Sciences* 99, no. 8 (2002): 5207–11.

43. L. A. Adamic and B. A. Huberman, "The Web's Hidden Order," *Communications of the ACM* 44, no. 9 (2001): 55–59.

44. Neuman, *Future of the Mass Audience*; B. Winston, *Media Technology and Society: A History from the Telegraph to the Internet* (New York: Routledge, 1998).

45. Gerhart, "Do Web Search Engines Suppress Controversy?"

46. B. Wellman, "The Three Ages of Internet Studies: Ten, Five, and Zero Years Ago," *New Media and Society* 6, no. 1 (2004): 123–29.

47. Ibid.

48. Rogers, *Information Politics on the Web*; Park, "Hyperlink Network Analysis," 49–61.

49. M. Tremayne, "The Web of Context: Applying Network Theory to the Use of Hyperlinks in Journalism Stories on the Web," *Journalism and Mass Communication Quarterly* 81, no. 2 (2004): 237–53.

LOKMAN TSUI

The Hyperlink in Newspapers and Blogs

> Following are links to the external Web sites mentioned in this article. These sites are not part of the *New York Times* on the Web, and the *Times* has no control over their content or availability. When you have finished visiting any of these sites, you will be able to return to this page by clicking on your Web browser's "Back" button or icon until this page reappears.[1]

The hyperlink poses a dilemma for news organizations. On the one hand, links can be very useful in their ability to directly link to source material, such as public reports or official transcripts, in providing support for a news article. Considering that trust in what the people hear, see, and read has been steadily declining since the 1980s, the ability of the hyperlink to link a claim to its source can increase transparency of the news and subsequently restore some of the credibility of the mass media.[2] On the other hand, news editors may fear to link to Web sites over which the news organization has no control, as the preceding disclaimer from the *New York Times* exemplifies. While the disclaimer itself is no longer used, it does nicely capture an anxiety regarding the clarity of boundaries in the digital space. Yet newspaper editors worried about readers' confusion may also consider that competition with blogs in the "marketplace of attention"[3] may have made concern about linking moot. Most definitions of blogs include the hyperlink as one of its characteristics, suggesting that bloggers are not at all constrained by the attributional worries that might concern newspaper editors.

These comparisons may seem logical, but it must be said that no research or writing exists on the norms that bloggers or workers at the online divisions of newspaper firms hold toward use of the hyperlink. In fact, there are few studies of the ways hyperlinks are used by online news organizations in the coverage of news areas, such as politics. Such explorations are almost nonexistent regarding bloggers. The purpose of this essay is to report on a systematic comparison of the ways a sample of leading newspapers and blogs used hyperlinks. My central finding is that while the blogs link heavily to external Web sites, some major newspapers barely link at all, and others link exclusively to themselves. The strategies that explain these findings and their implications for democratic deliberation are topics deserving of further academic and public discussion.

How News Directs Attention

News has always been and is still a crucial means for organizing and directing our attention to valuable information. It distinguishes itself from other forms of public knowledge in its claim to truth. Crafting the news, journalists buttress the claim to truth by relying on the use of factual information. Facts, according to Tuchman, are "pertinent information gathered by professionally validated methods specifying the relationship between what is known and how it is known."[4] It is this process of sourcing, which includes fact-checking and verification, that defines news vis-à-vis other forms of public knowledge.[5] However, the process of sourcing has traditionally been problematic in terms of transparency. How do we know whether the journalist really did verify sources properly? Tuchman argues that the notion of objectivity is a crucial strategy journalists developed to establish a relationship of trust with the public. Well known and widely accepted, for example, is the "two source" rule. It stipulates that a journalist has to check with at least two different sources before publishing something as fact.

Professionalism, objectivity, and a code of ethics all factor in the journalist's strategy in a bid for the public's attention and trust. These conclusions are drawn from what are considered a set of classic newsroom ethnographies.[6] Obviously, notions of objectivity and professionalism continue to guide the production of news. However, considering that these ethnographies were conducted decades ago, do they still provide a comprehensive picture of how newsrooms function today? While we don't know for sure, it is doubtful regarding online news. A crucial difference in the way online news directs our attention is through the use of the hyperlink. The hyperlink allows news providers to suggest which voices are worthy of our attention and which voices are not. The hyperlink also is able to support the facticity of news, because of its inherent ability to specify "the relationship between what is known and how it is known," simply by providing a link to the source. With over 70 percent of the U.S.

population having accessed online news, it becomes paramount to have a better understanding of the production of online news and the role the hyperlink plays in it.[7]

How Online News Directs Our Attention

> People trust the *New York Times* and *Washington Post* and link to them, but there are a huge number of people who are going outside the bounds of traditional media to these new media forms to get their information and, more importantly, to participate in the discussions around news and topics. (David Sifry, blogger and CEO of Technorati)[8]

Digital network technology has drastically altered the social conditions of speech.[9] It has enabled the change from a situation where journalism as a practice is constrained by technology and reserved for a select few to a situation where barriers to publish are lowered to such a degree that Hartley argues that now "everyone is a journalist."[10] Jenkins similarly describes the rise of what he calls a "convergence culture," which is blurring the lines between old and new media and is resulting in "a changed sense of community, a greater sense of participation, less dependence on official expertise, and a greater trust in collaborative problem solving."[11]

This change in the cultural environment is perhaps best exemplified by the incredible rise in popularity of blogs. Many definitions of blogs point to the notion of a Web site with regularly updated entries, presented in reverse chronological order. Most definitions include the hyperlink as an important and even essential characteristic of what constitutes a blog.[12] Herring distinguishes different genres of blogs, ranging from blogs that function as personal diaries to blogs that link to, comment on, and cover news.[13] While most blogs (65 percent) do not make claims to be a form of journalism, they do mention that they sometimes or often practice journalistic standards, such as including links to original sources (57 percent) and spending extra time to verify facts they want to include in their postings (56 percent).[14] Some research has framed the relationship between bloggers and journalists as adversarial. Others suggest that the question of bloggers versus journalists is over and that the two have a synergistic relationship.[15] Lowrey, for example, suggests that a division of labor exists between the two, with bloggers relying on the work of journalists and taking up what they fail to cover at the same time. Because of a relative lack of institutional constraints, bloggers can afford to be specialized and partisan; to cite nonelite sources; and, in general, to cater to a niche audience.[16] At a conference panel on blogging, journalism, and credibility, Rosen stated: "One of the biggest challenges for professional journalists today is that they have to live in a shared media space. They have to get used to bloggers and others with an independent voice talking about them, fact-checking them, overlooking them, and they no longer have exclusive title to the press."[17]

Clearly, the boundaries of what constitute news are blurring, and we need to have a more inclusive understanding of online news that goes beyond what is offered by the traditional mainstream media.[18] This sentiment is echoed by Jenkins, who argues that it would be "a mistake to think about either kind of media power in isolation."[19] Phrased in terms of the imperatives of media firms, the question is this: now that news is increasingly being created and read online, how have strategies for gaining public attention and trust adjusted according to the possibilities the Internet as a new medium offers? As a fundamental characteristic of the Internet, the hyperlink stands at the center of this subject.

The Functions of the Hyperlink for Newspaper Sites and Blogs

In its most basic form, the hyperlink makes it possible to connect one Web site to another. Due to its open-ended character, the hyperlink is a simple yet powerful tool that can be employed for many uses. The meaning of the connection is not implemented in the hyperlink itself and must often be inferred from the context.[20] With regard to the possible functions the hyperlink can take on in online news, we can distinguish between linking for two purposes: citation and reciprocity.

Citation

Perhaps the most classic function of the hyperlink is to use it for citation.[21] In its ability to connect a claim directly to its source, the hyperlink creates transparency in "the relationship between what is known and how it is known," something Tuchman has referred to as the defining feature of factual information. Much of the strength of the claim, however, still depends on the credibility of the source it is linked to. This might explain the reluctance to link to external Web sites, since there is no control over either their content or availability, as the previously quoted disclaimer from the *New York Times* exemplifies. As an existing news organization with an already well-established reputation, linking to less credible, external Web sites might form a threat rather than an opportunity. It becomes paramount to distinguish between internal links, which are considered safe, and external links, which there is no control over. One way to do this is to put a firewall between internal and external links; in practice, this means clearly marking what is internal and external—for example, by adding a disclaimer and clearly positioning the links outside the news article. Another way would be to dispense with external links altogether.

Reciprocity

The second function of the hyperlink is to foster relationships of reciprocity. Blogs in particular seem to depend on a strategy of reciprocity, of exchanging links, to build up both credibility and popularity. When asked by an audience member at the conference "The Hyperlinked Society" what he could do to have his blog mentioned and linked on Jay Rosen's popular blog PressThink, Rosen, a professor of journalism at New York University, answered that his best bet was to link to his Web site first.[22] Many search engines build on this concept of reciprocity. Measuring the relevance of a Web site through the number of incoming links is the basic idea behind PageRank, a crucial part of the success of Google as a search engine. It is also the basic idea behind Technorati, a search engine that keeps track of what is happening in the blogosphere. It measures which blogs are the most popular by their number of incoming links—by how many other Web sites link to them. The leading political blogs receive well over ten thousand incoming links from other Web sites. This includes such blogs as Michelle Malkin (10,240 incoming blog links) and group blogs, such as the Huffington Post (15,007 incoming blog links) and Daily Kos (11,475 incoming blog links).[23]

Incoming links are not just valuable for blogs, however, but also may carry great value for the traditional mass media. The idea of measuring incoming links—the idea behind PageRank and Technorati—is similar to a concept Tuchman has called "the web of facticity." It is the idea that facts can be supported and validated by other related facts, cross-referencing each other. Tuchman was certainly not referring to the World Wide Web back in 1978, but the idea of a "web" of facticity gains an added layer of meaning in the context of the hyperlink and online news: it is now possible to make the web of facticity explicit through the examination of the use of hyperlink in news articles. In other words, a journalist is now able to write a story with factual information and directly link the fact to the source, showing the public explicitly how that journalist got to know what she or he got to know. In turn, the story can be validated by other Web sites linking to it.

In addition to considerations regarding audience understanding of the facts of a story or opinion piece, important commercial concerns regarding reciprocal linking may guide news Web sites and blogs. All newspaper sites and many blogs carry advertising. The price of the ads goes up with the number of people who come to the site and, often, by the time they spend on the site. Newspaper sites consequently have an interest in keeping readers in their territory for as long as possible, and we might assume that external linking would work against that. Bloggers also have an interest in keeping readers, but their desire to rank highly in blog search engines so that people will visit them may lead them to follow Jay Rosen's previously noted advice and link to other bloggers.

Previous Research on Linking

Research on news production in the digital age has been sparse, with little attention being paid to the role of the hyperlink.[24] No writings examine the norms and strategies that the people who edit news or blog sites have toward links. A handful of studies do look at the presence of hyperlinks on newspaper sites. In a study published in 2002, Barnhurst concludes that online newspapers rarely make any use of hyperlinks in news articles, with more than 75 percent having no link at all.[25] Dimitrova and others found in 2003 that the destination of hyperlinks to an external Web site only happened in a stunningly low 4.1 percent of the total number of hyperlinks in newspaper articles.[26] This seems to be in line with the findings of Tremayne, who reports a steady decline in the proportion of external links over the period of 1999–2002.[27] Note, though, that these investigations were conducted during the Web's early years, and the current robust environment for the Internet might have brought changes in newspaper organizations' online procedures.

What about blogs? Contrary to what might be a general sense, by people who follow blogs, that heavy interlinking is widespread, Herring finds that about only half (51.2 percent) of the blogs that she surveyed link to other blogs, with even fewer (36.1 percent) linking to news sites.[28] However, she also notes that this number is likely to be skewed by the high number of blogs that act as personal diaries, many of which do not link to other Web sites. One might expect the blogs that link to, comment on, and cover news to display a strategy that links heavily to other Web sites. Herring's sample, however, does not include enough of these political blogs to say anything (statistically) significant about what their typical linking pattern would be like.

For this study, I am particularly interested in link patterns of political blogs as an alternative form of online news. Political blogs are interesting because many of them are stars of the blogosphere, attracting the most attention. Shirky argues that blogs follow a distribution that closely resembles a power law, meaning a winner-takes-all situation, where a small minority of the total number of blogs gets the majority of attention, while there is a long tail of the remaining blogs that does not get the amount of traffic remotely near those at the top.[29] A significant number of blogs at the high end of the power law distribution consists of these political blogs. Although the size of their audience is not quite comparable to those of the mass media, they are rapidly gaining influence.

Besides anecdotal evidence, however, there has been surprisingly little empirical research looking at link patterns of these leading political blogs. An exception is a study done by Adamic and Glance, who found in 2005 that the top forty political blogs refer to the mainstream media about once every post and referred to other blogs only one post out of ten.[30] This result, however, might not be fully generalizable, as it sampled posts during the 2004 presidential election, a time where it is particularly likely for blogs to link to coverage in the mainstream media. That the top forty political blogs linked more often to the mainstream media than to other blogs is particularly striking because these political blogs live and die by the link.

The goal of this study is to address some of the gaps in the literature on hyperlinks. It seeks to answer two sets of questions. First, is the hyperlink used at all in online news; and if so, to what Web sites do they link, in what way, and how often? Second, from the specific ways hyperlinks are used or not used, can we infer strategies regarding editorial control, the desire for high site ranking, and the interest in keeping people on the site?

Study Design and Method

I examined the online editions of four leading newspapers and five leading political blogs. The newspapers selected were the *New York Times*, the

Washington Post, USA Today, and the *Los Angeles Times.* The five political blogs selected were the Huffington Post, Michelle Malkin, Daily Kos, Crooks and Liars, and Think Progress. These five blogs were listed as the five most popular political blogs by Technorati based on the number of incoming links.[31]

The study focused on the coverage of political news in two periods, together making up one full week. The first period was March 1–4, 2007. The second period was March 26–28, 2007. By focusing on two distinct periods, the hope was to limit issues of periodicity bias. Political news was chosen because this type of news provides many opportunities to link to external sites.

The news articles and blog postings were downloaded on March 4, 2007, for the first period and on March 28, 2007, for the second period. Starting from the front page of the politics section for the newspapers and the front page of the political blogs, all articles and postings were downloaded and saved. This was critical due to the habit of newspapers to put older articles behind (sometimes locked) archives.

Answering the research questions required a content analysis of the news articles and blog postings. Two units of analysis were used: the article and the hyperlink. This design was chosen to make the content analysis more functional by breaking down the articles into hyperlinks and to aggregate them back again once the analysis was finished. The articles were coded for the following categories: URL, date of story, author, title, and source. Another code sheet was developed to capture the characteristics of hyperlinks. Links were coded for URL, label (the underlined text that is being linked), placement (inside or outside the article body), destination (internal or external Web site), category of the destination Web site (blog, mainstream news site, governmental or other institutional site, and other), and type of content being linked to (text, video, photo, audio, or contact information—e.g., an email address). The destination Web site was coded for four categories: blog, mainstream news, government or other institution, and other.

For the purposes of this study, a blog was defined as a Web site with regularly updated entries, presented in reverse chronological order. A "mainstream news site" was a Web site of any major news organization; when in doubt, a site was coded as other. The category "government or other institution" included any Web site by any government or other major institution, such as Gallup; when in doubt, the Web site again was coded as other. Other destination Web sites who did not fit in any of the other categories were coded as other.

All collected news articles and blog postings were analyzed for content. Hyperlinks were coded insofar as they were deemed relevant to the news article or blog posting. The decision of what was deemed relevant was left to the coder but specifically excluded tags, trackbacks, and comments. Tags were defined as links that are used to categorize the news article, often located outside the main body of the article and internally linked. The justification for exclusion here is that they are not used for the purpose of citation or reciprocity. Trackbacks and comments were excluded to eliminate issues involved with the lack of conformity across newspapers and blogs in offering these two functionalities. To determine intercoder reliability, three news articles or blog postings for each day for each newspaper or blog were randomly selected and coded. The average intercoder reliability was established at 0.97 for the news articles and blog postings and at 0.87 for the hyperlinks, using Krippendorff's alpha.

Findings

Do leading newspapers and political blogs link heavily? The answer seems to be yes. The total number of articles coded was 806, and the total number of links was 3,876, with a mean number of 4.8 links per article. Two newspapers, the *Los Angeles Times* and *USA Today*, were exceptions to this. *USA Today* had, despite the highest number of articles, only a little more than one link per article. The *Los Angeles Times* had even fewer links, on average only one link per three articles. The political blogs and the other two newspapers, the *Washington Post* and the *New York Times*, all linked frequently in their political news articles. Surpris-

TABLE 1.   Frequency of Links

Source	Number of Links	Number of Articles	Mean Number of Links Per Article
LA Times	11	37	0.3
USA Today	196	180	1.1
Think Progress	424	117	3.6
Crooks and Liars	356	76	4.7
Washington Post	429	73	5.9
Michelle Malkin	193	30	6.4
Huffington Post	1,114	163	6.8
Daily Kos	726	89	8.2
New York Times	427	41	10.4
Total	3,876	806	4.8

ingly, it was not a blog but the *New York Times* that linked the most of all, with more than ten links per article on average.

Do the leading newspapers and political blogs link to external Web sites? Here is a stark difference between the newspapers and the blogs in this study. The political blogs all linked heavily and also linked heavily to external Web sites. More than a third of the links of the Huffington Post and Daily Kos and over three-quarters of the links of Think Progress and Michelle Malkin pointed to external Web sites. This is in sharp contrast with the newspapers. While both the *Washington Post* and the *New York Times* linked heavily in their news articles, they linked almost exclusively to themselves. Less than 1 percent of the links in the political news articles of the *New York Times* pointed to external Web sites, while only 3 percent of the links in the political news articles of the *Washington Post* did so.

How many links are placed outside the main body of an article? The leading newspapers all placed well over half of their links outside the main body. The leading political blogs, however, seemed to exclusively place their links within the body. The exception was the Huffington Post, which placed well over two-thirds of its links outside the main body. How many links placed outside the main body of the article also point to external Web sites? Here the picture is very clear: practically none of those in this study were linked to external Web sites.

Finally, when blogs link externally to Web sites, to what kind of Web sites do they most often link to? The newspapers were here omitted from this analysis, considering that only the blogs linked to external Web sites. In roughly one-third of the cases, the political blogs linked to other blogs, with Michelle Malkin (42.4 percent) and Crooks and Liars (47.5 percent)

TABLE 2.   Destination of Links

Source	Number of Links to External Web Sites	Number of Links	Percentage of Links to External Web Sites
New York Times	3	427	0.7
USA Today	4	196	2.0
Washington Post	13	429	3.0
LA Times	3	11	27.3
Huffington Post	395	1,114	35.5
Daily Kos	273	726	37.6
Crooks and Liars	202	356	56.7
Think Progress	320	424	75.5
Michelle Malkin	151	193	78.2
Total	1,364	3,876	35.2

TABLE 3.   Placement of Links

Source	Number of Links Outside Article	Number of Links	Percentage of Links Placed Outside Article	Percentage of Links Placed Outside Article to External Web Sites
New York Times	225	427	52.7	0.0
USA Today	181	196	92.4	1.0
Washington Post	277	429	64.6	0.0
LA Times	7	11	63.6	0.0
Huffington Post	766	1,114	68.8	0.0
Daily Kos	0	726	0.0	0.0
Crooks and Liars	0	356	0.0	0.0
Michelle Malkin	9	193	4.7	0.0
Think Progress	0	424	0.0	0.0
Total	1,465	3,876	37.8	0.0

TABLE 4.   Categories of Externally Linked Web Sites by Percentages

Source	Blog	News	Gov.	Other
Michelle Malkin	42.4	27.8	4.6	25.2
Crooks and Liars	47.5	16.8	6.0	29.7
Think Progress	26.9	42.5	10.3	20.3
Daily Kos	28.6	38.1	12.1	21.3
Huffington Post	28.9	21.8	7.6	41.8
Mean	34.9	29.4	8.1	27.7

in particular being fond of linking to other blogs. The blogs also link frequently to mainstream news Web sites, including those of the *Washington Post* and the *New York Times.* Crooks and Liars (16.8 percent) linked the least to mainstream news Web sites, while Think Progress (42.5) linked the most frequently to mainstream news Web sites. A moderate number of the links were directed toward governmental or other institutional Web sites. Michelle Malkin (4.6 percent) linked the least frequently to such cites, while Daily Kos (12.1 percent) linked to them the most often. Finally, a fair share of their links went to other Web sites that did not fit into one of the three categories (blogs, mainstream news sites, and governmental or other institutional sites).

Discussion

J. D. Lasica, a media critic, blogger, and citizen media expert, has lamented the sparse use of the hyperlink by journalists.

> Equally important—and still underused, in my view—is the ability to link to source materials, transcripts, public records and other original documents to buttress an article's reporting. In this age of public mistrust of the media, such steps enhance a news organization's credibility. In my freshman year at college my journalism professor told us that the first rule of good journalism is: Show, don't tell. So: Don't tell readers to trust you. Show them the goods.[32]

Is Lasica's lament valid? The findings of this study show that it is a mixed bag for the leading newspapers. While the *Los Angeles Times* and *USA Today* still do not rely on the hyperlink much, the *Washington Post* and, in particular, the *New York Times* certainly do not underuse the hyperlink, as this study has shown that they link heavily in their news articles. However, Lasica is correct in his sense of the lack of use of the hyperlink by journalists to source original material, or what he refers to as "showing the goods." Even though the *Washington Post* and the *New York Times* link heavily, they also only exclusively link to themselves.

The leading newspapers do not use the hyperlink in their political news coverage for the purpose of citation. This is particularly unfortunate given the nature of political news, which affords many opportunities to link to external sources. Blogs, by contrast, link heavily and also link heavily to external Web sites. But how do we know that they use the hyperlink for purposes of citation and not for reciprocity? In cases when the political blogs link externally to other blogs, we cannot tell for sure. A blog might link to another blog to back up a claim but might also do this in the hope that the other blog will link back. However, the political blogs also link frequently to mainstream news Web sites. In this case, we can be pretty sure that the political blogs link for the purpose of citation. As this study has shown, there is zero expectation that the mainstream news Web sites will actually consider linking back to the blogs.

So why are newspapers reluctant to link to external Web sites? Although further research on the institutional processes behind online news production is needed, the findings of this study add support for several hypotheses that seek to explain the lack of external links. First, the study suggests little support for the hypothesis that the reluctance to link to external Web sites results from fear of losing control because it might threaten credibility. In the past, as the *New York Times* disclaimer has shown, links to external sites were often placed outside the main body of the news article; nowadays, both the disclaimer and the links to external sites are gone. But there really is no particular reason to hesitate linking externally for fear of losing credibility, as there are many credible Web sites that could be linked to. Pointing to press releases from the White House Web site might be useful to readers, for example. The fear of losing control, then, might be because of gatekeeping purposes. Dimitrova and others have previously suggested this second hypothesis.[33]

A third reason sometimes mentioned for mainstream news organizations' slowness to pick up on the potential of new technology, such as the hyperlink, points to technical or organizational inertia. The idea is that it takes time to get used to the new online environment. But inertia is clearly not the reason for news organizations' reluctance or even refusal to link to external Web sites. Tremayne has shown a clear decline in the number of external links over the years,[34] and the findings of this study confirm this trend. Ironically, it seems that the more comfortable newspapers grow with the Web, the more inclined they are not to link to external Web sites and, instead, to link only to themselves.

That leaves a fourth possible suggestion for the lack of external links: newspapers' fear of losing advertising revenues by sending people out of their sites. It seems a reasonable possibility, though more research is needed to make this claim definitive. In general, more work is needed to validate the findings presented here and to determine why newspapers virtually ignore the use of links for citations. The point is not merely an academic one. In view of the importance of the *New York Times*, the *Washington Post*, *USA Today*, and the *Los Angeles Times* online as well as offline, the way these news organizations draw attention to and verify ideas ought to be a topic of concern to anyone interested in expanding the quality of democratic discourse in the digital age.

NOTES

I want to extend my gratitude to Dr. Joseph Turow for his guidance and valuable feedback and for giving me the opportunity to work with him. I also want to thank Brigitte Ho and Anne-Katrin Arnold for their insightful comments and help with coding. All errors in this essay remain, of course, mine.

1. Quote from *New York Times* disclaimer retrieved from Mark Glaser, "Open Season: News Sites Add Outside Links, Free Content," *Online Journalism Review*, October 19, 2004, http://www.ojr.org/ojr/glaser/1098225187.php (accessed March 23, 2007).

2. Pew Research Center for the People and the Press, *Online Papers Modestly Boost Newspaper Readership*, 2006, http://people-press.org/reports/display.php3? PageID=1069 (accessed March 23, 2007).

3. See the essay by Webster in this book.

4. G. Tuchman, *Making News* (New York: Free Press, 1978), 82.

5. B. Kovach and T. Rosenstiel, *The Elements of Journalism: What Newspeople Should Know and the Public Should Expect* (New York: Crown, 2001).

6. Tuchman, *Making News;* H. J. Gans, *Deciding What's News: A Study of "CBS Evening News," "NBC Nightly News," "Newsweek," and "Time"* (New York: Pantheon, 1979); M. Fishman, *Manufacturing the News* (Austin: University of Texas Press, 1980).

7. For the latest information on how many people use online news, see Project for Excellence in Journalism, *The State of the News Media 2007*, http://www.sta teofthenewsmedia.org/2007/narrative_online_audience.asp?cat=2&media=4 (accessed April 23, 2007).

8. Quote by David Sifry cited in J. D. Lasica, "Transparency Begets Trust in the Ever-Expanding Blogosphere," *Online Journalism Review*, August 12, 2004, http://ojr.org/ojr/technology/1092267863.php (accessed March 24, 2007).

9. J. M. Balkin, "Digital Speech and Democratic Culture: A Theory of Freedom of Expression for the Information Society," *New York University Law Review* 79, no. 1 (2006), http://www.law.nyu.edu/journals/lawreview/issues/vol79/no1/ NYU101.pdf.

10. J. Hartley, "Journalism as a Human Right: A Cultural Approach to Journalism," in *Journalism Research in an Era of Globalization*, ed. M. Loeffelholz and D. Weaver (London: Routledge, 2005), 39–51. Also see D. Gillmor, *We the Media: Grassroots Journalism by the People, for the People* (Sebastopol, CA: O'Reilly, 2006).

11. H. Jenkins, *Convergence Culture: Where Old and New Media Collide* (New York: New York University Press, 2006), 208–9.

12. R. Blood, *The Weblog Handbook: Practical Advice on Creating and Maintaining Your Blog* (Cambridge, MA: Perseus, 2002).

13. S. C. Herring et al., "Conversations in the Blogosphere: An Analysis 'from the Bottom Up,'" in *Proceedings of the 38th Hawaii International Conference on System Sciences* (Los Alamitos: IEEE Press, 2005), 107–18.

14. A. Lenhart and S. Fox, *Bloggers: A Portrait of the Internet's New Storytellers* (Washington, DC: Pew Internet and American Life Project, 2006), http://www .pewinternet.org/pdfs/PIP%20Bloggers%20Report%20July%2019%202006.pdf (accessed April 24, 2007).

15. J. Rosen, "Bloggers vs. Journalism Is Over," PressThink, January 21, 2005, http://journalism.nyu.edu/pubzone/weblogs/pressthink/2005/01/21/berk_essy.ht ml (accessed April 24, 2007). Also see J. D. Lasica, "Blogs and Journalism Need Each Other," *Nieman Reports* 57, no. 3 (2003): 70–74.

16. W. Lowrey, "Mapping the Journalism-Blogging Relationship," *Journalism* 7, no. 4 (2006): 477–500.

17. Quote by Rosen cited after R. MacKinnon, "Blogging, Journalism, and Credibility," *Nation*, March 17, 2005, http://www.thenation.com/doc/20050404/ mackinnon (accessed April 24, 2007).

18. J. B. Singer, "Who Are These Guys? The Online Challenge to the Notion

of Journalistic Professionalism," *Journalism* 4, no. 2 (2003): 139–63; M. A. Deuze, "The Web and Its Journalisms: Considering the Consequences of Different Types of Newsmedia Online," *New Media and Society* 5, no. 2 (2003): 203–30.

19. Jenkins, *Convergence Culture*, 212.

20. For the sake of simplicity of argument, I am omitting developments with regard to the Semantic Web, which seek to add layers of meaning onto the hyperlink.

21. See the essay by Halavais in this book.

22. Videotaped panel discussion at the conference "The Hyperlinked Society," Annenberg School for Communication, University of Pennsylvania, June 9, 2006, available at http://appcpenn.org/HyperlinkedSociety/download/HyperLinked_Panel1_Full.wmv.

23. Retrieved from Technorati as of April 4, 2007. See http://www.technorati.com/pop/blogs/.

24. P. J. Boczkowski, *Digitizing the News: Innovation in Online Newspapers* (Cambridge, MA: MIT Press, 2004); E. Klinenberg, "Convergence: News Production in a Digital Age," *Annals of the American Academy of Political and Social Science* 597, no. 1 (2005): 48–64.

25. K. Barnhurst, "News Geography and Monopoly," *Journalism Studies* 3, no. 4 (November 2002): 477–89, http://www.ksg.harvard.edu/presspol/research_pub lications/papers/working_papers/2002_2.pdf.

26. D. V. Dimitrova et al., "Hyperlinking as Gatekeeping: Online Newspaper Coverage of the Execution of an American Terrorist," *Journalism Studies* 4, no. 3 (2003): 401–14.

27. M. Tremayne, "News Websites as Gated Cybercommunities," *Convergence* 11, no. 3 (2005): 28–39.

28. Herring et al., "Conversations in the Blogosphere."

29. C. Shirkey. "Power Laws, Weblogs, and Inequality," in *Reformatting Politics: Information Technology and Global Civil Society*, ed. J. Anderson, J. Dean, and G. Lovink (London: Routledge, 2006), 35–42.

30. L. A. Adamic and N. Glance, "The Political Blogosphere and the 2004 U.S. Election: Divided They Blog," in *Proceedings of the 3rd International Workshop on Link Discovery* (New York: ACM, 2005), 36–43.

31. Retrieved from Technorati as of April 4, 2007. See http://www.technorati.com/pop/blogs/.

32. J. D. Lasica, "How the Net is Shaping Journalism Ethics," July 2001, http://jdlasica.com/articles/newsethics.html (accessed March 24, 2007).

33. Dimitrova et al., "Hyperlinking as Gatekeeping."

34. Tremayne, "News Websites as Gated Cybercommunities."

ESZTER HARGITTAI

The Role of Expertise in Navigating Links of Influence

In this essay, I focus on how the influence of links may be mediated by the skills and expertise that both content producers and viewers are able to mobilize when using the Internet. My main argument is that while lots of factors influence how links are presented on the Web and how users respond to the content that shows up on their screens, people's Internet user abilities remain an important and understudied aspect of navigating links of influence. Both content creators and content users (readers, listeners, viewers) can benefit from a more in-depth understanding of how the Web works. Since such skills are not randomly distributed among the population, certain content providers and content users stand a better chance of benefiting from the medium than others. Relevant know-how will help producers attract attention to their materials. Savvy about the medium will assist users in sidestepping potentially misleading and malicious content.

Links' control over what people see is less of a factor in the online behavior of savvy users than it is with those who know less about the Internet. Knowledgeable users know how to interpret various types of links and are able to approach information seeking in a myriad of ways. While some people are considerably dependent on what content is presented to them by aggregators and content providers, others can sidestep many supply-side decisions by turning to alternative ways of browsing the Web's vast landscape. Both provider and seeker have the potential to influence which links will matter to any particular user's experience in the course of a particular information-seeking incident or when confronted with particular content. My main argument is that the weight of how much of this relationship is influenced by the provider versus the user shifts based on the savvy of actors at both the supply and demand sides of the equation.

I start the essay by discussing why links matter and the main types of links that exist on the Web, including a brief consideration of how the presentation of sponsored search engine results has changed over time. In the first section, I also consider the types of manipulations that content presenters can employ in order to attract more attention than would otherwise be possible. Then I introduce the concept of user skill, providing examples of what we know regarding people's Internet uses in order to argue that expertise is an important component of how user attention is allocated to online content and how people navigate links of influence. I end by discussing what questions remain about predictors of user savvy and the type of research that would be helpful in answering them.

Why Links Matter

From the early days of the Web, hyperlinks have allowed users to move from one page to another, finding content either with intent or through serendipity. While there are other means of getting to material on the Web, links remain an important way for users to move around online, whether within a known site or by venturing to new destinations.[1] Links are important precisely because they allocate user attention. They can have both positive effects and negative ones. By driving much needed eyeballs to material, they can spread updates about important health matters, draw attention to significant political issues, encourage people to donate to a cause, or help small businesses and independent artists thrive through sales of items that would not otherwise have the chance of garnering attention were it not for the low cost of online presentation.

But links can also have negative consequences. Too much popularity can overwhelm a system and make the material at least temporarily inaccessible. More important, drawing audiences to unsubstantiated rumors can lead to harmful outcomes in people's lives. Links can compromise relationships, personal and professional. An article in the *Washington Post* reported on an incident that damaged a recent law school graduate's career advancement.[2] Some negative comments left on a message board by anonymous commentators about a candidate showed up prominently when users did a search on the candidate's name. Employers are turning to the Web to gather information about applicants, so having negative comments show up high on the result list when searching on a particular name can have significant repercussions.[3]

To counter such incidents, one can now turn to a whole new set of professionals to help achieve desirable rankings on search engines. Experts in search engine optimization (SEO) work with both businesses and indi-

viduals to maximize the chances of a good position on search engine results pages. Interestingly, much of the advice given by such professionals
is of the kind that a somewhat more nuanced understanding of how the
Web works makes relatively simple to implement. This is one area where
the importance of online skill comes into play from the perspective of
content providers. Those who know more than others about how to
achieve prominent exposure can respond to situations like the one just
described relatively quickly and at low cost. The perceived influence of
links has jump-started a new profession centered on the idea that organizations and individuals need help and are willing to pay to improve the
positioning of links that pertain to them.

Link Types and Manipulation

Links matter in a broader sense, beyond direct issues of corporate or personal reputation. To understand how, it is important to highlight the
many ways in which we can categorize links from their location on a page
to their source, from attached financial incentives to design principles.
Technically speaking, all hyperlinks are created equal. They can be easily
inserted into any page with the simple code <a href="http://abc.xy">text
or image</a>. At the same time, the potential of links to influence users'
actions differs based on the way they are actually used. Consequently, a
discussion of how a particular type of link relates to content presentation
and user activity is worth consideration.

    Of course, there are several ways one can arrive at a Web page without
clicking on a link; these include, for example, using a bookmark or favorites listing or typing a URL in the location bar of the browser.[4] A
common form of moving from page to page, however, does involve clicking on a link. The simplest type of link is one that connects to additional
information about a detail in some text that constitutes the main content
on a page. There are also links whose main purpose is to facilitate navigation. They are not part of core content on a page. Rather, they exist
solely to guide people to a destination. These links range from directory
categories on large portal sites, such as Yahoo, to sidebar menus on Web
sites of all sizes and complexity. These two types of links share one feature: for the most part, they are a relatively steady part of the site on
which they are located. Obviously, pages can be edited easily, and links
may change as a result. But these kinds of links have fairly stable positions, and producers of these sites maintain a say over their specific placement.

In a substantively different category are links that show up on aggregator and recommender sites. These links are not based on one content producer's decisions. Rather, placement is determined by the link's popularity among users. Sites such as Digg and Reddit are examples of this presentation and organization. Any registered user can submit a link that then gets added to the pool of sites made available for users to browse. If enough site members support the link and it gains popularity relative to other submissions, it makes it onto the cover page of the site and garners increasing amounts of attention. These links are not stable the way the previous set of links are. Rather, their position and potential to be clicked changes rapidly with input from users. Thus, while visiting Reddit one minute will yield a certain link list, revisiting it a few minutes later will result in a different set of links.

Another category of links is comprised of those on search engine results pages. Here, the main purpose of the page is to redirect the user to content elsewhere. Such links depend on the proprietary algorithms used by search engine companies to rank pages. Results may be based on relevance and quality—however these two concepts are understood in a given context—but they may also be dependent on financial considerations. Search engines sometimes sell prominent placement on their results pages. Some search engine companies, like Google and Yahoo, also have systems set up where players large and small can bid for placement on their ad link section. Those links can usually be found on a sidebar next to the unsponsored ("organic") search results, although they are occasionally also included within the organic listings.

Another form of sponsored links tied to search results shows up on a plethora of Web sites that have affiliations with ad placement programs offered by ad-serving companies, like Google and Yahoo. These ad links appear on sites across the Web covering numerous topics targeted at diverse communities of users. There is no standard for where they are placed. They can be embedded within the main body of text on a page or on the sidebar, depending on the preferences of the publisher of the page. It is customary for these ads to be accompanied by a note that identifies them as such, but this information is not always clearly visible.

Are such sponsored links ever effective in gaining users' attention? Evidence suggests that they are. One of the most successful Internet companies, Google Inc., has launched numerous products over the years, only very few of which have been profitable to date. One of its most important products is the AdWords program that supplies links to affiliates. Each time someone clicks on such a link, both the owner of the Web site and

Google itself, as ad system provider, make money. Without people clicking on such links regularly, the company could not have achieved the revenue stream it has.

Whether users are clicking on these links because they are the most relevant for their needs is another matter. Layout and context of the links can, at times, be confusing or outright deceiving. Some sites display ads very clearly and mark them as such. Others are not as forthcoming about the source and reasons for the links. Take, for example, the case illustrated in figure 1. The Web site featured in this illustration focuses on photo editing. In a prominent place on its welcome page are some smaller images with links right below them. The links are ads, in this case from Yahoo's ad network. However, this is not immediately obvious. Looking at the rightmost picture, one notices an image of dishes, and the link below this picture states "San Francisco Dish." Clicking on the link, despite appearances, has nothing to do with the image of dishes displayed on the page. Rather, the link goes to an advertisement for an American Express program. The images are randomly rotated in what seems to be an effort to entice clicks despite little connection between the images and the links below them.

As suggested by the earlier examples, search engines play a special role in allocating user attention to links and thus online content, given that they are some of the most popular destinations by users.[5] Over time, there has been a considerable amount of change in how links are included and presented on search engines. John Battelle does a nice job of tracing the history of changing search engine results pages.[6] Initially, search engines just brought up sites that included at least one of the search terms entered by the user. As the Web grew, the default Boolean operator "OR" was replaced by "AND," resulting in search engines now returning results that contain all terms in a user's query. Changes also occurred in the financial domain of searching. Goto.com was the first search engine to allow payment for search positioning. These practices of the service were quite explicit. The amount of money the featured link sponsor would pay upon a click by the user was made public and listed right next to the link. Figure 2 depicts a screen shot taken on June 6, 2001, during the online browsing actions of a forty-one-year-old woman using Goto.com for searching.[7] Note the cent amounts next to the links. This example shows results to a search query for the phrase "lactose intolerance." The top advertiser was willing to pay thirty cents per click. Then there is a sharp drop, with the following links going for seven, six, five, and four cents, respectively. This explicit manipulation of search engine results caused

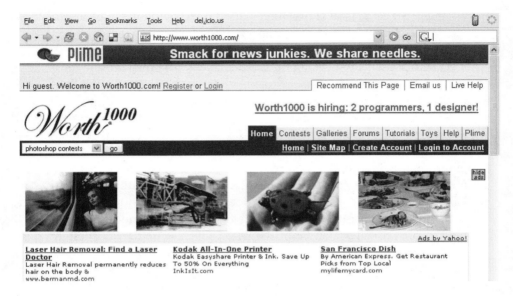

Fig. 1. Example of ad links presented in a confusing manner at www
.worth1000.com (2007)

considerable stir in the industry. Ironically, later manifestations of sponsored links have included even less explicit mention of what the advertisers may have done to achieve their products' ranking. Despite the initial
resistance by many, this practice has become commonplace across search
engines.

What determines which links feature prominently on results pages?
Detailed information about search engine rankings is proprietary information, so it is difficult to answer this question.[8] However, there are some
generally understood factors that influence rankings, and this is precisely
the type of know-how on which the SEO industry has been built. At the
most basic level, search engines rely on programs to crawl the Web to
create an index of Web site content.[9] When a query is submitted to a
search engine, the service returns sites that include the requested terms
and possibly considers whether the specified terms are in the title or in
various tags (underlying information about the page file), possibly with
attention to their position on the page. Of course, in most cases, there are
numerous pages that meet these criteria. Search engines use additional
information to rank results. An important factor, introduced in the late
1990s by Google founders Sergey Brin and Larry Page, concerns the reputation of the page on the Web.[10]

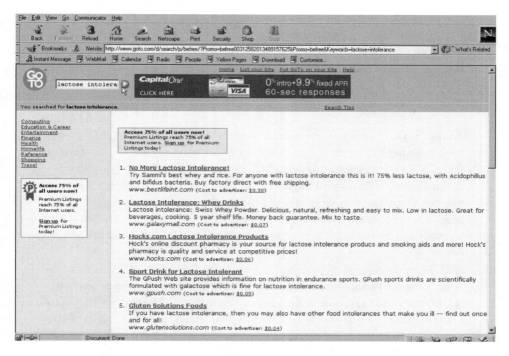

FIG. 2. Screen shot of a Goto.com search engine results page (2001)

To explain the basic idea behind this reputational system, I will draw on an analogy. Imagine a classroom full of students. Each student is liked by some people, and each student, in turn, likes some other students. Let us assume that Brigid is the most popular student, because most people in the class like her. There are two students who are also liked by quite a few students: Sam and Jamie both get the affection of several classmates, although not as many as Brigid. While Brigid is friends with Sam, Brigid does not care much for Jamie, and this is widely known, since she rarely socializes with Jamie. If an outsider came into the classroom and asked a student whether she should befriend Sam or Jamie, most students would likely suggest Sam. The reason is that although Sam and Jamie are liked by the exact same number of people, Sam is also liked by the most appreciated student in class, Brigid. A vote of confidence from Brigid plays an important role in the evaluation of the students in the context of a larger group. Now, let us replace the students in this story with Web pages, the sentiment of liking a person with a link going from one page to another. If we thus translate the story to Web pages and search engine rankings, the main idea is that having many links pointing to you and especially having ones from popular, established and well-regarded sites is valuable (these aspects of a site would, again, be determined based on some of the linking features of the site).

Search Engine Manipulations

Knowing that linking is important to search engine rankings, it is possible to engage in practices that may help boost a site's position on a results page. There are various ways in which content producers and distributors can influence the amount of attention their content manages to attract online. Many of these concern the manipulation of search engine rankings. The goal is to drive traffic to one's Web site, and this is often done without any regard to the needs of users who may then end up on the page.

The term "Google bombing" refers to the practice of manipulating search engine results by aggressively targeting links to a specific site with the same anchor text where the anchor text refers to the text that links to another page. Several such movements have been documented over the years. Bar-Ilan analyzed some of the most popular ones and identified their sources to be varied, ranging in motivation from personal (e.g., for people with common names wanting to be the first result in response to their names) to political (e.g., links to a page denying the existence of the "Arabian Gulf" despite the use of that name by some for the "Persian Gulf"), humorous (e.g., a search for "French political victories" yielding a link to a spoof search engine page on "French military defeats"), or financial.[11] Users achieve surprisingly high rankings for specific sites in these cases by organizing a movement of people linking to a specified page using a particular term as the anchor text. If the Google bomb is successful, future searches on the anchor text will yield the page that was being targeted by this effort.

While many Google bombs have a larger social or political purpose, some are much less controversial and simply target the popularization of a private individual's ranking on the search engine. For example, freelance journalist and photographer David Gallagher decided in 2002 that he wanted his site to have the top spot in the results listings in response to a search on his name.[12] This was not a trivial goal, given that many people share his name, including a Hollywood actor. Nonetheless, in a few months, he achieved his goal and remained in the top spot for three years, occupying the second position as of this writing.[13]

Mobilizing many people to help out with a Google bomb requires a convincing story to motivate participants. Political or humorous motives seem to work well. Commercial ones from which only a handful of people or entities benefit are less likely to gain wide popularity; in such a case, boosting a site's rankings is left to the actions of just a few people. This is where sites like splogs come in. Splogs, or "spam blogs," are Web sites that include nothing but links with one of two purposes: either they are filled with revenue-generating links, or they feature links to a site with the same goal as the links just described in the Google bombing scenario. The sole purpose of these sites is to come up high on search engine results and then make money by getting people to click on revenue-generating links.

Search engines have been vulnerable to such practices. Google often lists splogs prominently on its results pages, including in the top ten results. For example, at the time of this writing, a search on the words "origami tulip" yields a link to http://www.origamitulip.com in the top ten results on Google but not on any of the other top three engines. Curiously, however, there is no material on this Web site that directly addresses folding paper into tulip shapes. Instead, the page is completely made up of links that point off-site. This is precisely the type of site that has no original content (at the time of this writing) and simply contains links pointing elsewhere.

Staying ahead of such empty and confusing content is a cat-and-mouse game between spammers and search engines. However, while search engines catch up with the imaginative, ever-evolving approaches of spammers, users are caught in the middle, having to deal with the resulting confusion. One approach used by spammers is setting up for-profit sites that mimic government sites but use the suffix ".com" rather than ".gov" in URLs, as in "whitehouse.com" instead of "whitehouse.gov." Many users do not understand the distinction between different top-level domain names (here ".com" versus ".gov") and thus are vulnerable to clicking on the wrong link when faced with several seemingly interchangeable options. Analyzing the methods by which users find tax forms, I found that many are derailed and confused by profit-making ventures that claim to assist with tax forms but, in the end, do not include relevant information.[14]

Whether splogs and other such sites continue to mislead users is a question of how well search engines and other aggregators can stay ahead of such malicious practices, in addition to what extent users understand such practices. A paper looking at the source of spam redirection content found that just a few sites are responsible for a large portion of spam content.[15] Ironically, the Google-owned free blog-hosting site Blogspot appears to be one of the most spam-infested sites, hosting thousands of splogs. In a related realm, people (or, often likely, automated robots or programs) leave strategic comments on blogs to drive traffic and rankings to their sites. When a user leaves a comment on a blog, the username is often linked to a site specified by the user. In this case, the spammer includes a link to the site that is being promoted. Many of the splogs previously mentioned gain popularity precisely through this practice. Once a splog is set up, the next step is to create links to it by leaving comments on legitimate blogs with good search engine rankings, so as to boost the splog's reputation.

User Expertise with Links

Whether vying for people's attention as the provider of information or looking for the most relevant material to meet one's needs as a user, links are at the forefront of how user attention is allocated to content on the Web. Consequently, exploring how users interpret and approach them is crucial for a better understanding of how attention is allocated online, why some content gets audiences while other content does not, and why some people are better than others at finding content of interest to them. This is an area that has only begun to be investigated. My research and studies by others suggest that users differ with respect to their know-how about the Internet, the sources of various links, and the motivations behind their placements. To get a feel for the nature and importance of what people do and do not know about hyperlinking, it is useful to explore the topic through three categories: general user savvy, users' understanding of search engine rankings, and users' understanding of links in e-mails.

General User Savvy

Based on data I have gathered over the years, it is clear that people differ considerably in their understanding of various Internet-related terms and activities, and these abilities are not randomly distributed across the population. Here, I will draw on various studies to illustrate these differences. Based on surveys administered to hundreds of mostly first-year college students at a diverse urban public research university in the winters of 2006 and 2007, I found that even members of the wired generation are not necessarily savvy about terms that are important for informed Internet use and understanding links in particular.[16] While most students exhibit a relatively high level of familiarity with mainstream terms, such as *spam* and *bookmark*, know-how is much lower when it comes to terms relating to more recent Web developments, such as *widget* and *malware*. Moreover, this knowledge is not randomly distributed. Students who scored higher on their college entrance exam (measured by their reported American College Testing score) and students whose parents have higher educational levels reported a higher level of familiarity with both mainstream and more advanced Internet-related terms.[17]

Surveying such a highly connected population is especially relevant since students represent the wired generation and thus make it possible to control for exposure to and experience with the medium. The fact that some people are not necessarily knowledgeable about Internet-related terms and activities despite high levels of connectivity and frequent usage suggests that mere exposure to and use of the medium does not result in savvy users. As per the findings already cited, students' socioeconomic background is related to their online know-how. This suggests that those in more privileged positions are more likely to understand their online actions well and thus are less likely to be derailed by confusing content presentation.

Knowing how to interpret URLs is an important part of user abilities. Understanding how a user can tell whether a site is secure is an essential part of staying secure when submitting certain types of information to sites, such as financially sensitive data. In a questionnaire administered to hundreds of undergraduate students in the winter of 2007, I gathered information about a related know-how. First, it is important to note that this is truly the wired generation. On average, respondents in this study had been online for over six years, and the majority (88 percent) reported using the Internet more than once a day. When asked to rate on a five-point scale, ranging from "strongly disagree" to "strongly agree," how confident they feel about "knowing the difference between http and https"—the latter of which signals to users that they are on a secure site—only 18 percent agreed with the statement. Over half (57 percent) disagreed (over a quarter of the full sample disagreed strongly) suggesting that many young adults even among the wired generation are not fully aware of how to be really safe in their online actions, since it is not clear that they could tell when they are on a secure site. While the relationship is not large, there is a statistically significant positive correlation between parents' education and reported level of know-how concerning "https," and there is a similar relationship with college entrance exam scores.

Understanding Search Engine Rankings

Regarding the special case of understanding how search engines make decisions about what content to display, some surveys have collected data on users' understanding of the practice of sponsored versus paid search results. Findings from these studies suggest that people are not particularly savvy about the behind-the-scenes aspects of search engines. For example, when asked in one study whether they were aware of the distinction between paid and unpaid results, the majority of adults interviewed (62 percent) indicated that they were not.[18] These findings were mirrored by another study, asking similar questions, where 56 percent of adult respondents did not know the difference between the two types of results.[19] Moreover, findings suggested that this know-how is not randomly distributed among users, as men and younger adults claimed to be more informed about this aspect of search engines than women and older users. Howard and Massanari also found that more experienced users were considerably more confident in their ability to tell apart paid and unpaid content on search engines.[20]

How do members of the wired generation respond to similar questions? I asked about related issues in a study I conducted in the winter of 2006 on a group of 150 undergraduate students at a private research university. These students had been, on average, Internet users for over seven years, and 98 percent of them claimed going online several times a day, signifying that the Internet is very much a part of their everyday lives. Among them, over 37 percent claimed never having heard about the fact that search engines are "paid to list some sites more prominently than others in their search results." Following up, all of the students in the sample were asked, on a four-point scale, how important they think it is that search engines tell users about this practice "in the search results or on an easy-to-find page on the site." Less than a quarter (24 percent) found this to be "very important," with an additional 46 percent considering this practice "important." Over 24 percent, however, thought this was "not too important," and a remaining 5 percent found it to be "not at all important."

There are limitations to what we can learn through surveys, so using other methodologies to address these questions can be helpful as well. Follow-up observations can help shed some light on the extent to which students understand links. Drawing on data from a study conducted in 2007, figure 3 shows the action of a first-year female college student at an urban public research university in response to a search query looking for

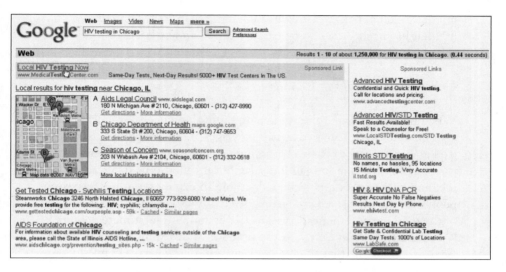

FIG. 3. Screen shot of a study participant's selection of a sponsored link result (2007)

HIV testing options in the city of Chicago. The respondent entered "HIV testing in Chicago" into the search box at Google.com and was presented with a list of results, including a highlighted link explicitly designated as sponsored and numerous ad links on the right side of the screen. She clicked on the sponsored link at the top of the page, right below the query box. This page did not yield the desired information.

When asked, later, to explain her choice here, the respondent stated: "I know that the ones that are in here [points to sponsored link section], they're the most relevant to what I'm looking for." There was no mention of sponsorship in her response. Later, in an effort to see whether she would say more about this, she was asked to recount how she learns what she knows about search engines. She stated that it comes "from using it frequently for school and for when you have to do homework." This response was fairly generic and suggests that her assumptions have received no external validation by other sources (whether people from her social networks or other resources). In the end, there is no basis for her assertion that the highlighted link is the most relevant result. It may be on occasion, but it is not always. Certainly, in this case it was not, as it led to a confusing site that did not include information on what she was seeking. Overall, it seems that this user does not have a good grasp of how search engines make decisions about what results to display. This user seems to put quite a bit of trust in Google's rankings, regardless of outcome, a finding that has been shown to be true for other student users of this service as well.[21]

Understanding Links in E-mails

When we think about links, we tend to think about clickable words or images on Web sites. Links in e-mail messages are increasingly common as well and pose a set of their own unique challenges. It can be convenient to receive a link in an e-mail message, but it can also be dangerous. The medium of e-mail is especially vulnerable to exploitation, because some people assume that seeing the name of a trusted source in the "From" line of the message automatically means that it contains legitimate content.

The term *phishing* refers to the practice of directing a user to a Web site other than one that the link and surrounding message context would seem to suggest, with the goal of extracting sensitive information from the user. For example, many users receive messages claiming to be from a bank (e.g., Chase) or an online commerce-related Web site (e.g., eBay or PayPal).[22] These messages ask users to follow the provided link and then the instructions on the Web site to which the link leads. The instructions often ask users to enter their username and password into a form secretly monitored by the malicious originators of the message. Once users have shared their login data, they may be exposed to fraudulent activity by the scammers.

Given technological advances, it is relatively easy to configure an e-mail message so it seems to be sent from a source other than the actual sender, resulting in what seems like a legitimate note to the recipient. However, once the user clicks on the included link, it may well lead to a malicious Web site. How many users are aware of these malevolent practices? In my surveys of a diverse group of undergraduate students, I asked respondents to indicate their level of understanding about the term *phishing*. (This question was part of a longer survey item asking about a myriad of terms, an item validated in earlier work as a good measure of people's actual online skills.)[23] In both 2006 and 2007, the reported level of understanding was extremely low: 1.6 and 1.7, respectively, on a scale of 1–5. Placing the term *phishing* in the context of other terms is also revealing. From among over twenty-five terms presented to the student sample in both years, *phishing* was one of the least understood. The survey included other terms, from the widely understood (e.g., *spam* and *bookmark*) to the less recognized (e.g., *tagging* and *tabbed browsing*) and the largely cryptic (e.g., *torrent* and *widget*). Nonetheless, all of these were claimed to be better understood by students than the term *phishing*. As with other types of Internet know-how, understanding phishing exhibits a statistically significant positive relationship with a student's score on a college entrance exam.

My findings are mirrored by data collected on people's understanding of Internet-related terms by the Pew Internet and American Life Project.[24] That organization's survey of a national sample of adult Internet users found that 15 percent had never heard of the term *phishing* and that 55 percent were "not really sure" what it meant (that survey only allowed three answer options, so the results of these studies—mine and Pew's—are not directly comparable). Of course, it may be that people understand the malicious practice and simply do not know the term that is used to describe it. It is possible to test this using a more nuanced method.

To examine the extent to which people are cautious about messages they receive, I have been presenting some college student study participants with hypothetical e-mail scenarios. Respondents are asked to read supposed e-mail messages and indicate how they would respond to them. Answer options include anything from reporting the message to IT support as fraudulent to following the instructions outlined within and forwarding the note to friends or family. There is also the option of choosing "other" and explaining what one might do, such as click on the link and check where it leads. Respondents are requested to check all of the actions in which they would engage upon receipt of the e-mail.

There are three messages in the study, one of which is made to look just like the e-mails students on this campus receive from the university through its official announcement list, including the appropriate sender and subject line conventions. The e-mail instructs recipients to log into a site and type in their username and password. The specified site address looks like a page on the university's Web site (i.e., it begins http://www .university.edu/admin/ . . .). The way this experiment is set up, the message is not clickable, so it is not possible for students to verify to what Web page the link actually leads. They are asked to indicate what they would do if they received this e-mail in their mailbox, by marking off all possible actions. Interestingly, very few suggest that they would contact technical support or verify where the link leads, and based on twenty-six cases, no one mentioned checking the address of the destination Web site. Over half of the students indicated that they would follow the instructions in the message and would click on the link and do what the destination page instructed, although a few did add that they would concurrently contact the IT department for more information.

Even when links are labeled as sponsored, users do not realize that they may not be the most relevant (of course, on occasion, they may be). Take the case of a thirty-seven-year-old woman who had been using the Internet for eleven years, was frequently online, and participated in a study conducted on average adult users in the spring of 2006 in a suburban town. While searching for information on lactose intolerance, she clicked on a sponsored result that showed up at the top of the search engine results page. This link led her to a site that did not include the information of interest to her. She then returned to the original results pages and proceeded to click on another result (this time the top result under the heading "Web Results" on the AOL search results page). She was directed to a page with the necessary information.

As a next step, she was asked to look for recipes that are acceptable for lactose intolerant people. She clicked on a link that was listed on the bottom of the previous page she had been viewing. This link was located under the heading "Sponsored Links." The link led to a page with the following statement in the midst of lots of graphics: "We're sorry, the page you were looking for was not found" (fig. 4). Below this statement were several links whose sponsorship was obvious to the trained eye but much less so to this particular user. She clicked on one of them and proceeded off-site to a page that no longer had anything to do with her original intent of finding a recipe that is suitable for lactose intolerant people. Based on her comments about the resulting page, however, it was clear that she did not realize this. She seemed to assume she was still on the original site at which she had started out her exploration. She was therefore confident that the recipe she had found was acceptable for lactose intolerant people, when, in reality, it was not. This is an example of the limited extent to which people understand where links lead them and of how they can be sent from one site to a completely different one, often due to strategically placed sponsored links that do not address the user's intent and may be interpreted as something other than what they really are.

Discussion

Relying on data collected using various methods, the empirical evidence presented in this chapter suggests that many users are not particularly familiar with the behind-the-scenes issues of Web content organization and presentation, issues related to how they may be navigating links of influence. Internet users differ considerably regarding their online savvy and their understanding of link navigation in particular. This know-how

FIG. 4. Strategically placed sponsored links (2006)

is not randomly distributed: on the contrary, socioeconomic status variables exhibit a statistically significant relationship with online savvy. Take, for example, the young woman who expressed considerable confidence in the relevance of a sponsored link on a search results page. She is a first-generation college student with parents who have no more than a high school education. This relationship between parental education and Internet skill seems to be consistent across several studies.

Despite some statistically significant relationships between user attributes and skill measures, it is safe to say that not enough work has been done in this domain for us to understand in depth what processes contribute to people's online abilities. We know, from earlier work and findings discussed in this piece, that information-seeking abilities and spelling mistakes are related to socioeconomic status,[25] but we know much less about link savvy in particular. We need better measures of this concept, especially survey items that can be administered to larger numbers of users for statistical analyses and generalizable results. Also, we need to go past individual user attributes to explore the role of users' social surroundings in their online behavior.

Links play a crucial role in how attention is allocated to material online, in what content becomes popular, and in what information is seen only by a few people. Links help users meet everyday needs ranging from the trivial to the profound. Given that people vary in their abilities to understand the sources of different links and their relevance, and given that these skills are not randomly distributed, some users are better positioned to use the medium efficiently and to their benefit, while others are more likely to be misguided and possibly even to fall into malicious traps. Links are important, but their potential influence on users is mediated by the level of expertise people bring to their online pursuits. Since those in more privileged positions seem to exhibit higher-level savvy, the Internet may be contributing to social inequalities rather than alleviating them, despite the many opportunities it makes available, theoretically, to everyone.

NOTES

1. Here, it is worth noting that I use the terms *audience, consumer, user, reader,* and *viewer* interchangeably. The level of agency associated with these terms may differ, but this not being the central focus of the chapter, I do not discriminate among them on that basis.

2. E. Nakashima, "Harsh Words Die Hard on the Web," *Washington Post,* March 2007.

3. K. Shea and J. Wesley, "How Social Networking Sites Affect Employers, Students, and Career Services," *NACE Journal* 66, no. 4 (2006): 26–32, http://www.naceweb.org.

4. E. Hargittai, "Classifying and Coding Online Actions," *Social Science Computer Review* 22, no. 2 (2004): 210–27.

5. D. Fallows, *Search Engine Users* (Washington, DC: Pew Internet and American Life Project, 2005).

6. J. Battelle, *The Search* (New York: Penguin, 2005).

7. E. Hargittai, "How Wide a Web? Inequalities in Accessing Information Online," PhD diss., Department of Sociology, Princeton University, 2003.

8. Battelle, *The Search.*

9. Ibid., 20–22.

10. S. Brin and L. Page, "The Anatomy of a Large-Scale Hypertextual Web Search Engine," *WWW7 / Computer Networks* 30 nos. 1–7 (1998): 107–17.

11. J. Bar-Ilan, "Google Bombing from a Time Perspective," *Journal of Computer-Mediated Communication* 12, no. 3 (2007), article 8, http://www.jcmc.indiana.edu/vol12/issue3/bar-ilan.html.

12. D. F. Gallagher, "Top of the Heap," *Business 2.0* (2002), http://www.business2.com/articles/mag10,1640,41488,00.html.

13. Bar-Ilan, "Google Bombing."

14. E. Hargittai, "Serving Citizen's Needs: Minimizing Online Hurdles to Accessing Government Information," *IT and Society* 3, no. 3 (2003): 27–41.

15. Y. M. Wang, M. Ma, Y. Niu, and H. Chen, "Spam Double-Funnel: Connecting Web Spammers with Advertisers," paper presented at Sixteenth International World Wide Web Conference, Banff, Canada, May 8–12, 2007.

16. E. Hargittai, "A Framework for Studying Differences in People's Digital Media Uses," in *Cyberworld Unlimited? Digital Inequality and New Spaces of Informal Education for Young People*, ed. N. Kutscher and H.-U. Otto. (forthcoming).

17. Ibid.

18. Fallows, *Search Engine Users*.

19. iCrossing, How America Searches, 2005, http://www.icrossing.com.

20. P. N. Howard and A. Massanari, "Learning to Search and Searching to Learn: Income, Education, and Experience Online," *Journal of Computer-Mediated Communication* 12, no. 3 (2007). http://www.jmcm.indiana.edu/vol12/issue3/howard.html.

21. B. Pan, H. Hembrooke, T. Joachims, L. Lorigo, G. Gay, and L. Granka, "In Google We Trust: Users' Decisions on Rank, Position, and Relevancy," *Journal of Computer-Mediated Communication* 12, no. 3 (2007). http://www.jcmc.indiana.edu/vol12/issue3/pan.html.

22. M. Huffman, "'Phishing' Scam Takes New Tack," *Consumer Affairs*, March 2007, http://www.consumeraffairs.com/news04/2007/03/phishing_tactic.html.

23. Ibid.

24. L. Rainie, *Public Awareness of Internet Terms* (Washington, DC: Pew Internet and American Life Project, 2005).

25. E. Hargittai, "Hurdles to Information Seeking: Spelling and Typographical Mistakes during Users' Online Behavior," *Journal of the Association for Information Systems* 7, no. 1 (2006), http://ais.aisnet.org/articles/default.asp?vol=7&art=1; E. Hargittai, "Second-Level Digital Divide: Differences in People's Online Skills," *First Monday* 7, no. 4 (2002): 1–18.

SETH FINKELSTEIN

Google, Links, and Popularity versus Authority

Suppose one wished to search through the data available on the Internet to find some information. Often, a user searches for Web pages associated with some particular keywords. However, the number of Web pages available is enormous. Whether millions or billions, the number of items that could potentially be read vastly exceeds any human capacity to examine them. This fundamental mathematical fact creates an opportunity for a solution by the use of automated assistance: that is, a search engine.

A search engine typically contains an index of some portion of all available existing pages and a means of returning an ordered subset of the available pages in response to a user query. Given that users likely wish to examine as few results as possible, the ordering of the results in response to the user query has become a subject of intense interest. The number of pages that merely contain the desired keywords could still be many thousands, but the user may start to lose patience when examining more than a few results.

Thus, primitive implementations of returning all pages that contain certain keywords, in an order based, perhaps, on the age of the page or on when the page was placed in the search engines database, work poorly in terms of returning results that are significant to the user. A major advance in quality of results was the PageRank algorithm of the Google system.

> Academic citation literature has been applied to the web, largely by counting citations or backlinks to a given page. This gives some approximation of a page's importance or quality. PageRank extends this idea by not counting links from all pages equally, and by normalizing by the number of links on a page. This innovation proved to be extremely successful. By taking into account the link structure among a network of pages, and employing a measurement based on the results, the structure of links was used in part to impose a structure of relevancy. However, this practice of using links as a metric for meaning has proved to have many complicated social effects.[1]

In sociological terms, it was insightful of the Google creators to realize that a popular answer would be a popular answer; that is, if someone were to search for the term *widget*, a popular answer, for the purpose of seeming to fit the needs of the searcher, would be to look for a popular page in some sense. For example, a frequently referenced (linked) page likely had some appealing or attractive aspect to many people. So when that page was returned to a searcher as a result, it would then likely have a similarly appealing or attractive aspect to that searcher.

A very naive initial concept of the functioning of PageRank in a search would include the following steps:

1. Select all pages containing the target term.
2. Order this subset by the size of their PageRank.
3. Return the top results of this ordered subset.

Some reflection would quickly show this model to be untenable. For example, the page that happened to possess the highest PageRank would then appear as the first result for a search on every word it contained, the page with the second highest PageRank would dominate for another set of words, and so on. Obviously, these results might not be very meaningful responses for the search words. Additional criteria for ranking pages for search terms must therefore be introduced, to prevent a small number of pages from dominating the results. Such criteria can include looking for large numbers of the search term; use of the search terms in emphasized or special contexts; or, crucially, hyperlinks from other pages that use the search term in the anchor text of the hyperlink.

The anchor text criterion is particularly powerful. If many people or a few prominent people refer (link) to a page with the desired term, that page is likely to be a good result to return for the desired term. So a somewhat more refined search algorithm would include the following steps:

1. Select all pages containing the target term or that have the target term in the anchor text of links to the page.
2. Calculate the number of links to the page containing the target term and the number of times the term appears on the page, as well as the PageRank.
3. Order the results by a weighted combination of the preceding factors.

As the algorithm becomes more and more elaborate, the addition of an increasing number of factors can create many unintended consequences.

As the various ranking aspects interact with each other, several small factors can combine to be equivalent to a large amount of another factor; or, inversely, a very high scoring on one particular basis may overwhelm negligible amounts of every other score. Crucially, all such quantitative criteria do not convey any sense of quality, as to whether the page might be considered good or bad from a perspective based on truth or merit (in an academic sense). While syntactical analysis of page elements (determining how many keywords are present, where they are, and whether they have any special attributes) is easy, semantic analysis (determining what the elements mean) is hard. There can be a confusion of quantitative with qualitative value, or popularity with authority.

Both the nature of the page-ranking activity and its uses underscore the importance of seeing search results as a value-laden process with serious social implications. The following pages will elaborate this idea by exploring three propositions. First, searching is not a democratic activity. Second, searching inherently raises the question of whether, when searching, we want to see society as we are or as we should be. Third, the current norms of searching, based on popularity, are not an appropriate model for civil society.

PageRank and Democracy

It's common to think about the technical examination of a network structure in terms of a political system imposing social structure. The analysis of relevancy in terms of popularity lends itself to an easy analogy of voting and democracy. But an analysis of the fundamental driver of Google's approach, the PageRank, reveals the problems with this analogy.

> PageRank relies on the uniquely democratic nature of the web by using its vast link structure as an indicator of an individual page's value. In essence, Google interprets a link from page A to page B as a vote, by page A, for page B. But, Google looks at more than the sheer volume of votes, or links a page receives; it also analyzes the page that casts the vote. Votes cast by pages that are themselves "important" weigh more heavily and help to make other pages "important."[2]

Someone might simplistically think that a democratic practice implies that one link is one vote and might then mentally equivalence that idea to a concept of everyone having equal power. But the ranking algorithms are rarely simple direct democracy. They're akin to "shareholder democracy" as practiced in corporations: that is, each person doesn't have a single vote; rather, individual voting power varies by orders of magnitude (for corporations, this depends on how many shares are owned by the shareholder). The votes are more like weighted contributions from blocks or interest groups, not equal individual contributions. One link is not one vote, but it has influence proportional to the relative power (in terms of popularity) of the voter. Because blocks of common interests, or social factions, can affect the results of a search to a degree depending on their relative weight in the network, the results of the algorithmic calculation by a search engine come to reflect political struggles in society.

A Proxy for Societal Importance

The outcome to these political struggles via searching can be quite real. Being highly ranked is the end result of a complex algorithm that is often taken as a proxy for societal importance. Inversely, being lowly ranked can doom a source to marginalization. One response to this concern may be that searching is necessary because of the "information overload" in contemporary society.

While information overload may be a modern cliché, there has always been too much information, ever since the days of cavemen grunting around the campfire, when more occurred at a tribal council than could be effectively retold to an absent hunter. The need to summarize events—to present important (according to some definition) information in a short, accessible form—is hardly new. Many issues surrounding search engines can in fact be framed as instances of long-standing journalistic problems. The universe of available information needs to undergo a winnowing process that can be described as selection, sorting, and spinning, according to the following model:

1. Selection: Which items are important?
2. Sorting: In what order should the items be presented?
3. Spinning: How should one view the items in context?

Compare this description to the colloquial summary of journalism as determining the who, what, when, where, why, and how of an event. For both journalism and search engines, crucial decisions are made as to what results to present to the end user, from among an overwhelming set of possibilities. And both have a concept of objectivity in theory but also inescapable problems with values that enter the decision-making process.

Consider the following passage, where a journalist outlines his education in the algorithm used for determining newsworthiness of traffic accidents, in the era before civil rights reforms took hold.

> The unwritten guidelines for reporting fatal automobile accidents were more complicated, the rough rule of thumb being: No n[-]gg[-]rs after 11 p.m. on weekdays, 9 p.m. on Saturdays (as the Sunday paper went to press early). Fatal highway accidents were reported without regard to the color of the deceased until these home edition deadlines: To get a late story in the final editions required making changes, and by tradition only white traffic deaths were considered worth submitting. The exception to this rule was in the area of quantity: If two black persons died in a late evening auto crash, that event had a fair chance of making the news columns. Three dead was considered a safe number by everyone, except those reporters who were known to be viciously anti-Negro. Most of us, of course, considered ourselves neutral or objective in that regard. Yet none of us questioned the professional proposition that the loss of a white life had more news value than the loss of a black life.[3]

The journalist describes determining newsworthiness by weighing various factors, such as number, time, and (crucially) social influence. All these factors might be calculated in a "neutral or objective" manner (by asking what time an accident was, how many people are dead, and what their color was). But by taking into account the relative weight (like PageRank) of race, social judgments are incorporated in the results of "news value."

Censorship and Search Links

Sometimes authorities don't want links to be made or, at least, to be visible. Perhaps contrary to a naive impression, there are specific cases where the results of a search are affected by government prohibition; that is, search results that might otherwise be shown are deliberately excluded. The suppression may be local to a country or global to all Google results.[4]

Search engines do not simply present a raw dump of a database query to the user's screen. The retrieval of the data is just one step. There is much postprocessing afterward, in terms of presentation and customization.

When Google "removes" material, often it is still in the Google index itself. But the postprocessing has removed it from any results shown to the user. This system can be applied, for quality reasons, to remove sites that "spam" the search engine. And that is, by volume, certainly the overwhelming application of the mechanism. But it can also be directed against sites that have been prohibited for government-based reasons.

One very simplistic model of links in the world is that all nodes are ideally visible to all other nodes. But search engines act as sources or portals for a set of links. So suppressing sites in search results will be an ongoing battle.

As We Are or As We Should Be?

Some of the debate over search results echoes ancient descriptive versus prescriptive philosophical conflicts. Should the world be presented as it is (at least as created through the particular search algorithm) or as it should be? The two case studies that follow highlight how Google's approach to the world raises this issue to sometimes emotional heights.

Case Study—Chester's Guide to Molesting Google

What if the terms sometimes used to find an innocuous site are also linked to a site that seems to be associated with child predators? Such a situation led to "moral panic" and a newspaper censorship campaign to have a site removed from both its host and the Google search index. The uproar turned out to originate from a single page of text of "sick humor."

An article headlined "Sick Website Taken Down" in the U.K. *Chester Chronicle* reported: "People power and The Chronicle have won the fight to get a sickening paedophile site—in the name of Chester—removed from the web."[5] Almost every fact in that article was wrong: the targeted site was not a pedophile site; the Google search index is not the Web. But the confusions of the people involved in this campaign (which ranged up to U.K. members of Parliament) are revealing. The article related:

> Councillors and readers were disgusted earlier this month when we told how a disturbing site could be accessed after innocently typing "Chester Guide" into the popular search engine run by Google.
> This week, the US firm agreed to remove the site, entitled "Chester's guide to picking up little girls," after receiving complaints from our readers.
> The move also comes after Cheshire Constabulary's paedophile unit alerted the Internet Watch Foundation. . . .

However, they urged objectors to bombard Google and the Internet service provider Marhost.com with complaints.

A driver of the controversy was apparently that the same words that would naturally be used to find material about the town of Chester were also featured on a page of extremely tasteless material. Thus some sort of association or connection was implied. Of course, extreme bad taste is not illegal. Contrary to the inflammatory description, all that was being returned was a page of very low humor. Bizarre tastelessness makes the rounds of the Internet every day and even has a genre of books devoted to it (e.g., *Truly Tasteless Jokes*). But contrast these statements from the same article:

> Google's international public relations manager, Debbie Frost, said . . . :
> "When an illegal site is discovered, search engines like Google will remove such sites from their indices in order to abide by the law."
> "After our investigation, we have determined that the site in question is illegal and therefore it will be removed from our index."
> . . . John Price, leader of Chester City Council, was furious when we informed him of the site's existence.
> This week, he said: "It's great news the site has been removed. Good riddance to bad rubbish. However, we must now be vigilant and make sure it does not come back."
> Chester MP Christine Russell was also outraged and immediately agreed to demand a change in the law to make such sickening sites illegal.

Crucially, no judicial process seems to have been applied in Google's determination. There was certainly no judicial avenue of appeal, no public evidence record to examine. One might argue that there was little value to the page that was removed from the index, but the implications of such a removal can be troubling.

Case Study—*Jew Watch*

While Chester's problem of a popular link that yielded unfortunate search results may sound unique, it is not. One of the most well-known examples of complex issues of unintended consequences and social dilemmas is the high ranking of an anti-Semitic Web site, Jew Watch, for Google searches on the keyword "Jew." The Web site describes itself as "keeping a close watch on Jewish communities, organizations, monopoly, banking, and media control worldwide." The front page contains such categories as "Jewish-Zionist-Soviet Anti-American Spies," "Jewish Communist Rulers & Killers," and "Jewish Terrorists." It is unarguably a site devoted to anti-Semitic "hate speech." However, such material, though repulsive, is completely protected under the U.S. Constitution's First Amendment, though other countries may consider it illegal.

For a long time, this objectionable site was the first result in a Google search for the keyword "Jew." As reported by ZDNet:

> The dispute began . . . when Steven Weinstock, a New York real estate investor and former yeshiva student, did a Google search on "Jew." . . . Weinstock has launched an online petition, asking Google to remove the site from its index.[6]

After the controversy had been in the news for some time, Google posted an explanation of the search result.

> A site's ranking in Google's search results is automatically determined by computer algorithms using thousands of factors to calculate a page's relevance to a given query. Sometimes subtleties of language cause anomalies to appear that cannot be predicted. A search for "Jew" brings up one such unexpected result.[7]

The explanation was in part aimed at defusing charges that Google was anti-Semitic and had deliberately placed a hate site in a high search ranking. Such a charge is completely unfounded. But the problem is more closely outlined by the Anti-Defamation League's analysis: "The longevity of ownership, the way articles are posted to it, the links to and from the site, and the structure of the site itself all increase the ranking of 'Jewwatch' within the Google formula."[8] While Google did not in any way promote the hate site, there is more to the ranking than "subtleties of language." The Google system was, in effect, used by the site to promote itself.

Another site, Remove Jew Watch (www.removejewwatch.com), was set up to launch a petition to "get Google.com to remove Jewwatch.com from their search engine." Other people tried to have different sites rank higher for the keyword "Jew." But Jonathan Bernstein, regional director of the Anti-Defamation League, noted that "one can stumble across plenty of Holocaust denial Web sites by simply typing 'Holocaust' into Google." He added: "Some responsibility for this needs to rest on our own shoulders and not just a company like Google. We have to prepare our kids for things they come across on the Internet. This is part of the nature of an Internet world. The disadvantage is we see more of it and our kids see more of it. The advantage is, we see more of it, so we're able to respond to it. . . . I'm not sure what people would want to see happen. You couldn't really ask Google not to list it."[9]

It might be noted, however, that Google will place sites on certain blacklists if they are illegal. A search for the keyword "Jew" in some country-specific Google versions (in Germany and France) shows Jew Watch removed from Google.[10] And in at least one situation (the "Chester's guide" case mentioned previously), Google has blacklisted a site that was not illegal. But that way lies madness, and Google has sound reasons to duck the issues as much as it can. The problem will not disappear, and there will be constant pressure from various groups.

Ironically, all the controversy probably raised the rank and relevance of the Jew Watch site within Google's algorithms, at least temporarily. Most important, people who made hyperlinks to the site for the purposes of reference added to the number of links to the site on the Web, which could have contributed to raising its search ranking. For a while, the site lost its service provider and, since it was not available, dropped in ranking; but then it rose back up (around April 22, 2004). Eventually, the Wikipedia entry for the word "Jew" took over the top position for a search on that word, and attention to this case subsided. But as hate groups realize the power that comes from prominent placement in searches, the topic will certainly be revisited. As an ironic aside, during the height of the controversy, one neo-Nazi was apparently jealous of all the attention received by a like-minded rival, so he tried to generate a campaign to ban his own site, presumably so publicity and anticensorship sentiment would give that site similar prominence. The campaign failed, but it illustrates the extremes of convoluted political maneuvering that can be found in the topic.

To some extent, the high position of the Jew Watch site in search results for the keyword "Jew" can represent a kind of plurality dominance over diluted opposition. If one were to ask what the most prominent associations with the word "Jew" are, anti-Semitism would sadly have to be significant. And it would by no means need to have anywhere near a majority share to be returned as a first result. If, hypothetically, anti-Semitism were the association 19 percent of the time and there were nine other slightly different positive associations that each had 9 percent of the remaining time, being the greatest single identifiable block could give it a ranking of "most popular" in some algorithmic sense. This is the popularity versus authority conflict all over again. A site that has a plurality of weighted link votes need not be accurate or even inoffensive to the population outside that group.

Moreover, if a goal is to return relevant results, anti-Semites also use search engines, and a hate site counts as a correct result to them. In a sense, Google argued that it was performing a descriptive function in reflecting relative prominence for a search term, against the tangle that would develop if it was prescriptive in its results. But a contrary point of view is that an algorithm that gives high ratings to hate sites is by definition flawed in some way and should not be justified merely by the fact of being an algorithm. At least, if the choice is made that a dominant plurality result is correct, even if it is sometimes offensive, it should be recognized that there are significant social implications of such a choice.

Intentionally or unintentionally, the Jew Watch site had done search engine optimization for the keyword "Jew." In extreme forms, an optimization activity turns into "Google spamming," where search engine spammers try to get irrelevant pages to rank highly in order to obtain profit from ad clicks. The activity can reach a point of doing significant damage to search results, and it has generated some drastic countermeasures, where harsh antispam actions cause problems with legitimate sites. But significant self-promotion can be done short of spamming, and search engine optimization is merely puffery, not fraud.

A different form of linking to game Google is a practice known as "Google bombing" (defined at Wordspy.com as "setting up a large number of Web pages with links that point to a specific Web site so that the site will appear near the top of a Google search when users enter the link text"). Technically, this manipulates Google search results by hyping the ranking factor associated with the words used to link to a site—for example, using the phrase "miserable failure" to link to a biography of President George W. Bush or connecting the phrase "out-of-touch executives" to Google corporate information. From a Web site's standpoint, Google bombing is the mirror image of search engine optimization, where a site seeks to rank highly for desired keywords.

Search engine optimization for political ends is a largely unresearched area. Google bombing is now a crude process, done for laughs. In the future, it might well involve much more serious political dirty tricks. Indeed, political campaigning is at heart a process of manipulating information, and as search engines become more important as sources of information, we can expect more and varied creative attempts at their manipulation.

PageRank Selling and Commodification of Social Relations

The factors that Google uses to rank pages have long been a target for financial ends. Once any sort of value is created by a link, there's an immediate thought that a market can be created to monetize that value. While many people think of linking as a purely social relationship, it's quite possible to have such expressions of social interconnection be subverted for commercial purposes.

But search engines cannot simply let the market decide the value of a link. That would eventually produce pages of results that are nothing but advertisements, which would then drive users away from the search engine. Those would not be popular results—advertisements tend to be unpopular (even if they are sometimes effective in generating business). Moreover, paying for links on the Web usually competes with the search engine's own paid advertising program. So a search company has an incentive to disallow outright sales of links, while marketers have an incentive to attempt to buy as much influence as possible.

A crude way to do such buying of links would be to seek out high-ranking pages and offer payment for placement. But such pages are relatively easy to monitor, and internal ranking penalties can be applied if a site owner is found to be participating in such practices. More sophisticated schemes are being refined by companies that offer independent Web writers (bloggers) small amounts of money to write about products on the writer's own Web site. These arrangements are commonly discussed in terms of traditional journalistic ethics regarding sponsorship or disclosure. The idea is that if the writer discloses that the article is a paid placement, the reader can then apply the appropriate adjustment to the credibility of the content.

However, such a traditional framework misses an important aspect of the exchange. In the case of PageRank selling, the sources of the ranking will not be evident. It won't matter what the writer says about the product or what the reader thinks in terms of trusting the article, as the ranking algorithm will see only the link itself. If the accumulated purchasing of links eventually results in a high ranking, that process will be virtually invisible to the searcher. In a way, this is a disintermediation of the elite influencers—commodifying their social capital—and a reintermediation of that influencing process with an agency specializing in the task. Instead of courting a relatively few A-list writers who are highly valued for their ability to have their choice of topics echoed by many other writers, the lesser writers can be purchased directly (and perhaps more simply and cheaply).

Even for prominent writers who would decline an explicit pay-for-placement deal, the many ways linkage can be purchased (literally or metaphorically) leads to controversy over proper behavior. For example, one company, FON, set off a round of discussion by having many advisory board members who were also widely read Web writers.[11] But the tiny company also got publicity from another source: influential commentators on the Internet who write blogs—including some who may be compensated in the future for advising FON about its business. Though an appropriate journalistic disclosure was made almost everywhere in this case, the aspect in which the social was intermingling with the commercial remained unsettling. A focus on disclaimers often assumes a certain background in separation and avoidance of conflict of interest and is insufficient when those strictures are no longer in place. While blurring the lines between business and friendship is not at all a new problem, the shifting systems of attention sorting and seeking are now bringing these issues to notice in new contexts.

To put it simply, there's an old joke that runs as follows:

BILLIONAIRE TO WOMAN: Would you have sex with me for a million dollars?
WOMAN: Well . . . yes.
BILLIONAIRE: Would you have sex with me for ten dollars?
WOMAN: What kind of a girl do you think I am?
BILLIONAIRE: We've already determined that. Now we're just arguing over the price.

Two factors make up the humor in this joke: commerce itself and amount. The obvious aspect of the joke is that there are two categories of interactions, commercial and social, between which there is not supposed to be any overlap, regardless of the dollar amount at stake. A less-often-remarked aspect is that there is indeed a "class" division between high-priced commercial and low-priced commercial.

Future controversies may present a real-life version of that joke that might go roughly as follows:

COMPANY TO BLOGGER: Would you write about me for advisory
    board membership?
BLOGGER: Well . . . yes.
COMPANY: Would you write about me for ten dollars?
BLOGGER: What kind of a flack do you think I am?
COMPANY: We've already determined that. Now we're just arguing
    over the price.

Is a few dollars the same as an advisory board membership? No—there's a class division, in that an advisory board membership is high-class and expensive, while a few dollars is tawdry and cheap. But there's also a problem when executive "escorts" criticize street prostitutes.

The Nofollow Attribute

There's a public relations saying (attributed to many people) that goes, "I don't care what the newspapers say about me as long as they spell my name right." The concept is that any mention, positive or negative, is helpful in terms of recognition. Links have a somewhat similar phenomena, where any link, even originating from a page making negative statements about the site, can help build the site's search ranking. This is a particular pernicious issue in the case of hate sites (as discussed earlier), as any publicity for the sites tends to generate more links to the sites even if the publicity is negative. A link, by itself, cannot distinguish fame from infamy.

One attempt to address this dilemma has been the introduction of a special attribute, nofollow, to try to distinguish the purely referential aspect of a link from any implied popularity or importance of the site that has been referenced.[12] If you're a blogger (or a blog reader), you're painfully familiar with people who try to raise their own Web sites' search engine rankings by submitting linked blog comments like "Visit my discount pharmaceuticals site." This is called comment spam. We researchers don't like it either, and we've been testing a new tag that blocks it. From now on, when Google sees the attribute (rel=nofollow) on hyperlinks, those links won't get any credit when we rank Web sites in our search results. This isn't a negative vote for the site where the comment was posted; it's just a way to make sure that spammers get no benefit from abusing public areas like blog comments, trackbacks, and referrer lists.

The results of this attribute have been mixed. It certainly has prevented many blog owners who have open comment areas from inadvertently adding to spam pollution. But even if some link spammers have been discouraged, more than enough remain undeterred so that the problem of spammers is still overwhelming. While many blogs have automatically implemented the nofollow attribute on all links in their public areas, a large number of spammers will apparently spam anyway—finding it more efficient to be indiscriminate, perhaps, or in hopes of benefiting somehow in any case.

Businesses That Mine Data for Popularity: Not a Model for Civil Society

From a political standpoint, one might hope that the use of the nofollow attribute regarding hate sites would lower their rankings as people who mention them unfavorably discourage linking. But the use of this attribute in linking requires both knowledge of its existence and some sophisticated knowledge of how to code a link (as opposed to using a simple interface). So while this way of separating meanings is helpful overall, it is complicated enough to carry out so that the problem is not substantially addressed in practice.

Moving from the specifics of the nofollow attribute to the more general impact of links on people's consciousness, it should be clear by now that Google-like approaches to searching, which base rankings on the popularity of links, tend not to question the society's basic hierarchy. One initial simplistic way of thinking about link networks is to somehow lump all nodes together, as if there were no other structure for determining who received links. But since many links are made by people, all the prejudices and biases that affect who someone networks with personally or professionally can affect who they network with in terms of hypertext linkage. One writer described this (often gender-based) cliquishness in the following manner:

> Point of fact, if you follow the thread of this discussion, you would see something like Dave linking to Cory who then links to Scoble who links to Dave who links to Tim who links to Steve who then links to Dave who links to Doc who follows through with a link to

Dan, and so on. If you throw in the fact that the Google Guys are, well, guys, then we start to see a pattern here: men have a real thing for the hypertext link. . . .

[Later] When we women ask the power-linkers why they don't link to us more, what we're talking about is communication, and wanting a fair shot of being heard; but what the guys hear is a woman asking for a little link love. Hey lady, do you have what it takes? More important, are you willing to give what it takes?

Groupies and blogging babes, only, need apply.[13]

Recall that popularity can be confused with authority and that a link from a popular site carries more weight to a search engine. The self-reinforcing nature of references within a small group can then be a very powerful tool for excluding those outside the inner circle. Instead of democracy, there's effectively oligarchy.

The best way, by far, to get a link from an A-List blogger is to provide a link to the A-List blogger. As the blogosphere has become more rigidly hierarchical, not by design but as a natural consequence of hyperlinking patterns, filtering algorithms, aggregation engines, and subscription and syndication technologies, not to mention human nature, it has turned into a grand system of patronage operated—with the best of intentions, mind you—by a tiny, self-perpetuating elite. A blog-peasant, one of the Great Unread, comes to the wall of the castle to offer a tribute to a royal, and the royal drops a couple of coins of attention into the peasant's little purse. The peasant is happy, and the royal's hold over his position in the castle is a little bit stronger.[14]

In fact, rather than subvert hierarchy, it's much more likely that hyperlinks (and associated popularity algorithms) reflect existing hierarchies.[15] This is true for a very deep reason—if an information-searching system continually returned results that were disturbing or upsetting, there would be strong pressure to regard that system as incorrect and change it or to defect to a different provider. As can be seen in some of the discussions earlier in this essay, even isolated anomalous results can draw angry reactions. Subversive results would not be acceptable.

The positive results from data-mining links for popularity are certainly impressive but have also inspired flights of punditry that project a type of divinity or mystification into the technology. *New York Times* columnist Thomas Friedman wrote an op-ed column entitled "Is Google God?" where he quoted a Wi-Fi company vice president as saying:

> If I can operate Google, I can find anything. And with wireless, it means I will be able to find anything, anywhere, anytime. Which is why I say that Google, combined with Wi-Fi, is a little bit like God. God is wireless, God is everywhere and God sees and knows everything. Throughout history, people connected to God without wires. Now, for many questions in the world, you ask Google, and increasingly, you can do it without wires, too.[16]

However, in contrast to the utopianism, there is much research to show that the mundane world is very much the same as it ever was. Hindman and his colleagues note: "It is clear that in some ways the Web functions quite similarly to traditional media. Yes, almost anyone can put up a political Web site. But our research suggests that this is usually the online equivalent of hosting a talk show on public access television at 3:30 in the morning."[17]

Link popularity is itself no solution to problems in governance. Determining what opinions are popular is usually one of the least complicated political tasks. But what if the results are hateful or are manufactured by an organized lobbying campaign? How much weight should be given to strong minority views in opposition to the majority? These questions, which determine the character of a society, are not answered by merely listing the popular opinions and options. Moreover, some of the lessons learned from such businesses are arguably exactly the wrong lessons needed for a pluralistic democracy, where you cannot simply ban the minority that isn't profitable. Unfortunately and maybe self-provingly, that is not a popular position.

NOTES

1. S. Brin and L. Page, "The Anatomy of a Large-Scale Hypertextual Web Search Engine," *WWW7 / Computer Networks* 30, nos. 1–7 (1998): 107–17.

2. Google Inc., "Our Search: Google Technology," 2007, http://www.google.com/intl/en/technology/.

3. W. Hinckle, *If You Have a Lemon, Make Lemonade* (New York: Putnam, 1974).

4. B. Edelman and J. Zittrain, "Localized Google Search Result Exclusions," http://cyber.law.harvard.edu/filtering/google/; Seth Finkelstein, "Google Censorship—How It Works," http://sethf.com/anticensorware/general/google-censor

ship.php; BBC News, "Google Censors Itself for China," http://news.bbc.co.uk/
1/hi/technology/4645596.stm.

5. "Sick Website Taken Down," *Chester Chronicle*, February 21, 2003,
http://iccheshireonline.icnetwork.co.uk/0100news/chesterchronicle/page.cfm?ob
jectid=12663897&method=full&siteid=50020.

6. D. Becker, "Google Caught in Anti-Semitism Flap," 2004, http://zd
net.com.com/2100-1104-5186012.html.

7. Google Inc., "An Explanation of Our Search Results," 2004, http://www
.google.com/explanation.html.

8. Anti-Defamation League, "Google Search Ranking of Hate Sites Not Intentional," 2004, http://www.adl.org/rumors/google_search_rumors.asp.

9. J. Eskenazi, "No. 1 Google Result for 'Jew' Is Fanatical Hate Site—for
Now," 2004, http://www.jewishsf.com/content/2-0/module/displaystory/story_id/
21783/format/html/displaystory.html.

10. B. Edelman and J. Zittrain, "Localized Google Search Result Exclusions,"
2002, http://cyber.law.harvard.edu/filtering/google/.

11. R. Buckman, "Blog Buzz on High-Tech Start-ups Causes Some Static,"
2006,   http://online.wsj.com/public/article/SB113945389770169170-0DZ4wQf
felheiC5fe4GISe73UwQ_20070209.html.

12. Google Inc., "Preventing Comment Spam," 2005, http://googleblog
.blogspot.com/2005/01/preventing-comment-spam.html.

13. S. Powers, "Guys Don't Link," 2005, http://weblog.burningbird
.net/2005/03/07/guys-dont-link/.

14. N. Carr, "The Great Unread," 2006, http://www.roughtype.com/
archives/2006/08/the_great_unrea.php.

15. J. Garfunkel, "The New Gatekeepers," 2005, http://civilities.net/TheNew
Gatekeepers.

16. T. Friedman, "Is Google God?" 2003, http://www.cnn.com/2003/
US/06/29/nyt.friedman/.

17. M. Hindman, K. Tsioutsiouliklis, and J. Johnson, "'Googlearchy': How a
Few Heavily-Linked Sites Dominate Politics on the Web," 2003, http://www.cs
.princeton.edu/~kt/mpsa03.pdf.

Part 2: Hyperlinks and the Business of Media

Preface to Part 2

Part 2 focuses on the ways media and marketing organizations use linking as they face new challenges in the digital environment. Martin Nisenholtz, senior vice president of digital operations for the New York Times Company, provides an account of the ways the *New York Times* has been reconfiguring itself to succeed in the new age. This meant recognizing the need to become comfortable with new ways to reach out to readers as well as with opening the paper's vast archive to search engines.

Like so many publishing businesses, most of the *Times*'s online revenues come from advertising. The three essays that follow reflect the importance of marketers in shaping new media—and the role hyperlinks play in that. Tom Hespos argues forcefully that the advertising industry needs to come to terms with the drastic changes the Internet and the hyperlink have brought about in human communication processes. Hespos states that advertisers have lost the control they previously had in their interactions with customers, now that the Internet not only enables consumers to find competing information but also allows them to connect to the opinions of other consumers. Consumers now talk to each other and also talk back to the advertisers. Hespos sees this as an opportunity rather than a threat and stresses the need for advertisers to take advantage of the unique capabilities of new media.

Stacey Lynn Schulman continues the topic with thoughts on how the advertising industry should start dealing with an environment where the consumer is increasingly at the center and in control. She says that consumers expect advertisers to know who they are and what they like, and while, in many cases, they are willing to give up privacy for personalization, it is crucial to know where to draw the line between what is acceptable and what is not. She points out that one of the opportunities afforded by the digital environment is the untapped potential of online communities for marketing research. The next logical step up for marketers is to create their own online communities that connect the brand to customers in order to win their loyalty.

Eric Picard, continuing the spirit of the essays by Hespos and Schulman, talks about the challenges advertisers face as a result of digital and network technology. His essay reflects on the changing economics of attention and describes the shift in advertisers' buying from time slots to "impressions." Whereas in the past, the advertiser simply had to select a time slot to find the right audience, Picard shows how technological advances have made it possible for the audience to "watch content whenever and wherever they like," resulting in a fragmentation of the audience. He concludes that with the content world changing to one where the audience is in control, advertising strategies have to adjust and adapt accordingly.

Marc Smith takes off where the previous four essays end and focuses on the innovative possibilities new technology will have for the ways people relate to one another as well as to media and marketers. Structuring his essay around the concept he calls the "hypertie," Smith predicts how mobile devices with wireless technology that increasingly become aware of themselves and their location will lead to a drastic reconfiguration of our day-to-day interactions. Social ties will become more digitized, visible, and archived, and this in turn will allow us to interact in many ways hitherto impossible. Smith illustrates what is now possible with these new linking technologies. He describes name tags that automatically exchange data with other tags based on the common interests of the wearer. Also in testing are mobile devices that are fully equipped with a diverse range of sensors, including accelerometers, thermometers, cameras, and Bluetooth radio, to keep track of every movement of the user.

The ability of Smith's futuristic gizmos to follow people wherever they go certainly resonates with the goals that Hespos, Schulman, and Picard exhort marketers to pursue—as well as with the reasons they express caution regarding customer privacy. It's less clear what implications such a linked world will have for the development of the New York Times Company and the gamut of other media firms that are trying to find their audiences across technologies and across time and space. Will highly particularistic knowledge of audiences change the creation of news and entertainment? Will media companies serve not just different ads to people but different editorial content as well? To what extent will people's preference for customized material change the nature of their conversations with others—and so the shared discourses that may be crucial to a democratic society? The essays in part 2 lead us to examine these questions.

MARTIN NISENHOLTZ

The Hyperlinked News Organization

The Way We Were

In *The Making of the President, 1972*, Theodore H. White observed: "It is assumed that any telephone call made between nine and noon anywhere in the executive belt between Boston and Washington is made between two parties both of whom have already read the *New York Times* and are speaking from the same shared body of information."[1] The news has always been used as a catalyst for shared ideas. Baby boomers remember the era of Walter Cronkite. Sitting around the dinner table, families watched CBS news during the Vietnam War, talking about and often arguing about the war as the "magic of television" brought battlefield images into their dining rooms. The telephone, the postal service, and even the fax machine enhanced these connections. During the 1980s, it was common for people on commuter trains to cut articles out of newspapers and then fax them around to colleagues. Perhaps they would later discuss these articles on the telephone.

The patterns that defined these predigital interactions were hard to see, the trails left behind ephemeral. The news itself was "packaged" exclusively in analog format—whether in a nightly broadcast, a daily newspaper, or a weekly or monthly magazine. But the idea that these news packages were merely "one-way" delivery devices from top-down journalistic institutions to waiting masses is simplistic. Every day, specific articles were used for discussion fodder. And influential newspapers, particularly the *New York Times*, would be used by other media outlets to form the basis for their stories, amplifying and extending the journalism far beyond the printed page. This ecosystem created meaningful linkages through the technology of the day.

The Dawn of Internet News

It is not surprising, therefore, that the World Wide Web was initially used as a mere extension of existing behavior. News Web sites circa 1996 were mostly simple extensions of the printed product. The copy flowed out of the publishing systems into formatted pages to be made available to a growing number of Internet users. Message boards were established by most of these sites to encourage discussions about the articles. With few exceptions, the sites were published every twenty-four hours (perhaps augmented by wire copy throughout the day), and they were mostly "walled gardens," or repurposed online versions of the print product.

Beginning in 1996, the *New York Times* experimented with a section of its site called CyberTimes (see fig. 1). A young reporter named Lisa Napoli invented a column called Hyperwocky that insinuated many links throughout the articles she wrote. These were early forms of interactive journalism, nascent ways to begin insinuating the broader Web into the fabric of an article. But for the most part, readers weren't ready; networks were slow, and the real benefits of linking were abstract. The message boards were off in their own "ghettos," where only the most fervent and involved readers posted messages. There was no integration between articles and the social tools that might bring those articles directly into a conversation.

Of course, there were no easily usable syndication technologies to allow for multiple sources to exist in a single environment. Portals like Yahoo had developed highly useful aggregation services, but for the most part, the narrowband networks of the day favored shorter articles and breaking news. The wire services, particularly the AP and Reuters, became the cornerstone of the portals' news services. The absence of syndication standards mandated that business development deals and complex technology arrangements were often required to share content.

All of this led to an assumption on the part of news providers that they were creating electronic versions of their analog products, that the main benefit of the Web was its distribution capability. This was a world without "side doors"—in other words, the typical usage pattern would show readers arriving at the home page (much as they would pick up a paper and look at the front page first or start viewing a broadcast at the "top" of the hour) and then proceeding to read the online newspaper or broadcast. At the most innovative sites, there would be frequent news updates, so that users would return to the home page throughout the day and click through to read the stories. The idea that some readers would come to article pages from somewhere else on the Internet was a function of mar-

FIG. 1. Early NYTimes.com home page showing CyberTimes feature

keting. These were the days of "anchor tenancies" on AOL, where Web sites would pay tens of millions of dollars for favored positions that would deliver users. Only the "voodoo economics" of the dot-com boom, when businesses were valued on "eyeballs" rather than profits, made these agreements workable. News organizations that were part of traditional media companies, including the *Times*, couldn't play this game. In 1999, NYTimes.com had only 1.3 million monthly unique visitors on average. We were failing to harness the underlying fabric of the networked world. Our Web sites were created in HTML, but the world was not ready for the true power of hypertext.

Questions and Answers

The power of the Internet is its social fabric. By 1998, the *Times* recognized that it needed to find a bridge between news and community. This was during the first great era of community on the Internet, when sites like GeoCities and Tripod were being sold to portals for billions of dollars. But these community sites had nothing to do with journalism. By and large, they were like (mostly static) online vanity license plates.

At the *Times*, we had conceptualized the idea of a "knowledge network" that would combine our journalism with what our users knew; in other words, we would attempt to "unlock" the knowledge inherent in our very literate user base and, where appropriate, to combine that knowledge with our journalism. This sounds vaguely like the description of a Web log, but blogs were still in the future. Instead, we thought of social utility as questions and answers. During this pre-Google era, our users were going to Web sites like AltaVista to find answers, but we thought that "human search" would grow rapidly as the network effects of "people helping people" kicked in. Given our vast archive of content, we planned to find ways for our users to supplement their answers with our journalism. So, for example, if someone in the network asked for advice on great restaurants in Paris, our users could supplement their own answer with a Paris restaurant article that was stored in our archive.

In order to execute this plan, we acquired a sophisticated knowledge-management firm based in Cambridge, Massachusetts, called Abuzz. Abuzz had built an "adaptive routing" technology that "learned" from the link structure of human behavior in the system. People who would frequently answer questions about wine, for example, would be regarded as "expert" in this area. Behavior was complemented with ratings from other users. In the end, the technology would identify the handful of most knowledgeable users against almost any question from among millions of prospective answerers in the network.

For the first time, a journalistic organization was looking at the Web as a network, rather than as a mere distribution mechanism to deliver its content. Articles or even parts of articles could be used in the context of a conversation—in this case, one that involved answering a stranger's question on the Internet. The underlying link structure of a user's behavior would create a hierarchy of expertise or a predictive approach to quality.

Unfortunately, Abuzz and the *Times*'s knowledge network fell victim to poor timing. Advertisers at that time were skittish about buying community inventory, even though it was very topic specific. Several years later, Google's AdSense product would solve this problem, but with the dotcom bust and deep advertising recession of 2001, the Abuzz experiment was terminated.

The Rise of Aggregation

While the *Times* and other newspaper companies were placing their content online, entrepreneurs were building sites that took advantage of both the distribution power of the Web's open standard and the hyperlinked nature of the medium itself. The most important of these companies, founded by Jerry Yang and David Filo, was Yahoo. Yahoo's core value contribution, like that of several of its competitors, was to structure the Web into discrete categories, serving not as a creator of content but as a directory pointing users to others' content. The recognition that the Web was, first and foremost, a platform on which to share documents and even conversations goes back to its invention by Tim Berners-Lee. Berners-Lee, a scientist at CERN (the European Organization for Nuclear Research), built a generalized platform to share and discuss documents. Yahoo and its peer companies extended a part of this vision by creating a framework around which these documents could be organized on a global scale. Soon, the company extended this aggregation notion into news and ultimately became the world's largest Web news service, without creating any content.

Yahoo built this early position in news by understanding the essential character of the Web—that its value was as much in the aggregation and sharing of links as in the distribution of content. The explosion of choice and personalization, now harnessed by Yahoo and others, overwhelmed many mainstream news organizations. This soon led to the emergence of a new kind of Internet company—the portal—that offered a broad range of services under a single brand umbrella.

The Dawn of Web 2.0

Web 2.0 has become a buzzword without much meaning, but the folks who coined the term—Tim O'Reilly, John Battelle, and others—saw something fundamentally different emerging from the ashes of the dotcom bust. O'Reilly, in particular, has taken pains to create a substantive definition of the idea. His diagram in figure 2 depicts its many components.

In his post "What Is Web 2.0?" O'Reilly writes, "Google is most certainly the standard bearer for Web 2.0."[2] But as figure 2 shows, there are many broad aspects to the concept that have gotten lost, as Web 2.0 has been simplified in the popular press as the mere description of the post-bust era or reduced to the concept of "social networking." From the perspective of the hyperlinked society, the most interesting aspect of O'Reilly's diagram is the user positioning, the idea that users now control their own data. This has many implications and relates to the hyperlinked news organization in profound ways. Notions of user participation, online identity, reputation, and the "granular addressability of content" have all begun to change users' expectations of what a news service should

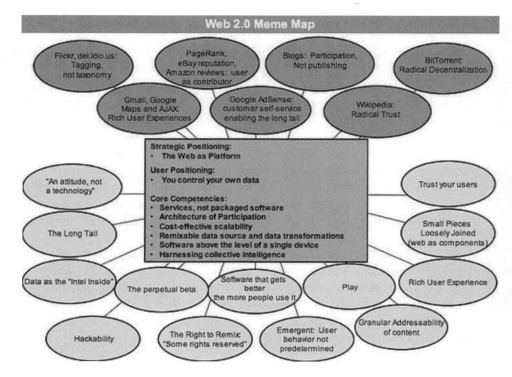

FIG. 2. A meme map of Web 2.0 developed at a brainstorming session. (From http://www.oreillynet.com/pub/a/oreilly/tim/news/2005/09/30/ what-is-web-20.html.)

be. In turn, new forms of content creation and aggregation have exploded, as the gradual de-portalization of the user experience pushes users from the head of the "long tail" to its edges.

From One to Three Ways to Experience News

Only ten years ago, there was essentially one way to experience news: from the editor's perspective. This was true in newspapers, on television, and by radio. Editorial judgment came exclusively from professionals who had spent their careers in journalistic institutions, such as the *Times*.

While some disagree, there is little evidence that the editor's perspective isn't both highly valued by readers and necessary in a complex democracy. But this perspective has now been joined by the Web 1.0 idea of aggregation and, more recently, by the Web 2.0 notion embodied by James Surowiecki in his book *The Wisdom of the Crowds*. The idea that readers, by voting en masse on which stories and events are most interesting or important, are now becoming a kind of editorial collective force is embodied in Web 2.0 companies, from giants like Google to more recent entrants like Digg and Memeorandum.

Fewer than 60 percent of the inbound links to NYTimes.com come from users who type the organization's URL into a browser or who link from a bookmark. The rest come from the distributed Internet, and a third of those come from Google alone. Google has become a vast content distribution system, its PageRank algorithm using the underlying link structure of the Web to act as a massive editorial filter.

In the case of Digg, users vote stories up or down, resulting in a highly dynamic, continuously updated stream of news content that readers can then share and comment on. Pages throughout the Web now include Digg tags (among others) that prompt users to submit stories. Digg evolved from the fabric of the Internet and the urge that users have to participate and interact. The fact that 75 percent of Digg users are male perhaps suggests something about its appeal, but it nonetheless is attracting millions of users every month.

In the case of Memeorandum, the service draws news content—mostly on politics—from around the Internet and associates this content with discussions taking place in the blogosphere. Whereas Digg is a kind of news voting system, Memeorandum is a huge, distributed authority engine, drawing content from across the whole Web. It is a kind of anti-walled garden, as so many Web 2.0 applications seem to be, taking advantage of the openness of the Web and the underlying associations embedded in its link structure.

Shamu Is Back!

Traditional news organizations are also tapping into the "wisdom of crowds" by creating new ways for news content to surface on the home page. At the *Times*, the most popular of these new forms of authority is the "most e-mailed" list.

In June 2006, the *Times* published a story by Amy Sutherland entitled "What Shamu Taught Me about a Happy Marriage." In brief, the story is about a woman's attempt to change unpleasant aspects of her husband's behavior using animal training techniques. The story quickly shot to the top of the most e-mailed list and stayed there for weeks. A fun story buried somewhere in the vastness of the *Times* was now—based solely on the fact that thousands of readers were e-mailing it around—appearing on our home page day after day, attaining an afterlife that would have been impossible just a few short years ago.

But the story doesn't end there. On January 10, the *Times* published a list of most e-mailed articles for the year, and right at the top of the list was the Shamu piece. Yet again, it was catapulted into the most e-mailed list, given a new lease on life based on its popularity six months earlier. The day before the list was published, the article generated 511 page views. Two days after it was published, it generated 94,637 page views. That week, Shamu generated over 600,000 page views—a testimony to how alternate taxonomies and the "wisdom of crowds" can drive enormous interest in even the most obscure news story.

Now, the *Times* is syndicating its most e-mailed list to other sites. Blogs can now use it as a "widget" to offer their readers a view into the *Times*'s most popular content. In this way, our journalism spreads across the Internet and around the world.

The "granular addressability of content" referred to by O'Reilly in his Web 2.0 post is playing out across the *Times* Web site. The *Times* pioneered the use of RSS as a way to allow users to subscribe to just those topic feeds that are of greatest interest. The reader is now using the distributed nature of the Web to assemble a personal news experience, linking to sources from across the Internet.

"Hi, I'm Art Buchwald, and I just died."

O'Reilly's diagram notes that blogs are forms of participation, not publishing. The best blogs draw links from around the Web to create a rich stew of commentary, reader participation, and conversation. Blogs are the most successful new medium since the video game, with over 50 million people now publishing.

Blogs are often put at odds with traditional media. How often do we hear, "When will blogs replace newspapers?" Actually, blogs and news sites are highly complementary. In fact, according to Technorati, the *Times* was the most blogged source in the world last year. This means that bloggers were using our content as the fodder for conversation. Millions of readers come to the *Times* through blogs, offering us an immense source of new distribution. This is why we were early pioneers in RSS— because by allowing users from across the Web to remix our content for their own needs, we actually enlarge the audience for the *Times* by a very large margin. This is the inherent paradox of the hyperlinked news organization—it can get much larger and has more impact through its disintegration. Part of the reason the *Times* now has the largest newspaper Web site by a significant margin is our early recognition of this phenomenon.

The phenomenon is illustrated perfectly by happenings following our recent introduction of The Last Word—a series of video obituaries that are created with the subjects while they are still alive. The first of these was on Art Buchwald. He begins the interview by saying, "Hi, I'm Art Buchwald, and I just died."

Two days after it launched, a reference to The Last Word could be found on Fred Wilson's blog. (Fred is a well-known venture capitalist who blogs on a diverse array of topics under the heading "Musings of a VC in New York.") On his blog, the headline "The Last Word" was accompanied by a description of the Buchwald obit. But Fred didn't find out about the obit at the *Times*. In the body of his description, he wrote, "Found this on Fred Graver's blog." I had never heard of Graver's blog, so I went there, and, indeed, Mr. Graver wrote, "The NY Times has done something wonderful," and he offered a full description of The Last Word and a link to the Buchwald obit.

But guess what? Graver didn't seem to find the obit on the *Times*, either. He pointed to another blog, PaidContent.org, as the source and offered a link to that site. PaidContent.org is a well-known site covering the world of new media. Staci Kramer, a writer for the site, described the Buchwald video this way: "It's an excellent example of what newspapers can do to translate their print personalities into an online blend of words, video, audio, stills and links." Did Staci find the video on the *Times* site? Apparently not, because she pointed to Romenesko, a fellow who's been writing on newspapers on the Internet for many years—a blogger before blogging.

The point is that Web content is part of a huge, swirling "conversation" taking place across the Internet twenty-four hours a day, seven days a week, in every corner of the earth. The Art Buchwald obit was enormously enlarged by being a part of that conversation. It was found and linked to from one writer to another. Surely, many people discovered it on the *Times* site as well, but over time, far more will have found it through the link structure of the Web itself.

The Iceberg

As O'Reilly points out, no company better embodies the principles of Web 2.0 than Google. The very nature of its PageRank algorithm is to use the "wisdom of crowds"—the underlying link structure of the Web—as a kind of mathematical voting machine for which documents are of the highest relevancy and quality given a particular search. In his book *The Search*, John Battelle refers to this underlying database as the "database of intentions," because the searches that people execute across the planet tell us everything from how "university students in China get their news" to where "suburban moms get their answers about cancer."

In a world where millions of people are searching for news and information every day, it has become critical for news organizations to be found. It is notable that some news organizations around the world are seeking payment for these links. They view the indexing of their headlines and summaries as a violation of copyright. Moreover, they argue, the search firms, by aggregating and structuring the Web, gain all the economic advantage, while the content providers, without whom the search firms would offer no value, are marginalized.

This is an understandable reaction, but the likely result of this protest will be to further diminish the impact that these news organizations have on their readers. As searching becomes the primary interface on the Web, it is more important than ever for news content to appear in the results. In part, this has motivated the *Times* to create Times Topics, a new area of the site that exposes all of the *Times*'s vast archive of content to search.

In many ways, the *Times* Web site can be viewed as an iceberg. The exposed content—the daily *Times* and associated Web features—is the tiny tip of something much larger. Most of the *Times* content is actually under the surface, buried in the archive. It is a vast storehouse of articles that goes back before the Civil War, to 1851. By dividing this content into tens of thousands of topical categories, from Mao to Madonna, and by exposing all of these topics to search engines, content that is rarely or never used by ordinary readers is revitalized and brought to the surface. Moreover, Times Topics is being developed as an open database, with quality controls built into the editorial process. This means that content will come not just from the *Times* but from other sources throughout the Web and from the community of users who have interest in the topics.

The Challenge

While the increasing disintegration of the packaged news experience brings millions of new users into the hyperlinked news organization, the problem is that many of these users are so ephemeral as to be of no prac-

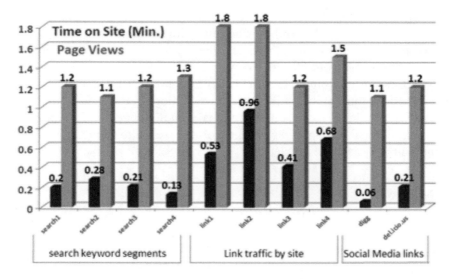

FIG. 3. Time on site and page views

tical economic benefit to the provider. Traffic from sites such as Digg can be of very low quality, as measured by user involvement. SiteLogic has done an analysis of inbound links from different kinds of Web referrals. Their analysis is striking.

Figure 3, showing inbound links to a single blog, suggests that while inbound links from all sources translate to relatively "light" reader engagement, those from Digg are of the lowest quality. Digg users spent only 3.6 seconds on this particular site and looked at one page. But even the inbound links from search referrals were of relatively little consequence. The principle challenge that news organizations have in this hyperlinked world is to convert these "flyby" users into more serious readers. As the SiteLogic analysis demonstrates, much of this traffic has almost no economic value to the news provider. As people increasingly turn to Web 2.0 mechanisms to find information and to communicate, news organizations must discover tactics to deepen engagement with these users.

Fortunately, the strong brand of the *Times* is a magnet for almost 60 percent of our inbound users. And a deeper analysis of our search referrals suggests that many users get to the *Times* by searching for it. Of the top fifteen natural inbound search links in December 2006, twelve resulted from some version of the keywords "*New York Times.*" Two non-

Times keywords, "Saddam Hussein" and "James Brown," were public figures who died in December. The remaining keyword was "Wii"—the popular Nintendo gaming console. The overwhelming majority of the links thus came from readers trying to find the *New York Times* itself by searching for it. Nonetheless, the future is clearly one in which news organizations must embrace the hyperlinked nature of the Internet to find and embrace readers from all sources. We can no longer depend fully on our traditional packaged view of the world, if we are to survive and prosper in the hyperlinked society.

NOTES

1. Theodore H. White, *The Making of the President* (New York: Bantam, 1972), 346.
2. Tim O'Reilly, "What Is Web 2.0?" http://www.oreillynet.com/pub/a/oreilly/tim/news/2005/09/30/what-is-web-20.html?page=1.

TOM HESPOS

How Hyperlinks Ought to Change the Advertising Business

The advertising industry is an interesting bird, owing largely to the fact that it was one of the first business sectors to experiment with the Internet and one of the last ones to realize why the Internet is important. As I write this, thousands of advertising industry executives still don't understand why the Internet and hyperlinking are important. They think they know why, and most of them will spout off a few canned lines about "consumer control" when asked about the Web, but they often don't fully comprehend the weak explanations coming out of their own mouths.

To grasp how hyperlinking has changed the advertising business, one must accept two fundamental truths, one of which logically follows from the other:

1. Hyperlinking has changed the fundamental dynamic of human communication.
2. This change in dynamic has altered how advertising functions within the context of the communications landscape.

The first fundamental truth is something that quite a few people, both inside and outside of the advertising business, have trouble swallowing—and with good reason. It's an incredibly broad statement—the kind an MBA candidate might back up with a thesis paper hundreds of pages long. But it's certainly true.

Allow me to illustrate with an example. A few years ago, I decided to make treasure hunting my new hobby. My family had given me a cheap metal detector from Radio Shack for my birthday that year, and I had some limited success with it on the beach near my house. One morning, I managed to uncover a small pile of change and some jewelry and was bitten by the bug. I was convinced that if I upgraded my metal detector and consulted some of my fellow treasure hunters, I might be more successful.

Think about how I might have addressed this challenge in the pre-Internet days. Gathering information about this niche hobby would have been a real challenge. I probably wouldn't have mustered up the courage to stop one of those solitary treasure-hunting nerds as he walked down the beach, intently listening for a signal in his headphones. Those people look like they want to be left alone.

There's nothing like getting information about a hobby right from the source, and in the pre-Internet era, my information choices might have been limited to finding stores that sold metal detectors and asking the (biased) shopkeeper, scouring the library for (outdated) books on the subject, or trying to find a magazine for hobbyists. None of these options gives me what I really want—both immediate gratification and accurate information. The Internet does.

To find out more about treasure hunting, I first did a Google search. Google pointed me toward a site called TreasureNet, where I read about the hobby and later interacted with enthusiasts on an online message board. There, I learned which metal detectors were best suited to my needs and where to get the best bang for my buck when I decided to upgrade. I perused a lot of valuable information on the site, but the best information came from my fellow enthusiasts, many of whom were happy to share their recommendations, experiences, and pitfalls I should avoid.

I learned all about this hobby using the Internet. The important thing to realize is that I didn't simply use the Internet to read static articles I could have found in a magazine. Nor did I use it only to price metal detectors like I might in a paper catalog. I got the most out of the Internet when I used it for the reason it's different from every other medium on the communications landscape—as a facilitator for human communication.

It's this concept that is at the core of how hyperlinking has changed the dynamic of human communication. The Internet has allowed us to connect not only with information but with each other. One would think that high-paid executives who purport to be experts in communication would understand that. Ironically, it's this concept that most advertising executives have trouble understanding. Most don't "get it" because of the institutional inertia of the advertising business itself.

Advertisers and advertising agencies have traditionally operated under the erroneous assumption that they control how their products and services are perceived by people. To many advertisers and agencies, messaging to consumers is the solution to nearly every marketing problem. The advertiser and the agency have information to communicate to consumers, and they push this information out through a variety of media—television commercials, ads in magazines and newspapers, billboards, radio commercials, and direct mail, just to name a few. Institutional inertia is a defining characteristic of the advertising business. Entire media empires have been built on this push model. Even David Ogilvy, the patron saint of advertising, owes his success to it. His canonical text *Ogilvy on Advertising* is one of the most widely read books in the business, and it's rare to find an advertising industry executive who hasn't read it.[1] (My dog-eared copy sits in my home office, on a shelf reserved for books that are frequently referenced in my weekly Web marketing column.)

If you thumb through *Ogilvy on Advertising*, you'll find a ton of information about the dynamics of the push model but almost nothing about two-way media and how to construct compelling campaigns within a media world where customers talk back. The back cover of my edition is littered with bullet points about how to make money with direct mail, about how to create advertising that "makes the cash register ring," and about television commercials that sell. There's nothing about how to handle a deluge of customer feedback or even about how to respond to an e-mail from a customer who is frustrated about a defective widget. Still, *Ogilvy on Advertising* is required reading for anyone hoping to make a career in the advertising business, and that tells us that many advertising agencies and their clients remain overly focused on the push model of communication. Meanwhile, the fundamental shift in the dynamic of human communication brought about by hyperlinking favors the conversational approach over the one-way push model. Push has been falling out of favor for more than a decade, and advertising agencies haven't exactly been quick to adjust.

One might think that agencies would try their hardest to be the first to figure out the best way to market in the age of the hyperlink. Certainly, if an agency could break away from the pack by showing unparalleled success in online marketing, it would stand to make a great deal of money. Regrettably, such efforts are not common, mostly because agencies think they've figured out how to approach interactive marketing, when they truly haven't. For most agencies, the answer to the interactive question involves completely ignoring the two-way nature of interactive media and attempting to force it into a box filled with a wide variety of one-way media. To many agencies, the Internet is yet another channel by which commercial messages can be disseminated to the masses, and they say damn the whole business of what happens when customers decide to talk back. You can see this systematic reengineering of the Internet in action when you take a look at the variety of models in use for advertising within interactive channels.

This reengineering of the Internet didn't start taking place until the commercial explosion of the World Wide Web at the tail end of 1994. The pre-Web Internet was a place where a hyperlink was as likely to connect you with other human beings as to connect you with a piece of information. E-mail discussion lists, Usenet newsgroups, bulletin boards on CompuServe—all were providing opportunities for people to connect with one another around like interests and lifestyles. This represented a shift in how people used communications media. Rather than simply consume it, they participated in it. While this model for accelerated human communication still exists today, advertisers tend to emphasize the one-way model and underwrite content development, putting online conversation in the role of second fiddle.

After the Web came onto the scene, commercial marketers jumped on the bandwagon in droves, encouraging the growth of the informational aspect of the Internet over the social aspect. Advertising revenues funded content development through a variety of tactical approaches toward advertising, all based on the old push model. The first of the advertising models to emerge was paid hyperlinking. Advertisers paid well-trafficked Web sites to carry what amounted to hyperlinked ad messages in areas where people might see them. Aside from the ability to easily move to the advertiser's Web page with a single click of the mouse, these ads were no different from classified ads in newspapers. Then came the ad banners. Advertisers learned to take advantage of pictures and animation, but the push model prevailed. Again, aside from providing easy access to the advertiser's Web site, the banner ad was no different from forms of push media that already existed—in this case, billboards. Then banner ads got crazy. Some had functionality, like store locators, built right into them. Some contained sound. Yet others expanded beyond the space allocated to them on a Web page, increasing the profile of the messaging and, by most accounts, really ticking people off. (Is it any wonder that one of the first companies to bring over-the-page ad formats to the Web was called Eyeblaster?)

The trend continued with some of the more modern ad formats. Sponsored search results on Google, Yahoo, and MSN are no different from paid hyperlinking, which is itself scarcely distinguishable from classifieds. Audio content on the Internet is peppered with thirty- and fifteen-second spots—direct analogs of radio commercials. Clicking on a video clip on CNN's home page usually brings up a thirty-second video spot for an advertiser. The ad runs for thirty seconds before it gets to the news clip the user requested in the first place. Yep, it's a TV commercial.

Along comes Web 2.0, which was supposed to bring about a new era in human communication. The next stage is ostensibly about connecting directly with the customer through social networking and two-way media, yet advertisers stubbornly cling to the push model. Just look at how many marketers have handled social network initiatives in places like MySpace. The "solution" seems to be all about creating pages for advertising mascots, which agencies then attempt to promote with more push advertising and paid hyperlinks. Advertisers also struggle with presences on YouTube, often opting to place their television commercials there in hopes that young people will see them. Today, if I search YouTube for the keyword "Mitsubishi," some of the results returned are video files of Mitsubishi commercials. They get a few thousand views, have a decent rating, and garner one or two comments. But if you were to look at some of the fan-generated Mitsubishi pages on YouTube, you would find higher ratings, pages upon pages of comments, and many more views. This is so because these pages are merely conversation starters that help Mitsubishi fans congregate around a common interest. As for the straight commercials, they're all push, and 99 percent of them fail to leverage the two-way nature of the medium that arose from the hyperlink.

See what I mean? While the rest of us are using the Internet in ways that bring us closer together, the advertising industry is hard at work trying to force the Internet into the box currently inhabited by media like television, magazines, and direct mail. Most advertisers prefer a world in which people absorb their advertising messages and buy a product without talking back to the company that sells it to them.

This still begs the question, if making the most of Internet advertising involves teaching advertisers how to talk directly with their customers rather than at them, why hasn't someone done it yet? Remember that institutional inertia I wrote about earlier? It's a lot more deep-seated than simply being blind to the back channel. The economic models of the advertising business reflect a bias toward the push model as well.

Currently, an advertising agency stands to make a lot more money on the recommendation and deployment of a twenty-million-dollar television campaign than from a twenty-million-dollar interactive campaign. A television buy of that size might net an agency eight hundred thousand dollars in fee and commission revenue, with much of that adding to a significant bottom-line profit. An interactive messaging buy usually nets an agency significantly less, with many more interactive professionals needed to staff the account. Why? In general, television campaigns take a lot less work to pull off successfully. Three or four people could handle a campaign this size, setting the campaign up to run and then communicating the results back to the client before moving on to help another client with another TV initiative. An interactive campaign of the same size requires more maintenance. As interactive campaigns run, they are continuously optimized by moving media weight from site to site and placement to placement in order to achieve the best results. Interactive campaigning also requires a very complex skill set that draws from both the technology and media worlds. Labor costs more, and there's a lot more labor involved. Does a TV buy net more than an Internet buy because the latter is more labor intensive, or are there other reasons—such as (sometimes) commissions on TV buys but not on Internet buys? In other words, why does this difference exist? Quite simply, interactive messaging is a less profitable business for ad agencies.

Now, factor in the notion of using the Internet for what it's good for—direct communication with customers. Agencies might not know how to do that just yet, but they know it will require more people spending more time to service the account, possibly calling the account's profitability into question. So while the answer to figuring out interactive marketing might be staring advertising agencies in the face, it goes largely ignored, owing in large part to uncertainties in the economic model. That's the bad news. The good news is that there are two schools of thought. While the traditionalists of the advertising business continue to cling to the push model, new thinkers are challenging that model's effectiveness and are developing new ways of doing business that could address profitability concerns. I call them conversationalists.

The conversationalists see how hyperlinking has changed communication, and they believe that the changes brought about by hyperlinking will make their mark not only on the Web but on every medium that will emerge over the course of their lifetimes. They believe the primary function of new media is to connect people meaningfully with one another and not merely to carry one-way commercial messages. They see the lengths to which ordinary people will go just to dodge the flurry of messages heading their way every day (think spam filters, PC-based ad blockers, or simply throwing out the junk mail before opening it). And they think they can fix it.

Many of these folks, coincidentally, are refugees from advertising agencies large and small, from the biggest of the Madison Avenue behemoths to the small independent boutiques. They see how push advertis-

ing becomes less effective year after year, and they believe that advertisers need to make changes in the way they do business to accommodate
the expectations of Joe Websurfer. Among those changes is an investment
by companies in resources that will allow them to meaningfully participate in the dialogue unfolding on the Internet about their products, services, brands, and product categories. They need to free up time for
people working at their company who are familiar with their products,
services, and policies to participate in that dialogue. Some have dubbed
this investment concept a "Conversation Department," and it's designed
to give people who buy products and services a human being to connect
with, rather than an empty advertising message. Once a company with
something to sell can contribute meaningfully to a conversation on the
Internet, it can deliver on what Internet users expect from it. To do that,
conversationalists need to fight decades' worth of institutional inertia and
billions of dollars' worth of transacted business. Perhaps the only way
they can do that is by demonstrating the power of a more direct approach
to addressing customer concerns and questions.

There are millions of conversations taking place right now on the Internet—on blogs, social networks, bulletin boards, and other Internet
communities (including virtual worlds like Second Life)—that have
something to do with unaddressed needs. All of them owe their very existence to the building block we call the hyperlink. The only substantial
thing standing between advertisers and success in addressing these needs
is a scalable way to take a personal and human approach to participating
in these conversations. Right now, companies like Nielsen, Cymfony, and
Technorati are providing new ways for companies to listen to these conversations. They sift through blogs, message boards, and other online
forums and apply algorithms to determine relevance to an advertiser's
brand, product, or category, providing advertisers with intelligence on
how and where people are talking about them. With such technological
solutions to assist with the Herculean task of keeping up to date on what
people are saying about a brand, there's clearly an opportunity for advertisers to find a nonpush way of addressing them.

Given the sheer volume of the conversation, it's much easier for a small
company to participate, and many small companies do. For instance, AccuQuote, which provides life insurance through online channels,
launched its own blog in 2006 to provide a focal point for conversation
about topics related to life insurance. The CEO, vice president of marketing, and other top-level managers contribute to the blog. They also
follow up every comment and question personally. The AccuQuote brand

is much less well-known than, say, Chevrolet, and their category tends to generate less conversation than the automobile category. So it's much easier for AccuQuote to keep up with comments and conversation than it would be for Chevy to do the same if they wanted to follow up on every comment posted to the GM Fastlane blog. The conversationalists' best hope thus might be to demonstrate the power of participation through a number of success stories with smaller companies. If there's a scalable approach that will allow larger companies to easily participate, the success of small companies will drive the interest of larger ones.

If we believe that hyperlinking brought about a fundamental change in the way human beings communicate, then we might also come to the conclusion that the changes brought about by hyperlinking have yet to be felt in a significant way within the advertising business. There are a lot of companies out there that are still clinging to push, and when we reach a tipping point, the advertising industry is in for yet another period of upheaval. This time, it will make the chaos brought about by the commercial explosion of the Web in 1994 look insignificant in comparison.

In the end, I think advertising has about a dozen years before the conversationalists revolutionize the business as we know it. Admittedly, this isn't characteristic of the sweeping, immediate changes that disruptive media like the Internet tend to bring about. However, as of this writing, we've waited more than a dozen years for the Web advertising business to chip away at institutional inertia to the point where advertisers spend more on the Web than they do on, say, billboard advertising. Simply put, advertising won't be as eager to kill off its own cash cow than we might expect, even with cold, hard facts staring it in the face. It will take time. Yes, hyperlinking has brought sweeping change to the advertising business, but we haven't seen anything yet.

NOTE

1. David Ogilvy, *Ogilvy on Advertising* (New York: Crown, 1983).

STACEY LYNN SCHULMAN

Hyperlinks and Marketing Insight

It seems that everywhere we turn these days, marketers and advertising professionals are talking about "putting the consumer at the center." They speak of understanding the consumer's needs and desires, crafting finely tuned segmentation studies, and using equal parts art and science to accurately pinpoint the right media environments for brand messages. Gone are the days when advertising told consumers what they needed and why (remember simple chronic halitosis?).

So why have marketers begun to prick up their ears? Although advertising has always focused to some degree on modeling (if not outright manufacturing) consumer behavior, today's emphasis on the value of consumer preference is less about competitive edge and more about survival. Technology's advances have given rise to a cacophony of amusements that compete for attention amid increasingly facile tools for avoidance. The result is an ultrasavvy, self-indulgent consumer who moves nimbly between a state of continuous partial attention and complete immersion in highly relevant media experiences. Today, consumer interaction with media (and thus brands) is self-styled, so won't marketers who capture consumers in their immersive moments win? The answer is partly.

Every effort to understand the consumer's lifestyle, patterns of consumption, and media habits culminates in a well-crafted creative campaign and a selective media plan that will be both effective and efficient. This is typically where the rationale for consumercentric research ends. The problem is that the effort marketers typically pour into "holistically" understanding the consumer in a "360-degree way" culminates just short of the critical insight we need today to truly connect. Identifying the relevant, engaging media vehicles is only half of the equation. Consumers have come to expect us to know who they are and what they like. Playing on that level is simply the price of entry. When we demonstrate, however, that we understand why they like it, we are welcomed into a relationship. The why is the critical second half, and marketers who embrace and activate this knowledge win.

Know Me, Know My Desires . . .
Just Don't Invade My Privacy

The problem with getting at the why is that the exploration requires extensive, qualitative consumer research at a time when no-call lists are gaining traction. Syndicated research is battling dwindling cooperation rates each year, while fragmented consumer segments demand bigger and better respondent samples. And we're not even sure we're always getting accurate information. Survey data, in any form, carries some degree of bias. From questionnaire design to focus group "leaders," bias can be introduced into the process at almost any access point. If the industry is to turn itself toward a larger scale of softer, qualitative research methods to get at the why, then new research methods need to be explored and supported.

Additionally, consumers are well aware of marketing efforts to track their behaviors and purchases, and in many cases, they will gladly give up privacy for convenience and personalization. The slippery slope is to know when and where the line is. The debate over personalization versus privacy illustrates the increasingly dichotomous world of marketing efforts to serve and communicate with consumers. In response to an increased demand from consumers for personalized attention, companies are providing greater choice, convenience, and customization in all types of products and services. The trend spans all levels of technological integration and is evident in media (satellite radio and podcasting), in online commerce (frequent shoppers now expect Amazon-style recommendations), and even in the store (Wendy's allows consumers to choose one of three sides for their value meals). The fact that this high level of personalized service and communication requires that consumers share with marketers richer data about their needs and preferences creates the second diametrical aspect of the consumer-marketer relationship: consumers are increasingly wary of providing too much information, for fear that their privacy will be compromised. The consequences of decreased privacy in today's world can mean, at best, an e-mail inbox overstuffed with unsolicited offers for "natural male enhancement" products, to, at worst, identity theft and a crippled credit rating.

Companies that exceed customers' expectations for personalized service and use appropriate timing and personalization in their marketing communications are richly rewarded. Isn't that what consumercentric research is all about, after all? With e-mail, Internet, cable, broadcast, and print advertising, the relevance of the content to consumers and the extension of the brand deeply into the experience is the home run we're looking for. The right combination of marketer-collected data sets and contextual qualitative analysis should yield a complete understanding of the why, but not in mass-sized quantities. Efficiencies lost in a more complex process of creating messaging, planning, and buying media are surely gained in a higher rate of connection with and therefore conversion of potential consumers.

The Hidden Link

One of the more exciting avenues for research has become the vastly unexplored intersections of online consumer communities. Today, those intersections exist robustly on the Internet in Web logs, discussion groups, and chat rooms. In those spaces that are not password protected and are thus "open to the public," a wealth of passive, free-form consumer sentiment is waiting to be mined.

Hyperlinks are the glue of these online communities, forming digital footprints of the way individuals make connections. Through a simple selection to include, exclude, or just follow a link in our daily online interactions, we passively telegraph the way we see the world, what is important to us, to what degree, and why. This information on a person-by-person level can be deconstructed and reassembled into meaningful groupings—or target markets—for advertisers. Smaller than mass audiences, but more efficient than one-to-one connections, these dynamic target markets promise more relevant, meaningful methods to connect consumers and brands in the future.

For years, the marketing community has depended on multiannual, expensive, longitudinal surveys of consumers in which respondents recalled their own behavior. Hyperlinking provides a map of actual behavior that expresses not only what purchases we make but what passions and concerns we have. In many ways, harnessing the power of hyperlinks unlocks the hidden link marketers have been seeking between many disparate sources of information. Media preferences, brand preferences, attitudinal disposition, and consumption habits are still primarily measured in separate studies by separate research vendors. By following and segmenting the patterns of hyperlinking, they can now be rolled into a single-source, behavioral composite of core consumer segments.

The Massive Myth Yields to the Finer Slices of Life

Over the past ten years, the advertising and marketing industry has lamented the degradation of the mass over the rapid advancement of technologies that challenge their ability to reach many consumers at once (proliferation of media channels) or even at all (commercial avoidance technologies, e.g., personal video recorders).[1] Somewhat paradoxically, as advertisers have begun to embrace the value of one-to-some marketing strategies, individuals have become enthralled with the newfound soapboxes that allow them not only to be channels in and of themselves but also to revel in the popularity of their postings (how many people are linking to their blog) as well as boast their number of "friends." In a world where big business has resolved to celebrate a more intimate connection with its audience, the audience has become enthralled with the potential robustness of its cohort set.

What can be at the source of such need for notoriety in society today? As technology speeds our ability to connect to the world, it simultaneously disassociates us from the neighbor next door. Everyone is a member of a global village but is woefully disconnected from the local infrastructure that historically defined "community." We're able to be intimately involved in events happening millions of miles away because we can manage the rote aspects of our daily lives—banking, bill payment, shopping—without ever making contact with a real person. The extreme example is the global citizen who'll step over the neighborhood homeless on the way to the ATM to empty his pockets for tsunami victims. We are at once connected and disconnected.

Twenty years ago, media scholars like Herbert Schiller pointed out that Main Street had been usurped by the suburban mall as the point for the intersection and exchange of ideas.[2] Almost in parallel, our real-world communities began to unravel, as membership in organizations from PTAs to bowling leagues showed marked declines.[3] Today, the intersection and exchange of ideas is still happening, but it's not at the mall or at the bowling alley; it's on the Internet. The emergence and proliferation of Web logs (Blogger), social networks (MySpace, Facebook), and online landscapes (Second Life) have become virtual surrogates for the real-life communities we've detached ourselves from.

For marketers, the crisis of community is important not so much because they seek new halls within which to capture consumer interest but because the concept of community is linked to that of identity. In fact, the two concepts are linked in the virtual space just as they are in the physical space. Erik H. Erikson, who popularized the notion of identity in his writings from the 1960s, called out the need for community in affirmation of the self: "The functioning ego, while guarding individuality, is far from isolated, for a kind of communality links egos in a mutual activation."[4] Any advertising scholar will tell you that while a product gets into your consideration set for simply fulfilling what it says it does, ultimate selection against its competitive set of products is based in emotional connection—and that requires deeper understanding of a more personal nature. It requires a linkage between the product's values and the consumer's personal identity.

Until recently, the industry has been able to identify the intersection of these values and instill that essence within the creative aspects of their advertising, but when it came down to buying media space, we were right back to looking at consumers in two slices—age and sex. While you might be able to make a case for significant differences between men aged eighteen to twenty-four as a group and women aged fifty and over as a group, you'd be hard pressed to validate that all women aged fifty and over share the same values, passions, and concerns. And therein lies the promise of marketing to the unmassed.

The Community-Identity Junction

Today, our individual identities exist within two types of communities—the physical and the virtual. While the expression of the self in the physical world has always been through a combination of personal signals (from what we say, to what we wear, to how we move), the virtual world is characterized by links and references to broader-known elements of the culture. In this way, TV shows, brands, and bloggers alike become markers of individual identity when referenced or hyperlinked.

In a very simple model (fig. 1), we can imagine a balance of identity production and community participation in today's society.[5] True to Erikson's thinking, both aspects exist individually and in concert with a larger community base. The difference today is that the "links" are hard coded as opposed to simply psychological. An individual MySpace page is viewed and reviewed by the self as well as by a larger MySpace community.

Living between identity production and community participation in this model is the mediated self. This is the critical space in which our identities are crafted by the symbols we choose as representations of our

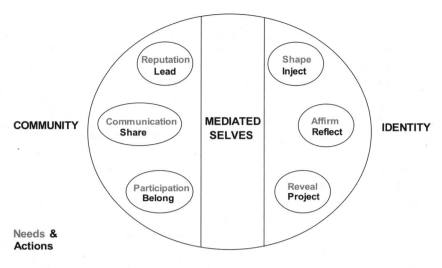

Fig. 1. Mapping the community-identity junction: needs and actions

true selves. The mediated self exists between identity and community precisely because it acts as a double-sided filter, simultaneously affirming and reflecting our personal values. It is the expression of identity through the use of materials or symbols that are generally more widely known to a larger group—logos, musical styles, favorite TV shows, links to other content, and so on.[6] The mass-produced cultural products of our time are a welcome common ground in a sea of disconnectedness—and for this reason will never truly disappear from society. Absent a true physical interaction, individuals will need these mass-understood symbols to shape, affirm, and reveal themselves within a community in which they want to belong, share, or lead. Hence our virtual (and physical) selves today are "mediated," as brands and the cultural industries flex their muscle and are either ignored, adopted, or discarded as potential markers of identity.

Practical Applications

Hyperlinking insights can be used by marketers to identify appropriate media vehicles for their advertisements and product placements or even in selecting celebrities for product endorsements. Consider, for example, a community of small business entrepreneurs. As a small business advertiser, you may want to reach these potential consumers within a small business context that is specific to your services. Alternatively, you may want to reach out to them in their leisure time, where they may be less guarded and more open. In either case, capturing and categorizing the hyperlinks of an online sample of small business owners could provide both types of insights.

In one study, a sentiment analysis was conducted across thirty targeted Web sites related to small business, from January to March 2006.[7] The sites were chosen for both quality and depth of conversation, from a set of small business forums, discussion groups, and blogs. Nielsen Buzz-Metrics provided the technology to mine the conversations and categorize the sentiment. In figure 2, the percentages in the pie chart represent conversations related to small business topics and are based on the raw number of messages as a percentage of the total messages captured ($N = 3000$). The chart at right depicts the personal passions of twelve hundred unique small business owners who visited the thirty sites monitored in the pie chart at left. This data was culled from ComScore and provided an opportunity to map the online behaviors of small business owners outside the core focus of business concerns. Each of the columns lists the areas in rank order according to the statistical measure at top. The shading of the boxes allows for a quick visual understanding of where commonalities exist across statistics.

Beyond simply accessing the insight from preexisting online communities, marketers are beginning to create their own communities in ways that entertain, inform, and provoke interaction. Some of these are very robust (P&G's Tremor), while others seek to entertain in line with their brand's values (Coca-Cola's Chill Factor). Perhaps one of the most enlightened examples is Toyota's Hybrid Synergy microsite. Rather than ply consumers with online video testimonials and stagnant statistics, the site mined its own database of existing customers and visually represented their motivations for acquiring the hybrid vehicles. The result is a compelling visualization of consumer sentiment representing the various links that brought the new owners to investigate the product, and it will grow organically as more Toyota hybrid owners contribute to the site.[8]

Media organizations, by contrast, can use intelligent links to better package the assets within their portfolio of content offerings. Instead of selling the mass of impressions that are delivered through the content pages of MySpace, News Corp could be mining its community for any links to News Corp content that are placeholders for our virtual identities. How does a group of users who feed on a steady diet of *American Idol*,

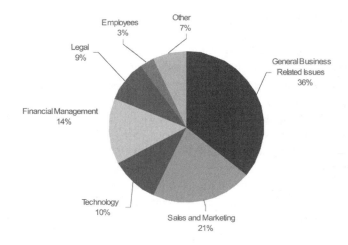

REACH	ENGAGEMENT	SBO FOCUS	PURCHASE
General News	Auctions	Online	Travel
Multimedia Entertainment	Online Gambling, Games	Food	Apparel
Music	General News	General News	Consumer Packaged Goods
Personal Finance	Banking	Movies	Consumer Electronics
TV	Sports	Health	Event Tickets
Movies	Kids' Entertainment	Personal Finance	Books, Magazines
Tech News	Personals	Travel	Music, Movies, Video
Books	Apparel	Music	Home & Garden
Auctions	Personal Finance, Travel	Home	Sports & Fitness

FIG. 2. Small business owners' concerns versus personal passions

for example, differ from those who quote and link to Bill O'Reilly? And do either currently subscribe to *TV Guide* or have a DirecTV system in their homes? Fan cultures that aggregate in social networks like MySpace are gold mines of information not only for connecting the dots between content assets in a media organization's portfolio but for linking program preferences to product and brand affinities. How many of those self-pro-

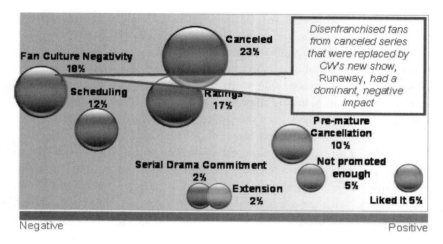

Fig. 3. Deconstructing the demise of the CW's *Runaway*. The percentages are based on the number of messages per total messages ($N = 84$) culled from several hundred entertainment message boards, discussion groups, and blogs after the show's premiere (September–November 2006).

claimed *Idol* fans are also commenting on Dove's Real Beauty campaign or the newest Samsung cell phone? In one community database, marketers can simultaneously prove the brand connections with media content for advertiser clients; develop prospect lists for deals involving content integration; mine ideas for the next prime-time drama project; and deconstruct our latest failures—as in the case, depicted in figure 3, of the demise of the CW's show *Runaway*.[9] The true benefit is not in the size of the potential audience but in the ways we can better understand the segments that exist within.

Listen, Enable, Engage for Insight (Not Just Impact)

Online consumer expression—whether through blogs, uploaded video, or embedded links—has created viable prisms with which marketers can move beyond the mass and engage consumers in a dialogue about their brands. In our world of rapid-fire change and immediate gratification, however, self-control is likely to emerge as the differentiator between success and failure. Marketers eager to be first or to ride the crest of the social community du jour without taking the time to listen and learn are at risk of disenfranchising the very consumers they're trying to woo.

Consider a case study of *American Idol 2*.[10] One aim of the study was to explore the drivers of engagement, by which the researchers meant the elements that attracted people to the program. I led a team at Initiative, a media buying and planning firm, that conducted a multitiered quantitative and qualitative analysis of the show's fans. Critical to the analysis was understanding the why. What was it about the show that fans connected to the most? How did the marketers associated with *American Idol 2* successfully or unsuccessfully harness the why to communicate their brand messaging? To answer, we actually created a special environment called "Shout Back" with the FOX and Fremantle teams on the official *Idol* fan site. This area allowed us to both query fans on specific questions of interest and allow them to free-form rant about the show. We then mined all of the free-form data to get at the most prevalent concepts. We analyzed the comments of more than fifteen thousand fans who discussed the show on the Web. Our goal was to extract the elements that they most frequently mentioned as attracting them to the show.

Figure 4 identifies the core engaging elements of *American Idol 2*—as noted by the fans over the course of the final five weeks of the series. In a surprising twist, what we would have considered the most "engaging" proposition—the interaction via a voting mechanism—was not the dominant element. In fact, it was the least engaging element. The personalities of the judges and the bonds established with the contestants proved to be much more powerful connection points with viewers.

In figure 5, Initiative mapped the major marketers to the core engagement drivers, highlighting the fact that Coca-Cola and Ford accurately tapped into the most resonant elements of the show, while AT&T focused on the least engaging element, the voting. Both Coca-Cola and Ford used the core personalities of the show within their creative. AT&T, on the other hand, used a *Legally Blonde*-esque actress as the core character in a spot featuring an *American Idol* voting campaign. Each week, the young blonde character would deliver a feverish, high-pitched appeal to the show's viewers to vote for their favorite contestant through AT&T SMS text messaging—and the core fans of the show translated the "ditziness" of the AT&T character as an affront to their commitment to the show and their "fanhood." They felt as though AT&T was making fun of their entertainment choice. The AT&T spot became clutter. The proof, of course, is in the data (fig. 6).

The *American Idol 2* case study is but one example that points out the return on investment (ROI) of enabling versus disruptive communica-

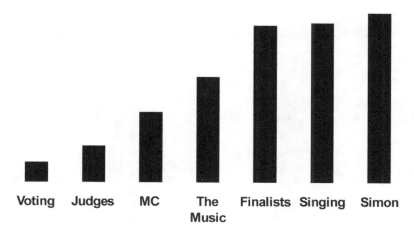

Fıɢ. 4. Attributes of engagement—*American Idol 2*. (From Initiative/ MIT/FOX/Hindsite—April/May 2003 Expression Research.)

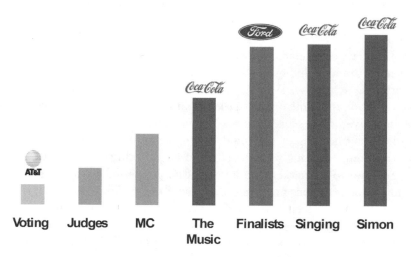

Fıɢ. 5. Leveraging program equities—*American Idol 2*. (From Initiative/ MIT/FOX/Hindsite—April/May 2003 Expression Research.)

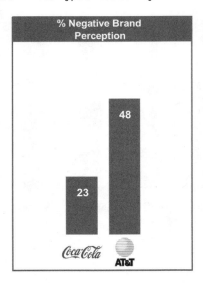
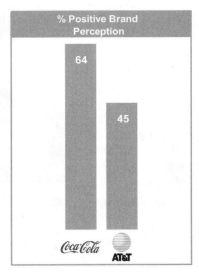

Fig. 6. Doing it right makes a difference—*American Idol 2*. (From Initiative/MIT/FOX/Hindsite—April/May 2003 Expression Research.)

tion. Initiative calculated the two marketers' performances along its proprietary Brand Value evaluation system, which measures the impact of marketing actions on a brand's core value statements. While both marketers made the same on-air marketing investment around *American Idol 2*, Initiative's tools scored Coca-Cola at a +64, while AT&T delivered a −16. Doing nothing at all would have generated a zero score. In other words, doing it wrong was worse than doing nothing at all.

So how should marketers embrace the new hyperlinked society for maximum benefit to consumers and their own bottom lines? Research shows that they should listen to the new dialogue, enable the immersion into the new technology, and engage consumers for insight (not just impact).

Listen to the Dialogue. Gone are the days of marketing monologue. With so much expression happening online, marketers can only learn. Collecting sentiment passively arms advertisers with better intelligence to build better products and bring them to market in more relevant ways for consumers.

Enable the Immersion. The plain truth is that when we sit down in front of the TV set or open up a magazine, we want one of two things— to be informed or to be entertained. What we don't want is to be advertised to. The technology at our fingertips—digital video recorders, video on demand, and so on—makes irrelevant content a disruption to our engagement with the experience we seek. The marketing challenge today is not only to communicate the brand without disruption but to harness the insight from inside the community culture in a way that actually enables engagement and creates goodwill.

Engage for Insight (Not Just Impact). Marketers might think that, armed with better intelligence and the next great idea to engage consumers, we need only find the right immersive application in the right environment. This assumption would be wrong. Wise marketers will make their investments in the new consumer dialogue work for them in the future, not just in the moment. Asking consumers to write your next Superbowl commercial may make you appear to embrace user-generated video, but the real value is gained from deconstructing how, why, and in what contexts those same consumers chose to highlight your brand, its attributes, and the competitive set.

In Conclusion

The fabric of real communities in American life is slowly being rebuilt with virtual threads in online communities. Those threads are the building blocks of a new social ecology in which brands can derive critical insight on consumer experience as well as serve as markers of identity in both the real and virtual landscapes. Our desire for connection sets up our media experiences in today's world as proxies for "community," providing the depth of experience and interpersonal connections we crave as a result of our fractionalization. Hyperlinks passively provide the understanding of how and why online communities form and, importantly, what drives individual engagement. Through effective use, marketers can actualize a less-is-more strategy, diverging from the one-size-fits-all mass tactics and moving toward accurately addressing a range of smaller target groups. Armed with a richer qualitative source of insight, marketers can then more readily move consumers from consideration to purchase.

NOTES

1. Michael Lewis, "Boom Box," *New York Times*, August 13, 2000, late edition, sec. 6.

2. Herbert Schiller, *Culture, Inc.: The Corporate Takeover of Public Expression* (New York: Oxford University Press, 1989).

3. Robert D. Putnam, *Bowling Alone: The Collapse and Revival of American Community* (New York: Simon and Schuster, 2000), 57, 112.

4. Erik H. Erikson, *Identity, Youth, and Crisis* (New York: Norton, 1968), 224.

5. Stacey Lynn Schulman, "The Community-Identity Junction" (paper presented to the Interpublic Group of Cos, New York, September 15, 2006).

6. TouchGraph, Live Journal Browser, http://www.touchgraph.com/TG_LJ_Browser.html (accessed February 28, 2007).

7. The Consumer Experience Practice with ComScore, Nielsen Buzzmetrics, "Small Business Owner Study" (internal corporate presentation, May, 2006).

8. Toyota Hybrid Synergy, Advertising Microsite Home Page, http://www.toyota.com/vehicles/minisite/hsd/?s_van=http://www.toyota.com/hsd &ref= (accessed February 28, 2007).

9. Stacey Lynn Schulman, "Future Thinking" (paper presented at the Family Friendly Programming Forum Conference, Los Angeles, November 28, 2006).

10. Stacey Lynn Koerner, "Consumer-Centric Research: Insight from the Inside Out," *Hub* (Association of National Advertisers), May–June 2005, 10–13.

ERIC PICARD

Hyperlinking and Advertising Strategy

Hyperlinking lets people control their own destiny—lets them drive their way through a media experience. It lets them choose their own path, focus on what interests them, and ultimately consume media at their own pace—on their own terms. This is a radical change from the relatively passive way that people have been consuming television. And it is a pretty big change in the way that people consume written words—the difference between a newspaper and a Web page. On the Web, hyperlinking is as simple as clicking on a piece of text or graphic to visit another page or document. But the act of hyperlinking is more profound than this: it is the act of controlling media consumption and applies just as well to "old-school" behavior like channel surfing with a remote control.

Most media are funded by advertising, and the majority of the media industry has always been driven by the economic machine of advertising. It is critical to understand the impact that consumer control will have on traditional ad-funded media. Broad estimates by analysts and experts have set an expectation that digital video recorders (DVRs) will decimate the television advertising industry because a large percentage of DVR users skip over advertising—the numbers have ranged from 30 to 80 percent in various studies. And if media do not figure out how to adapt to a consumer-controlled world, where hyperlinking is a "native" activity, the analysts are right. When the audience can fast-forward through television ads, advertisers will need new advertising scenarios to provide them with value if they are to justify continued ad spending.

Television is the best illustration of the major changes about to take place. So let's spend a few minutes learning about advertising in the "old world"—the world where content was delivered linearly while the audience leaned back and consumed it. In this world, the process of selling and buying advertising was driven by scarcity of advertising opportunity for any time slot.

In the old world, television was linear. Each time slot was filled with a fixed number of channels that a person could choose from at any given viewing moment. If you were a television executive before cable (let's say in 1978), there were only the three networks—ABC, CBS, and NBC. Prime time ran from 8:00 p.m. through 11:00 p.m. eastern time, so there were three one-hour or six half-hour time slots available to program television content against for each night of the week. The job of a television programmer back in those days was based on pitting the right offering against a limited set of competitors. Since a consumer could only watch one show at a time and since each household typically only had one television, there would be a clear winner for each block of time on a per-household basis.

In those days, the job of media buyers at advertising agencies was relatively simple. If they had a new product to launch, they knew that they could get their message in front of the vast majority of the U.S. population with a few simple media buys. With a few phone calls and negotiations, they could put their ads up and reach a huge number of people. For decades, the jobs of television programmers have remained relatively the same—if more complicated by the number of available channels growing from a handful, to dozens, to hundreds of channels competing for the same linear time slots. The programmer looks at what the competition is running in a given time slot and makes a decision about what show to run against that universe of shows running across cable and broadcast channels. If they do a good job of programming content, they will capture a large audience that is desirable to advertisers.

Simultaneously, the job of media buyers has become more and more complex as audiences have fragmented across all of the various channels. But the job is still relatively the same—the goal remains to find a show with the right mix of audience to match the profile of the product you are trying to sell, then to get your message in front of that audience. A media buyer's job is to find the biggest audience matching their campaign goals for the lowest price, and this task is quite complex when the available audience is so highly fragmented across so many television channels during every time slot.

The currency used in advertising is the gross rating point, or GRP. In television, the Nielsen ratings are used as the currency of advertising. Every television show is rated by the market it penetrates and assigned a rating based on the percentage of households that show reached. So in the most basic terms, if a television show reached 10 percent of the total audience, it would have a rating of 10 GRPs. If an advertisement ran in that show one time, it would get 10 GRPs, and if it ran twice during the same show, it would get 20 GRPs.

When a media buyer negotiates a price for any given piece of advertising, the buyer is negotiating against GRPs. The seller will guarantee a specific number of GRPs for a television spot, and the buyer fits together all the various ads in their campaign to reach a specific number of GRPs across all shows they've purchased ads in. Once the show runs, Nielsen ratings are compared to the guarantee given to the buyer. If the show exceeded the number of GRPs sold to the buyer, the buyer got a good deal. If the show fell below the number of GRPs sold to the buyer, the seller must offer a "make good" of some kind, usually giving away more advertising to cover additional GRPs.

This existing landscape of a linear schedule coupled to a formula based on reach (the number of people an ad is exposed to) and frequency (the number of times each person saw the ad) is about to shatter. The "art" of programming a show for a specific time slot is about to become obsolete, for in the hyperlinked world we live in, the audience can watch content whenever and wherever they like. In the very near future, all television will be available on demand. It will be delivered in numerous ways to numerous devices, and the advertising will not be scheduled to a specific time slot for the entire audience of a show.

Ultimately, the DVR is a bridging technology—it lets the audience forcefully excise the linear content and make it nonlinear. As long as content continues to be delivered in a linear-only scenario, the DVR will be a popular solution. But ultimately, the content will simply be made available in a nonlinear on-demand way that does not require bridging technology.

Beyond the DVR, numerous other TV consumption methods are about to blossom. Next-generation cable solutions, such as IPTV, will make almost all content available on demand through a simple set-top box, over a broadband connection. Video delivered to mobile devices over wireless broadband and downloaded to handheld media players will flourish, enabling place shifting as well as time shifting of content.

Once this huge change in audience behavior has propagated, the way that TV programmers think about their business will shift pretty quickly. They will transition to an approach much like we see today on the Internet. Internet advertising has shown us how to buy and sell media in a nonlinear way. On the Internet, content is consumed according to the whim of the audience, and all advertising is delivered dynamically. That means the decision about which ad to show to the specific audience member viewing a Web page is made at the very moment that the page is viewed. This model is how all advertising will be bought, sold, and delivered in the future.

Rather than buying a spot and then waiting to find out how many people watch the show an advertisement ran in, a buyer will negotiate a fixed number of advertising "impressions" (one ad delivered to one television set is one impression) for a fixed period of time. In the old world, if an advertiser wanted to reach one million males between the ages of eighteen and thirty-four, the media buyer would place ads into content that young males typically watch and would try to achieve a GRP rating that gave them their reach of one million people. In the new world, the media buyer could buy a fixed number of impressions across a specific date range. The buy could be associated to a specific set of content that appeals to the demographic of the audience they are trying to reach, or they could buy impressions that are targeted by the ad-serving system based on all sorts of data sources, ranging from geography to audience profile data.

In many ways, this makes the job of buyers more straightforward—they simply buy volume of ads instead of relying on the notoriously distrusted data coming out of the Nielsen ratings. But what happens to the television network programmer in this new, dynamically delivered, consumer-controlled world? In some ways, the job of a programmer becomes much simpler. There will no longer be an artificial scarcity of audience, since the audience will choose to watch whatever they like at any time of day. There will be no reason to agonize over the competition's placement of shows on the same time slot, since the concept of a programmed time slot will go away. Ultimately, the best content will always drive the biggest audience, and the available audience for every piece of content will become immensely larger.

In the old world, where one television show might be running at the fixed time slot of, say, Tuesday night at 8:00, there would be a fixed audience size of people who were actually available on Tuesday at 8:00 to watch TV. That audience was fragmented across all the various channels running content at that exact time. If a very popular show were running opposite the content in question, that content was by nature limited in the number of people who could possibly see it. Suddenly, in this new world, content that is desirable to a large audience has an opportunity to shine. And when the ads are delivered dynamically and sold by volume instead of time slot, the television programmer has an opportunity to sell many more ads for more money than they ever could in the old world. Ultimately, in this world, it becomes about the content—not about strategically running that content at the "right time of day." Quality content will gather an audience and will therefore gather ad revenue. The old methods of programming and media buying will shift, and this requires both new strategies and new technologies to manage the buying and selling of media.

TV programmers will need much better access to analytics of the available audience to ensure that their programming decisions are providing quality content that attracts the biggest possible audience. We'll likely see networks making bigger bets on content investments that align well with each other, either to capture a big chunk of a specific demographic or to spread across the spectrum more evenly. Production houses ultimately will have more power in this world, where distribution is less of a barrier and where successful production firms can self-fund speculative content creation. These production studios may even "win," in that the costs of distribution could drop away significantly and the lack of legacy investment may enable them to be more nimble.

We'll likely see more content tie-ins, with interwoven story lines across multiple shows that will attract the audience to watch content they wouldn't have seen in the past. In a nonlinear consumption model, this becomes much easier—the audience will simply flow from one show to another, not having to wait a week and hope that they have the time slot free. The content world will change, and the advertising models and strategies will change with them.

But there is a problem. So far, the technology that has enabled the audience to be in control has also enabled them to skip over advertising. This fact has caused widespread panic among the programmers and media buyers alike. But those of us in the field of advertising strategy are less concerned. We know that advertising technology will need to adapt to compensate for this new world.

When the ads delivered to any given person are targeted to his or her demographic and behavioral profile and even to preferences that person has intentionally exposed, the advertising will be more relevant and less obtrusive. Existing ad-serving technologies from the online advertising world are now being extended to include these scenarios. Targeting technologies will extend to include a comprehensive profile of an individual's interests and media consumption habits—in completely anonymous and privacy-appropriate ways—across all media. Tracking what someone is searching for online or which sites they visit will create an anonymous profile of that person's interests. Those interests can be segmented out and compared to advertiser goals. Then the ads can be delivered to the right person across all media.

On the format side of the ad business, we will see big changes. Rather than restricting the audience from fast-forwarding over TV advertising, we will let them fast-forward over an ad but will show a "down-level" ad experience, such as a five-second version of the same ad, while they fast-forward. More interactive formats will evolve, giving the audience the ability to hyperlink from a short version of the ad into a longer version of the ad. We will let them request more information or choose their own path through the narrative of an ad. And all sorts of new unforeseen controls will fall into their hands.

Many technology startups playing in the cable advertising space today are testing and developing these scenarios. We will see the winning solutions emerge in the market over the next few years. As the next-generation scenarios become reality, the chaotic change settles out, and the new technologies and platforms propagate, a new age of advertising will dawn—an age where the audience is in control. Ultimately, the power of hyperlinking will completely transform media and advertising as we know it.

MARC A. SMITH

From Hyperlinks to Hyperties

A new form of hyperlink is emerging, the "hypertie," which bridges the gap between links created in computational media and those authored in the physical world when people interact with one another and the objects around them. The hypertie is an innovation in the interaction order, the result of the merger of existing social practices of association with the technical affordances of mobile networked information systems and the existing hyperlink infrastructure. A new era in social life is arriving when the ties that bind people can be inscribed with decreasing effort into forms similar to the ways hyperlinks create connections between re-sources on the Internet and World Wide Web. New mobile devices rep-resent a novel innovation in an otherwise slow-to-change realm of social interaction—face-to-face encounters. The result is a shift from a social world in which much is ephemeral to one in which even the most trivial of passings is archival.

The Interaction Order

The sociologist Erving Goffman coined the term *interaction order* to label the realm of face-to-face naturally occurring social interaction.[1] Most so-cial life takes place in this medium through various means of self-presen-tation and perception. Body posture and adornment, speech, inscription, and proximity are resources used to present oneself and interpret the pre-sentations of others. Goffman studied this realm as a distinct domain of sociological inquiry and found a range of structural properties and prac-tices. In Goffman's eyes, people actively make presentations to one an-other, laboring with costumes, sets, and props to give a particular kind of impression to other people. Simultaneously, in slips and gaffes, through involuntary responses like blushing or eye motion, people also give off impressions that others are highly attuned to discovering and interpreting. This dance of symbols—authored intentionally and not, exchanged between actors in shifting roles with shifting audiences—is the setting for much of Goffman's vision of the social world. He highlights a complex landscape with sophisticated signaling and artifacts.

Tie signs comprise one element of the interaction-order landscape that Goffman describes in his book *Relations in Public*.[2] Tie signs are practices that indicate linkages between social actors and artifacts and that signal the nature of the relationship between them. Holding hands with someone is a good signal that you know them. Less explicit links are also commonly recognized as marks of a common bond or prior history. Shared costume, language, mannerism, and insignia are all good ways to tell if someone is from "around here" and is expressing a tie to a geographic region or social status. Related work from Edward Twitchell Hall defined and explored a realm he labeled "proxemics"—the study of proximity and orientation among social actors.[3] Hall highlights the ways cultures generate norms about how far different types of people should stand apart from one another, who has rights to look at whom, and how and when physical contact is permitted.

In the history of the interaction order of the sort that Goffman and Hall describe, there have only been a few significant innovations. The basic equipment of speech and costume is an integral part of human societies. Amphitheaters expanded the population that could usefully interact in one place. Breakthroughs like calendars and clock time allowed separated individuals to converge in space and time to engage in interaction. Innovations such as clocks and maps enhanced people's ability to both navigate and coordinate their actions. Innovations in the past century or so—the telegraph, radio, telephone, television—are predominantly technologies for interaction at a distance, not altering the primary (face-to-face) interaction order itself.

The Web hyperlink, while it doesn't directly impact face-to-face interactions, does point toward technologies that will do that. The hyperlink is a specific form of tie between resources or entities represented in computational media. These links, in aggregate, now affect most areas of commerce and culture. They are a new means of inscription for relationships, revealing connections that were previously latent or represented in ways that could not be aggregated and searched easily. When these ties are inscribed in computational media, new applications become possible for building connections, evaluating others, and gaining status and value from the accreted history of prior relationships. In contrast, many forms of social tie signs have been ephemeral or stubbornly physical. They have also lacked easily generated digital traces that describe their presence and dimension. Bridges, contracts, handshakes, and shared opinions are hard to catalog, aggregate, analyze, and track in near real time. In contrast to the digital qualities of hyperlinks, social ties remain mostly analog in nature.

That is beginning to change. The growth and widespread adoption of computer-mediated communication channels and their widespread adoption illustrates a major way that the social world is becoming "machine readable." Social networking sites (like MySpace and Orkut), Web discussion boards, e-mail lists, private instant messaging, and such emerging channels as graphical worlds are all examples of the expansion of the interaction order into machine-readable media. But they also illustrate the limits of these tools for impacting the primary interaction order of face-to-face encounters. Some edge toward the interaction order, as when people use mobile phones or laptops to instant message or e-mail one another while in the same meeting or room. But much of the activity of the face-to-face interaction order is not inscribed in a systematic and widespread manner.

Ties in computational media take on new attributes that are distinct from ties in the physical world. Computational ties are machine readable; can be collected from a wide range of ongoing events and systems; and can be aggregated, searched, and analyzed in ways that reveal patterns and connections not previously visible. The patterns that emerge from the analysis of machine-readable linkages have a range of practical applications, from enhancing searches of the World Wide Web to predicting toll fraud on the commercial phone network. Hyperlinks, one of the most visible forms of computational tie, impact commercial and social practices in multiple ways, driving many toward search engine optimization, which seeks to optimize the visibility of Web content to prospective partners. If Web content is created that is not well linked to, the investment in its creation is likely to underperform. The concept of "Google juice" expresses the need for explicit approaches to building positive patterns of linkage that stand as a proxy for many leading search engines for value.

In view of their critical role in commerce, hyperlinks have become a new form of currency. Links to and from sites act as forms of endorsement and sources of traffic. When a high-traffic, high-status site links to another site, it acts as implicit endorsement and yields increased visibility for the target site. The result is often more traffic to the target site and increased ranking in search engine results. Since higher-ranked results often correlate with increased traffic and since traffic rates often map to revenue, more inbound links of the right quality can equal greater income and value for a Web site.

Social network systems have become a rapidly growing form of computer-mediated social space. Systems like the SixDegrees launched by Andrew Weinreich in 1997, Friendster, LinkedIn, Plaxo, Orkut, Facebook, and MySpace—and, increasingly, any system for end-user content creation—have provided a means for individuals to link to other users of the same or related systems. The results are webs of associations that trace the connections between tens of millions of users, all explicitly authored at keyboards with mice and big screens. Studies of these systems have revealed highly structured behaviors, or roles, being performed by users who occupy positions within an ecosystem of actors. These desktop- and laptop-bounded systems are about to spill over into the physical world. The interaction order is changing as these systems are extended into the site of face-to-face interaction, the "synapse of society," the gap between people when they associate.

The Hypertie

The hypertie expresses relationships in a form that is similar to hyperlinks and is different in kind and quality from the ways such social ties have previously been expressed. Social ties are widespread, created whenever people or other entities share or exchange resources. In some cases, these exchanges leave behind durable artifacts that represent the previous or continuing existence of the tie. A bridge is a good example, but so are artifacts like trade contracts, shared languages, and written citations linking one textual work to another. Among some animals, chemical pheromones are another form of tie, linking nest mates and conveying information about resources like food and water. Simple behaviors toward common objects, like two people emerging from a swimming pool at different times and using the same suntan oil, can indicate the presence of a linkage between two people.

The mobile digital device, the replacement for the cell phone, is a recent and emerging innovation in the interaction order in that it enables novel forms of tie signs to be created and displayed. The mobile device is the first artifact that is aware of events in the interaction order to any extent. Its awareness takes place through the device's use of a number of sensors, such as radios, GPS, infrared light, and sound. These sensors allow the detection of other similarly enabled mobiles in the device's proximity. Given the intimate association of many mobile devices with individuals, these technologies allow for the mechanical sensing of the presence of people and the creation and inscription of ties—perhaps better thought of as hyperties—in increasingly implicit, passive, automatic, and pervasive ways.

The emergence of mobile devices in the forms of cell phones, PDAs, MP3 players, cameras, personal video players, and navigation devices like GPS provide a new platform for the creation of a range of novel classes of devices able to author finely detailed social ties. As the sensor capacities of these devices are developed, their ability to note their location in absolute terms as well as in terms of proximity to similar devices will become highly accurate and widespread. And given the personal nature of these devices, detecting them is a reasonable proxy for detecting a person, with some useful levels of precision. In some cases, existing widespread technologies like Bluetooth and WiFi, while suboptimal for a variety of technical reasons, provide an already broadly available base for devices to sense the presence of one another. Wireless devices can be programmed to monitor the ongoing stream of passing equipment like themselves, each of which is often provided with a unique identifier. When these data are stored and analyzed, the result is a self-documenting social world in which casual encounters are noted with the same detail as long-term relationships. Projects like the Jabberwocky system from Intel Research, along with commercial systems like nTAG and Spotme, explore this implicit hypertie concept.[4] These and other related projects and products are described in the next section of this essay.

When mobile devices are widespread, social ties can be authored and inscribed in a number of ways, most of which are passive and without explicit intervention by the participants. Machines accomplish this sensing in two broad ways; they can directly link to one another, sensing the presence of other radios, light beacons, or sound sources. Alternatively, machines can independently determine their location using a variety of technologies—from GPS to terrestrial radio and other location beacons—and can share that information with a common repository such that their proximity can be calculated from the joint data set and reported back to the mobile devices.

Hypertie Systems

Here are capsule descriptions of early examples of hypertie systems.

"Life logging," a concept championed by Gordon Bell at Microsoft Research, describes a set of technologies that allow a large number of people to continuously capture many aspects of their lives from cradle to grave. The resulting data, compiled from video and audio recordings as well as from the capture of, for example, every keystroke, mouse tap, GPS reading, and heart rate data point, would amount to a manageably low number of terabytes. The recognition of people in the resulting data stream is just one of the many applications being considered for exploiting this new data resource. Given the existing commercial availability of terabyte storage for a few hundred dollars (and dropping rapidly) and the low cost of low-end video cameras and microphones and other sensors, the prospects for the vision of complete life logging seem bright. I here describe the fragments of this vision that are already in demonstration form and a few that are already in more stable commercial forms of use.

Trace Encounters, deployed at the Ars Electronica conference in Linz, Austria, in 2004, was a system built around a small computerized tag in the form of a lapel pin, which contained an infrared mechanism for exchanging data with similar devices. When one person wearing a tag encountered another person who also wore a tag, each transmitted a string of data that represented the wearer's interests and prior encounters. The result is a display of one or more LED lights that indicated to what extent two individuals shared common interests, perhaps encouraging the individuals to engage in interaction to discover their shared interests. When an individual's tag came into range of a PC at a base station, it also provided information about its previous encounters with people wearing other tags, which was collected and aggregated with information from all other tags that linked to the base station. The resulting data set painted a macropicture of the encounters between each tag and thus between each person who attended the conference and consented to wearing the tag.

The nTAG system is a commercial product that extends the core concepts explored in the Trace Encounters system by making the device's display of information far richer. The nTAG device was designed to be worn in the same way a name tag at a conference would be displayed, replacing the paper name card with a thin LCD display. Where Trace Encounters displayed only a series of LEDs, nTAG displayed grayscale text and images, allowing the device to send more sophisticated messages beyond the general rate of overlap between two user's profiles. The extra signaling space was used to exchange information about topics that were of possible mutual interest, creating a kind of context-aware form of the "ticket to talk" concept described by sociologist Harvey Sacks. "Tickets to talk" are signs or behaviors that invite others to engage in conversation. A sports team's emblem, particularly when worn far from their home city, is an example of a ticket that invites a kind of recognition behavior. The nTAG "ticket" is more aware of the context, displaying specific messages depending on the viewer, behaving much more like their socially aware wearers, who also shape their interaction presentations to their interaction partners. Subsequent to a meeting, users of nTAG can recall a list of who they interacted with and for how long, highlighting the frequent short meetings and significant long ones.

Spotme is a related commercial product available predominantly in Europe. The Spotme device is a handheld, similar in form to a PDA and not intended for worn display the way the nTAG device is. The handheld device uses radio frequency (RF) communication rather than the infrared (IR) technology used in Trace Encounters and early versions of the nTAG system. The use of RF rather than IR has important implications; IR is a line-of-sight technology that requires that two devices be within modest range (ten feet or so) and in proper orientation toward one another in order to exchange data. These limitations are also affordances in that they require that social proximity and orientation be achieved prior to the exchange of data. In contrast, RF systems are often omnidirectional and may have greater range than IR systems. The absence of direct line-of-sight requirements for the exchange of data mean that those devices and their bearers need not be as aware of one another or even in sight to connect and exchange data. This means that RF devices can exchange data between people otherwise separated by walls that may or may not be desired. Spotme also generates "dwell time" reports on who the user interacts with and for how long.

The Jabberwocky project explored an alternative RF mechanism, Bluetooth, widely available on millions of mobile devices worldwide, to illuminate the population of social beacons already present in the wilds of the Bay Area of California.[5] Bluetooth radios are designed to discover other Bluetooth devices in order to facilitate the pairing of devices like headsets and phones. An unintended consequence of this design is the ability to monitor the region of ten to thirty feet around a radio for the presence of any other Bluetooth devices. Since many users of Bluetooth devices make their radios discoverable or never changed the default settings with which the device shipped, an avid listener to the Bluetooth bands is able to hear a wide range of radios emitting identifiers that often reveal aspects of their human owner's identities. The Jabberwocky system processed the aggregate data about past discoveries of Bluetooth radios and presented users with a "familiarity" display that indicated how many people nearby were people ever previously seen.

SenseCam is a prototype device developed in the Microsoft Research laboratory in Cambridge, England.[6] The device resembles a digital camera the size of a credit card and has significant enhancements in the form of sensors. Accelerometers, thermometers, visible and IR cameras, and Bluetooth radios are combined in the SenseCam to provide the device with the means of recording ongoing sensor data and then determining when to take a picture. Its programming selects for volatility events, or points of transition between states, such as generated when a walking person comes to a halt or when a sitting person stands and begins to walk. When worn from rise through to bed, the result is between two hundred and four hundred photographs of the transition points in each person's day. Research involving the SenseCam's utility in therapeutic contexts explored their use by Alzheimer's patients. Initial findings showed improved recall of prior events when each user reviewed the day's images and events each evening. SenseCams are likely to be able to detect one another and, through techniques like facial recognition, to identify people seen by the person's device throughout the day. These sightings could be transformed into the kinds of social reporting delivered by systems like nTAG and Spotme.

SlamXR, a research project developed in the Microsoft Research lab in Redmond, Washington, is a project that explores the automatic inscription of space-time trails and hyperties. It extends the scenarios explored in the other hypertie systems described here, in that it incorporates a range of sensors in addition to the radios and IR beacons used in other devices. Sensors like accelerometers, thermometers, altimeters, GPS, and devices that measure biological input (e.g., heart rate and blood oxygen levels) are increasingly affordable and miniaturized and may soon become standard features of many consumer mobile devices. Each sensor has a capability to measure aspects of the user's state in surprisingly refined ways. Accelerometers measure acceleration, or movement. A three-axis accelerometer can generate data about the patterns of force applied to it and, by extension, to its owner. Motions like standing, sitting, walking, and riding in a variety of vehicles all apply distinct force patterns that can be machine interpreted and identified with high levels of accuracy. The forces applied to a person by an elevator ride and an airplane are very distinct. Recording the output of an accelerometer over time results in a continuous map of a person's (or their device's) motions. Research using accelerometers suggests that rich diaries of activity can be generated cheaply and efficiently for vast numbers of people. Combined with GPS and related technologies like altimeters (which help correct altitude errors that are often generated by GPS devices), a package of sensors can locate a person precisely on the surface of the planet while simultaneously characterizing the range of forces and motions applied to that person. The recent release of a joint effort between Apple's iPod product and a Nike running shoe is an early intimation of this trend.[7] The Nike + iPod product is intended to measure a runner's footfalls and thus map the runner's exertion over time. This data is recorded on the iPod and can later be uploaded to a shared Web application where people can contrast their progress with others. When combined with biological sensors that determine, for example, heart rate, temperature, and blood oxidation, a detailed picture of where a person is and what their physical state is can be generated at reasonably low (and dropping) costs. SlamXR highlights the ways hyperties can be created even in the absence of direct device-to-device detection. Colocation can be calculated based on individual devices' reports of their location. Interestingly, this allows hyperties to be created even when colocated individuals are not cotemporal; that is, people who were where you were but not when you were there can be linked together by matching their location data without regard to time.

Implications of Hypertie Systems

Some affordances of these technologies are already relatively clear. Copresence is about to be increasingly automatically documented in such a way that our blurry social backgrounds will likely resolve into a detailed pattern of passing profiles, while our primary relationships will be documented in remarkable detail. As even casual crossings become increasingly visible, existing patterns that are latent or previously ephemeral are made visible and available for collection, aggregation, and analysis. Once generated in machine-readable form, sensor data can be merged with a wide range of other data and correlated with selected collections of traces from other people or groups. From credit and census records, to crop and weather patterns, to Web browsing and system configuration patterns, mesostructural and macrostructural patterns will emerge from the collective behavior of millions of people moving through the spaces and places they inhabit. The result is a kind of explosion of social science data that is unprecedented.

The resulting data will have many implications. One in particular is the amenability of hypertie data to social network analysis. This form of inquiry focuses explicitly on the patterns created by ties or links between people or any kind of entity. The resulting directed graph data structures are considered to be social networks when people are in the population of connected entities. These networks can be complex and large and can be summarized in a number of ways that capture dimensions of their level of interconnection and the key people or nodes that occupy significant roles as indicated by their patterns of connection with others. The resulting analysis can highlight the range of different roles people play in the social world and show their change over time, making individual behaviors visible at the population scale. Social network analysis, when fed sufficient data, can create a more global view of a society's interlocking social networks than has even been perceived by any individual observer.

The digital quality of these observations introduces other issues as well. Once collected within the context of a specific social setting, these observations are likely to be available to people a world away. The erosion of control over audience is a critical shift that is already in play as people upload video captured from mobile devices to video sharing sites on the Internet, making the potential audience for an event far larger than the population present at the actual occurrence. Given Goffman's focus on the careful crafting of interaction presentations for the specific audience, loss of control over the possible audience is a significant hurdle. Almost any event can be recast into a less flattering frame, increasing the uncertainty and risk of social encounters. Alternatively, the possession of a personal "black box recording" of moment-by-moment events allows for a counterperspective to be offered providing a different framing of the event (i.e., "I did not say that and here is the tape to prove it").

The sum of these changes could be considered to be a kind of pervasive inscription revolution, an era in which practices of inscription explode to include almost all human actions. The signs of the expansion of inscription are visible in the behavior patterns seen in many online services. For many of these systems, the hurdle to cross for minimal active contribution has been systematically reduced over time. Early systems, like e-mail, required active contributions of content in order for a user to be visible in the space. A widespread concern was for the disproportionate numbers of "lurkers," read-only users who contributed no visible content. Over time, computer-mediated interaction systems have evolved so that the hurdles preventing users from leaving traces in systems are smaller, allowing the act of "viewing" a piece of content to be visible to others. Making objects into "favorites," adding someone to a watch list, and similar features allow people to browse content as before but now leave a series of traces behind that are visible to others. As a result, writing is easier than ever: we are all writers now, if only because reading is now writing. Few systems allow for the unnoticed and unreflected consumption of content. Such behavior is valuable, socially and practically interesting, and cheap to collect. In such a situation, privacy issues are sharpened. The walls have ears and eyes, and others' eyes and ears are now high-fidelity and archival.

NOTES

1. E. Goffman, *Relations in Public: Microstudies of the Public Order* (Harmondsworth: Penguin, 1972).

2. Ibid.

3. E. Hall, *The Hidden Dimension* (New York: Doubleday, 1966).

4. "Jabberwocky," http://www.urban-atmospheres.net/Jabberwocky/.

5. Ibid.

6. "Current Project—SenseCam," http://research.microsoft.com/sendev/proj ects/sensecam/.

7. "Nike + iPod," http://www.apple.com/ipod/nike/.

Part 3: Hyperlinks, the Individual and the Social

Preface to Part 3

The essays in this section explore what it means to live in a hyperlinked society, a world where individuals and information are increasingly connected and linked to each other. In a philosophical essay, David Weinberger makes a strong case for the morality of links. Links are good, he says, because they allow us to share the existence of others and their ideas. However, whether we decide to use the hyperlink for good or bad will be ultimately up to us. The other essays in this section explore the ways links connect people to each other and the social implications of those connections.

Stefaan Verhulst relates linking to the future of mapmaking. He notes that maps help us make sense of the world, much as links do, and that it is dangerous to take both for granted. Mapmaking, he says, is a process that has inherent biases and power structures that we need to question, particularly because maps mediate the ways we experience reality. New tools, such as Google Earth, that create maps by linking to databases that use information from the Web can lead to positive and negative developments for society.

Jeremy Crampton is more positive than Verhulst about the possibilities the democratization of mapping will bring. Whereas maps were once the exclusive domain of an elite few, advances in technology and open standards have allowed many more people to produce, combine, and contribute maps. What is new about the tools now used is that they often rely on open standards and make use of widely distributed data sets. This allows for what has come to be known as "map mashups"—the act of collaboratively linking data to create new maps. With the linked technology now available to the wider public, maps are increasingly being made and used by grassroots organizations for advocacy purposes.

In her essay, Lada Adamic considers different faces of the hyperlink. Hyperlinks often reveal communities that are created on the basis of shared interests. She finds, for example, that niche hobbies are good predictors of relationships. Adamic also finds that the same is true in the commercial space: niche products enjoy the highest success of being propagated. In addition, Adamic looks at the hyperlink's role in creating political communities and finds important relationships between political preference and the connections blogs make to one another.

The final two essays of the book continue to explore the implications a hyperlinked society has for political democracy. Markus Prior examines whether hyperlinks are "weak ties." Weak ties, a concept borrowed from social networks, are relationships that reduce social fragmentation because they allow diverse groups to connect to each other. However, while access to a diversity of information is greater than ever, ironically there are signs that an increase in the choices we have in the media actually leads to higher levels of political fragmentation. Matthew Hindman takes another tack to exploring the implications of a hyperlinked society for the public sphere. Whereas some writers, such as Yochai Benkler, argue that the Internet has lead to a wider public sphere, Hindman argues that this is not necessarily the case. He challenges the "trickle-up theory" of blog inclusiveness and brings data to show that only a handful of voices receive a disproportionate amount of attention.

Hindman's essay opens up more questions than it answers, and that is a fitting end to this volume. The hyperlink and the technologies that enable it are only in their infancy. While the writers in this book point to many avenues into which links will take society in the years to come, there will undoubtedly be enormous surprises. Even more important than their prognostications, however, are the questions and perspectives the essayists present. We hope that these provocative ideas will transcend technologies to ignite important streams of discussion and research about hyperlinking and society for years to come.

DAVID WEINBERGER

The Morality of Links

Links are good. I believe that. And I'm not indifferent to the statement, the way I am to the vast majority of facts with which I agree, such as "There is a worm somewhere in our front lawn" and "Venus Williams plays tennis better than I do." The Web, as an infrastructure built of links, brings me joy and even an occasional sip of hope. I just don't know exactly what it means to say that links are good.

1.

Atomic bombs are bad. Not every conceivable use of atomic bombs is bad. There is a reasonable case to be made that using one to kill one hundred thousand civilians in Hiroshima was a good thing to do. We don't have to agree about this. I personally do not think it was, but I'm not as certain as I once was. Even so, that nudging of my position about the bombing of Hiroshima[1] has not nudged my belief that atomic bombs are bad.

As everyone knows, technology is not good or bad in itself. The iron maiden, that instrument of medieval torture, would be mighty handy if you tipped the spikes with life-giving medicine and gently closed the door part way on a patient of some sort. Or perhaps they would make the perfect planters for an herb that can save lives. Or make up your own example. Despite the ability to dream up good uses for iron maidens, I'm still willing to say they're bad.

But a funnel is not bad. Why, I've used one myself, to pour oil into a car engine. And if you respond that given the fuel inefficiency of car engines, funnels are bad, then let me tell you about the time I used a funnel to filter out the cork remnants from a delightful but cheap wine, to be drunk in moderation. And if delightful but cheap wine is not good, then nothing is. But funnels are also used in a form of "waterboarding," a contemporary form of torture sanctioned by my government. Even so, my belief that funnels are not bad remains unshaken.

Likewise, I do not believe rocks, sticks, or bricks are bad, although they have been used to commit unspeakable and at times unimaginable acts of evil. The difference between funnels, rocks, sticks, and bricks, on the one hand, and iron maidens and atomic bombs, on the other, is obvious. The difference does not lie in the intention of the creators, for those intentions don't adhere to the objects. Besides, what was the intention of the creator of rocks and sticks? Rather, the difference lies in what the social psychologists call affordances, that is, what these objects enable you to do. Funnels and bricks let us do many, many good things. Funnels let us transfer materials with little spillage. Bricks let us build structures that keep us warm and safe. Sticks and rocks have so many affordances that it's silly to even try to list them. But atomic bombs and iron maidens have fewer affordances. Their main ones result in pain and destruction. They're bad, even if we're just using an atomic bomb to prop open a door so an ambulance can get through. Their good uses are the exceptions.

If you see a problem in the preceding argument and it really bothers you, then you're a philosopher, whether you're willing to admit it or not. A philosopher reads the preceding and sees essentialism lurking beneath the surface. Essentialism, a doctrine that springs officially from Aristotle, picks out one definition—or meaning or use—among the many possible and gives it ontological priority. Essentialism says that there are many ways an atomic bomb can be used but that the real way is to blow things up. Essentialism says that a funnel can be used as a hat for the Tin Man but that its real use is to transfer pourable materials. In the previous paragraph, when I picked out some affordances over others, I was evaluating the moral character of objects by choosing one particular affordance over others. But since we no longer believe in essentialism—who is the privileged person or Person who gets to choose which use is the real one?—my assignment of moral properties to things is really just a shorthand for saying that we usually use funnels for good purposes and usually use (or intend to use) atomic bombs for bad purposes.

I am not an essentialist. But I am also not so blinded by philosophy that I've become an idiot.[2] There is some sense in which the use of funnels for transferring materials is more important than their use as hats. Things are like words. They have meaning, but that meaning isn't single-voiced and exclusive. Even so, we almost always understand words and things well. We rarely run into a word that genuinely stumps us, and we rarely encounter things that we stare at blankly, saying: "What the heck is that? Is it a car part or something I can eat?" It happens, but it's rare. Nor do we ever run into a word or thing that we insist can mean only one thing. The word *elevator* usually refers to one of those up-and-down conveyances, but if someone talks about an elevator as part of an airplane wing or as a type of mood-altering drug, we don't stare blankly as if the person just said "Umphlitz." Likewise, when our child uses a funnel as a musical instrument, we don't snatch it from the child's hands and send him or her for a time-out for violating the funnel's essence.

Things and words do not have meaning apart from us. But in their involvement with us, they have meanings that are neither as baked in, universal, and unalterable as essentialism would have us believe nor as arbitrary and willfully changeable as we sometimes would like to believe. Bring together the affordances of things, our needs and desires, and our ways of thinking, and you come up with an inevitable sense that although funnels aren't really hats or musical instruments, they can be used that way. We need a middle ground that lets us prefer certain meanings and uses but that acknowledges other meanings and uses—a middle ground that also lets us talk about how what we bring to the party can reveal what's true and real about the things we encounter.

Eleanor Rosch's work provides this middle ground. In the 1970s, she showed empirically that we make sense of the world around us by clustering meanings rather messily around prototypical examples. A robin or a sparrow is a prototypical bird, whereas a penguin or an ostrich is not. Penguins and ostriches are birds, of course, but they're not great examples of birds. They are part of a loose-edged cluster of birds that's formed not around a definition but around examples as clear as robins and sparrows. Likewise, a funnel is a cluster of meanings and users, some of which are prototypical—pouring motor oil, transferring cooking ingredients— while others are out at the edge of the cloud of meaning. Over time, a funnel might become prototypically something we wear or blow through, just as salt has gone from a precious substance to the most common of edible commodities. And perhaps someday atomic bombs will be used primarily as a way to dig canals or power spaceships. At that point, I'll say atomic bombs are good, and we'll all chuckle about how we were once so primitive that we actually thought they were bad. But now isn't later. Now atomic bombs are bad.

How do we know that? As usual, that question really comes down to how we can explain ourselves if someone disagrees. After we've spent hours arguing and have started to pick up the empties, the fundamental question is this: is the world better off for having atomic bombs; or iron maidens; or funnels; or rocks, sticks, and bricks?

Or links?

2.

Links are more like sticks than like funnels. There are so many ways to use them that there are few prototypical uses. Perhaps the most prototypical is the Web page that links to another because it's on a related topic. But that's not much more prototypical than saying a stick is part of an old branch. In fact, it's worse than that. There are so many different reasons one page refers to another: to dig further into the same topic, to explore the topic more broadly, to explore a topic that's related but not the same, to see an example of a site that doesn't understand the topic at all, to get further evidence that what the page says is right, to propitiate an acquaintance, to get paid for running an ad someone clicked on. There are as many ways to link as there are to use a stick.

This occurred because Sir Tim Berners-Lee made sure there was only one way to link two pages. The HTML code that creates the link that shows up on the page as blue and underlined (typically) has no standard way of saying what the relationship is. A link to, say, www.martinlutherk ing.org is encoded in HTML as <a href="http://www.martinlutherk ing.org">MLK</a> and would show up on the Web page as a clickable "MLK" link. Nowhere in that code is there a place for the linker to note that www.martinlutherking.org is a hate site created by a racist organization called Stormfront.[3] Berners-Lee's aim was to make linking as simple as possible. His success is evident in the hundreds of billions of links already created. If a Web page's author wants to explain the nature of the relationship to a page recommended, he or she can put an explanation into the text of the page: for example, "Here is a godawful, frightening, hateful page masquerading as a straightforward biography." Whatever type of relationship an author can put into words can be expressed on the page. And when words don't work, the page can contain pictures and music. So the HTML code that expresses the link says nothing about the nature of the link, but the page that displays the link can say volumes.

Tim Berners-Lee has been working for years on a way of enriching the HTML code with more of the meaning of the link. That's called the Semantic Web. But we don't have to wait for it before we can talk about whether links are good or not, for links as they exist for humans are what's written on the page, not the HTML code intended to be seen and used by computers. The vast majority of those human links have a meaning—a semantics—that's at least somewhat explicit and obvious given their context; that is, the meaning is explicit and obvious to a human reader, even if a computer gets nothing more from them than a "Go fetch!" imperative.

We could perform an analysis of those links to get a sense of what sort of connections they're drawing. If the vast majority of them are embedded in text that consists of variations on "I hate that other site!" then my belief that links are good might be shaken, especially if the pages hosting those links were the most popular ones. But that's an unlikely outcome.

Besides—and more important—the goodness of links comes not from the quality of the pages they point to or the semantic contexts in which they're embedded. The goodness of links operates a level below that. So even if all the links on the Web were negative and hateful, I think I'd say not that links are bad but that there's something very nasty about us human beings. How else could we explain how we took something as useful as a stick and only figured out how to poke people in the eyes with it?

3.

How long have we been arguing over issues of abortion rights, gay marriage, capital punishment? How much longer do we have to continue before we'll just give up on the hope of resolving them?[4] The length and ferocity of these arguments are strong empirical evidence that hotly fought moral debates cannot be settled.

This might lead us to despair, except we have equally strong empirical evidence that most moral issues do not need debate. Is it wrong to lie? Yes, unless you have a good reason. Is it wrong to punch someone in the face? Again, yes, except in special circumstances. Someone who lies for no reason and punches people in the face randomly isn't worth arguing with. He or she is only worth avoiding.

Our moral behavior and our ability to engage in moral argument are grounded in the same facts. You can't be moral if you don't recognize that there are other people with interests. If they're mere cartoons to you, even if you happen to be honest when making change and avoid slapping innocent babies, you're not yet moral. You're just a rule follower. To be a moral person—as you and I and just about everyone we know are—you have to be aware not only that there are others but that they care about what happens to them.

This assumption is built into the Golden Rule enunciated by Hillel the Elder and Rabbi Akiva[5] and by a certain better-known rabbi who came after them. To imagine yourself in someone else's shoes is not just to imagine seeing the world from that person's point of view but, more important, to care about the world the way that person does. If all you can see is that other person's intellectual framework, then what you've understood is nothing. What counts is seeing how the world matters to the other person. That person would feel the pain your contemplated action might cause; he or she cares about the effect of your action on his or her career, children, guppy. This caring about what happens is at the heart of morality.[6] Without it, morality becomes a mere set of rules. With it, the rules become rules of thumb we only consult when we have trouble sorting out the jumbled ways our actions matter.

Just a little unpacking of the Golden Rule reveals the obvious premises of moral life. If we want to see whether links are good per se and not just if they link to good stuff, we need to take a moment—here, a paragraph—to state the obvious.

The Golden Rule tells us that the possibility of morality itself depends on three fundamental facts: we share a world, that world matters to others, and the fact that it matters to others matters to us. If we remove any one of these three facts, the world isn't moral in any way we can recognize. Remove the first and what we do has no effect on others. Remove the second and it doesn't matter to others what we do to them. Remove the third and it doesn't matter to us what we do to others. (These are the views of solipsists, sociopaths, and really twisted sociopaths, respectively.) Put these three facts together and we live in a world in which our behavior is constrained because what we do affects others who also care about what happens to them.

Some moral principles can be derived from this infrastructure: it's good to consider the interests of others; it's good to try to understand others and what matters to them; it's good to let that understanding move us. These principles don't help us settle many disputes, because there are times when we need to frustrate the desires of others, and these principles don't tell us where the lines should be drawn. We should go back to the lesson that our world experience has taught us: we are never going to come to complete agreement, even as we slowly—oh so slowly—make progress as a species in, say, turning the tide against slavery and the subjugation of women.

But here I'm not trying to come up with universal laws of morality that can be trotted out to settle all the tough cases facing us. That would be useful if I were trying to decide whether most links are good or which types of links are good. But my purposes here are one level down. I want to see if there is anything about the structure and nature of links themselves that lets us say reasonably that links are good. Or, to be more exact, is there anything about their structure and nature that explains why at least some of us (I, for example) have a strong sense that links are good.

There is. If morality is based on our caring that we share a world with others to whom that world matters, then in acting morally, we turn toward that world with others. They point out to us that the world is this way or that and matters in that way or this. Making the comment "Hey, I'm trying to hear the movie!" reminds the person behind you that you're sharing a world that matters to you. Of course, it's unlikely to be very effective, since a person talking on a cell phone in a theater probably already knows you're trying to watch the movie but doesn't believe or doesn't care that his or her conversation is disturbing what should be your reasonable expectations for noise in a theater. Nevertheless, your instinctive comment leans on the right lever, trying to get your antagonist to see how the world looks and matters to you. In different circumstances, you might make more progress by engaging the person in conversation: "I'm just curious about why you think it's OK to take a call while in a crowded theater. Do you not know that we can hear you and it distracts us from the movie?" Maybe you won't get anywhere, but you're likely to get further than with your simple expostulation.

We sometimes make progress in morality by feeling the feelings of others, but we make more significant progress by understanding how the world appears such that it evokes those feelings. Sympathetic understanding is more powerful than mere empathy because it gets at more of the truth. Parents' grief for their child, for example, includes not just the universal grief parents feel but is embedded in an understanding of how the world occasioned the grief. Was it a wanton act of cruelty, part of a divine plan, a mere accident? These simple categories do not suffice. They merely sum up an event saturated with particularities. Our moral sense can go as deep as the world itself in understanding how things matter to those affected. Their grief is conditioned by and conditions all in their world. Everything matters differently.[7] In this sense, then, morality is an infrastructure of connection in which we allow ourselves to care about how the world matters to others. That is formally the same as a description of the linked structure of the Web.

After all, what do we do on the Web? We link. No links, no Web. In linking, we send people to another site (assuming we aren't the sort of narcissists who link only to themselves) where they can see a bit of the world as it appears to another. We send our visitors to other sites because we think those other sites will matter to them. Our site probably explains why we think it will matter to them and how it matters to us, even if that explanation is "Here's a trashy site I hate." Pointing people to a shared world, letting how it matters to others matter to us—that's the essence of morality and of linking.

4.

Morality and the Web have the same basic architecture? Holy Toledo! That means the Web is the same as morality. Surely the Web can't be that important. I must have slipped off the rails and crashed into the thickets of overstatement and Web utopianism.

I don't think I have. (But, then, of course I would think that.) It would be an overstatement if I were claiming that only the Web has this moral architecture. But despite the fact that Morality 101 is taught as a discrete course in college, the moral realm is not an isolated segment of human experience. If it were, it would indeed be a coincidence straining credulity if links happened to mirror its structure. But if morality is in fact the basis of human experience—or, to switch metaphors, if it permeates experience—then it's not too surprising that what we build for ourselves reflects that experience. Some of what we build reflects it more than others, but everything we build reflects it somewhat. It has to. We build things on purpose, and our purposes are always formed with awareness that we share a world. Outside of the odd cases where we build something purely for our own use and without a care for how it will affect others, we create in public and almost always for a public. If you manufacture funnels, you do so in order to help others achieve their purposes, thus implicitly acknowledging that we share a world with others who have interests.

But the moral structure of funnels is not in a funnel itself the way the Web's moral structure is in the Web. There is something special, but not unique, about the Web's moral architecture. The tools by which we communicate tend to reflect the moral architecture more explicitly than do funnels, sticks, and atomic bombs, because communication itself has the structure of morality: by communicating with each other, we turn toward the world that we share and that matters to both of us. I try to show you how the world matters to me, I attempt to understand how it matters to you, and we try to share more of the world. In communicating, I'm acknowledging not only that the world shows itself to both of us but that it matters to both of us. So as a communication medium, the Web is already structured morally.

The Web brings three new characteristics. They are not radically new—for what is?—but they are new enough to be worth noting. First, the Web is global in scope—and increasing its actual reach at a remarkable pace. Second, the Web turns the steep hill of broadcasting into a huge plain bordered by a cliff—once you're on, you're pretty much equal with everyone else, although if you're not on, you're pretty much off entirely. Third, the Web brings persistence not just to our communications but to the relationships our communications note; that is, the Web brings persistent links. In this, it is profoundly unlike other publishing media. Even if the cost of printing paper books went to zero, it would still be difficult to follow a reference from one book to another. In fact, if the cost went to zero, the number of books would increase exponentially, and thus there would be more books than ever between you and the book referred to in a footnote. The great importance of the Web is not that it lets us publish but that it lets us link. And linking does exactly what morality wants us to do: turn toward the world we share and see how it matters to one another.

That certainly does not mean that every link would make Mother Teresa proud. It could easily turn out that the majority of links on the Web point to ads or porn sites. That's why we have spent the past ten years inventing ways to guide one another to the sites that matter to us (including to ads and porn, if that's what you're looking for). The chief method is to say in the text why a reader should click on the link— "You've got to see this hilarious video!"—but we also are busily creating techniques that use the preferences and behaviors of social groups, that analyze patterns of text, that make random stabs in the dark. We are not done innovating—not by a long shot. The potential for understanding— and for letting the world matter to us in new ways—is just too great.

5.

So if saying that links are good is the same as saying that the world is better off with links than without them, and if their goodness resides not just in the quality of the links we're making for one another but in their very structure, in what way are we better off? I think there are two ways.

First, the value of the linked structure of the Web is primarily potential; that is, it is a giant affordance that we may do good or bad with. But it's not potential the way a stick could potentially be used to prop open a car hood. The Web is a potential that we're actively creating and expanding. The potential is the sum of the relationships embodied in links. It is a potential we can traverse any time we're near a browser. It is a potential that can be explored and "mined." There is nothing "mere" about this potential. It is, so to speak, a real potential, existing and at our fingertips. Fundamentally, it is a potential for seeing how the world matters to others around the spinning ball we share.

Second, we're better off with links because, whether we think about it explicitly or not, every time we click on a link, we take a step away from the selfish solipsism that characterizes our age—or, to be more exact, that characterizes how we talk about our age. We've invested so much in building out the potential of the Web. We've posted tens of billions of pages and created links in numbers that multiply that score. So many of us are so absorbed in this new world that researchers wag their fingers, worried that we're withdrawing from the "real" world.[8] The Web's reach makes it clearer than ever that the world we share is in fact the entire world, not just our cozy corner of it. The Web's links make it unavoidable that we care about what matters to others, even if we care in the mode of hatred, fear, and ridicule. The world has never seemed so "intertwingled," to use Ted Nelson's phrase, and that awareness is a good thing. In fact, it is the very basis and embodiment of morality itself: allowing how our shared world matters to others also matters to us.

Links are good.

NOTES

1. I've purposefully left the bombing of Nagasaki out of this account because it is so much harder even to attempt to justify.

2. I achieve my idiocy in other, subtler ways.

3. Geeks know that link code actually can contain additional metadata, including a phrase like "Hate site hosted by Stormfront." But there is no agreement about how to encode such data, beyond Google's use of the nofollow tag, which lets a page author indicate that he or she does not want search engines to mistake a link to a page as an endorsement of its worth.

4. A. K. M. Adam uses this empirical argument to make the case for what he calls "differential hermeneutics," according to which maintaining we're right no longer necessarily entails maintaining that everyone else is wrong. He presents his case in "Integral and Differential Hermeneutics"—a chapter in *The Meanings We Choose: Hermeneutical Ethics, Indeterminacy, and the Conflict of Interpretations*, ed. Charles Cosgrove (Edinburgh: T and T Clark, 2004), 24–38—which you can read online at http://akma.disseminary.org/06Adam.pdf. It is also the theme of his *Faithful Interpretation* (Minneapolis: Fortress, 2006).

5. They formulated the Golden Rule in its negative form: don't do to others what you would not have them do to you.

6. The idea that caring is as central to our being as rationality and understanding was the great corrective Martin Heidegger brought to twentieth-century Western philosophy.

7. See Elizabeth Edwards's *Saving Graces: Finding Solace and Strength from Friends and Strangers* (New York: Broadway, 2006) for a very personal and moving example of this.

8. I use quotes here because there is, of course, only one world.

STEFAAN G. VERHULST

Linked Geographies: Maps as Mediators of Reality

Maps, just like hyperlinks, help us make sense of the world. As individuals, we use them to get between places, to determine our location, to find a store, and, with the advent of the Global Positioning System[1] and ubiquitous computing, perhaps to track a loved one. As policy makers or business leaders, we use them to determine decisions involving, for instance, the allocation of resources geographically. Through maps, we grasp reality. But do maps also shape our reality and our behavior? Do they determine the world we see and live in?

This essay suggests that, in addition to acting as mirrors for the world, maps also act as mediators to the world: they contextualize and frame our perceptions of reality. Despite their frequent claims to scientific and technical neutrality, maps, it is suggested, are inherently subjective; whether consciously or not, they contain the biases of their creators.

Such observations about the subjectivity of maps have been made by others. As I show in the first section of this essay, there is a tradition of research and inquiry—sometimes called "critical geography"—that seeks to reveal (and question) the inherent biases, power structures, and distortions contained within maps. But the subjectivity of maps has become a more pressing issue—and is perhaps changing in character—as a result of new developments, such as GPS, geographic information systems (GIS),[2] and consumer-oriented Web 2.0[3] tools like Google Earth.[4] These new technologies and applications increasingly deepen mapmakers' ability to create links between databases and visual interfaces. The results are fundamentally altering the way people see and relate to the world around them.

In the course of such linking activities, the very concept of a map, once limited to a representation of the physical world, is changing. The extensive use of data sets and other tools now allows visual representations of a variety of demographic, climate, and other nongeographic information. In addition, we are awash with "maps" of phenomena like the human genome and social relations; and, of course, the hyperlink itself is part of a larger attempt to map the Internet. Many of these maps are user-generated (mashups), and while this may democratize the process of mapmaking, it also raises important questions about authenticity and reliability.

All these developments require a rethink of how we view and approach maps. They require sustained research and systematic analysis. One of the goals of this essay is to provide the analytical foundations for such research and analysis. The aim is to understand how maps are changing as a result of new technologies, such as the hyperlink; more generally, the essay explores how maps mediate (or frame) reality and how that process of mediation is itself being transformed with changes in mapping technologies and tools.

The first section of this essay provides a historical perspective on the role of maps and, in particular, of their inherent subjectivity. Although not a systematic literature overview, it also discusses some of the analytical methods of "critical geography." The second section considers the concept of mediation: maps, it is argued, function as mediators, shaping our perceptions of reality and thus behavior. The third section considers how, much as in earlier technological revolutions, the role of intermediaries is changing today; it discusses some new mapping tools and their key features. It seeks to provide an overview of some of the key ways in which new mapping tools—particularly those that are technology enabled—are different from earlier ones. The fourth section discusses how these new features and tools are changing our perceptions of and interactions with the world. The section represents an attempt to understand how reality is being linked, framed, and mediated in a new mapping environment.

The new features outlined in the third and fourth sections suggest only some of the dramatic changes underway in mapmaking. Technology is moving so fast, and end-user behavior is adapting equally rapidly; it is difficult to categorize—and certainly to forecast—all the important transformations underway. This essay should, therefore, be seen as a starting point—an attempt to think through some of the new ways in which maps are mediating reality and to provide an analytical framework with which to approach mapmaking in a "linked age."

Maps in History

The history of mapmaking is a fascinating tale that sheds light on world history, politics, culture, and economics. It begins in ancient Egypt and

Babylon, where the earliest maps have been found, and continues through the publication of Ptolemy's famous (if mistaken) *Geography* and on to the more accurate Renaissance maps. Perhaps one of the best known mapmakers in history was Gerardus Mercator, whose Mercator projection revolutionized mapmaking.[5] Mercator, realizing that sailors who followed a straight line on their compasses would in fact plot a curved course, redefined the lines and paths of navigation on the globe. His projection proved invaluable for sailors and helped usher in an era of global travel and conquest.

Yet for all the importance of Mercator's contribution, it is important to realize that his famous maps were not, in fact, accurate. For example, on a Mercator projection, Greenland (with a surface area of around two million square kilometers) appears larger than Africa (which has a surface area of thirty million square kilometers). There are a number of other distortions, too, which were necessary in order to create a projection that would be useful for sailors. Indeed, the full title of the map is "A New and Enlarged Description of the Earth with Corrections for Use in Navigation."

This title is extremely important to keep in mind. For, as Wood, Kaiser, and Abramms argue in their book *Seeing through Maps*, "all maps have a purpose." They further argue: "Every map is a purposeful selection from everything that is known, bent to the mapmaker's ends. Every map serves a purpose. Every map advances an interest."[6] This purpose determines the form of the map and its relationship to reality. Indeed, the purpose of a map—which may reflect the mapmaker's biases or subjectivities—determines the reality depicted by the map.

Mercator's biases, intended to aid navigation, are relatively benign (although he has sometimes been accused of furthering racism and colonialism). But this isn't always the case: as several scholars have argued, a number of instances can be found in which a map's description of reality serves a far less benign purpose. Mark Monmonier describes some instances in his book *How to Lie with Maps*; Brian Harley, often considered the father of modern "critical geography," expresses similar sentiments throughout his writings, arguing in 1988, for instance, that "as much as guns and warships, maps have been the weapons of imperialism."[7]

Maps as Mediators

Others, too, have pointed out that maps not only serve to represent reality but can shape it. For example, cartography has been implicated in the

Nazi propaganda project before and during World War II.[8] In addition, cartography has been implicated in colonial and postcolonial usurpations of native rights in the Americas. Conversely, authors have also shown how native people have used cartography to reclaim their rights and cultural heritage.[9]

These are only some of the many examples that suggest how maps can shape or mediate reality. Thus, Harley urges us not to take maps for granted, not to accept their apparent neutrality at face value. Instead, he urges us "to read between the lines of the map, to discover the silences and contradictions that challenge the apparent honesty of the image."[10] Jean Baudrillard, upon whose writings Harley based some of his work, famously argued in *Simulacra and Simulation* that the map has come to precede the territory.

One useful analytical tool that can help us understand how maps shape reality is the concept of mediation. This concept has a long pedigree in the history of media studies, and it has been used by a range of authors and theorists to help understand how our experiences of reality are determined by the media and technologies (the intermediaries) through which we access and analyze reality. Elsewhere, for instance, I have argued that the twin notions of mediation and intermediaries can prove highly useful in analyzing both our understanding of reality today and, perhaps as important, how that understanding is being changed as a result of technical changes.[11]

Other media critics and authors have also written extensively on the concept of mediation. For Silverstone, mediation is a "fundamentally dialectical notion, which requires us to address the processes of communication as both institutionally and technologically driven and embedded."[12] Alternatively, mediators have been conceived of as "gatekeepers,"[13] as "mirrors" or "holograms,"[14] or as "interlocutors" and "informed interpreters."[15]

Frame analysis, too, can be applied to understanding the concept of mediation and the role of intermediaries.[16] Indeed, Gitlin, writing from a theoretical standpoint on the general role played by intermediaries, provides a highly useful and relevant description of the interpretive role played by maps and of their relationship to reality. "Frames," he writes, "are principles of selection, emphasis and presentation composed of little tacit theories about what exists, what happens, and what matters."[17]

We have seen, in some of the examples already discussed, how such acts of framing can be implicated in colonial or other projects that harm traditionally underrepresented groups. Of course, not all acts of framing and mediation need be harmful. But it is important to keep them in mind: to be aware of them and to understand how they shape our perceptions—and experiences—of reality. We need to realize that through mapping, we are engaged in codifying our existence, using our values and beliefs about the world. Such awareness is all the more important in the context of a rapidly changing technical and media environment; in such an environment, as I have elsewhere argued,[18] the nature, role, and function of mediation is being dramatically altered. By extension, so is the way we interpret and experience reality. Ultimately, the increased realization of the mediating qualities of maps can also be applied for changing our paradigms and, hence, potentially changing the world for the better. As such, mapmakers can become change makers.[19]

The remainder of this essay examines the changing nature and function of intermediaries in a new media and technical environment. The next section examines some of the precise ways in which new technologies are changing maps and mapmaking. The section following that discusses how these changes are altering our experiences of reality.

New Mapping Technologies: Key Features

Mercator and other early mapmakers created their maps at a very different time—and for very different purposes—than modern mapmakers. Yet their era was similar in one respect: like today, the popularity and usefulness of maps was being driven by a technological revolution. For Mercator, the technology in question was the printing press, which made it easy to print and distribute multiple copies of a map. This led to a democratization of sorts, in which average citizens were newly empowered to sail the world and spread global commerce. Indeed, Mercator's maps coincide with the advent of a form of globalization and the accompanying spread of merchant-driven colonialism.

The advent of the printing press changed not just the role played by maps but that of the media more generally. In the terms of this essay, we can say that Mercator's era was witnessing a dramatic transformation in the role played by intermediaries: suddenly, within the span of just a few decades, average citizens' experiences of reality were fundamentally transformed. To be sure, reality was democratized by the advent of what today might be called the mass media; at the same time, people's understandings of the world—and of themselves—became entangled and imbricated with an early form of capitalism. As Benedict Anderson has pointed out, the advent of "print capitalism" ushered in a new way of "imagining" and conceiving of the nation-state (and thus a fundamental pillar of personal identity and selfhood). These changes affected a variety of methods of communication—including, but not limited to, maps.[20]

In much the same way, we are witnessing today a technical revolution that is changing the role played by a wide variety of intermediaries. The rise of the Internet and of networking technologies more generally is up-ending traditional notions on the role of the media and the relationship between production and consumption. Our reality is to a significant extent shaped by search engines and blogs; our interpersonal relationships are determined by e-mail and cell phones. These tools did not even exist a couple decades ago; today, they play critical intermediary functions in our lives.

These changes have affected all forms of media; maps have not been an exception. In particular, the role played by maps has been changed by the increasing interactivity of content and applications, the advent of digital-ization and satellite-provided positioning data, and the rise of the Inter-net (and the attendant revolution in consumer-driven content and appli-cations).[21] The growing popularity of GIS, through which various forms of data can be represented in a meaningful way to aid with analysis and decision making, also represents a new way of conceptualizing and creat-ing maps—indeed, GIS has led to an entirely new kind of map, one that represents not only geographic elements but demographic, historical, cli-matic, economic, and various other social or cultural phenomena.

It is worth considering, in somewhat greater detail, some of the key developments that have changed the mediating function played by maps. These key features, briefly described here, include nongeographical data, real-time and mutable data, and links and thick description. Later in this essay, I define some of the social, cultural, economic, and political changes that have resulted—in effect, how these new mediating features of modern mapmaking change our perceptions of reality.

Nongeographical Data

Today's maps are, to an unprecedented degree, driven and shaped by data unrelated to physical location. Of course, it could be said that some ear-lier maps were, to an extent, similarly shaped by data. John Snow's famous nineteenth-century London maps, which he used to identify the source of a cholera epidemic, are a case in point.[22] But today's maps are not just shaped by an unprecedented quantity of data; they use data in very different ways. Indeed, as we shall see, the real-time, interactive, and linked maps of today integrate data in a way that would have been unimaginable to Snow and his mapmaking colleagues, who patiently and painstakingly plotted health figures by hand on a paper grid.

Perhaps more fundamentally, today's mapmakers have access to radically different types of data than their predecessors. The ready availability of GPS, in particular, has revolutionized (and democratized) mapmaking. In addition, mapmakers today have access to various different kinds of data—their ability to create maps from demographic, social, cultural, climatic, and various other kinds of nongeographical data has led to a proliferation of so-called geographical information system (GIS) maps and, as we shall see, has transformed the way in which maps represent reality.

GIS maps, in effect, permit mapmakers to move beyond mere visualizations of the physical world. They enable a mapping of the social worlds, contextualizing geography within a variety of nongeographic descriptions. GIS leads to a form of what anthropologist Clifford Geertz famously called "thick description." It dramatically changes the ways in which modern maps represent and frame reality.[23]

Real-Time and Mutable Data

The use of data sets has also led to a proliferation of what we might call real-time maps. Unlike the static maps of old, generated in a cartographer's office and propagated in a fixed form to users, today's maps have the ability to adapt themselves to new realities and to change by the second. Needless to say, this mutability of maps (itself a new characteristic) applies not so much to geographic features as to social, cultural, economic, and other demographic features. Nonetheless, as we shall see, the mutability of maps has a strong influence on the way we perceive our world.

Links and Thick Description

The rise of the Internet and the growing use of maps on the network have resulted in a number of maps containing links—either to other maps or to other nonmap forms of information (such as those derived, for example, from GIS data).[24] A key feature of such maps is that, unlike old paper-based maps, they are not self-contained; that is, the information they offer is no longer limited to the map itself. Perhaps another way to put this is that such maps are connected to the world. As such, they offer a fuller (or "thicker") description of the world. In this sense, they very much exceed the descriptive capacities of paper maps.

Interactivity

A final, yet vital, feature of new maps is their interactivity. Links provide one example of this phenomenon: they allow consumers to interact with the map by clicking on or otherwise selecting information. Other forms of interactivity include the ability to add reviews or opinions, to add sites or locations to the map itself, or to select a particular location for further exploration by zooming in on it. All of these options offer very different experiences than those offered by traditional maps. By allowing map readers to interact with the map, interactivity brings the map and its viewer closer; it closes the distance between representations of reality and the experience itself of reality.

New Maps, New Realities

How do these various properties of modern maps change the way we experience and perceive reality? If, as I have suggested, maps mediate our understanding of the world, and if all maps offer a subjective take on the world, then how is the world being shaped in an era of data-driven, interactive and real-time maps? This section discusses some key ways in which our perceptions of the world and our paradigms are being transformed by the new mediating function of maps.

New Realities

Perhaps one the most fundamental changes lies in the ability of maps to create, as it were, new realities—realities that are not solely defined, as in traditional maps, by topography and geographic features. Maps of poverty, maps representing political affiliations, climatic maps—all these forms of "thick description" show us and help us understand the world in a new way. Thick description, it might be said, helps us visualize and experience new (virtual) spaces. As mentioned already, new maps are capable of describing far more than their predecessors.

In addition to these virtual spaces, which remain affiliated with the geographic maps of old, new technologies have also led to conceptual maps that have no relationship to geography. Today, for example, there are a number of different visualizations of the Internet or of the human genome.[25] These visualizations do not map the geographical world or its geographic entities as we typically conceive of them; yet in their representations of new concepts and ideas, they lead us into new worlds and realities. New conceptual maps, in effect, are redefining the way we think of and live in our world. They are shaping our mental maps. Here, the traditional role of intermediaries is being dramatically extended: they no longer simply frame or "augment" reality; they actually invent new realities.[26]

Interdependence

Today's maps are particularly effective at mapping the interdependence and networked nature of our world. Whereas traditional maps represented sovereign nations and thus reinforced a sense of isolation and geographic separation, modern maps, through their use of links and other technical features, depict a far more interconnected world.

Social networking maps—for example, those that create communities of affiliation, or so-called six-degree maps, are good examples. These maps allow individuals in different countries to establish effectively "neighborly relations"; they bring the world closer, shrinking distances and defining virtual communities that traverse geography. These virtual communities, it could be said, are the new nations of modern maps: based more on affiliation and common interests than geographic proximity, they dramatically change the way we see and experience our world.

Serendipity

New maps, especially those that bring out the interdependence of the world, frequently have a strong element of serendipity; they introduce an element of chance into daily life that can greatly widen the horizons of everyday life. Such serendipity is most evident when social networking sites on the Internet are linked to digital maps.[27] Using such geographically specific community sites, strangers meet and develop shared communities of affiliation; their horizons—their notions of the world—are being widened. Every time a new friend is made or a new community created through a digital map, the individuals "consuming" the map become part of a new reality.

There is another aspect to serendipity: modern maps mean that our worlds are no longer fixed. As noted earlier, the linking of data sets and maps means that maps are mutable, constantly in flux. This constant change also affects the way we see and experience the world; it adds an element of newness, of unpredictability, to everyday life.

Democratization of Reality

New maps also permit a democratization of reality. In an Internet- and technology-driven era, maps and mapmaking are no longer the province of specialists. This "democratization of cartography" has its skeptics, who worry about quality and accuracy.[28] But if mapmaking is inherently subjective and if maps inevitably represent a subjective interpretation of the world, then it might be considered important for cartography to allow for a multitude of realities. In this sense, we could speak of a multiplicity of mediating functions: traditionally, intermediaries often limited (by framing and thus constricting) reality; now there exists the possibility of reality being extended and enriched through a multiplicity of points of view and intermediaries.

The democratization of cartography is particularly important (and beneficial) in the case of maps visualizing traditionally underrepresented groups. We have seen how mapmaking, as a profession, has sometimes been implicated in colonial bias or other forms of subjectivity that privilege dominant groups. Early on, GIS mapping was accused of a similar bias. John Pickles's edited collection *Ground Truth* was, for instance, vital in establishing a connection between GIS tools and power. He and other scholars have argued, for example, that maps can be used as tools by the privileged to maintain their privilege.[29] As with other mediators, maps can control the way we see reality and hence control points of view that may be seen by some as disruptive to their position.

Such arguments have led to what is sometimes referred to as "critical GIS" or "public participation GIS" and to a flood of offshoots, including "gendered GIS."[30] What all these approaches have in common is an understanding of the role of power in generating maps and an effort to reach out to traditionally underrepresented groups in the process of mapmaking. Thus, participatory GIS has been used to empower residents of American inner cities to create more representative systems of town planning, for instance, as well as for culturally sensitive forest management in Africa.

To take but one example, Hoyt, Khosla, and Canepa write of a participatory GIS project in New Delhi slums, held in the late 1990s, that contributed to community and urban development. In particular, data was collected to create new GIS maps that revealed shortcomings (and sources of the shortcomings) in the municipal water network; these maps encouraged citizens to demand better access to the network and ultimately contributed to greater development and sanitation. A further consequence of the project, which arose as a result of increased citizen awareness, was an increase in political accountability. The new maps helped uncover lapses in government delivery and encouraged citizens to demand better treatment.[31]

It is important to realize that such efforts do not result simply in new or different kinds of maps. Participatory GIS introduces new voices into mapmaking and, as a result, into our processes of decision making; ultimately, it affects the way we act in and see the world. Thus, the democratization of cartography can result in new and more representative understandings of our world.

All the World's Personal—Too Personal?

The preceding discussion has made clear many of the potential benefits of new mapmaking technologies. But new technologies also pose new dangers or at least difficulties. One of the further ways in which new technologies can be said to have altered reality is by blurring the boundary between the personal and the public: when individuals' data (e.g., phone numbers or addresses) are linked with widely available maps, the personal in effect becomes public. This alters notions of identity and how identity is being negotiated; that is, your map may become your identity. This can have its benefits (e.g., new friends, new communities of affiliation), but it also poses certain risks, particularly to personal privacy and even security.

The so-called secondary use of "mapped" personally identifiable information—uses that differ from the initial purpose of mapping—may be even more worrisome. The growing use of tracking tools and data only heightens this risk. Today's maps offer the potential for virtually unlimited intrusiveness. This risk was dramatically heightened recently in Argentina, when it came to light that authorities there were using Google Earth to catch tax evaders. Using Google satellite images and Google Earth Pro, the tax man for the Buenos Aires province was able to locate 1,184,030 square feet of allegedly undeclared property (amounting to approximately half a million dollars in unpaid property taxes). Likewise, in the United States, there have been recent reports of the Arkansas police using Google Earth to identify marijuana fields in order to punish the man responsible for harvesting the marijuana.

As the use of satellite imagery expands, and with the inevitable spread of ubiquitous computing and sensor technologies, similar uses of mapping tools for surveillance and law enforcement are likely to increase, posing serious challenges to individual privacy. Some of these challenges may be surmountable. In some cases, particularly when it comes to law enforcement or national security, we may feel that the benefits outweigh the potential risks and dangers to privacy. In other cases—those that are linked with the use of geozoning for marketing, price discrimination, and political campaigning—we may feel a loss of autonomy. Nonetheless, in all cases, it is essential that the public (and policy makers) understand the potential risks posed by new technologies. Without an adequate public discussion that may inform a new policy and regulatory framework, privacy may be seriously eroded. Indeed, as Michael Curry argues in an essay titled "The Digital Individual and the Private Realm," modern mapping technology presents "challenges to the possibility of privacy itself."[32]

Security

Concerns have also been raised that new mapping tools may pose a security risk by giving terrorists access to high-resolution images of sensitive sites. Such concerns have surrounded the Google Earth application in particular and have been heard across the globe, from security-conscious governments in India, South Korea, Australia, Thailand, the United Kingdom, and the Netherlands.[33] In the United States, too, concerns have been raised about the potential use of Google Earth by al-Qaida and other terrorist groups. For example, in 2005, Queens assemblyman Michael Gianaris complained to Google, suggesting that the images being provided were too detailed and posed a serious security risk.

Google has, on occasion, responded by blurring or reducing the level of detail in certain images. While this may address some of the security concerns, it raises equally grave concerns about the public's right to information. The situation is similar to that of the privacy rights already discussed: much as potential erosions of privacy need to be seriously concerned and weighed against the potential benefits of new technologies, so the security risks posed by new technologies need to be weighed against the risks of censorship and limits on information flows.

Conclusion

As the preceding discussion has made clear, new intermediaries, particularly new mapmaking technologies, are fundamentally altering our relationship to reality. Many of these changes are positive. Indeed, this essay has made clear many of the exciting and positive contributions that can be made by modern technologies. New maps can widen our horizons, build new social and political affiliations, improve policy and industry decisions, and democratize perceptions of the world.

As always, however, technology is a double-edged sword: we must be aware of the potential pitfalls along with the benefits. Developments associated with the Internet, in particular, have a tendency to be swept up in waves of euphoria. But the potential privacy and security risks need serious consideration, too. We need to systematically consider and weigh the potential benefits against the dangers of new mapmaking technologies. And we need to put the emergent trends in mapmaking and navigation within a broader context of technological and societal developments underpinning our "linked age." Indeed, how we will use and experience the Internet will be transformed in three ways: the ways we will use and manage personal identity information, the ways new "borders" will be negotiated in cyberspace, and the ways new mediating tools are transforming the way we perceive reality. Linked with map technology, new tools for identity management can empower users tremendously (e.g., by providing contextual and customized information) but can equally lead to intrusive surveillance, if not governed properly. The combination of geolocation technologies with filters may provide for islands of highly relevant information or generate a balkanized landscape of censored information. Tools used for searching and for access control (e.g., management of digital rights), along with recent developments in virtual (game) environments (e.g., Second Life), especially have the potential to "frame" our reality differently. Again, the integration with map technology has the potential to alienate certain groups from a shared sense of "reality," with all kinds of unforeseen implications.

The need for systematic analysis makes it all the more important to develop an analytical and research framework through which to approach and understand developments in modern cartography. This essay has attempted, in a modest way, to lay the foundations for such an approach. In particular, I have suggested that the notions of mediation and intermediaries could prove helpful in understanding the role of maps in shaping reality and how that role is changing.

NOTES

1. The Global Positioning System (GPS) is a satellite-based navigation system made up of a network of twenty-four satellites placed into orbit by the U.S. De-

partment of Defense. GPS was originally intended for military applications, but in the 1980s, the U.S. government made the system available for civilian use.

2. Geographic information systems are collections of computer hardware, software, and geographic data for capturing, managing, analyzing, and displaying all forms of geographically referenced information. See http://www.gis.com/whatisgis/index.html.

3. Tim O'Reilly, "What Is Web 2.0: Design Patterns and Business Models for the Next Generation of Software," 2005, http://www.oreillynet.com/pub/a/oreilly/tim/news/2005/09/30/what-is-web-20.html.

4. See http://earth.google.com/.

5. For a history of mapmaking, see http://www-gap.dcs.st-and.ac.uk/~history/HistTopics/Cartography.html.

6. D. Wood, W. L. Kaiser, and B. Abramms, *Seeing through Maps: Many Ways to See the World*, 2nd ed. (Amherst: ODT, 2006), chap. 1, http://odtmaps.com/pdf/SeeingThroughMaps_Chapter1.pdf?REFERER=GSI.

7. Quoted in M. H. Edney, "The Origins and Development of J. B. Harley's Cartographic Theories," *Cartographica* 40, nos. 1–2 (Spring-Summer, 2005): 1; Mark Monmonier, *How to Lie with Maps* (Chicago: University of Chicago Press, 1996).

8. M. Monmonier, "Mapping under the Third Reich: Nazi Restrictions on Map Content and Distribution," 2005, http://www.sunysb.edu/libmap/coordinates/seriesb/no2/b2.htm.

9. For discussions, see M. Sparke, "A Map That Roared and an Original Atlas: Canada, Cartography, and the Narration of Nation," *Annals of the Association of American Geographers* 88, no. 3 (1998): 463–95. See also M. Sparke, "Between Demythologizing and Deconstructing the Map: Shawnadithit's New-Found-Land and the Alienation of Canada," *Cartographica* 32, no. 1 (1995): 1–21.

10. Quoted in Edney, "Origins and Development," 1.

11. S. Verhulst, "Mediation, Mediators, and New Intermediaries," in *Media Diversity and Localism: Meaning and Metrics*, ed. P. Napoli (Mahwah, NJ: Erlbaum, 2005), 113–37.

12. R. Silverstone, "Mediation and Communication," in *The Sage Handbook of Sociology*, ed. C. Calhoun, C. Rojek, and B. Turner (Thousand Oaks, CA: Sage, 2005), xvi, 590.

13. K. Lewin, "Frontiers in Group Dynamics," part 2, "Channels of Group Life; Social Planning and Action Research," *Human Relations* 1, no. 2 (1947): 143–53; D. M. White, "The Gatekeeper: A Case Study in the Selection of News," *Journalism Quarterly* 27, no. 4 (1950): 383–90.

14. J. Baudrillard, *Simulations* (New York: Semiotext(e), 1983), 66.

15. D. McQuail, *Mcquail's Mass Communication Theory* (Thousand Oaks, CA: Sage, 2000).

16. E. Goffman, *Frame Analysis: An Essay on the Organization of Experience* (New York: Harper and Row, 1974); T. Gitlin, *The Whole World Is Watching: Mass Media in the Making and Unmaking of the New Left*, 2nd ed. (Berkeley: University of California Press, 2003); R. M. Entman, "Framing: Toward Clarification of a Fractured Paradigm," *Journal of Communication* 43, no. 4 (1993): 51–58.

17. Gitlin, *The Whole World Is Watching*.

18. Verhulst, "Mediation, Mediators, and New Intermediaries."

19. Comments by Stefaan Verhulst, at the conference "The Hyperlinked Society," Annenberg School for Communication, University of Pennsylvania, June 9, 2006.

20. B. Anderson, *Imagined Communities*, rev. ed. (London: Verso, 1991).

21. For a whole set of examples of the new generation of maps, see http://www.directionsmag.com/mapgallery/.

22. S. Johnson, *The Ghost Map: The Story of London's Most Terrifying Epidemic—and How It Changed Science, Cities, and the Modern World* (New York: Riverhead, 2006). For information on Snow and his maps, see http://www.ph.ucla.edu/epi/snow.html.

23. For some examples of GIS maps and their social relevance, see http://www.esri.com/news/arcnews/spring04articles/social-sciences.html and http://pus.sagepub.com/cgi/content/abstract/15/4/411.

24. The proliferation of links is evident in a road map that links to the Web sites of the various commercial establishments shown on the map, for instance, or in a traveler's map that links to reviews of and articles on various tourist sites.

25. For an interesting take on maps of the Internet, see http://jcmc.indiana.edu/vol5/issue4/dodge_kitchin.htm.

26. This "invention of reality" is not always a positive development. The power of naming—the ability of maps to will a nonexistent entity into reality simply by naming—was evident recently when Google Earth, relying on a short-lived name from the period of World War II, mistakenly labeled a mountain in Bavaria as "Mount Hitler." This mistake, which virtually invented a reality for the mountain, was strongly protested by local residents.

27. For an example of such a site, see http://www.43places.com.

28. "New Technology Helping Foster the 'Democratization Of Cartography,'" *ScienceDaily*, October 5, 2006, http://www.sciencedaily.com/releases/2006/09/06 0920192549.htm.

29. John Pickles, *Ground Truth: The Social Implications of Geographic Information Systems* (New York: Guilford Press, 1995).

30. For discussions of these and other concepts, see D. O'Sullivan, "Geographical Information Science: Critical GIS," *Progress in Human Geography* 30, no. 6 (2006): 783–91.

31. L. Hoyt, R. Khosla, and C. Canepa, "Leaves, Pebbles, and Chalk: Building a Public Participation GIS in New Delhi, India," *Journal of Urban Technology* 12, no. 1 (2005): 1–19. Further examples can be found at http://www.shef.ac.uk/~scgisa/spoleto/weineretal.pdf.

32. M. R. Curry, "The Digital Individual and the Private Realm," *Annals of the Association of American Geographers* 87, no. 4 (1997): 681–99.

33. For a description of some of the concerns, see http://www.mcwetboy.net/maproom/2005/09/google_earth_pr_1.php.

JEREMY W. CRAMPTON

Will Peasants Map? Hyperlinks, Map Mashups, and the Future of Information

In this essay, I examine the changing dynamics of how maps and information are interlinked. I argue that for most of its history, mapping has been the practice of powerful elites—the sovereign map.[1] Nation-states, governments, the wealthy, and the powerful all dominated the production of maps, and knowledge of the world emanated from the elites for the benefit of the elites.[2] This history is now being challenged by the emergence of a new, populist cartography, in which, through new forms of linking, the public is gaining access to the means of producing maps.

This is certainly not an isolated development. It is part of a larger movement of counterknowledges that are occurring in the face of ever-increasing corporatization of information, such as the consolidation of the news media into the hands of a few global multinationals and their dominance by fairly narrow interests. The Internet and Web, blogs, and the "netroots" (online political activism) are all reasons for this "people-powered" control of information.[3] In this essay, I focus on some of the exciting new developments that can help create, visualize, and disseminate geographical information. I also note a number of obstacles that impede widespread dissemination of these tools.

Popular versus Populist Cartography

Maps are a powerful way of knowing about the world and have always involved linking certain types of information to spatial representations of that information. Evidence of map use dates back to earliest historical times (Greece, Rome, and Mesopotamia). Map popularity has fluctuated: at certain times, the public has embraced maps; at other times, maps were only made due to new geographical discoveries and technologies, without explicit demand by the public. However, if we look at these occasions, they all share something in common; they were popular but not populist events. In popular mapping, the control of geographical information remains in the hands of an elite. In populist mapping, by contrast, the public not only has access to maps as an end product but can control the means of production of maps. This populist project is a truly radical historical departure that has the potential to change the future of information. It faces some difficult challenges and obstacles, which I shall discuss.

Historical Examples of Popular Mapping

During the sixteenth century, as new territories were being explored, an explosion of new maps became available from the big European cartographic publishing houses, such as Ortelius. The map of the world produced by Ptolemy in the first century AD was rediscovered and republished in the mid-fifteenth century with very little modification. The Behaim Globe of 1492 (the oldest surviving globe) was indicative of knowledge at the time in that it obviously omitted the Americas but also pushed Asia eastward by 1500 miles, making it far more reachable from Europe. It is thought that this mistake confirmed Columbus in his enterprise of the Indies. If Columbus did not see that globe, he would be familiar with its general content as a navigator himself (and one who had a brother in the mapmaking trade), from world maps and maps of ports along the coast (known as portolan charts).

Subsequent to the "Columbian encounter,"[4] however, information about far-flung territories and continents came in thick and fast, and publishers vied with each other to produce the most up-to-date maps. Juan de La Cosa, who sailed with Columbus, was the first European to map the American continent (1500), while Martin Waldseemüller's map of 1507 (recently purchased by the Library of Congress for ten million dollars) was the first to name it. The Flemish cartographer Mercator invented his eponymous projection in 1569, still in use in classrooms today. The sixteenth century also saw Abraham Ortelius issue the first modern atlas, the *Theatrum Orbis Terrarum* (Theater of the World) by combining maps into book form in 1570. It was Mercator, however, who coined the word *atlas* (for his collection in 1595). John Smith's map of Virginia of 1608 is also well known and includes a drawing of Chief Powhatan, father of Pocahontas. As these selected examples testify, the importance and number of maps and cartographic publications during this period cannot be underestimated, and they were embraced by the public. Every educated person considered their library incomplete without atlases and maps.

A different kind of popular mapping emerged during the nineteenth century. In this case, the new knowledges were not of territories but of science. Many types of "thematic" maps that then developed—such as proportional symbol, dot distribution, choropleth, and isoline maps—form the basis of today's mapping and GIS software.[5] John Snow, for example, considered today to be the father of epidemiology and a keen exponent of the geographical nature of disease, is famous in both geography and public health for his work that used mapping to analyze the cholera epidemic.[6] Snow's map identified the very water pump that was the source of the cholera–infected water. This was a full three decades before the germ theory of disease was accepted in the 1880s.

With the rise of industrialization and urbanization, the modern state mapped out a host of problematic subjects: crime, education, divorce, birthrates, education, poverty, disease, the distribution of languages, and new immigrants. All these topics received treatment at the hands of the century's political scientists, protodemographers, geographers, and governments. Even Florence Nightingale used data graphics to convince skeptical British officials that dirt and disease killed more men than fighting did.

Many of these maps were published in a new kind of atlas, the "statistical atlas." It mapped not territory but, rather, the nation's human resources. Based on the census, it was aimed not just at officials but at the educated public. The first American statistical atlas was printed in sufficient numbers for both the public and libraries to purchase it.[7] New editions were issued every ten years in time with the census.

But interest in knowledge of places had not disappeared; in line with the new scientific knowledges, it was oriented inward, at the home territory. As Schulten describes in her fine account of the Rand McNally mapping company,[8] in America, at least, the continent was still relatively unexplored. By the time the "closing" of the American frontier took place in 1893,[9] maps were required for the emerging automobile industry.[10] The American Geographical Society (AGS), founded in 1851, and the National Geographic Society (NGS) also provided the public with prodigious quantities of new maps and explorer's accounts. These were popular with the public, if not among more serious-minded academics.[11]

The world wars of the twentieth century also stimulated a renewed public appetite for maps. During World War II, many Americans followed the progress of the war on wall maps, an activity encouraged by President Roosevelt himself. Such popular outlets as *Fortune* and the *Los Angeles Times* published incredible new maps by Richard Edes Harrison and Charles Owens suited to the "air age," featuring views over the polar ice caps and perspectives of Europe as seen from Moscow.[12] The war itself was not short on propaganda maps, often dropped in the thousands from the air over enemy territory.

Countermapping

The preceding examples demonstrate that the popularity of mapping has waxed and waned historically in conjunction with new demands for maps or new opportunities for maps. Noticeably, map popularity is associated with the production and dissemination of new knowledge by elites (the state, the wealthy). As maps are deeply cultural phenomena, this geographical knowledge does not exist in a sociocultural vacuum. Mapmakers share a top-down approach; information is disseminated from a cadre of cartographic experts to a largely ignorant public. This public has no control over what information is provided, when it is provided or in what form, how much it costs to access it, who can access it, the possibility of challenging this information and getting other information, and so on; that is, the system was profoundly undemocratic.

The fact that the distribution and circulation of geographic information was constrained in this way should not surprise us. The control of information and knowledge for the benefit of a political elite has been a hallmark of information for as long as there has been information, as writers on public opinion have long pointed out.[13] Nevertheless, parallel to this control has been a current of opposition and critique, which in cartography takes the form of countermapping.

The idea of countermapping is to reverse power asymmetries. Maps can be created by small groups, communities, and even individuals to achieve goals not otherwise possible. They can be used by those in developing countries to work against dominant Western information. They are "counter" to the prevailing structures of power, especially those deployed by the state. For example, countermapping has been used in conservation to show that the way some areas are mapped affects their status as protected areas.[14] Some spaces that include indigenous people with non-Western cultures might be construed as uninhabited and a candidate for environmental protection in ways that would disrupt their lives or ignore local knowledges. While biodiversity and species loss are critical ecological factors, the simple protection of areas can also be merely an extension of state control to the exclusion of local actors. Countermapping can be employed to give voice to these actors, whether they are in East Africa or impoverished American urban neighborhoods.

Indeed, one of the earliest examples of countermapping (although no term yet described it) was performed during the 1960s by the radical geographer Bill Bunge in urban areas, such as Detroit.[15] Bunge's maps were produced with groups in the inner city struggling for civil rights and safe neighborhoods. One famous example mapped out rat bites on neighborhood children; another showed clusters where children had been hit by cars.

Countermapping often employs the very tools that have previously been used to assert dominant power relations. For example, in community GIS (sometimes known as participatory GIS, or PGIS), local communities may use cheap or Web-based GIS tools to map out neighborhood resources (e.g., community centers, parks, and open spaces) to resist development. PGIS is a grassroots phenomenon with the goal of empowering traditionally disempowered groups. "Map or be mapped" might be its motto.

Countermapping is an attempt to create maps based on different kinds of knowledge that explicitly embrace a political, partisan point of view. Countermappers claim that all maps have such points of view. Maps are not "mirrors of nature" that reflect knowledge but sites of knowledge production. Knowledge is created not in isolation but in conditions that privilege some knowledge over others.

These ideas have proven to be very influential in understanding spatial representations, and they parallel research in other areas, such as spatial cognition. For example, children appear to go through a process of understanding spatial relations as a creative process. As two leading investigators succinctly put it, "maps are creative statements about the world, not merely degraded versions of it."[16] Sarah Elwood, a leading researcher of PGIS, has argued that the conditions of spatial knowledge production are political.[17] This does not mean that maps and GIS are biased; it means that knowledge is produced under conditions of power. Here we are close to a well-known idea in the work of Michel Foucault, that of "power-knowledge." Foucault said that knowledges are usually produced under certain conditions of power and that some knowledges are privileged while others are "subjugated." For example, he speaks of "a whole series of knowledges that have been disqualified as nonconceptual knowledges, as insufficiently elaborated knowledges, knowledges that are below the required level of erudition or scientificity."[18]

Relevant for our purposes here is that sometimes counterknowledges can emerge and provide the basis for a critique of the prevailing way of doing things, likened by Foucault to an "insurrection" from below.[19] The most obvious parallel to this insurrection are the "netroots," a term coined in 2002 by Jerome Armstrong to describe the online grassroots political community. Armstrong has stated that he was attracted to "the whole netroots to grass roots type of political activism that the Internet enabled."[20] Armstrong and Markos Zúniga wrote that they were "crashing the gate" of establishment politics.[21]

The netroots has some interesting parallels to countermapping. It is organized from the bottom up and distributes messages through blogs and other social networks.

> The principal value of the blogosphere is that it democratizes our political discourse almost completely. Anyone can become a "pundit," find an audience, report facts, create a community of like-minded citizens and activists, and influence the public discourse—all without having to mold oneself into what is demanded by the *Washington Post* and without having to care about pleasing the editors of *Time* magazine.[22]

To democratize "discourse" meaningfully in the case of mapping requires tools that are accessible to as many people as possible, the knowledge to use those tools, access to relevant data, and the ability to analyze and display that data on maps. In the next section, I discuss the development of these tools and what they mean for the future of geographical information.

The "Democratization of Cartography"

It turns out that when we talk about "the world's information," we mean geography too.
  —Google

Up until the 1980s, it had always been assumed that maps were essentially devices that communicated information that had been gathered and processed by the expert cartographer. As the historical examples previously cited testify, this had been the case for hundreds of years. The craft of cartography had a guildlike status, requiring years of training and the mastery of specialized techniques. These ideas about how maps worked were formalized in the postwar years by Arthur Robinson, a professor of geography at the University of Wisconsin–Madison. Robinson provided the conceptual apparatus of what later became known as the Map Communication Model (MCM), which explains mapping as a process of communicating information from the map expert or cartographer to the map reader. The information is acquired, marshaled, and selected by the map expert and set down on the map.

It is a very top-down model. For example, the cartographer-expert might acquire information on the distribution of crops across the Midwest, select and arrange the information (e.g., into categories of different crop types), and then symbolize it cartographically (e.g., as a dot distribution map). The map reader-novice then absorbs the information.

However, there were problems with this model. Cartographers had no way to decide how to present the information or even if their maps were being understood. Robinson's insight came in paying attention not only to the way the information was laid out (symbolized) on the map but to the abilities of the map reader to absorb it. His keystone work issued a call for research into "the physiological and psychological effects" of map design.[23]

This idea was based on that of one of the most influential scientists of the twentieth century, Claude Shannon. Shannon is the progenitor of communication (or information) theory.[24] This theory is at the heart of our digital devices, such as computers. Shannon recognized that information was "countable." Using his methods, it became possible to count the maximum amount of information that it was possible to transmit through a particular channel,[25] such as a map. Shannon showed that communication could be improved if the "signal" (the information) was maximized and the "noise" (the unwarranted distortions or errors) could be minimized. This signal-to-noise ratio (SNR) is still used today in information theory to measure the quality of a communication. Using communication theory, Robinson cleared the way for the development of the map communication model in the late 1960s. By 1972, this model was firmly established in the discipline, with the International Cartography Association (ICA) establishing "the theory of cartographic communication" as one of its terms of reference.[26]

By the 1980s, however, there were a number of pressures on this account of mapping. For one thing, public control of information became more possible with the arrival of inexpensive desktop computers and the first mapping software. Mapping programs had been around since the 1960s and were later to prove very influential. The Harvard Laboratory for Computer Graphics, for example, nurtured early developments in

GIS.[27] But they were cumbersome, limited to expensive equipment, and required sophisticated programming skills. They were also very crude in appearance. By the 1980s and the advent of the Apple Macintosh (a platform quickly embraced in the graphic design, publishing, architecture, and cartographic communities), a new form of mapping—desktop cartography—was possible.

As a graduate student, I can still remember the thrill of those first Macs. The department taught cartography the "old" way (darkroom, camera, and photographic chemicals) until the late 1980s. Students were expected to buy ink pens and master free-form drawing on mylar as they had done for decades—in his 1948 cartography guide, Raisz had included a chapter on how to avoid smudging your ink.[28] Now one could guarantee a straight line of constant width with a flash of the mouse.

Cartographers quickly realized that these new tools afforded new mapping possibilities. At the time, scientists were working on "scientific visualization," a set of approaches for visualizing scientific data. In geography, this became known as geovisualization.[29] Typically, visuals are of secondary importance in science or are only used to communicate findings—the "knowns." By the late 1980s, scientists and cartographers realized that visualization could be a research tool to explore data to find hidden patterns. These exploratory tools focused on discovering the "unknowns" in a data set. Today, the GIS business is believed to generate anywhere from four to ten billion dollars a year,[30] and the geospatial global business is possibly as large as fifty billion dollars a year.

Very large data sets, such as satellite imagery of deforestation, could now be interactively "data mined" for significant patterns without requiring prior knowledge of the situation. The power of the visual graphics was that they could display huge amounts of data at once. Today's Google Earth (GE) is an offshoot of this work—it provides a visualization of the earth with which the user can interact in any number of ways (zooming scale, adding or subtracting data layers, measuring distances, calculating directions, etc.). Both desktop mapping and visualization moved the production of mapping from the hands of the elite into those of the public. Mark Harrower, a leading proponent of populist cartography, has observed:

> One of the themes of my profession right now is the democratization of cartography. . . . Mapping used to be a job of the elite, the Rand McNallys and National Geographics of the world. Now people are taking it upon themselves to map their passions.[31]

In other words, desktop mapping and geovisualization provided the beginnings of new forms of people's mapping. But the true democratization of cartography would only arrive with the advent of new advances in Web technology, often referred to as Web 2.0 functionality, such as massively distributed and hyperlinked data sets, mashups, and customizable open-source tools. These tools are profoundly different from their precursors because they allow collaboratively linked mappings.

Populist Mapping Applications: Web 2.0 and Web-Based Mapping

Google Earth

With the release of Google Earth in the summer of 2005, it became apparent that there was a tremendous public appetite for visualizing geographic information. GE-like tools had existed in scientific GIS for some years (and Vice President Al Gore had outlined an early vision of digital earth in 1998),[32] but Google's popularity was far greater. The key to Google's success lay in providing open access to Google Maps, known as an application programming interface (API). Using this API, members of the public could "hack" (i.e., modify) these maps and link them up with their own data.[33] The results are known as map mashups.

Google Earth is a data visualization tool—it does not perform analysis, run models, or manipulate data (create buffers, merge one layer with another, etc.). It provides realistic imagery and 3-D pictures rather than the abstract cartographic symbolization of traditional mapping. Despite these aspects—or, rather, because of them—Google Earth is easy to understand and is "natural" looking (although no view from space would ever look like GE).

Google Earth and other map open-access APIs are highly collaborative and provide fertile ground for other data to be linked and geographically visualized. For example, Google Earth now sweeps through Wikipedia and automatically makes maps of places mentioned in the articles (through Placeopedia). Google has created a feature that maps all the places mentioned in books and puts them into a Google map mashup. These maps give you a chance to see not only how "platial" (how rich in geographical reference) but also how concentrated or distributed the book is. "Where" does the book focus? Is it Westernized? Is it oriented to Europe and North America? One could also compare the maps from two different books on the same topic (e.g., the spread of a disease, like HIV or SARS) to see if they tell different stories.

Google has also implemented a layer of information called the Geographic Web, in which people can annotate the earth with their photographs or place descriptions. As with the Wikipedia project, Google seems to have realized a project that works because of user collaboration and contributions—data now come from the bottom up rather than from the top down.

Census Bureau Data

Every ten years, the United States collects reams of data about its population and the places people live. Additional data is collected on an annual basis. All sorts of topics can be mapped, including income, race, age, gender, ethnicity, and occupation. The census is probably the most important single source of sociodemographic data about America today, and its findings inform policy analysis and decision making of all kinds. All this data can be mapped—if you know how to navigate the Census Bureau's labyrinthine databases.

The bureau offers an online mapping tool called the American FactFinder, which is useful for an initial visualization of the data. The display is quite small however. Most serious users download the raw data sets and process them with GIS. Both of these approaches restrict usage of the data. Recently, a different approach was developed that allows users to interactively display census data without having to have GIS expertise. The tools to do this are distributed across the network, thus providing access for many more people than if it were desktop based. This is the Social Explorer project, based at Queens College at the City University of New York, in association with the *New York Times*. Social Explorer provides an easy-to-use interface to huge quantities of complex census data dating back as far as 1940.

Political Applications

Republicans still control the maps.
   —Chris Bowers, MyDD.com

There is now some intriguing mapping evidence that suggests that access to, control of, and dissemination of geospatial information is changing political participation.[34] While much political discussion occurs in the traditional, or "mainstream," media, much is now also held in the emerging arena of blogs. Blogs now constitute a significant and noteworthy component in today's political landscape. Blogs and online political activism (the netroots) now play important roles in campaigns for getting out the vote (GOTV) and "getting out the dollar" (especially in online fund-raising). Since the 2004 elections and the success of Howard Dean and such organizations as MoveOn.org, the intersection of netroots and politics has only become stronger.

Working alongside and often in conjunction with the netroots are a range of mapping and GIS tools now available for the public. These tools often rely on making linkages between different kinds of things: for example, between different sources of data (e.g., between Google Maps and the U.S. Census Bureau or the Federal Election Commission) and between different software programs (e.g., between GIS and Google Earth). These linkages, effected through open-source software and APIs, mark a potentially new phase of political activism and collaboration characterized by more democratic access, control, and production of information and knowledge; a more local "micropolitics"; and potentially a way to break the hold of establishment "big money" incumbents.

For example, the FairData Web site provides community-based interactive maps for the whole nation down to level of precincts and census block groups.[35] These data are linked to open-source mapping APIs, such as Google Maps, for visual display. Users can pan and zoom across the maps and display different layers of information (the site uses a sophisticated online GIS as a back end to the Web pages). For a GOTV effort, community organizers can create maps of the number of nonvoters by precinct. In the map of Philadelphia in figure 1, the voting turnout is shown for each precinct, allowing the GOTV team to target nonvoting neighborhoods.

The map shows that turnout varied quite considerably across the city and was below 40 percent in many areas. These areas can then be targeted by the GOTV effort. The maps can also show individual households that did not vote for even more targeted efforts. As far as I am aware, these are the first tools available to the public that were previously only compiled by political parties in secret political precinct maps.

Do these tools by themselves mean that the political landscape is now more democratic? Not necessarily. Foucault's reminder (mentioned earlier) about power and knowledge is nowhere more salient than in the re-

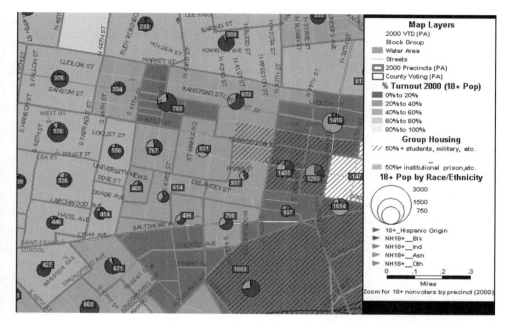

FIG. 1. Percentage turnout in a Philadelphia neighborhood by voting precinct, compared with race and ethnicity. (From www.fairdata2000.com.)

lationship between the military and digital mapping and geovisualization. The size of the military investment in GIS, such as the geospatial intelligence (GEOINT) community, is not known but was formally recognized in the creation of the federal National Geospatial-Intelligence Agency (NGA) in 2004, and the military's doctrine on GEOINT has been described in recent reports.[36] Because GIS has historically been largely associated with government and industry (e.g., the GEOINT 2006 symposium was keynoted by the director of national intelligence, John Negroponte), there are many who view GIS as being just another mechanism of government control and surveillance.[37]

Pickles argues that many of the new mapping capabilities are wonderful.

They provide more powerful tools for local planning agencies, exciting possibilities for data coordination, access and exchange, and permit more efficient allocation of resources, and a more open rational decision-making process.[38]

Yet he concedes that these systems are taking place in a larger context of economic production and a "culture of military and security practices."[39] Trevor Paglen, a geographer at Berkeley, has investigated many of these "hidden geographies" and even provided a map mashup of the CIA's "extraordinary rendition" flights.[40]

Open-Source Access to Geospatial Data

The development of open-source data and tools is very attractive to those who seek to avoid political and cultural associations and retain control over the maps. For example, Microsoft offers MapCruncher, a technology that allows anyone to make their own map mashup in about ten minutes. NASA offers a global map projector—you can take any map and project it automatically. One listing gives over 230 ongoing open-source GIS projects (http://opensourcegis.org/).

One obstacle faced by the open-source mapping community is that many map data layers are protected by copyright, especially in the United Kingdom (the United States does not copyright federal data). The national mapping organization of the United Kingdom, the Ordnance Survey, can regulate these data through licenses. In response, the OpenStreetMap is a wiki-based collaborative mapping project to create mapping coverages that are copyright free (under the Creative Commons license).

Participants in the OpenStreetMap project take GPS systems with them wherever they go and then upload the recorded routes into the system. In the beginning, parts of the project were based on old copyright-expired maps. Other users who do not have GPS can edit or annotate the uploaded maps. (A courier company in London has also provided tracks of virtually all London roads.) For more inaccessible areas, such as Baghdad, the project has made an agreement with Yahoo to use its aerial imagery. This will provide digitized map layers of all features (roads, rivers, railroads, parks, etc.), which can be used in many different applications—for example, the data can be exported to Google Earth for wide viewing and distribution.

A "slippy map," in the Google Maps style, allows users to browse across the map and zoom in and out to specific cities. The level of detail is at near-professional levels, which poses the real challenge of these projects: will they provide competition for the traditional top-down providers of geospatial information? It at least seems likely that open-source mapping will provide a parallel alternative set of publicly available data, but it does not seem likely that they will replace traditional data providers.

Another obstacle is that data providers sometimes curtail or suppress data that they have. The most well-known instance of this involves Google's imagery of India, China, and Korea. In these countries, Google has agreed to degrade the quality of imagery for certain military sites. (Other countries, such as Indonesia, have declined to make this request, stating that the reduced quality would simply indicate where such sites are located.) The sensitivity of this practice was illustrated when questions were asked in the U.S. Congress about Google's provision of imagery rather closer to the United States.[41] Google revealed that in September 2006, they had replaced newer imagery of the devastated city of New Orleans with pre-Katrina imagery. Google responded that they continued to provide the newer imagery (which is actually lower quality) on a special Web site. However, Google's alterations to imagery, sometimes at the request of foreign governments, raises questions about the future of information supply.

Community and Participatory Mapping

When groups of people come together to address a problem, they can leverage economies of scale. Think of the online social networking communities, such as del.icio.us, Diggit, and Slashdot. In mapping, this leveraging has often taken the form of community or participatory mapping, which I already discussed in the context of countermapping.[42]

Scientific Applications of Map Mashups

Scientists are now using collaborative mapping tools to visualize and bring to light spatial patterns of things as diverse as bird migration patterns or the spread of the SARS virus and to demonstrate how logging will affect downstream communities.[43] As we have seen, open-source geospatial APIs, such as Google Earth and Yahoo Maps, are popular and powerful tools. This point has not been lost on scientists, who are increasingly turning to these tools in order to visualize and communicate data. For example, Declan Butler, a senior reporter at *Nature*, regularly posts KMZ (Google Earth) files in articles showing the occurrence of avian influenza A (H_5N_1) and other public health issues.

Another fascinating application has been produced by the American Association for the Advancement of Science (AAAS) as part of its Science and Human Rights Program. The Geospatial Technologies and Human Rights (GaTHR) Project uses high-resolution global satellite imagery to examine areas of the world that are otherwise impossible to access, such as Darfur in Sudan. In 2004, this imagery confirmed the extent of ethnic cleansing in this area, and it is now available as GE layers. The AAAS says:

> The QuickBird imagery used by the Department of State and US-AID, together with other high-resolution imagery, has proven especially valuable as it can show damage to small houses, orchards, fields, and other features. Given the unequivocal time of image acquisition it can authoritatively document changes to these features, and in printed form the imagery helps compile and synthesize witness reports during interviews.[44]

Such a project can, of course, benefit from traditional GIS, but its public outreach and dissemination component is significantly improved by using publicly assessable outlets of data visualization. The GaTHR project also works with members of the human rights community (e.g., Amnesty International) who may not have access or expertise in costly technology.

> Geospatial technologies potentially offer human rights researchers and advocates a significant new tool for assessing human rights violations and monitoring developing crises in geographic areas where it is difficult to send observers. . . . These tools may also provide compelling documentation to encourage intervention and to determine responsibility. The initial phase of this project will enable AAAS to evaluate the potential uses and to determine the most feasible way to develop and disseminate these technologies within the human rights community.[45]

GE and similar applications, such as NASA's World Wind and Microsoft's Virtual Earth (VE) 3D, do not provide "real-time" data as many people believe (except in special circumstances). But they are vitally important for looking at "change detection" (comparing imagery between different time periods). Change detection can show whether villages or buildings have been razed to the ground, for example—as the AAAS found in Zimbabwe, despite governmental silence.

Barriers for Linking Geospatial Data

Interoperability

There are still many barriers to the use of open-source geospatial tools, map mashups, and map hacking. Some of these are technological—for example, ensuring that different software can operate with each other, or interoperability. The development of widely accepted standards and metadata is the most workable solution to this problem. We are currently in a situation analogous to the many standards for high-definition DVDs. They all work, but not necessarily together. Efforts such as the Open Geospatial Consortium (OGC), an international consortium of governments, universities, and corporations, can promote standards and interoperability to a certain extent in a top-down model. The biggest problem here is not getting software to connect but getting the data and metadata into standard forms.

Institutional Barriers

As we have seen, there are presently two different realms of mapping and GIS data: GIS and Web-based mapping. The GIS industry is having to catch up to the popular applications, such as GE and VE. In the last year or so, programs that link between popular traditional GIS applications have appeared: an example is the Arc2Earth program, which links ESRI's ArcGIS and GE. GIS companies, after largely ignoring programs for digital earth visualization because they did not provide analysis, are now struggling to quickly catch up and leverage the tremendous popularity of Web-based mapping. A major breakthrough in thinking came when ESRI realized that they needed not just an exporter from ArcGIS to GE but one from GE to ArcGIS—that is, that you could bring pretty "pictures" into industrial-grade GIS to do serious work.

Another institutional barrier arises from the corporatization of information. The Internet has undergone tremendous corporatization over the last ten years, not solely in terms of content, but also in terms of ownership of the mechanisms of distribution (the cables and phone wires). In particular, there is mounting concern over the erosion of "net neutrality." The concern is that Internet providers might no longer treat all Internet traffic equally. End-users, for example, may experience differential access to Web sites in accordance with fees that the sites and end-users may have paid (or not paid). This "tiered" access would resemble the current model often adopted by cable providers, whereby consumers receive different TV channels according to the package they have purchased. The fear is that access to content per se or even differential speeds of access to content (faster or slower) may become the norm on the Internet. One model to circumvent this is to switch to open-access WiFi broadband, but even the provision of that access is ultimately cable bound.

Advocates of tiered information access argue that it is a typical financial model found in many businesses. Proponents of net neutrality argue that the concept of business models should not apply to the provision of such an important source of information. The debate over net neutrality is currently being fought out in competing legislation at state and federal levels and is undoubtedly going to remain an important issue in the next few years.

The Digital Divide

The digital divide is a measure of access to the digital information economy. It includes access to technology (hardware and software) but also to knowledge itself (education). Recent research has demonstrated that the Internet is not free of the geographical restraints of the physical world.[46] These divides occur at a plethora of scales: within a city, within a region, within a country, and between one country and another. For example, according to figures from the United Nations, Internet access rates are 19 per 1,000 people in sub-Saharan Africa; in high-income OECD countries, they are more than 30 times higher, on average 563 per 1,000.[47] But even within the United States, broadband access (required for many of today's Internet applications) is currently installed in about 45 percent of homes—a high proportion, but certainly not at saturation level.[48]

The digital divide is enduring in the sense that new technologies are constantly being produced and constantly being spread unevenly. Each time we invent a great technology, we ironically also produce inequalities. As Shirky has argued, "diversity plus freedom of choice creates inequality, and the greater the diversity, the more extreme the inequality."[49] As the Internet increases in size and diversity, inequalities will also increase and replicate the digital divide patterns already found in the physical world.

Research also shows that there are some remarkable geographies of hyperlinks between blog clusters on the right and the left of the political spectrum. Looking not at the cross section of all blogs but, rather, at those that carry the most readership (the A-list bloggers), Adamic and Glance found that in the months preceding the 2004 U.S. presidential election, the degree of interaction between liberal and conservative blogs was very low. Both blogospheres linked mostly within their own communities and not across the political divide.[50]

Conclusion: Can Peasants Map?

Many obstacles to digital access, such as the digital divide and net neutrality, are not, at base, technological issues that can be addressed through market incentives; rather, they are complex sociopolitical problems. Lack of access to online information parallels the very underserved populations it could benefit. Community and participatory GIS, the netroots, and Web-based mapping are therefore not likely to provide solutions for underserved populations to bootstrap themselves out of poverty. But if underserved and well-served communities work together, then problems can be more ably addressed. This is a big if, and as this essay shows, there are enduring divides and connectivities. After all, we live not in isolated communities but in a world of networks.

In his work on political Net-based activism, David Perlmutter explores the question of whether the online activism and the netroots are a representative constituency—specifically, whether bloggers are "the people." He points out that at the moment, the netroots are overwhelmingly young, white, male, well educated, and technologically savvy and are thus not representative of the population as a whole. As he put it, "peasants do not blog."[51]

In this essay, I have introduced a number of developments that both assist and create obstacles for access and usage of geospatial information. These tools are provided out of a genuine realization that the ways we visualize and understand the world around us—its places, geographies, and relationships—are undergoing a radical transformation. If the media (TV, newspapers, and news radio) has had to adapt and incorporate new models of information dissemination and participation, and if publishing is undergoing a similar transformation, then there would seem to be an equivalent transformation working on our mappings. The remaining questions, however, are to what degree, how much, and with what effects these tools will confront the obstacles and barriers. The answers to those questions will prove vital in deciding the future of information.

NOTES

1. C. Jacob, *The Sovereign Map: Theoretical Approaches in Cartography throughout History* (Chicago: University of Chicago Press, 2006).

2. D. Buisseret, *Monarchs, Ministers, and Maps: The Emergence of Cartography as a Tool of Government in Early Modern Europe* (Chicago: University of Chicago Press, 1992).

3. J. Armstrong and M. M. Zuniga, *Crashing the Gate: Netroots, Grassroots and the Rise of People-Powered Politics* (White River Junction, VT: Chelsea Green, 2006).

4. J. B. Harley, M. Warhus, and E. Hanlon, *Maps and the Columbian Encounter: An Interpretive Guide to the Travelling Exhibition; American Geographical Society Collection* (Milwaukee: Golda Meir Library, University of Wisconsin, 1990).

5. Maps that show geographical distributions (as opposed to road maps and general reference maps) can be categorized into several types. These maps are known generally as thematic maps and tend to show quantitative data. Isoline maps are basically contour maps (with lines of equal elevation) but can also represent abstract information (as in the familiar temperature map). Dot distribution maps show distributions of events or features with scatterings of dots (the more dots, the more features). Proportional symbol maps use size to indicate quantity (e.g., line width for traffic flows). Choropleth maps are one of the most familiar thematic maps. They take predefined areas (e.g., countries) and show quantity for each area (e.g., per capita income by country on a world map).

6. S. Johnson, *The Ghost Map: The Story of London's Most Terrifying Epidemic— and How It Changed Science, Cities, and the Modern World* (New York: Riverhead, 2006); T. Koch, "The Map as Intent: Variations on the Theme of John Snow," *Cartographica* 39, no. 4 (2004): 1–14.

7. F. A. Walker, *Statistical Atlas of the United States* (New York: J. Bien, 1874).

8. S. Schulten, *The Geographical Imagination in America, 1880–1950* (Chicago: University of Chicago Press, 2001).

9. F. J. Turner, *The Frontier in American History* (New York: Henry Holt and Company, 1921).

10. J. R. Akerman, "American Promotional Road Mapping in the Twentieth Century," *Cartography and Geographic Information Science* 29, no. 3 (2002): 175–91.

11. H. Clout, "Geographers in Their Ivory Tower: Academic Geography and Popular Geography in Paris 1931," *Geografiska Annaler Series B Human Geography* 87, no. 1 (2005): 15–29.

12. D. E. Cosgrove and V. della Dora, "Mapping Global War: Los Angeles, the Pacific, and Charles Owens's Pictorial Cartography," *Annals of the Association of American Geographers* 95, no. 2 (2005): 373; R. E. Harrison, *Look at the World: The Fortune Atlas for World Strategy* (New York: Knopf, 1944).

13. E. S. Herman and N. Chomsky, *Manufacturing Consent: The Political Economy of the Mass Media* (New York: Pantheon, 2002); W. Lippmann, *Public Opinion* (New York: Free Press, 1922).

14. L. M. Harris and H. D. Hazen, "Power of Maps: (Counter)Mapping for Conservation," *ACME* 4, no. 1 (2006): 99–130.

15. W. Bunge, *Fitzgerald: Geography of a Revolution* (Morristown, NJ: Schenkman, 1971); W. Bunge, "The First Years of the Detroit Geographical Expe-

dition: A Personal Report," in *Radical Geography*, ed. R. Peet (Chicago: Maroufa, 1969), 31–39.

16. R. M. Downs and L. S. Liben, "Through a Map Darkly: Understanding Maps as Representations," *Genetic Epistemologist* 16 (1988): 16.

17. S. Elwood, "Beyond Cooptation or Resistance: Urban Spatial Politics, Community Organizations, and GIS-Based Spatial Narratives," *Annals of the Association of American Geographers* 96, no. 2 (2006): 323–41; S. Elwood, "Negotiating Knowledge Production: The Everyday Inclusions, Exclusions, and Contradictions of Participatory GIS Research," *Professional Geographer* 58, no. 2 (2006): 197–208.

18. M. Foucault, *Society Must Be Defended: Lectures at the College De France, 1975–1976* (New York: Picador, 2003), 7.

19. Ibid., 9.

20. W. Safire, "Netroots," *New York Times Magazine*, November 19, 2006.

21. Armstrong and Zuniga, *Crashing the Gate.*

22. G. Greenwald, "Blogs, Alternative Political Systems, Funding," http://glenngreenwald.blogspot.com/2007/02/blogs-alternative-political-systems.html.

23. A. H. Robinson, *The Look of Maps: An Examination of Cartographic Design* (Madison: University of Wisconsin Press, 1952), 13.

24. C. E. Shannon, "A Mathematical Theory of Communication," *Bell System Technical Journal* 27, no. 3 (1948): 379–423, 623–56.

25. D. Mindell, J. Segal, and S. Gerovitch, "From Communications Engineering to Communications Science," in *Science and Ideology: A Comparative History*, ed. M. Walker (London: Routledge, 2003), 66–96.

26. L. Ratajski, "Commission V of the ICA: The Tasks It Faces," *International Yearbook of Cartography* 14 (1974): 140.

27. N. Chrisman, *Charting the Unknown: How Computer Mapping at Harvard Became GIS* (Redlands, CA: ESRI Press, 2006).

28. E. Raisz, *General Cartography* (New York: McGraw-Hill, 1948).

29. J. Dykes, A. M. MacEachren, and M. J. Kraak, *Exploring Geovisualization* (Amsterdam: Elsevier, 2005).

30. Daratech, "GIS/Geospatial Market Grew 17% in 2005 to Top $3.3 Billion," http://www.directionsmag.com/press.releases/index.php?duty=Show&id=14697&trv=1.

31. "New Technology Helping Foster the 'Democratization of Cartography,'" *ScienceDaily*, http://www.sciencedaily.com/releases/2006/09/060920192549.htm.

32. A. Gore, "The Digital Earth: Understanding Our Planet in the 21st Century," http://www.isde5.org/al_gore_speech.htm.

33. S. Erle, R. Gibson, and J. Walsh, *Mapping Hacks* (Sebastopol, CA: O'Reilly, 2005).

34. E. Talen, "Bottom-up GIS: A New Tool for Individual and Group Expression in Participatory Planning," *Journal of the American Planning Association* 66, no. 3 (2000): 279–94.

35. The FairData/FairPlan site is so vast that no description can really encompass it. It provides interactive maps, census data, precinct maps of registered nonvoters by race, racial profiling data, GOTV data, and much more.

36. United States Joint Forces Command, *Geospatial Intelligence Support to Joint Operations* (Washington, DC, 2007).

37. J. Pickles, *A History of Spaces: Cartographic Reason, Mapping, and the Geo-Coded World* (London: Routledge, 2004); N. Smith, "Real Wars, Theory Wars," *Progress in Human Geography* 16, no. 2 (1992): 257–71.

38. Pickles, *History of Spaces*, 148.

39. Ibid., 152.

40. T. Paglen, "Unmarked Planes and Hidden Geographies," http://vectors.usc
.edu/index.php?page=7&projectId=59; T. Paglen and A. C. Thompson, *Torture Taxi: On the Trail of the CIA's Rendition Flights* (Hoboken, NJ: Melville House, 2006).

41. Associated Press, "House Panel: Why Did Google 'Airbrush History'?" http://edition.cnn.com/2007/TECH/03/31/katrina.google.maps.ap/index.html.

42. Elwood, "Negotiating Knowledge Production."

43. S. Herhold, "Technology Builds Bigger Soapbox," *Mercury News*, December 3, 2006.

44. American Association for the Advancement of Science (AAAS) 2007. "Geospatial Technologies and Human Rights." http://shr.aaas.org/geotech/what canGISdo.shtml (assessed December 28, 2007).

45. E. W. Lempinen, "New AAAS Project Will Explore Geospatial Technology and Human Rights," http://www.aaas.org/news/releases/2006/0127geospatial .shtml.

46. J. Chakraborty and M. M. Bosman, "Measuring the Digital Divide in the United States: Race, Income, and Personal Computer Ownership," *Professional Geographer* 57, no. 3 (2005): 395–410; M. Crang, T. Crosbie, and S. Graham, "Variable Geometries of Connection: Urban Digital Divides and the Uses of Information Technology," *Urban Studies* 43, no. 13 (2006): 2551–70.

47. United Nations Development Program, *Human Development Report 2006: Beyond Scarcity; Power, Poverty, and the Global Water Crisis* (Basingstoke Hampshire and New York: Palgrave Macmillan, 2006).

48. L. Rainie and J. Horrigan, "Election 2006 Online," http://www.pewinter net.org/pdfs/PIP_Politics_2006.pdf.

49. C. Shirky, "Power Laws, Weblogs, and Inequality," http://shirky.com/writ ings/powerlaw_weblog.html.

50. L. A. Adamic and N. Glance, "The Political Blogosphere and the 2004 U.S. Election: Divided They Blog," *Proceedings of the 3rd International Workshop on Link Discovery* (New York: ACM, 2005), 36–43; see also Adamic's essay in the present volume.

51. D. D. Perlmutter, "Are Bloggers 'the People'?" http://policybyblog.square space.com/are-bloggers-the-people.

LADA A. ADAMIC

The Social Hyperlink

At first glance, the hyperlink—a simple sequence of characters serving as an address of a unique location on the World Wide Web—may not appear very social. Creating a hyperlink takes just one individual, as does bookmarking it, as does clicking on it. Yet very few people would create hyperlinks purely for their own use. Instead, they create them to help others navigate an information space in a way that they themselves would. They use them to express social relationships in a public space for others to see. They share hyperlinks as gifts—through e-mail and instant messages that share information and laughs—and so reinforce existing relationships. They direct hyperlinks at others in the hope of the hyperlink being reciprocated, and so they build entirely new online relationships. In essence, since the very inception of the World Wide Web, the hyperlink has acted as a social element.

Hyperlinking was used to express social relationships far before social networking sites (e.g., Friendster, Orkut, MySpace, or Facebook) appeared on the Web, before blogs and the popularity of blogrolls. The first incarnation of my own home page, circa 1995, included links to friends. But not until four years later, when a friend in graduate school pointed out (none too subtly) that she had linked to my home page from hers but that I hadn't reciprocated, did I start to wonder how many people had given in to such peer pressure and how widespread friendship hyperlinks were. I teamed up with Eytan Adar, who was a researcher at Xerox PARC at the time, and we crawled the home pages hosted by two universities: Stanford and MIT. To our surprise, we found hyperlinked social networks of over a thousand individuals at each university.[1]

In our study, we had discovered that what had been hidden before, the social relationship (accessible to the social scientist only through time-consuming individual interviews), now was in plain sight, for anyone to study. Home pages provided us not only with the social hyperlink but with text and URLs that allowed us to understand the context of the relationship. We sought to predict, from the information contained in each home page, which home pages would be linked to each other and which would not. The most predictive information was the presence of links to a home page of a shared contact. After all, social networks tend to be cliquish—a friend's friend is likely to be my friend as well. Other types of links and words were also found to be predictive: for example, membership in the same research group for graduate students and living in the same dorm or belonging to the same religious group for undergraduates. Beyond this, we found, for example, that cohabiting was more predictive of hyperlinks for MIT students than for those at Stanford. This corresponded to true differences in student life at the two universities: MIT students typically lived in the same dorm, fraternity, or sorority all four of their undergraduate years; Stanford had less of a fraternity/sorority presence, and most of the rest of the students had to reenter the housing lottery and relocate yearly.

Within a couple of years of our initial study of home pages, Stanford had its first exclusive social networking site, called Club Nexus. Its creator, Orkut Buyukkokten,[2] was a computer science graduate student. Club Nexus had much the same features as present-day social networking sites: friend lists, profiles, blogging functionality, matchmaking, search capabilities, and birthday reminders. It allowed its users to specify their interests and describe their personalities in their profiles. Fortunately, Orkut was interested in analyzing this rich data.[3]

In our second study, the hyperlinks we were studying had explicit social meaning: users were asked to enter their "buddies," and the site wove a web of social network hyperlinks. A popular activity on the site (one that persists in online social networking sites today) is exploring a person's network of friends, friends of friends, and so on by clicking on hyperlinks. Repeating our analysis of relationship prediction, this time with profiles entered into the site, we found, as one might expect, that team sports (e.g., synchronized swimming or crew) were far more predictive than sports that can be pursued individually (e.g., swimming or bicycling). Niche tastes (e.g., professional and technical books, gay/lesbian-themed movies, or gospel music) tended to be more predictive than general and popular categories (e.g., general fiction, comedies, or rock music). Though I will leave communities and niche tastes for now, I will return to this subject later in this essay, in the context of viral information spread.

In addition to finding attributes that would be predictive of friendship links, we also cross-correlated various attributes in the profiles themselves. Political science majors were more likely to think of themselves as attractive and lovable, while physics, math, and electrical engineering majors fulfilled the nerdy stereotype by being more likely to enjoy spending their free time learning and to describe themselves as weird. One of the most interesting features of Club Nexus to study was Nexus Karma. Users were given the opportunity to rate their friends on a scale of 1 to 4 on how "trusty," "nice," "cool," and "sexy" they were. By correlating the ratings a person received from others with how they described themselves (this self-description was not visible to other users), we found that those who characterized themselves as being "responsible" indeed received higher "trusty" ratings from others, but they also tended to receive lower than average "cool" and "sexy" ratings. When users described themselves as "sexy" and/or "attractive," their friends tended to concur by giving them higher "sexy" scores on average, but they also received lower "trusty" and "nice" scores. Finally, users who described themselves as "funny" received, on average, lower "nice" ratings. Perhaps they had made a few too many jokes at their friends' expense. This raises interesting questions about human nature and relationships. Is it indeed rare to find a friend who is attractive, funny, and nice at once?

These two studies, one of networks of personal home pages and one of a forerunner of the social networking Web sites that are now so prevalent online, were just the tip of the iceberg of the wealth of social network data that was to be placed and studied online. In this essay, I will highlight a few of my own online social networking studies that explored online community structure and information diffusion.

The Political Blogosphere

Shortly following the 2004 presidential election, I became curious how the political divide was reflected online. Back in 1999, I had examined the top search engine results corresponding to two opposing sides of the abortion debate and found pro-life Web sites to be more heavily interlinked than pro-choice ones.[4] I wondered whether either the liberal or conservative communities were better connected online. I contacted Natalie Glance, who created BlogPulse, a large-scale blog search engine at a startup called Intelliseek.[5] Natalie and I shared the same dissertation advisor, Bernardo Huberman, and it was during my visit to her research group at the Xerox research center in Grenoble that I had started analyzing the networks of home pages. She generously agreed to collaborate with me on the analysis of political blogs.[6]

As a first step, I crawled approximately fifteen hundred liberal and conservative blogs whose home pages and leanings I had gathered from online blog directories. The set was remarkably balanced between liberals and conservatives, very much in tune with the close race that fall. I then extracted the hyperlinks from the front page of each blog and created the social network shown in figure 1. It reveals a clear preference for liberal blogs to link to other liberal blogs and for conservatives to link to conservatives. Only about 10 percent of the links bridged the two communities. But before elaborating on these linking patterns further, I need to address the nature of a hyperlink in a blog.

Blogs are a very dynamic, yet structured, medium. Because of this, hyperlinks placed in different parts of the blog play rather different roles. On the one side (or, rather, the sidebar), there are blogrolls, lists of hyperlinks pointing to the blogs that this particular blogger reads. Whether or not the blogger actually keeps up with these blogs, the hyperlinks serve as a way for the blogger to identify with his or her friends, community, and interests.

Relatively speaking, in the context of continuously generated content, blogrolls are a fixture. They are faithfully shown to every reader visiting the blog and will remain unchanged unless explicitly modified by the author. Some exceptions include blogrolls that are automatically generated by RSS readers, such as Bloglines, but even they likely change only infrequently, as the blogger subscribes or unsubscribes from a blog's feed. Daily Kos, a prominent liberal political blog, recently commented that its blogroll, minor tinkering aside, was almost three years old.[7]

If blogroll links are fixtures, then in-post citations, hereafter referred to as citations, are both a permanent and fleeting connection. A citation to another blog within a post can refer to a blog in general or to a particular post on that blog. In the latter case, one blog might be continuing a conversation where another left off, agreeing, disagreeing, or elaborating on a thread. Unlike a blogroll link, a citation is time-stamped with the permalink of the post in which it was contained, and one can be rather certain that the citing blogger was reading and commenting on the other. But eventually (in many cases, rather soon), the post is archived and the citation is no longer on display. A conversation has taken place, but it has moved out of view. So although possibly a stronger indication of interest than a blogroll link, citations, unless periodically repeated, will become dated.

Of course, the citations need not be only to other blogs but, in principle, can point to any Web page. As much as bloggers consider their blogs a new kind of journalistic medium, they are still very much tied in

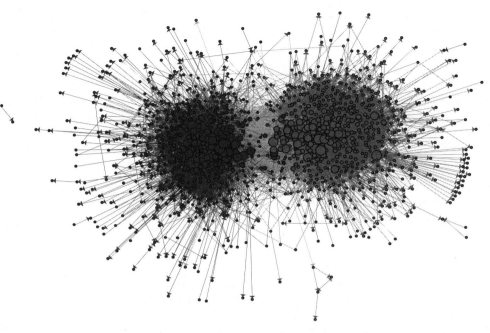

FIG. 1. Community structure of fifteen hundred political blogs, visualized using the GUESS network analysis tool. In the original figure, the colors reflect political orientation, red (right) for conservative and blue (left) for liberal. Orange (center right) links are citations of conservatives by liberals, and purple (center left) links are citations of liberals by conservatives. The size of each blog reflects the number of other blogs that link to it. (The original figure is printed in color in the jacket of this book.) (From Adar 2006.)

with the mainstream news sources. By studying the top forty political blogs during the three months preceding and two weeks immediately following the 2004 presidential election,[8] Natalie Glance and I found that bloggers referred to the mainstream media about once every other post but referred to other blogs only one post out of ten.

Because of the very timely nature of in-post citations, they can be used to filter the most interesting content on a daily basis. This was the concept behind Blogrunner, a site that contained a special feature that aggregated the conversations bloggers were having about specific *New York Times* articles. The *New York Times* acquired Blogrunner and now features a "most blogged" list of its own articles, along with a list of most e-mailed articles. Interestingly, or perhaps as might be expected, the articles that are most blogged about tend to have a political focus, reflecting the strong presence of political blogs in the U.S. blogosphere. For example, the five most blogged *New York Times* news stories on February 11, 2007, were "The Deadliest Bomb in Iraq is Made by Iran, U.S. Says," "Edwards Learns Campaign Blogs Can Cut 2 Ways," "Giuliani Shifts Abortion Speech Gently to Right," "Prewar Intelligence Unit at Pentagon Is Criticized," and "Congress Finds Ways to Avoid Lobbyist Limits." As anyone receiving links to news articles sent by family or friends knows, e-mail links tend to have more of a human interest flavor, frequently referring to articles on health, education, recreation, personal finance, or the environment. While the blogosphere was preoccupied with international and domestic politics, the person-to-person e-mail network filtered these five stories: "Troubles Grow for a University Built on Profits," "In Niger, Trees and Crops Turn Back the Desert," "How Green Was My Wedding," "Surf's Upscale as Sport Reverses Beach Bum Image," and "Day Out: Time-Traveling in Oxford, England."

Services such as BlogPulse and Technorati index a large portion of the blogosphere and are able to harness the collective writing and hyperlinking activity of blog authors to track any and all trends by reporting on the most popular URLs and tags contained in blog posts. One would not be able to keep track of the pulse of an online nation were it not for the unique property of blogs as pieces of content added in discrete, time-stamped intervals and for the power of aggregation over hundreds of thousands and even millions of blogs.

One may naively expect that sidebar links and citation links point in pretty much the same direction in about the same proportion. After all, bloggers would place their favorite news sources on their sidebars and refer to them in their posts when those news sources had particular articles they wished to comment on. In a sample of about fifteen hundred political blogs, we recorded the news sources that were linked to and found the expected division along party lines, with conservatives linking to the *National Review* and Fox News and with liberals linking to Salon.com. Links to relatively unbiased news sources (e.g., WashingtonPost.com and NYTimes.com), at around one hundred, were a bit less than those to the *National Review* (120) and Fox News (130) and a bit more than those to Salon.com (70). From this analysis, one might surmise that publications with a strong liberal or conservative bias captured about the same amount of attention as the largest and nominally unbiased news sources.

However, remember that many blogroll links serve as badges that bloggers may display as part of the profile they would like to reveal to their readership. Indeed, if we look at the frequency with which news sources are cited in the top political blogs of either leaning, the neutral news sources pull far ahead, with the most citations. The *New York Times* and *Washington Post* received fourteen hundred citations each from political blogs during this time period, albeit with slightly more liberals than conservatives citing them. In comparison, the *National Review* garnered only five hundred in-post citations, and Salon.com (accessible by subscription or day passes) received only two hundred citations. It appears that linking to news sources of one's own leaning may be a way of announcing one's preferences online but is not entirely reflective of where the bloggers are receiving their news from and what is prompting them to blog. This preference for a few top mainstream media sources is only apparent, however, when one considers the citations in aggregate over the period of several months, again pointing to differences in blogroll links and citations.

Criticizing and Selective Linking

Armed with sophisticated tools for processing natural language (tools that can identify people's names in text), Natalie Glance analyzed thousands of posts made by the top political bloggers and found who was being discussed in them. Remember that all of these posts were made in the short period preceding the presidential election, so the bloggers spent a considerable amount of time discussing the two candidates, George W. Bush and John Kerry. The liberals were responsible for a little over half of the mentions of Bush, and 59 percent of the mentions of Kerry were made by conservative bloggers. In general, liberal bloggers were predominantly discussing prominent conservatives and the Republicans in the White House, while the conservative bloggers were busily criticizing several liberals, with the greatest imbalance observed for those who were easy targets. Terry McAuliffe, who served as the chairman of the Democratic National Committee, had 140 mentions from conservative bloggers but only 47 from liberal ones. Laura Bush was rather more favored by the liberal bloggers, with 107 mentions versus 81 among conservatives. Michael Moore, who had garnered more sidebar links from liberal (as opposed to conservative) blogs, was predominantly discussed by the conservatives, 382 to 102. The liberals chewed out Secretary of Defense Donald Rumsfeld (193 to 37) and Secretary of State Colin Powell (160 to 48) and took easy aim at Zell Miller (174 to 33), the Democrat turned Republican senator who was backing President Bush for reelection. Established political figures who had held prior office were mentioned frequently but in more even numbers. Bill Clinton was mentioned over five hundred times, about 57 percent of the mentions being by liberals. Al Gore was mentioned about three hundred times, with an even split between conservatives and liberals. President Reagan, who had passed away earlier that same year, was mentioned 250 times, with an exactly even split.

Knowing that a lot of the discussion involves criticism rather than support brings us back to the question of the hyperlink. How much of the linking activity between the left and right blogosphere is criticism, and how much is support? If bloggers do find it easier to criticize major political figures than to support them, would, for example, liberal bloggers prefer to be criticizing opposing points of view expressed in the posts of conservative bloggers, rather than agreeing with other liberal bloggers? We see an overwhelming majority of hyperlinks falling between bloggers of similar political leanings. One possible explanation is that bloggers are primarily seeking validation for their own ideas and lending support to similar blogs. Another, rather likely explanation is that they are limiting their own exposure to opposing points of view by selectively reading the posts of those blogs they are already in agreement with. Yet a third possibility is that they do engage in criticism of disagreeing blogs but that they intentionally do not link to the content they are disagreeing with.

Bloggers face a dilemma. If they link to content they are criticizing, they can spare themselves reiterating the others' blog posts and continue to directly make their point. However, the bit of time saved means that they are exposing their readers directly to opinions opposite their own. In addition, they are indirectly boosting the score of that particular post and the blogger who wrote it. This is because citations are comprehensively monitored by many of the blog tracking services (Google among them). As a result, each citation increases the likelihood that a particular post will be read, whether because it will have a higher ranking in a search engine or because it may be included in a "most cited" list by a blog indexing site.

Whatever the reason, overwhelmingly, bloggers cited others on their own side, with a few exceptions. Figure 2 shows a visualization of the citation patterns of the top political bloggers prior to the election. The social network layout shows Andrew Sullivan drifting over into the liberal sphere. Indeed, during this period, Andrew Sullivan was criticized for being too liberal (he himself stated that he is a fiscal conservative but a social liberal). Glen Reynolds, author of the conservative InstaPundit blog, had very few links to give to the left blogosphere before President Bush's

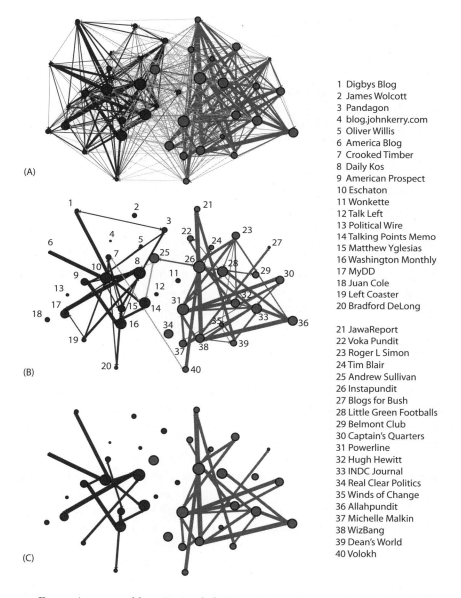

(A)

(B)

(C)

1 Digbys Blog
2 James Wolcott
3 Pandagon
4 blog.johnkerry.com
5 Oliver Willis
6 America Blog
7 Crooked Timber
8 Daily Kos
9 American Prospect
10 Eschaton
11 Wonkette
12 Talk Left
13 Political Wire
14 Talking Points Memo
15 Matthew Yglesias
16 Washington Monthly
17 MyDD
18 Juan Cole
19 Left Coaster
20 Bradford DeLong

21 JawaReport
22 Voka Pundit
23 Roger L Simon
24 Tim Blair
25 Andrew Sullivan
26 Instapundit
27 Blogs for Bush
28 Little Green Footballs
29 Belmont Club
30 Captain's Quarters
31 Powerline
32 Hugh Hewitt
33 INDC Journal
34 Real Clear Politics
35 Winds of Change
36 Allahpundit
37 Michelle Malkin
38 WizBang
39 Dean's World
40 Volokh

FIG. 2. Aggregate blog citation behavior prior to the 2004 election. In the original figure, color corresponds to political orientation, size reflects the number of citations received from the top forty blogs, and line thickness reflects the number of citations between two blogs. (A) All directed edges are shown. (B) Edges having fewer than five citations in either or both directions are removed. (C) Edges having fewer than twenty-five combined citations are removed.

reelection. One of the exceptions included his citation of Matthew Ygle-sias, a liberal blogger, when Yglesias had agreed with him about an esti-mate of civilian casualties in Iraq. The overall pattern appeared consis-tent. Bloggers would predominantly create hyperlinks to others they agreed with, who most often happened to be bloggers of similar political leaning.

Natalie and I had left open the question of whether, after the election was over, the political divide in the blogosphere may start to close. Shortly after we reported the results of our study in March 2005, our at-tention was called to what was seen as a new trend—perhaps a bridging of the left and right blogospheres. Bloggers on both sides were uniting for a cause, which was to defeat the bankruptcy bill before the Senate that would favor creditors and weaken the position of consumers. Ultimately, the bill was passed,[9] but for a brief period, many liberals and conservatives cited one another, if only to voice astonishment that they were, for once, in agreement. This shows that the shape of the political blogosphere can change in part because its link structure is so strongly affected by the in-formation that is flowing on it.

The fact that a single cause, such as opposition to a bill in Congress, can reshape the blogosphere brings us to question whether information flow was also responsible for the shape of the political blogosphere prior to the election. The shape we are looking at is an aggregation of hyper-links, but each of these hyperlinks is added at a given point in time. If we look at the citation patterns between the top blogs on either side as shown in figure 2, we observe that the conservative blogs cite one another more frequently and in a more decentralized way. On the liberal side, there are a few very popular blogs citing one another, but there is less dense inter-action overall. One interpretation may be that the conservatives are more cohesive, that they formed a stronger community. But another could be that they just had more information to share and filter. Remember that this was an exciting time for conservative bloggers. They were the ones who broke the story that the documents concerning President Bush's ser-vice in the National Guard, which had been touted as authentic on *60 Minutes* by Dan Rather, were in fact fakes. Rather than merely comment-ing on news that was reported in the mainstream media, the bloggers were making news, and this topic alone accounted for a large number of links between the bloggers. The liberals were relatively quiet about the topic—it wasn't their story.

The preceding example illustrates why one must be careful when drawing conclusions from a static snapshot about communities represented by hyperlinks (or from an aggregate snapshot, for that matter), because the hyperlink may represent association but may also represent a flow of information. That flow becomes frozen and archived but was once a flow nonetheless. Had those documents never been forged, we may have observed a less cohesive conservative blogosphere. Or perhaps it would have been just as cohesive, with more posts and cross-links devoted to some of the other topics.

As an illustration of the changing patterns of citation, consider two samples of blog data taken approximately six months apart. The first was a large data set released by Nielsen BuzzMetrics as part of the third annual Workshop on the Weblogging Ecosystem (WWE).[10] It covered a period of three weeks in July 2005 and sampled almost a million and a half blogs, with over a million blog-to-blog citations during that period. The second data set, provided as part of the TREC (Text REtrieval Conference) 2006 Blog Track, had a little over one hundred thousand RSS and Atom feeds from a sample of the blogs in the WWE data set. It spanned a period of eleven weeks from December 2005 to February 2006 and captured over sixty thousand citations between the blogs. Xiaolin Shi, a PhD student in computer science engineering at the University of Michigan, found, however, that of the pairs of blogs where one blog cited the other in the July 2005 sample, only 5 percent were citing each other again during the second time period.[11] This speaks, in part, to the infrequency of blog-to-blog citations but also points to the dynamic nature of information flow in the blogosphere. Blog ties that are active in one period, relating to a particular discussion, may be dormant during another period, when the discussion shifts elsewhere.

Communities

If the preceding discussion has left you with the impression that the hyperlink in the blogosphere is a fleeting thread cast about at random, this could not be farther from the truth. The hyperlink frequently reveals very real underlying communities—and not just those consisting of liberal and conservative bloggers. Although political blogs are among the most prominent in the U.S. blogosphere, many other communities form around different interests. Susan Herring and her collaborators at Indiana University were among the first to research blog communities and discover that densely interlinked regions of the blogosphere corresponded to topics such as Catholicism or homeschooling.[12]

Some interests, such as cooking or knitting, have the ability to span cities, if not continents. What brings people together is the interest itself, and it is unclear whether there are corresponding real-world relationships. However, communities defined by their geographic location have the potential for their members to meet in person, to have carried over real-world relationships into the blogosphere, or to transfer online relationships back into the real world. In the fall of 2005, Noor Ali-Hasan, then a graduate student at the School of Information at the University of Michigan, approached me about doing a master's thesis on the Kuwait blog community. To have something to compare against, she selected two additional communities, one being located in another small oil-rich Middle Eastern nation, the United Arab Emirates, and the other being completely different—the Dallas–Fort Worth (DFW) community in the United States. All three were self-identified communities, with a central site that listed all member blogs.

Over a period of several months, Noor meticulously tracked the three communities, using the Technorati and BlogPulse blog search engines to record any linking activity within the communities and across their boundaries. In the spring, she followed up with an online survey. Her aim was to track the expression of social relationships through blog links and comments. In the process, she discovered not only different linking patterns in the communities and different roles for different kinds of hyperlinks but also an interesting correspondence to the real-world demographics of the three corresponding countries.[13]

Interestingly, the residence and citizenship of each community varied in their uniformity. Ninety-eight percent of DFW bloggers were living in the United States, 95 percent were U.S. citizens, and 74 percent identified themselves as either white or Caucasian. In contrast, only 73 percent of the Kuwait bloggers resided in Kuwait, and 82 percent were Kuwaiti citizens, with a full 22 percent being Kuwaiti citizens but residing in the United States at least part-time. Finally, 82 percent of UAE bloggers resided in the United Arab Emirates, but fully 84 percent of them were nonnationals. This figure corresponds closely to the foreign population levels of 85 percent reported in the United Arab Emirates. Thus we see a significant demographic difference between the two Middle Eastern communities. In Kuwait, where around 60 percent of the population consists of foreign workers, the community is still overwhelmingly composed of Kuwaiti nationals; in the United Arab Emirates, where an even greater proportion of the population consists of foreigners, the foreigners have formed the blogging community. Many of the

UAE bloggers were likely to be professionals, with 85 percent holding an undergraduate degree and 37 percent holding a master's or other advanced degree.

There were other respects in which the two communities differed. The Kuwaiti blogs linked to one another more, with 6.25 in-community blogroll links and 2.08 citations on average during the six-month time period, compared to 2.65 blogroll links and 1.37 citations on average for the United Arab Emirates. However, both Kuwaiti and UAE blogs linked to each other more heavily than the DFW community, with 1.79 in-community blogroll links and 0.37 citations. Since the DFW blog community is largest, at over three hundred blogs, one might expect that blogs within it have more in-community blogs on their blogrolls. However, we found instead that the most linked-to blogs in DFW were the national A-list blogs for the United States: Dooce, Michelle Malkin, Power Line, and Captain's Quarters, the latter three being conservative political blogs. It turns out that bloggers in DFW were not stingier with their hyperlinks—they were sharing them with a broader sphere of blogs. Their community boundaries were porous, with 9 percent of the blogroll links falling within the community and the remainder going elsewhere. For comparison, almost half of the blogroll links from Kuwaiti bloggers went to other Kuwaiti bloggers. The blogroll links simply reflected the attention and relationships in the real world. Kuwait and the United Arab Emirates are two small nations (with populations of around three million people each) forming definite, but not closed-off, communities. The DFW area has a larger population (approximately five million) but is far less self-contained. A majority of the bloggers' attention drifts to other parts of the nation. On the other hand, reserving even one-tenth of one's links for geographically proximate blogs indicates the strong presence of community.

A further aspect in which the communities differed was their motivation for blogging. In the survey, bloggers were asked to check all reasons that motivated them to start blogging, including self-expression, keeping an online journal, being inspired by a friend's blog, finding new friends, and sharing news with friends and family. DFW bloggers were twice as likely (46 percent) to be interested in maintaining contact with their friends and family through blogging than either the Kuwait (26 percent) or UAE (23 percent) bloggers. This may be partly due to the desire of bloggers in Kuwait and the United Arab Emirates—countries with a lesser degree of freedom of expression—to blog under pseudonyms. Pseudonyms may stand in the way of keeping in touch with at least some friends.

Kuwait bloggers were most likely (23 percent) to be motivated by the desire to meet new friends, compared to 12 percent of UAE bloggers and only 3 percent of DFW bloggers. This may be partly due to the younger demographic of the Kuwait community or to a real desire to join a new community, which was reflected in the denser ties among Kuwait bloggers. Just because some bloggers did not indicate finding new friends as a motivation does not mean that they did not do so anyway. A Kuwait blogger commented on the survey: "Most of the Kuwaiti bloggers know one another, either directly (friends/relatives) or indirectly (friends of friends, friends' relatives, etc.). If they don't know one another, then they don't remain strangers for long. . . . I know of several people who used their blogs to make new friends in Kuwait." Even the DFW blog community, which I have so far portrayed as less cohesive than the other two, allowed bloggers to discover new relationships. One blogger wrote: "The DFW Blogs community was an incredible social network for me. I had recently moved back to the Dallas area when the group began. Through that group I was able to meet highly intelligent, talented, motivated, and creative people." In fact, one DFW blogger who didn't report meeting new friends as a motivation found her husband through the blog community.

In the survey, we specifically asked bloggers if they had made new friends through blogging. When asked to estimate the number of bloggers listed on their blogrolls whom they initially met through blogging but whom they now communicate with in person or by phone, e-mail, or instant messaging, the Kuwait bloggers listed a median of five, the UAE bloggers listed a median of four (approximately 20 percent of their blogroll), and the DFW bloggers listed a median of just three, although two DFW bloggers mentioned having met upwards of one hundred people through blogging.

How exactly does one meet people through blogging? In all three communities, there are organized face-to-face meet-up opportunities. One might imagine, however, that many relationships form much before bloggers meet in person. In the context of blogs, I have mentioned the hyperlink as an expression of a relationship, a mode of information flow. But the hyperlinks I have discussed so far are rather limited in their ability to support relationships. Blogroll links, though recording and expressing either a readership relationship or a social relationship, are neither dynamic nor interactive. In-post citations are very dynamic, as already discussed, but it is difficult to conduct a conversation with them. Sometimes, if blog A cites blog B, a trackback in the comments is attached to blog B's post and will point back to blog A. By following trackbacks, one may discover an interactive conversation. Not only trackbacks but direct comments to bloggers' posts support much of the bloggers' interaction.

Comments, however, are relatively difficult to gather automatically. Noor decided to gather them by hand and accomplished an impressive feat. She selected the two-week period surrounding the Kuwaiti emir's death in January 2006 and hand tagged 3,943 comments according to the content of the 468 blog posts (on eighty-nine blogs) that they were left on. Not all blogs allow comments, and even those who do may only selectively open up their posts for comments. But for those posts that allowed comments, the median number received was six. Clearly, a lot of the communication is occurring through direct commenting on blog posts. During this time period, the emir's death and the succession to the throne were important subjects of conversation, with a peak in commenting activity occurring exactly on the day of the emir's death. Another topic was that of a suspicion that a blog-hosting site was being intentionally blocked due to the political content of the blogs.

Although not always strictly containing a hyperlink, a comment represents an online connection. Frequently, it will contain a link to the blog of the blogger leaving a comment or may be left by a nonblogger or anonymously. In just the two-week period studied by Noor, there were twice as many blog-to-blog interactions through comments than over the entire six-month period through in-post citations. Blogroll links were still more numerous, but they may have been created years earlier and do not have the potential that comments have for repeated interactions. Even more interestingly, as shown in figure 3, the different kinds of hyperlinks only infrequently overlapped. Blogroll links and comment links coincided in only 15 percent of the cases, and only 3 percent of directed connections between blogs were expressed in all three forms: blogroll, in-post, and comment. Therefore, to study only one kind of hyperlink would miss out on the full interaction occurring among blogs.

The comments alone reveal some interesting patterns. First, there was a high degree of reciprocity in commenting. Among the Kuwait blogs, only 19 percent of in-post citations and 32 percent of blogrolls links were reciprocal among the Kuwait blogs, but 43 percent of the time, if blogger A left a comment on blog B, blogger B also left a comment on blog A. Nevertheless, these interactions are not entirely reciprocal, and the bloggers who leave the most comments are not necessarily the ones whose posts receive the most comments, or vice versa. As may be expected, there is a positive correlation ($\rho = 0.32$) between how many comments a blogger leaves on other blogs and how many comments they receive. But the correlation is even greater (ρ = 0.62) between how many comments a blogger leaves on their own blog and how many comments from others they receive. This suggests that some bloggers are good conversation starters and conversation maintainers around their own posts, while others may play the role of visitors and cross-pollinators by frequenting other blogs and carrying conversations there.

Community Boundaries and Information Diffusion

So far, I have mentioned that hyperlinks reflect communities and that they represent information diffusion as well. Now I'd like to argue that community boundaries may limit the spread of information even in the presence of hyperlinks that cross community boundaries. The evidence for this is only anecdotal at this point, but consider the following blog post: title "Blog," content "blog." It doesn't seem like much, but this post—made on April 7, 2006, by Jim Henley on his Unqualified Offerings blog—attracted over eleven hundred comments.[14] The comments became a self-parody of commenting behavior. I provide just an excerpt.

12. *Comment by Jon H—*
     April 8, 2006 @ 9:13 am
     Comment flaming other commenter for spelling error, which flame contains the requisite spelling error of its own.
13. *Comment by Michigan J. Frog—*
     April 8, 2006 @ 9:19 am
     Accidental double-post.
14. *Comment by Michigan J. Frog—*
     April 8, 2006 @ 9:20 am
     Accidental double-post.
15. *Comment by Michigan J. Frog—*
     April 8, 2006 @ 9:20 am
     Apology for accidental double post, wasting even more space.

This comment thread could have been enjoyed by almost any blogger, since it made fun of one of the most central blogging activities. However, when we look at the previous linking patterns of the bloggers citing this post, shown in figure 4, we find that many of them are on each other's

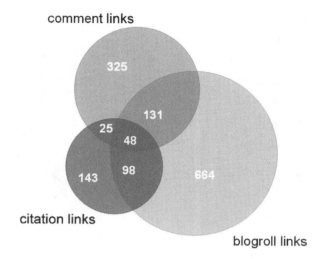

comment links

citation links

blogroll links

FIG. 3. Venn diagram illustrating the overlap in different types of blog ties (comments, blogrolls, and citations) for Kuwait blogs. (From Ali-Hasan and Adamic 2007.)

blogrolls or have previously cited one another—that is, they are part of the same blogging community. Due to its high popularity, the post eventually made it onto lists of "most blogged about" URLs, which is where I found it. A number of blogs at this point link to the original post, but they fail to set off cascades of their own. The bloggers find the post interesting enough to blog about, but since the original event did not happen in their own blog communities, it does not diffuse through them. Communities are relevant to the spread of information, since a piece of information that is relevant to one community's interests (e.g., knitting or French cooking) is likely to be of less interest in another community. Even if the information is not community specific, it may have a lesser likelihood of crossing community boundaries than of circling within them.

The Hyperlink and Viral Marketing

Thus far, I have discussed the hyperlink, the communities it builds, and the information that is spreading along it, but I have not mentioned the issue of money or profit. It is true that the very top bloggers can make a living by blogging these days, but the information that is spreading

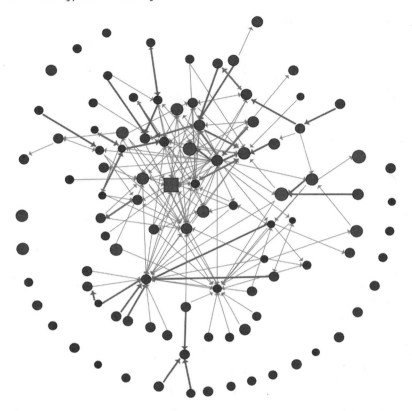

FIG. 4. Blogs (circles) citing a post (square) parodying commenting behavior. Thin lines represent previous citations and blogrolls. In the original figure, thicker, green lines represent directly attributed links regarding the particular post. The blogs are both colored and sized according to how soon they cite the post (with redder and bigger nodes cited earlier). (From Adar 2006.)

around tends to be news, opinion, cute photos, jokes, and personality quizzes. Increasingly, however, marketers are interested in capitalizing on the hyperlink and the underlying social network to promote their own products.

In the summer of 2005, Jure Leskovec, a computer science PhD student at Carnegie Mellon University, came to HP Labs for an internship with Bernardo Huberman and myself. With him came a large data set from an incentivized viral marketing program by an online retailer. This is how the program worked. When purchasing a product on the Web site, the customer had the option of recommending the product to their friends by providing their e-mail addresses. A hyperlink would be created and shipped off via e-mail to the customer's chosen recipients. If one of those recipients was the first to click on the hyperlink and actually make a purchase, he or she would receive a discount, and the sender would receive a credit for the same amount toward their purchase. The data set contained about sixteen million recommendations sent between four million customers on approximately half a million products.

Given such a wealth of data, we were able to discern several things. First, very few of the recommendations actually propagated virally. A large fraction of the recommendations terminated with the single individual who made the initial purchase and then unsuccessfully tried to recommend to one or more friends. Overall, the success rate (the probability that a sender received a discount) was around 2–4 percent, depending on product category. Occasionally, especially for some categories of DVDs, we observed large cascades involving dozens of individuals who bought a product as a result of propagating recommendations. Here, unlike in the case of memes that sometimes spread so readily on the Web, the cost of propagating the item was greater than simply copying a hyperlink—one needed to reach into one's pocketbook and purchase the product before e-mailing out a hyperlink recommending the product.

Nevertheless, we were able to make several interesting observations about the nature of viral marketing and social persuasion. The data was ripe with power laws, some of them simply displaying the long tail of product demand. But in this case, the usual 80/20 rule, where 20 percent of the products account for 80 percent of the sales, did not hold exactly. The tail was a bit fatter than that. The top 20 percent of the products accounted for only 50 percent of the recommended purchases, which means that the more niche-oriented products actually had a greater likelihood of being recommended than their overall sales would suggest. This brings us back to the importance of community in information flow. The most successfully recommended products tended to correspond to professional interests, such as law, medicine, engineering, or computer science. Organized contexts (whether they were school or places of work) were conducive to successful recommendations. But it wasn't just work or study that brought people together. Even within the category of books on religion, books corresponding to organized religion (e.g., Christian Bibles or prayer books) were more successfully recommended than books on new age topics and occult spirituality. Similarly, books on orchid growing, which tends to be quite organized online through Web sites and offline through orchid shows, are more successfully recommended than books on tomato growing, a pursuit that does not cause most people to form communities online or offline.

When we ran a regression on the success rates of recommendations for different products, we found that one variable, the number of senders, was most predictive and accounted for about 69 percent of the variance in success rate. Also significant were the number of recipients, the number of recommendations, and the price of the product. The coefficients for the number of senders and receivers were negative—meaning that niche products that appeal to a limited number of people are most successfully recommended. The coefficients for the number of recommendations and the price of the product were positive—indicating that small communities (with few senders and receivers) that are tightly knit (giving many recommendations) and that enjoy expensive products (which means the incentive discount for recommendation translates to greater savings) are the most suitable for viral marketing. This result may seem intuitive after the fact, but one's initial guess may have been that blockbusters like the *Harry Potter* books would be the ones most easily spread via viral marketing.

In addition to discovering the product categories and community characteristics that were conducive to viral marketing, we also examined the process from the point of view of the sender, the recipient, and the tie that links them together. First, we were interested in whether sending out more recommendations would be more likely to yield at least one successful recommendation. It did—up to a point. The likelihood of success increased initially as more and more recommendations were sent, but once they exceeded a dozen or so recipients, the success rate leveled off. This indicates that we may be able to influence some of our closest friends, but once we start spamming a large number of people, we get no additional gain. In fact, we see that the influence of influencers is limited.

Next, we examined how receiving multiple recommendations of the same product influenced a person. One might imagine that as more and more of one's friends recommend a particular product, one is more and more likely to purchase a product. In this case, we observed a stark difference between book and DVD recommendations. For books, if a person did not make a purchase after the first recommendation but received another, they were more likely to buy after the second recommendation. But once they received three or more and were still not buying, the probability that they did after any subsequent recommendation declined. Possibly, they simply had decided not to purchase the book, whether it was not of interest to them or they already had access to it in some other way than purchasing it from this particular retailer. For DVDs, we saw something quite different: as more and more recommendations were received, a person was more likely to make the purchase. This could be partly due to a phenomenon that occurred with DVD recommendations but did not, to our knowledge, occur with books. DVD aficionados, especially those favoring Japanese anime DVDs, could coordinate and exchange e-mail addresses online to obtain discounts. Subscribing to one of these forums could then flood the person's mailbox with recommendations, and they would be more likely to actually make the purchase, because they had subscribed in the first place. This kind of coordination is an interesting example of how the network may be affected by the information that is spreading on it. People who share common interests but otherwise are strangers contact each other by e-mail in order to receive discounts on products. The social network we see then is a mix of the true social network that existed prior to the viral marketing efforts and the one that was created for the express purpose of exchanging recommendations.

In addition to creating new ties, viral marketing can negatively affect existing ones. We observed that as more recommendations are exchanged between the same two people, their effectiveness decreases for both books and DVDs. For books, this happens after a few links are sent. For example, the first time a person receives a book recommendation from a friend, they might think, "My friend says I would enjoy reading this book, let me buy it and try it." The second time the person may believe their friend as well. But by the third and fourth recommendation, they may have started to distrust their friend's recommendations or started to believe that the friend is simply spamming them in order to get a discount. From this point on, the probability of following that person's recommendation will steadily decrease. We see that viral marketing may be weakening the very ties it is attempting to use, an observation that marketers looking to capitalize on social networks should heed.

Information Changes Even as the Hyperlink Remains the Same

Finally, I'd like to leave you with a funny story, one that shows the hyperlink's great potential not only to link together and spread information but also to twist it. In February 2004, Eytan Adar, Li Zhang, Rajan Lukose, and I had finished writing a paper on characterizing information diffusion in the blogosphere.[15] It was our good fortune that Amit Asaravala of *Wired* had interviewed us and had written an article about it titled "Warning: Blogs Can be Infectious."[16] The title reflected our finding that some information spreads readily through the blogosphere, with blogs getting information from other blogs. The *Wired* article was posted online at 2 a.m. on Friday, March 5, 2004. At 7:25 that morning, Slashdot picked up the story, with the humorous but also more provocative title "Bloggers' Plagiarism Scientifically Proven." By 9:55 that morning, MetaFilter covered the story with the even more sinister title "A Good Amount of Bloggers Are Outright Thieves." Eytan Adar, who was the lead author of the study, grew a bit concerned about the tone the stories were taking. After all, our research had just shown that information diffuses readily through the blogosphere and how one might predict where it will spread. He decided to write a brief FAQ right before lunch explaining what the study was really about, but having the good sense of humor that he has, he titled the FAQ "Do Bloggers Kill Kittens?" and essentially made a pun that every time a blogger steals a URL off of another blog, God smites a kitten. Sure enough, after lunch, several bloggers had titled their posts "Bloggers Kill Kittens!"

This story just goes to show that hyperlinks not only help information spread through the blogosphere but help it change and grow, as many individuals are able to use the hyperlink to thread together their evolving collective discussions. It also portrays bloggers as self-aware, sardonic, and lighthearted judges of their online social interactions. The hyperlink allows them to share, in a social way, their reflections on the world, but they are also very much aware that the same hyperlink, often borrowed, also reveals their social context—whom they are influenced by and what communities they belong to. This awareness and the basic human inclination to take in and share information will continue to shape the hyperlinked landscape of online spaces.

NOTES

1. L. A. Adamic and E. Adar, "Friends and Neighbors on the Web," *Social Networks* 25, no. 3 (2003): 211–30.

2. Orkut Buyukkokten went on to join Google, where he created the social networking site Orkut.

3. L. A. Adamic, O. Buyukkokten, and E. Adar, "A Social Network Caught in the Web," *First Monday* 8, no. 6 (2003), http://firstmonday.org/issues/issue8_6/adamic/.

4. L. A. Adamic, "The Small World Web" (paper presented at the European Conference on Digital Laboratories, Paris, 1999).

5. Intelliseek was subsequently acquired by Nielsen BuzzMetrics.

6. L. A. Adamic and N. Glance, "The Political Blogosphere and the 2004 U.S. Election: Divided They Blog," *Proceedings of the 3rd International Workshop on Link Discovery* (New York: ACM, 2005), 36–43.

7. http://www.dailykos.com/storyonly/2007/2/3/192341/1181.

8. We gathered posts from the top twenty liberal and top twenty conservative blogs, selected according to the number of citations they had received from the blogosphere at large during this period.

9. *Bankruptcy Abuse Prevention and Consumer Protection Act of 2005*, Public Law 109–8, *U.S. Statutes at Large* 119 (2005): 23.

10. E. Adar et al., "Implicit Structure and the Dynamics of Blogspace" (paper presented at the Workshop on the Weblogging Ecosystem, New York, May 18, 2004).

11. X. Shi and B. Tseng, "Looking at the Blogosphere Topology through Different Lenses" (paper presented at the International Conference on Weblogs and Social Media, Boulder, CO, March 26–28, 2007).

12. S. C. Herring et al., "Conversations in the Blogosphere: An Analysis 'from the Bottom Up,'" in *Proceedings of the 38th Hawaii International Conference on System Sciences* (Los Alamitos: IEEI Press, 2005), 107–18.

13. X. Shi and B. Tseng, "Looking at the Blogosphere."

14. http://highclearing.com/index.php/archives/date/2006/04/07/.

15. Adar et al., "Implicit Structure."

16. http://www.wired.com/news/culture/0,1284,62537,00.html.

MARKUS PRIOR

Are Hyperlinks "Weak Ties"?

More than thirty years ago, Mark Granovetter introduced the idea of "weak ties,"[1] defining them as interpersonal connections that are not particularly intense, close, or emotional. And yet weak ties serve an indispensable function: they hold together groups of people who do not otherwise have much in common and may not share the same view of the world. "Bridges" are particularly important weak ties, as they are the only links between different sets of individuals. Without weak ties and bridges, internally homogenous groups of people would be completely isolated from others outside their groups. Social interactions would occur only between like-minded people. Weak ties thus reduce social fragmentation.

The social and psychological forces that work against weak ties are powerful. It is generally more efficient to take advice from like-minded individuals.[2] People do not like disagreement and often seek to minimize the discomfort of experiencing it by avoiding it in the first place or by adjusting their attitudes to reduce the discomforting dissonance.[3]

In light of these pressures toward homogeneity, weak ties gain importance because they expose people to crosscutting views. They allow information to diffuse more widely and ideas to be exchanged between different groups of people. Weak ties "are the channels through which ideas, influences, and information socially distant from ego may reach him."[4] It is through weak ties that people encounter information that challenges their existing opinions.

Recent studies of weak ties in the political realm have offered different assessments of their ability to support civic discourse and deliberative democracy. Huckfeldt, Johnson, and Sprague find that encountering diverse opinions through weak ties is quite common and sustainable.[5] Citizens with weak ties develop more balanced, ambivalent political opinions. Although Mutz, too, shows that "hearing the other side" encourages appreciation of opposing points of view, she finds less disagreement in people's interpersonal networks to begin with.[6] Her results also reveal that crosscutting exposure can depress political participation. Yet both studies agree—in fact, take as their premise—that weak ties offer the best chance to encounter unexpected, unselected, and potentially conflicting opinions and facts.

Many observers fear that encounters with "the other side" through the media are becoming rare. Understanding interpersonal discussions is important for Mutz exactly because of the fear that media exposure is becoming increasingly selective. Although media can be a source of exposure to political opposition, "as the number of potential news sources multiplies, consumers must choose among them, and that exercise of choice may lead to less diversity of political exposure."[7] Paradoxically, increasing diversity of opinion in the aggregate could foster individual narrow-mindedness. And if the addition of only a few more television news channels threatens to have this effect, the consequences of online diversity seem exponentially more disturbing.

The capacity of different Web sites to link to each other offers a potentially consequential counterforce to this trend toward greater selectivity and fragmentation. Can hyperlinks, by connecting people who would otherwise go their separate ways in the sprawling new media landscape, prevent the kind of fragmentation that observers see looming large? In this essay, I sketch answers to two versions of this question. The first version of the question is the one commonly addressed by academics and commentators alike. Can anything be done to keep media users from exclusively exposing themselves to ideologically extreme media outlets that offer little information to challenge their existing opinions? Drawing on our experience with cable television and some early studies of Internet use, I conclude that the dangers of political fragmentation are probably exaggerated.

Bigger dangers to a healthy democracy lie elsewhere. Almost completely overlooked is the second version of the fragmentation question: can anything be done to keep media users from ignoring political information altogether? In a world where media content of many different genres and subgenres is abundantly available around the clock, tuning out politics is easy. Hyperlinks could make their greatest contribution to democracy in encouraging the politically uninterested. Unfortunately, as I will argue in the final section of this essay, this is the function they are least likely to serve.

Media Choice and Political Fragmentation

New media technologies give people more choice and the opportunity to customize their media use. The capacity to filter out content in advance has triggered a vigorous debate about the societal and political implications of new media. While some scholars emphasize the benefits of choice and customization,[8] others are alarmed by the potentially dire consequences of customization, fragmentation, and segmentation. Turow sees the emergence of "electronic equivalents of gated communities" and "lifestyle segregation."[9] Sunstein predicts the demise of "shared experiences" and increasing group polarization as media users select only content with which they agree in the first place.[10]

In the realm of politics and public affairs, fragmentation of news audiences has raised concerns because it might limit the diversity of arguments that viewers encounter and expose them to biased information. Sunstein conjures up a world of almost perfect selection in which media sources conform neatly and reliably with one's prior beliefs and expectations. Such constant and nearly exclusive encounters with points of view from like-minded people will, he argues, lead to group polarization. In Turow's view, the marketing strategies of advertisers, not technology per se, cause the fragmentation of society. Media offer specialized content and formats that allow advertisers to target desired populations more effectively, which "will allow, even encourage, individuals to live in their own personally constructed worlds, separated from people and issues that they don't care about or don't want to be bothered with."[11] Mutz and Martin have found the media to be more a source of exposure to political opposition than are interpersonal relationships.[12] Their study was conducted in the 1990s, however, and echoes the fear of increasing selectivity as more political outlets become available.

Audience fragmentation, the starting point for this debate, is empirically well established. As the number of television channels increases, the audience for any one channel declines, and more channels gain at least some viewers. Yet while audience fragmentation increases the diversity of media exposure in the aggregate, it tells us nothing about the diversity of individuals' media use. Individuals may take advantage of greater media choice either by watching a mix of many newly available channels or by "bingeing on their favorites."[13] Webster uses the concept of "audience polarization" to capture the concentration of viewing of a particular channel.[14] If a few viewers account for most of the channel's viewing, its audience is polarized. If viewing is distributed across a large number of people who individually make up only a small share of the channel's viewing, audience polarization is low. From the viewer's perspective, audience polarization is high when people watch a lot of a particular program format or genre and not much else.

For Sunstein's and Turow's predictions to be realized, audiences need to become not only more fragmented but also more concentrated. The danger lies not in rising audiences for politically biased news outlets per se but in exclusive exposure to outlets that are all biased in the same direction. Several important pieces of evidence suggest that fears of this kind of audience concentration may be exaggerated. Examining Nielsen audience data, Webster finds little evidence of overall audience concentration by channel. Instead, his data indicate a considerable overlap between audiences for CNN and the Fox News Channel (as well as other cable news channels).[15] Even heavy consumers of a particular television channel devote only a small fraction of their total viewing to that channel.[16]

According to Webster's data for February 2003, those who watched at least some FOX News spent 7.5 percent of their overall viewing time with the FOX News Channel but another 6 percent with the other four cable networks (CNN, CNN Headline News, CNBC, MSNBC). Viewers who never watched FOX News also spent less time, under 3 percent of their total television consumption, watching other cable news channels. Likewise, CNN viewers, who spent 4.7 percent of their viewing time watching CNN, devoted another 6.8 percent of their viewing to the other four cable channels, including 3.7 percent to FOX News. The 65 percent of viewers who never watched CNN also rarely watched other cable channels (for less than 3 percent of their total viewing time). MSNBC viewers—23 percent of the adult population who spent 3 percent of their viewing time with MSNBC—watched other news channels for an additional 9 percent of their total television use. For viewers who avoided MSNBC, that share is only 4.2 percent. Even though these averages may hide more polarized viewing patterns among small subsets of cable news viewers, they offer little support for claims that the fragmentation of the cable news environment fosters political polarization by encouraging selective exposure to only one side of an issue. Survey data and diaries of television viewing also indicate considerable overlap of audiences for Fox News Channel and CNN.[17]

Another indicator of overlap between cable news audiences is the exclusive "cume" rating, which records the number of unique viewers for a network that do not watch a specified set of other networks. In December 2004, for example, the cumulative audience for CNN was fifty-five million (i.e., fifty-five million different people watched CNN for at least six minutes on at least one day of the month). In reference to the other cable networks, CNN's exclusive cume in this period was only twelve million. In December 2004, twelve million people watched CNN for at least six minutes on at least one day and did not watch the FOX News Channel, MSNBC, CNN Headline News, or CNBC. The cumulative audience for FOX News in this period was fifty-four million, with an exclusive cume of fourteen million. MSNBC's cume was forty million, and its exclusive cume was seven million. Many cable news viewers routinely watch more than one news channel. In an analysis of cable television, it appears that many viewers do not tune out the other side. But what about selectivity online?

A recent test of Sunstein's hypothesis provides little evidence that users tune out opposing points of view. During the 2000 presidential campaign, a random sample of Americans received one of two multimedia CDs—one with all candidate speeches and advertisements, the other with a wide selection of media coverage of the candidates and the campaign. The use of these CDs, which was evaluated for study participants who returned a tracking file after the election, indicated that most people accessed both materials about the candidate with whose party they identified and materials about the opposing candidate. To the extent that participants engaged in selective exposure, they mostly did so by focusing on specific issues.[18] This evidence on how people actually search political information comports with their own assessments of what they are doing. Few Internet users say that they visit only sites that they know to be congruent with their political attitudes.[19] These results are not terribly surprising. Evidence for partisan selectivity in exposure to political campaigns has always been mixed at best.[20]

Although they suggest limited selective exposure along partisan or ideological lines, these results need to be viewed as preliminary. Webster's data are for the average cable news viewers. They do not rule out greater audience concentration on one particular news channel among the heaviest cable news viewers. Furthermore, we lack data to effectively assess selective exposure across media (e.g., the correlation between exposure to Fox News, conservative blogs, and conservative talk radio). It is clearly too early for a conclusive verdict on the level of political or ideological selectivity in our current high-choice media environment. The available evidence emphasizes, however, that the expansion of media choice alone will not automatically lead to greater audience polarization. Cable viewers mix CNN and the Fox News Channel despite the opportunity to do otherwise. Study participants evaluating the 2000 presidential candidates looked at both sides even though they could have easily concentrated on their favorite.

Even if political fragmentation is more severe than currently available evidence suggests, the consequences are not necessarily all bad. Ideologically tinted interpretations of political events still refer to a host of basic facts. Given the considerable barriers to persuasion among people interested enough to tune in,[21] exposure to either CNN or Fox News may inform viewers of current events and leave opinions largely unchanged. We value political learning in large part because it encourages voter turnout[22] and other forms of political participation.[23] There is no evidence that a slightly biased interpretation of the facts could not generate the same participatory benefits as a neutral presentation.[24]

The Concentration of News Consumption and Its Political Consequences

The same development that sparked the concern about audience polarization along ideological lines—the proliferation of media choice—also causes increasing segmentation between politically interested people and people who prefer nonpolitical entertainment content. The former access a lot of information and increase their already high levels of political knowledge. The latter can more easily escape the news and therefore pick up less political information than they used to. This type of audience polarization between news and entertainment fans has not received nearly as much attention as ideological audience polarization. Sunstein and the debate he prompted is primarily concerned that people may be following customized news and come to the polls with biased information. This debate passes over a more fundamental concern: people may not be following any news and may not show up at the polls at all.

In *Post-Broadcast Democracy*,[25] I have shown how cable television and the Internet have increased inequality in political knowledge and electoral participation by increasing involvement among news fans and decreasing it among entertainment fans. New media offer users greater choice and thereby add to the importance of individual motivations in seeking political information out of the mass of other content. Media content preferences—people's preferences over different media content—become very powerful predictors of political behavior in a media environment characterized by abundance of choice. In fact, their influence on knowledge and turnout already exceeds the impact of education and other resource variables, even though choice and the efficiency of choice are nowhere near their practical maxima.

Post-Broadcast Democracy offers several findings that can guide scholars in assessing the political effects of hyperlinks. First, selectivity with regard to program genre is at least as important as selectivity with regard to the ideological slant of one particular program type: coverage of politics. Second, growing segmentation between news and entertainment audiences is a result of voluntary actions that increase everyone's enjoyment of their media consumption. Segmentation increases because structure matters less than in the broadcast era, not because structure imposes segmentation. Third, political inequality is on the rise primarily because preferences increasingly determine exposure to politics, not because the "digital divide" prevents some people from accessing new media. Fourth, greater media choice polarizes politics, but not by turning ordinary people into partisan firebrands.

Even the concepts of audience fragmentation and polarization, as Webster defines them,[26] are too broad to be of use in evaluating the political implications of audience behavior. As these concepts are used in audience analysis, they refer to channels. Yet the political implications of changing audience behavior depend on fragmentation and polarization by and within genres. If people who used to watch the same entertainment programming now watch different entertainment programming, audience fragmentation and possibly audience polarization increase, but without any political implications. Even if former viewers of the same news program now watch different mainstream news programs, thus fragmenting the news audience, they still learn roughly the same things about politics. To the extent that exposure to political information motivates political participation, they would not seem to be less likely to participate than in the past. Fragmentation of the news audience need not doom civic life. And as discussed in the previous section, there are few signs of the potentially more dangerous development of audience polarization within the news genre.

Instead of selecting exposure on the basis of ideological content, media users are increasingly selective with respect to genre. Webster shows considerable concentration of cable news viewing.[27] In February 2003, about a quarter of the population tuned in to the Fox News Channel at least briefly. On average, these Fox News viewers spent 13.5 percent of their overall time watching cable news, compared to less than 3 percent for the other three-quarters of viewers. CNN viewers were a somewhat larger group, at 35 percent. They devoted 11.5 percent of their viewing total to cable news, compared to less than 3 percent for non-CNN viewers. MSNBC viewers, the smallest group, with 23 percent of all adults, also spent 11.5 percent on cable news, compared to 4.2 percent who did not watch MSNBC. As discussed earlier, the overlap between audiences for different news channels is considerable. People's content preferences and the concentration of political knowledge also support the conclusion that a relatively small segment of the population—probably less than one-fifth—have specialized in news content.[28] They consume so much news that average news consumption, average political knowledge, and average turnout have not dropped, even though a lot of people have tuned out politics altogether.[29] The most significant change caused by greater media choice is a heavier concentration of news consumption.

It is important to note that entertainment fans have voluntarily reduced their news media use. For them as for most others, more media choice means greater viewing, reading, and listening pleasures. Yet a corollary of greater media satisfaction is rising inequality in political involvement. Unlike most other forms of inequality, this one arises due to voluntary consumption decisions. Entertainment fans abandon politics not because it has become harder for them to be involved—many people would argue the contrary—but because they decide to devote their time to media that promise greater gratification than the news. The mounting inequality between news fans and entertainment fans is due to preference differences, not differences in abilities or resources. Strong and growing preference-based inequality is likely to persist even when (or if) resources are distributed more equally.

This conclusion is at odds with most discussions of access and use of online political information, which have focused largely on structural barriers to use. DiMaggio and others review several dimensions of the digital divide.[30] Mere access to the Internet is only one of many aspects of the divide. Differences in hardware, software, and connection speed all introduce additional inequality. Using the Internet in a library or at school is not the same as using it in one's own home. Demographic differences in access to the Internet persist today. Unlike broadcast television and radio, the Internet is a service that is available only for a regular fee, not a product that provides free access to media content after an initial purchase. Although the Internet reaches many Americans, some are still without access today. DiMaggio and others caution that it is not a foregone conclusion that almost every American will eventually have easy and efficient access to the wealth of political information online. The crucial point to realize is that access to new media is not the solution to the problem of political inequality but, rather, a contributing factor. Ironically, greater access to political information has reduced the share of Americans who are exposed to politics.

Lack of education and functional illiteracy are not the primary obstacles to learning about politics, either. Americans have become better educated, and news media have become easier to comprehend. Before television, during a period when formal education levels were much lower, an inability to comprehend political information posed a real obstacle to political learning. These same barriers to learning do not exist today. Television made the news easier to grasp. Streaming video online offers another source of political information for those with reading difficulties or an aversion to print news. A high school education should provide most Americans with the skills necessary to read and understand a newspaper. Although print media may still discourage some people by presenting politics in complex ways, the major fault line in explaining political engagement and participation has shifted to motivation.[31]

Audience concentration along the fault lines of news and entertainment not only exacerbates inequalities in political involvement; it also contributes to partisan polarization. It does so in a way that is entirely different from the ideologically selective exposure to highly biased political information that so many observers fear. As I show in *Post-Broadcast Democracy*, a preference for entertainment is negatively related to the strength of people's partisan attachments. The more interested citizens who take advantage of abundant political information and vote at higher rates are also more partisan. Citizens who become less likely to vote in our high-choice media environment because they prefer entertainment are predominantly politically moderate or indifferent. As choice increases, their share among the voting public declines, thereby raising the proportion of voters with deep partisan and ideological convictions. Greater media choice facilitates participation of the more partisan news seekers and abstention of the less partisan entertainment seekers. Hence, voting behavior would be less partisan if the expansion of media choice had not happened. Cable television and the Internet have polarized American elections by providing their audiences with more choice. One reason there are fewer moderate voters today is not because they have been converted by increasingly partisan media but because they have been lost to entertainment.

This explanation for increasingly polarized elections is very different from polarization through selective exposure to ideologically consistent content. It focuses not on the type of messages being sent but on the receivers of these messages. Independent of message content, the segments of the electorate that are exposed to news about politics are different today than in the past. Before cable television and the Internet expanded viewing choices, news and entertainment fans both received elite messages, and many were sufficiently motivated by them to go to the polls. Since then, more interested, more partisan citizens have become more likely to receive political information and vote, while moderates have become less engaged. Moderates do not make it to the polls anymore, whereas partisans just keep doing what they always did: voting for their party.

Together, these consequences of greater media choice shape the environment in which Internet users encounter hyperlinks. Hyperlinks are a central way to navigate a world in which a minority of people consume a lot of news while the majority avoids political information, a world in which media users quite easily access the content they want, a world in which partisans are increasingly overrepresented at the polling place because the less partisan have better things to do than learn about politics and vote. In assessing the impact of hyperlinks, it is important to remember that these consequences would have played out rather similarly without hyperlinks.

What (Not) to Expect from Hyperlinks

The title of this essay deliberately confuses a prominent sociological concept, weak ties, and an emblem of new technology, hyperlinks. Weak ties describe social interactions between individuals. Hyperlinks are structural links between media content. Clearly, hyperlinks are not weak ties. More precisely, then, the question is whether hyperlinks, much like weak ties, can encourage the exchange of ideas and information between individuals who do not share the same interests or political preferences. The answer depends on the disparity of interests that hyperlinks have to overcome. The likelihood is low that hyperlinks will connect distinct domains of interests. Within domains of interest—within the domain of politics, for example—hyperlinks stand a better chance of generating traffic.

The potentially most significant benefit of hyperlinks would be to bridge the mounting disconnect between people who are interested in politics and those who are not. As weak ties, hyperlinks may expose people to experiences they would not have sought out of their own interest and to Web sites that do not fit their content preferences. In this way, hyperlinks could more or less accidentally inform entertainment fans. In a media environment of abundant choice, where users follow their content preferences to either abandon the news or indulge in it like never before, can hyperlinks limit political inequality?

We can analyze new media effects on political inequality by making two different comparisons: one between the current Web, with its hyperlink structure, and a hypothetical Web without links (holding everything else constant); and a second between the old media environment in which structures imposed strong regularity on media use and our current new media environment. Both perspectives are valuable, but only the second comparison gives us a sense of the overall effect of the Internet on trends in political involvement. To assess the political impact of an Internet with hyperlinks, we need to understand both the effect of the Internet in general and the effect of hyperlinks in particular.

Two central findings in *Post-Broadcast Democracy* provide the context for assessing the impact of hyperlinks. First, the explosion of media choice—both online and through other media, notably television—multiplies the role of motivation in people's selection of content. Second, most people prefer some kind of entertainment to news, politics, or public affairs content. Increasingly, new media users read, watch, and hear the content they really like, but this content is rarely political. With or without hyperlinks, new media offer so much more content and so much more user autonomy that inequality in political involvement increases considerably.

Suppose for a moment that, all other things equal (including the availability of the Web), hyperlinks furthered political equality by encouraging exposure to politics among people who started their surfing on an entertainment Web site. This potential benefit of hyperlinks would be easily overshadowed by the mounting inequality caused by other aspects of new media. Hyperlinks are passive elements of the environment. They are fighting a losing battle against the motivational forces unleashed by media choice. Hyperlinks, especially those generated by search engines, do offer gateways to a wealth of political information and opinion—but primarily to those who are looking for information and opinion. And even if an avid entertainment fan comes across a hyperlink to a political Web site, that hyperlink typically has to compete with a variety of more entertaining links that are also just a click away. Hyperlinks that connect nonpolitical Web sites to political information sources attempt to pry users away from what they came to accomplish or enjoy online. The likely outcome is that intrinsic interest beats hyperlink. In short, holding together media users with widely varying content preference against the centrifugal forces of greater choice is too much to expect from a passive feature of the Internet.

Within a domain of interest, however, hyperlinks are more likely to be traveled. Hyperlinks between different sources of political information are still only passive structural features, but they will often be aligned with the general content preference of those who see them. If hyperlinks within the domain of political and policy-relevant information function as weak ties, they not only will limit ideological selectivity but may also strengthen political accountability.

As weak ties, hyperlinks can expose citizens to political positions they do not share and to political information they do not expect. Links may thus counteract partisan polarization that arises from ideologically selective exposure. Even though I have argued, based on rather limited evidence, that the dangers of political polarization through ideologically selective exposure have been overstated, it is still important to understand if hyperlinks can limit polarization.

The risk of polarization rises with exclusive exposure to ideologically one-sided opinion or biased information. Three kinds of people are likely to visit an ideologically extreme Web site: news junkies who enjoy the spectacle of politics, partisans who look for confirmation of their political opinions, and politically less interested Web users who end up on the sites by accident or perhaps even through a hyperlink on a nonpolitical Web site. News junkies will not content themselves with visiting just that one ideologically extreme Web site. Instead, they will access other sites and be savvy enough to find Web sites of different ideological shades. Exclusive exposure to only one side is unlikely for them, with or without hyperlinks. Hyperlinks might help partisans to find confirmatory opinions and information, but they are partisan to begin with, so polarization should change little.

That leaves the politically innocent as a victim of hyperlinks. Within the domain of news and political opinion, mainstream news Web sites and news portals, such as Google News or Yahoo News, are unlikely to send the innocent surfer only to ideologically slanted sites.[32] But we might expect hyperlinks on blogs or other Web sites with a political mission to contribute to politically one-sided experiences, just because conservative Web sites are more likely to link to other conservative Web sites, while liberal sites are more likely to link to liberal sites.

Hyperlinks have their interpersonal equivalent in the context in which people form their social networks. Like the composition of neighborhoods, hyperlinks make certain connections more likely without imposing them in a determinative way. Exposure to opinions of like-minded people may occur not because someone deliberately seeks out political agreement but as a side effect of accepting the most readily available discussion partner or Web site. Long ago, Sears and Freedman referred to this process as "de facto selectivity."[33]

De facto selectivity becomes powerful only when people wander around aimlessly. Even in New York's East Village, where most random encounters will be with liberals, you can find conservatives. Even if most hyperlinks point to politically congruent sites, you can still follow the link structure to opposing points of view. Typically, neither news junkies, who look for the most comprehensive political information, nor partisans, who look for a particular ideological slant, access political Web sites aimlessly. But when people choose their social encounters and their Web sites in quasi-random fashion—perhaps because they do not know what they are looking for or they do not care—both context and hyperlinks can lead to de facto selectivity. If political Web sites link predominantly to other sites featuring the same worldview and if users select among them arbitrarily, polarization may ensue even in the absence of any intention to tune out the other side.

How likely, then, is exclusive exposure to only one side as a result of aimless surfing among political innocents? Not very likely—for structural reasons and because of the aimlessness. Like news sites, blogs link to news stories more often than to other blogs, according to a study of forty of the most popular blogs during the two months preceding the 2004 presidential election.[34] Even blogs, the most politically opinionated quarters of the Web, thus do not automatically sustain ideological de facto selectivity.

When bloggers link to other blogs, they select predominantly ideologically consistent ones. Adamic and Glance find that 87 percent of all links by conservative bloggers led to other conservative blogs. For liberal bloggers, that number is 86 percent. Only a few prominent blogs, such as Andrew Sullivan or Wonkette, receive links from both sides of the political spectrum. Yet although blog-to-blog links are ideologically quite segmented, both conservative and liberal blogs link to many of the same mainstream news media. The three news sites to which the top forty blogs most commonly link (NYTimes.com, WashingtonPost.com, and News.yahoo.com) receive about 55 percent of their links from liberal blogs and 45 percent from conservative blogs. Links to news Web sites with more ideological reputations (e.g., Salon.com, TheNation.com, WashingtonTimes.com, and NationalReview.com) are much more strongly determined by the ideology of the blog, but the total number of links is decidedly lower as well. Hence, the number of links from the top twenty conservative blogs to the *Washington Post* Web site roughly equaled the combined number of their links to FoxNews.com, NYPost.com, and

OpinionJournal.com (the *Wall Street Journal's* editorial page online). Although the link structure of blogs is partly driven by ideology, a common core of references to mainstream media is clearly evident.

Irrespective of the precise partisan skew of the blogosphere, the theory that aimless surfing might lead to polarization assumes a set of rather inconsistent premises that make it unlikely. First, the politically uninterested user would have to access a political Web site. Second, the same user would then have to be interested enough to link to another political Web site but aimless enough to accept whatever the link structure offers. Third, our politically innocent user with some interest would have to navigate the Web in this fashion repeatedly but somehow always end up on sites with the same political slant. This is not an impossible scenario, but it does not fit the behavior we would expect from a casual visitor. Among media users with little political interest, hyperlinks may lead to ideological de facto selectivity over short periods of time, but aimless surfing should soon restore political balance.

The creation and use of hyperlinks by political junkies for the purpose of sharing and acquiring vast amounts of political information suggests another consequence for representative democracy. Hyperlinks may facilitate political accountability. This expectation builds on a model of citizenship proposed by Michael Schudson.[35] In Schudson's view, the ideal of an informed citizen who carefully studies political issues and candidate platforms before casting a vote needs adjustment. It is an ideal against which most citizens have always looked ill informed and ineffective. It also ignores an arena for citizenship that has expanded dramatically in the last fifty years. Both the growing regulatory powers of the federal government and the increasing role of litigation have extended the reach of politics into many areas of private life. This new dimension has added considerable complexity to the role of citizens, who now have the opportunity and the obligation to claim their rights.

Although Schudson does not deny the benefits of an informed citizenry, he considers it neither realistic nor necessary for citizens to be well informed about every aspect of their increasingly complex role in society. Instead, he proposes a modified model of citizenship, the "monitorial citizen." Rather than widely knowledgeable about politics, citizens merely need to "be informed enough and alert enough to identify danger to their personal good and danger to the public good."[36] In order to fulfill this "monitoring obligation," citizens "engage in environmental surveillance rather than information-gathering."[37]

Not all citizens can be effective monitors. Dedicated entertainment fans, in particular, may prefer not to be. According to Schudson, "in some ways, monitorial citizenship is more demanding than informed citizenship, because it implies that one's peripheral vision should always have a political or civic dimension."[38] For many Americans, the beauty of greater media choice lies exactly in getting rid of that "political or civic dimension," which used to creep in through the ubiquitous evening news or through the presidential debate that was hard to avoid. To those who enjoy staying informed, however, the high-choice media environment provides unprecedented resources to perform as monitorial citizens. News junkies consume a lot of information and do not mind the monitoring obligation. They take advantage of new media technologies to share and debate the results of the monitoring. Hyperlinks can thus make monitoring more effective.

If it is not necessary for all citizens to engage in monitoring (because some citizens can fill in as monitors for others), the expansion of media choice could actually make it easier to spot the "dangers" that Schudson writes about. Even as greater media choice creates a less equitable knowledge distribution, it could benefit representative democracy, if those who become more knowledgeable guide policy in a more "enlightened" direction. Hyperlinks can help to spread information quickly, allowing monitorial citizens to sound their alarms before it is too late.[39]

To what extent alarms will receive attention outside the monitoring class is less clear. The challenge will be to limit alarms to important matters, even when an efficient information environment produces many reasons for concern—some worthy of an alarm, others not.[40] Moreover, it is doubtful that news junkies will faithfully represent the interests of those who have tuned out politics. Demographically, news fans and entertainment fans are remarkably similar,[41] so their political views might correspond relatively well to the views of entertainment fans. But news fans are far more partisan and unlikely to advocate the moderate policy positions that entertainment fans seem to favor.

In sum, among the large number of citizens with a solid preference for entertainment, hyperlinks will do little to change political involvement. But by making it easier and more effective for news junkies to navigate the information-rich media environment, hyperlinks raise the potential for accountability. Whether this potential can be fulfilled depends at least in part on the assertiveness of linkers and linked in resisting both partisan and commercial distortions. If political Web sites link in a parochial and inward-looking way, monitoring will remain inefficient as a basis for accountability. An information environment in which the most prominent link goes to the highest bidder promises distortions of a different kind. A powerful influence works against these obstacles, however: the desire of news junkies to spend countless hours learning and linking political information, regardless of partisan or commercial value. That's what being a news junkie in a high-choice media environment is all about.

NOTES

I thank Scott Althaus and Matthew Hindman for their helpful comments on an earlier version of this essay.

1. M. S. Granovetter, "The Strength of Weak Ties," *American Journal of Sociology* 78, no. 6 (1973): 1360–80.

2. A. Downs, *An Economic Theory of Democracy* (New York: Harper and Row, 1957).

3. L. Festinger, *A Theory of Cognitive Dissonance* (Stanford, CA: Stanford University Press, 1957).

4. Granovetter, "The Strength of Weak Ties," 1370–71.

5. They refer to "low density networks," which imply the presence of weak ties. See R. R. Huckfeldt, P. E. Johnson, and J. D. Sprague, *Political Disagreement: The Survival of Diverse Opinions within Communication Networks* (New York: Cambridge University Press, 2004).

6. D. C. Mutz, *Hearing the Other Side: Deliberative versus Participatory Democracy* (New York: Cambridge University Press, 2006).

7. D. C. Mutz and P. S. Martin, "Facilitating Communication across Lines of Political Difference: The Role of Mass Media," *American Political Science Review* 95, no. 1 (2001): 111.

8. E.g., N. Negroponte, *Being Digital* (New York: Knopf, 1995).

9. J. Turow, *Breaking Up America: Advertisers and the New Media World* (Chicago: University of Chicago Press, 1997), 2, 7.

10. C. R. Sunstein, *Republic.com* (Princeton, NJ: Princeton University Press, 2001).

11. Turow, *Breaking Up America*, 7.

12. Mutz and Martin, "Facilitating Communication."

13. J. G. Webster, "Beneath the Veneer of Fragmentation: Television Audience Polarization in a Multichannel World," *Journal of Communication* 55, no. 2 (2005): 369.

14. Ibid.; J. G. Webster, "Audience Behavior in the New Media Environment," *Journal of Communication* 36, no. 3 (1986): 77–91.

15. Webster, "Beneath the Veneer of Fragmentation," 380.

16. I thank James Webster for sharing with me data he did not use in his article.

17. S. DellaVigna and E. Kaplan, "The Fox News Effect: Media Bias and Voting" (April 2006). NBER Working Paper No. W12169 available at SSRN: http://ssrn.com/abstract897023.

18. S. Iyengar, K. Hahn, and M. Prior, "Has Technology Made Attention to Political Campaigns More Selective? An Experimental Study of the 2000 Presi-

dential Campaign" (paper presented to the American Political Science Association, San Francisco, CA, April 2001).

19. P. DiMaggio and K. Sato, "Does the Internet Balkanize Political Attention? A Test of the Sunstein Theory" (paper presented to the American Sociological Association, Atlanta, GA, April 16, 2003).

20. Mutz and Martin, "Facilitating Communication"; D. O. Sears and J. L. Freedman, "Selective Exposure to Information: A Critical Review," *Public Opinion Quarterly* 31, no. 2 (1967): 194–213.

21. P. F. Lazarsfeld and B. Berelson, *The People's Choice: How the Voter Makes Up His Mind in a Presidential Campaign*, 3rd ed. (New York: Columbia University Press, 1968); W. J. McGuire, "The Nature of Attitudes and Attitude Change," in *The Handbook of Social Psychology*, ed. L. Gardner and E. Aronson (Reading, MA: Addison-Wesley, 1969), 136–314.

22. M. X. D. Carpini and S. Keeter, *What Americans Know about Politics and Why It Matters* (New Haven, CT: Yale University Press, 1996).

23. S. Verba, K. L. Schlozman, and H. E. Brady, *Voice and Equality* (Cambridge, MA: Harvard University Press, 1995).

24. This is not to say that bias creates no costs. Misinformation—caused by ideological commentary that misrepresents the facts, for example—can be pernicious and will obstruct collective decision making. See J. H. Kuklinski et al., "Misinformation and the Currency of Democratic Citizenship," *Journal of Politics* 62, no. 3 (2000): 790–816.

25. M. Prior, *Post-Broadcast Democracy: How Media Choice Increases Inequality in Political Involvement and Polarizes Elections* (New York: Cambridge University Press, 2007).

26. Webster, "Audience Behavior"; Webster, "Beneath the Veneer of Fragmentation."

27. Ibid.

28. Due to the impending U.S. military intervention in Iraq, news audiences were unusually large in February 2003, the month Webster analyzed. Weekly cumulative audiences in 2005 were closer to 20 percent for both CNN and Fox News and were under 15 percent for MSNBC and CNN Headline News.

29. Prior, *Post-Broadcast Democracy*.

30. P. DiMaggio et al., "Digital Inequality: From Unequal Access to Differentiated Use," in *Social Inequality*, ed. K. M. Neckerman (New York: Russell Sage Foundation, 2004), 355–400.

31. Ability has not entirely disappeared as an obstacle to political involvement. New technologies require new skills, such as knowledge of how the Internet is organized and how desired content can be located most easily. These skills are important in making the most out of the political resources available online. They are not evenly distributed across the population. See H. Bonfadelli, "The Internet and Knowledge Gaps: A Theoretical and Empirical Investigation," *European Journal of Communication* 17, no. 1 (2002): 65–84; DiMaggio et al., "Digital Inequality."

32. The Project for Excellence in Journalism examined thirty-eight different news Web sites and found considerable variation in the use of links to related stories or archival material. Web sites maintained by newspapers or electronic media outlets face an economic disincentive to link to competitors. News portals, in con-

trast, do not provide original content but offer links to other media outlets. Google News provides hundreds of computer-generated links to outside news stories, whereas human editors at Yahoo News offer their (abundant) selections. See Project for Excellence in Journalism, *The State of the News Media 2007* (Washington, DC, 2007).

33. Sears and Freedman, "Selective Exposure to Information."

34. L. A. Adamic and N. Glance, "The Political Blogosphere and the 2004 U.S. Election: Divided They Blog," *Proceedings of the 3rd International Workshop on Link Discovery* (New York: ACM, 2005), 36–43.

35. M. Schudson, *The Good Citizen: A History of American Civic Life* (New York: Free Press, 1998); M. Schudson, "Good Citizens and Bad History: Today's Political Ideals in Historical Perspective," *Communication Review* 1, no. 4 (2000), 1–20.

36. Schudson, "Good Citizens and Bad History," 22.

37. Schudson, *The Good Citizen*, 310–11.

38. Schudson, "Good Citizens and Bad History," 22.

39. J. Zaller, "A New Standard of News Quality: Burglar Alarms for the Monitorial Citizen," *Political Communication* 20, no. 2 (2003): 109–30.

40. W. L. Bennett, "The Burglar Alarm That Just Keeps Ringing: A Response to Zaller," *Political Communication* 20, no. 2 (2003): 131–38.

41. Prior, *Post-Broadcast Democracy*.

MATTHEW HINDMAN

What Is the Online Public Sphere Good For?

Almost from the moment the Internet became a mass medium, observers predicted that it would change the relationship between citizens and the political information they consume. According to numerous accounts, the Internet would function as a digital printing press, enabling any motivated citizen to publish his or her views for a potential audience of millions. The architecture of the Web would also instantly link citizens with diverse opinions to one another. This citizen-created hyperlinked content would not need to follow the biases, whims, and market demands that constrain traditional media. Without barriers to entry, the public sphere would become vastly broader and more representative.

Recent events have borne out at least some of this breathless, mid-1990s Internet boosterism. Internet sources are now a large and still rapidly growing portion of American's diet of political media. According to one recent study, 14 percent of the public relied primarily on Internet sources in the lead up to the 2006 midterm elections, which is double the percentage of four years earlier.[1] Citizens have also rushed to their digital printing presses with an eagerness matching the most optimistic predictions. Surveys have suggested that twelve million Americans maintain a blog, with about 10 percent of these blogs focused primarily on politics.[2] The most popular political blogs and political Web sites now claim far more readers than traditional opinion journals, such as the *Nation, National Review,* or the *New Republic.* In several prominent incidents, stories first reported in political blogs became the focus of sustained mainstream press coverage.

Against this backdrop, some scholars have revised, qualified, and extended early theories about how the Internet would transform the public sphere. Cass Sunstein's recent book *Infotopia* focuses on new collaborative models that allow citizens themselves to create and filter high-quality political information.[3] Richard Rogers similarly suggests that, despite its limitations, the Web is "the finest candidate there is for unsettling informational politics,"[4] offering citizens exposure to political points of view not heard in traditional media. Many scholars have focused on blogging as reason for optimism. Despite a critical assessment of online deliberative forums, Andrew Chadwick concludes, "The explosion of blogging has democratized access to the tools and techniques required to make a political difference through content creation."[5] While Daniel Drezner and Henry Farrell note that some blogs garner far more readership than others, they state, "Ultimately, the greatest advantage of the blogosphere is its accessibility."[6]

Yet perhaps the most prominent recent account in this vein is Yochai Benkler's *The Wealth of Networks.*[7] Compared to traditional media, Benkler suggests, the Internet allows for a broader, more inclusive and more densely linked public sphere. Like the other scholars already cited, Benkler argues that the Internet does not just place far more information in the hands of interested citizens; it transforms public debates by enabling online communities to use collaborative methods to create content, correct inaccuracies, and send readers to the most insightful commentators.

In this essay, I focus on Benkler's influential book to make two central claims. First, I suggest that his vision of the "networked public sphere" is partly correct and that the Internet is strengthening some democratic values. Benkler's account in particular illuminates important aspects of the Internet's impact on collective action, including the way it has made it easier to aggregate small contributions into a useful whole. There is also evidence that the Internet is strengthening public oversight by making "fire alarm" or "burglar alarm" models of citizenship more effective.[8] Finally, there is reason to believe that the Internet has made journalists and other political elites more accountable or at least more vulnerable. Former Senate majority leader Trent Lott and former *New York Times* reporter Judith Miller have both publicly laid the blame for their travails on bloggers' criticism.[9] The Mark Foley scandal that dogged Republicans during the 2006 midterm election seems to have been touched off by an obscure political blog that posted "overly friendly" e-mails between Foley and a former congressional page.[10] In these incidents, the evidence for the Internet's role is strong, and the political consequences have been dramatic.

Second, however, I argue that while the Internet is strengthening some democratic values, it has placed others at risk. Many continue to celebrate the Internet for its inclusiveness; others decry the medium for the same reason, worrying (as CNN president Jonathan Klein put it) that the Internet gives too much power to "a guy sitting on his couch in his pajamas."[11] I argue here that the underlying premise of both assessments is wrong. Inclusiveness is precisely what the online public sphere lacks. Part of the problem is the extraordinary concentration of links and patterns in online traffic. For example, several observers have suggested that a group of A-list political bloggers attract disproportionate attention. I argue here that even the emergence of a blogging A-list barely scratches the surface of online inequality.

I am going to develop this argument by targeting what I term the "trickle-up theory" of online discourse, particularly as it is formulated in Benkler's account of what he terms the "networked public sphere." As I have already suggested, Benkler's work merits special attention for several reasons. *The Wealth of Networks* is important in its own right, the culmination of nearly a decade of scholarship; yet Benkler's claims are also representative of those made by others. One of the virtues of Benkler's book is that it fully explicates key claims and assumptions that other scholars often gloss over. Benkler is also scrupulous about cataloging and responding to potential counterarguments.

Like many other observers, Benkler argues that the networked structure of the Web itself can compensate for inequalities in traffic and in the elite profile of those who publish the most read online political outlets. He describes blogs as an "ecosystem," in which even the smallest outlets have an important role to play. Insights or discoveries made by lower-ranking blogs can (in theory) travel up the hierarchy of online outlets, with the most worthy posts receiving a torrent of attention if they are linked to by the most prominent blogs. His account persistently reframes inequalities in egalitarian terms, recasting them as "collaborative filtering" or "meritocracy" in action. In what follows, I suggest that there are several reasons to be suspicious of the trickle-up theory of public debate advanced by Benkler and others. Thus far at least, public discourse online looks more like a multilevel marketing scheme than a Habermasian ideal.

What Is the Public Sphere For?

Before critiquing recent accounts of the online public sphere, it is worth placing such scholarship in a broader context. In recent decades and well before the rise of the Internet as a mass medium, there has been a resurgence of interest among scholars in the public sphere. Much of the initial credit for this belongs to Jurgen Habermas.[12] Yet what John Dryzek calls the "deliberative turn" in political philosophy now includes numerous theorists: John Rawls,[13] Joshua Cohen,[14] Carlos Nino,[15] Amy Gutmann and Dennis Thompson,[16] John Dryzek himself,[17] and Bruce Ackerman and James Fishkin,[18] to name a few.

Despite long-running academic disputes, the visions of deliberation authored by this group show strong commonalities. All look to enrich democracy beyond mere bargaining and aggregation of preferences. All suggest that everyone whose vital interests are at stake in a public decision should participate in making it and that true participation requires citizens themselves to engage in discussions with their fellow citizens. Most of these deliberative theorists have examined actual practices of deliberation in an effort to go beyond armchair theorizing. And though they differ in their emphasis, all of these theorists argue that properly conducted deliberation can produce both moral and epistemic advantages. On the one hand, deliberation is supposed to help discern empirical facts and moral truths and (ultimately) lead to the adoption of better public policies. On the other, deliberation is supposed to confer democratic legitimacy. Legitimate, or just, public policies are those that result (or at least could result) from properly conducted deliberation between equals.

This recent scholarship on deliberative democracy is particularly important in the context of the Internet, since scholars have frequently looked at the online public sphere through the lens that deliberative democrats have provided. In *Republic.com*, for example, Cass Sunstein explicitly evaluates online discourse by the standards of deliberative democracy—particularly through the standards articulated in his own previous work, which reads American constitutionalism as intrinsically deliberative.[19] Sunstein's worry—more prominent in *Republic.com* than in *Infotopia*—is that the Internet will fragment the public sphere that deliberative democrats depend on. Deliberation within "echo chambers" will promote polarization rather than respect and democratic legitimacy.

Like Sunstein, Benkler, too, relies on deliberative theorists in his efforts to evaluate the Internet's impact on political freedom. Rather than offer an ideal conception of democracy, Benkler instead asks, "What characteristics of a communications system are sufficiently basic enough to be desired by a wide range of conceptions of democracy?"[20] Despite this claim to minimalism, the political philosophers he names directly—Habermas, Ackerman, and Rawls—are nevertheless deliberative democrats of one stripe or another. Benkler singles out Habermas's views several times in order to support his own case. In addition to relying on Habermas for his initial definition of the public sphere, Benkler also echoes Habermas's critique of commercial mass media as reducing public discussion to its lowest common denominator.

Following Benkler and other recent commentators, most of this essay

is focused on discussions about blogs and other Web sites that are devoted to political commentary and advocacy. Yet it is worth emphasizing
at the outset that a normative defense of blogging is essentially a fallback
position. Initially, hopes about the Internet and public discourse centered
on new online collaborative forums, where citizens could discuss important public issues, often in real time, in a virtual space. Many such online
forums were constructed to reflect the norms and institutional guarantees
that deliberative democrats suggested.

Overall, however, reports about these experiments in online deliberation have been dismal. A few scholars reported small-scale successes.[21]
Yet these were the exception. Surveying a large set of diverse experiments
in online deliberation, Chadwick harshly concludes, "The road to e-
democracy is littered with the burnt-out hulks of failed projects."[22]

If the online forums that have largely failed were designed, from the
ground up, to meet both the practical and normative demands of deliberative theorists, the blogosphere was not. The enormous growth of blog
readership was a surprise even (as most have acknowledged) to the bloggers who have benefited most. This spontaneous growth and substantial
readership is, of course, central to blogging's power. But it also means
that the political blogosphere has features that deliberative democrats
would never have designed into it.

The Networked Public Sphere: Theory and Practice

Benkler relies on a definition of the public sphere derived from deliberative theory and suggests that these deliberative standards are a good yardstick (though perhaps not the only yardstick) with which to judge the Internet's impact. Yet Benkler is also clear that his vision is not a rehashing
of mid-1990s cyberutopianism, explaining that it is silly to dismiss the Internet simply because it failed to make "everyone a pamphleteer."[23] He
argues, quite reasonably, that we should evaluate the Internet against the
baseline of commercial mass media. The claim here is thus explicitly
comparative, placing online content against the backdrop of traditional
media.

Benkler positions his view of the Internet's effects between two distinct
criticisms of Internet content. On the one hand, early critics of the Internet worried that chaos and overabundance of content would make it impossible for citizens to gather information effectively. Benkler terms this
the "Babel" criticism.[24] On the other hand, later scholarship worried

about the opposite problem. With winners-take-all patterns in the structure of the Web and in online traffic, the fear was that the Internet would allow a small number of popular outlets to dominate, mirroring patterns found in traditional media.

In contrast to these two prevalent criticisms, Benkler stakes out what he terms the "Goldilocks" position, arguing that the level of concentration seen online is "just right."[25] Benkler's claim is that the networked nature of Web content provides adequate visibility within smaller communities, while also allowing quality content to filter up to a broad audience. At the micro level, Benkler argues, "Clusters of moderately read sites provide platforms for a vastly greater number of speakers than are heard in the mass-media audience."[26] Yet such clusters are egalitarian and not isolated: "As the clusters get small enough, the obscurity of sites participating in the cluster diminishes, while the visibility of superstars remains high, forming a filtering and transmission backbone for universal uptake and local filtering."[27]

Benkler's claims here are similar to those made by others. Sunstein's most recent work argues that "the blogosphere might be seen as a kind of gigantic town meeting."

> The presence of many minds is particularly important here. If countless people are maintaining their own blogs, they should be able to act as fact-checkers and as supplemental information sources, not only for one another but for prominent members of the mass media. . . . The blogosphere enables interested readers to find an astounding range of opinions and facts.[28]

Drezner and Farrell, in their study of blogs, also emphasize that widely read bloggers promote postings by more obscure bloggers.[29] Drezner and Farrell suggest that since journalists themselves focus their readership on top blogging outlets, a story that reaches an A-list site can jump to traditional media. Drezner describes blogger coverage of the CBS-forged document scandal (discussed in more detail later in this essay) as "like firing a flare," with blogs pointing out the story and traditional journalists investigating and fleshing out the details.[30] Journalists and bloggers themselves have also repeated such claims over and over. Bloggers such as Glenn Reynolds[31] and Hugh Hewitt[32] on the right and Jerome Armstrong and Markos Moulitsas Zuniga[33] on the left have all published books arguing that the Internet empowers "an army of Davids" and allows citizens to "crash the gates."

Yet such egalitarian hopes are problematic, as Benkler's "Goldilocks" account demonstrates. Benkler relies heavily on a piece of scholarship from NEC Research Institute to support his claim that clusters of Web sites are less concentrated—and thus more transparent—at the microlevel. In the article "Winners Don't Take All," Pennock and others look at clusters of Web sites in a variety of different categories, from online retailers and media Web sites to university Web sites and sites of photographers.[34] Benkler cites this research as the most important piece of evidence that we find more egalitarian patterns at the microlevel of the Web. Several other researchers and works cited by Benkler address the same issue but report apparently contradictory findings.[35] Benkler's rationale for accepting the ostensible conclusions of Pennock and others over those of other researchers is not made clear.

Given the significance of the research of Pennock and others to Benkler's argument, it is important to note that their claims seem to have been misread. Pennock and others do not contradict the much larger, well-established volume of literature concluding that most communities of Web sites are highly concentrated. Pennock and others model microlevel traffic by assuming that sites get some baseline number of hyperlinks just for being part of a community, while another—highly skewed—portion of their hyperlinks depend on their rank within the community.

Pennock and others do find that in some communities of content, sites seem to get a greater portion of links just for belonging. Still, the majority of categories they examine distribute more than 90 percent of their links according to winners-take-all patterns. Moreover, the groups of Web sites that Pennock and others find to be less concentrated are exceptional. The Web sites of professional photographers face natural geographical limits: you cannot hire a wedding photographer from Maine if you are having your ceremony in Florida. Links from one university Web site to another, another apparent exception, are parasitic upon real-world social networks that provide both horizontal and vertical visibility. For example, professors are likely to be aware of scholars at Harvard and Yale and Princeton, as well as scholars at nearby institutions.

Benkler also points to Drezner and Farrel,[36] arguing that their research confirms that political content is less concentrated than other online content, making it possible for political Web sites to provide adequate levels of visibility to numerous participants. Yet here again, "less concentrated" is a relative term. Drezner and Farrel are actually making a more technical argument, about whether the distribution of links and traffic among blogs better fits a power law or an extreme lognormal distribution. Even the smaller claim that Drezner and Farrel are making is contradicted by other research that Benkler cites. Adamic and Glance's finding that links among political Weblogs are distributed according to a power law distribution with an exponential cutoff seems difficult to refute.[37] Still, whichever claim is right is largely irrelevant to the questions that Benkler raises. Neither set of scholars disputes that political content online is overwhelmingly concentrated.

Yet even if we were inclined to accept the evidence of Pennock and others wholeheartedly, we cannot conclude that all online content automatically provides for "vast" numbers of "moderately read" Web sites. If there is variation in the structure of online content niches, the question is whether the content that Benkler cares about—political content and public discourse generally—looks like the distribution of either retail or photography Web sites. In partnership with researchers from the same NEC Research Institute unit that Benkler relied on, I have conducted research that provides one answer to this question.[38] Looking at categories of political Web sites focused on such issues as gun control, abortion, and the U.S. Congress, it does show that some categories of sites are more concentrated than others. Yet even though the study finds hundreds of Web sites in each topical community, the majority of links in each case are divided up between less than a dozen sites. According to the model of Pennock and others, all of these areas of political content look like the winners-take-all patterns found in online retailing and not at all like the more diffuse patterns found among photographers or university home pages.

Traffic Patterns and "Discourse Elitism"

Dividing up Web content into subcategories and sub-subcategories does not demonstrate the conditions Benkler lays out for "universal uptake." This same conclusion is powerfully reinforced by broad patterns of online traffic. Traffic analysis cannot give the level of detail provided by analyzing link structure. The reason is simple: even with a sample of millions of people, so few people visit the most obscure Web sites that traffic is difficult to measure reliably. This difficulty alone suggests a problem with Benkler's arguments. Still, traffic data gets more directly at concerns about visibility, and it does a better job of placing Benkler's claims about the public sphere in context.

One of the best sources of Web traffic data is Hitwise, an online competitive intelligence service. Hitwise partners with Internet service providers to track and analyze the behavior of their subscribers, allowing for highly detailed, clickstream data. Hitwise's sample includes data from ten million American households, and Hitwise tracks visits to more than eight hundred thousand of the most popular Web sites. Hitwise data thus allows us to look at traffic patterns even within content areas that are a tiny fraction of the Web's total traffic.

Markus Prior asserts earlier in this volume that the Internet and increasing media choice in general has amplified the importance of citizen motivation. Prior argues that citizens with little interest in politics and without firm ideological or partisan commitments have shifted away from political news and toward "soft," entertainment-driven content. The broad outlines of the Hitwise data are strongly consistent with Prior's argument. News and media Web sites are only a small portion of what citizens see online, accounting for only 3 percent of total Web visits. Online, public oriented content has to compete for attention with countless other materials. If most of what Americans are doing online has nothing to do with issues of public concern, this surely recasts Benkler's argument.

Looking more closely at these numbers raises even more questions. According to Hitwise data, Benkler's claim that Internet audiences are more dispersed than those for traditional media seems to be wrong. Internet audiences may be less concentrated than those for television, particularly with regard to news content. Yet despite growing use of online video, the Web remains overwhelmingly a text-based medium. A majority of the top news and media sites are online outposts of print publications, and even the sites of television news outlets (e.g., CNN or NBC News) distribute far more stories in print form than in video. In measuring audience concentration, print media therefore seems to be a more apt yardstick for comparison. Circulation data is readily available for all major U.S. newspapers and national magazines, courtesy of the Audit Bureau of Circulations, a private oversight organization.

In fact, audiences for online news are both more and less concentrated than audiences for newspapers and magazines.[39] Comparing circulation figures to site traffic shows that the most popular news outlets are even more important online than offline. The top ten media sites receive 29 percent of total site visits, whereas the top ten newspapers and the top ten national magazines receive only 19 percent and 27 percent of total circulation, respectively. More holistic metrics of concentration emphasize the same conclusion. Both the Gini coefficient and Herfindahl-Hirschman Index (HHI), the most commonly used metrics of concentration in the social sciences, suggest that online content is more, not less, concentrated than print media.

Concentration at the top is nevertheless only part of the story. Hitwise tracks more than thirty thousand media sites, and those ranked below 500 account for more than a quarter of the total traffic. Collectively, lower-ranked outlets thus receive far more attention online than they do in any traditional media. The Internet, then, is hollowing out the audience for online news, shifting eyeballs to the most and least popular outlets at once.

Partly, this counterintuitive result seems to come from exposing previously protected local monopolies to nationwide and even worldwide competition. The fate of online newspaper sites illustrates this problem starkly. Not only do the top ten newspapers get dramatically more of the total audience share online than in print, but it is overwhelmingly nationally prominent newspapers (e.g., the *New York Times*, the *Washington Post*, and the *San Francisco Chronicle*) that have a greater online market share; smaller newspapers, by contrast, have lost ground relative to their larger rivals. Controlling for potential confounding factors further strengthens this conclusion. Much content in local papers, for example, is provided by national and international wire services, such as the Associated Press or Reuters. Yet research by Paterson shows that here, too, online content provides less diversity than print media.[40]

Even if online news outlets were a larger portion of the total content and even if top online news outlets were less influential, Benkler's account would still face problems. Most important, the political content that citizens are exposed to on the Internet is still provided overwhelmingly by the commercial mass media. Benkler is kinder to the *New York Times*, the *Wall Street Journal*, and the *Washington Post*—organizations that "may credibly claim to embody highly professional journalism"[41]—than he is to local and regional newspapers. In this respect, shifts from local to national news outlets may be partly positive. Yet given how damning Benkler's critique of commercial media is, sending a proportionally larger number of eyeballs to the most popular news outlets does not seem like a step forward.

The content that Benkler is most interested in, then, is not news and media sites but the sites that Hitwise places in its "politics" category. Most of the specific examples that Benkler uses in his chapters on political freedom belong in this grouping. According to Hitwise, the politics category gets only 0.1 percent of total site traffic, less than one-thirtieth the traffic received by traditional news outlets.

We can argue all we want about what is going on with this one-tenth of 1 percent of all Internet traffic. But no matter how visibility within this niche is distributed, it is hard to see how such a small portion of the public's media diet can account for the positive effects Benkler hopes for. By way of comparison, Hitwise reports (as of February 2006) that 13 percent of all Web traffic goes to sites featuring adult content—outpacing visits to political sites by two orders of magnitude.

Figure 1 graphs the traffic among the top fifty political sites as of February 2006, according to Hitwise data. For that month, Hitwise tracked visits to 970 of the most popular political Web sites. Here, too, we see winners-take-all patterns that contradict Benkler's claim that visibility emerges within small enough categories of content. These top fifty sites account for 62 percent of political traffic. The top ten sites together receive as much traffic as the next forty sites combined. Yet as the figure shows, even the disproportionate amount of traffic received by these top sites understates their importance. Top sites in the community do seem to be functioning as filters, much the way that Benkler and others have suggested. In practice, this magnifies the influence of these top sites even beyond the disproportionate number of page views they receive. As with news and media sites, it is the "middle class" of outlets that seem to be missing.

Both of these features of online political audiences—concentration at the top and diffusion at the bottom—work against Benkler's claims. Even within the tiny politics niche, top sites have replicated a broadcast-style model of public attention. Moreover, those who get heard in the online public sphere are in many ways less representative and more elite than those whose voices were carried by traditional media. It is common to hear talk of an A-list of bloggers whose voices are disproportionately influential. Yet the top ten or top twenty bloggers who constitute the so-called A-list are only the tip of the iceberg.

This can be seen clearly in my forthcoming research that includes a census of top political bloggers.[42] Following the widely held belief that the 2004 general election was the moment that bloggers arrived as a political force, the census looked at all political blogs who had more than two thousand daily visitors as of December 2004, according to N. Z. Bear's Blogging Ecosystem project.[43] Through public sources and e-mail surveys, data was gathered on seventy-five of the eighty-six blogs that met this level of traffic.

Given that the United States is a nation of three hundred million people, it is striking that so few blogs attracted as much attention as a college newspaper. Nearly all of the bloggers in the sample had careers as lawyers, professors, journalists, senior managers, or technology profes-

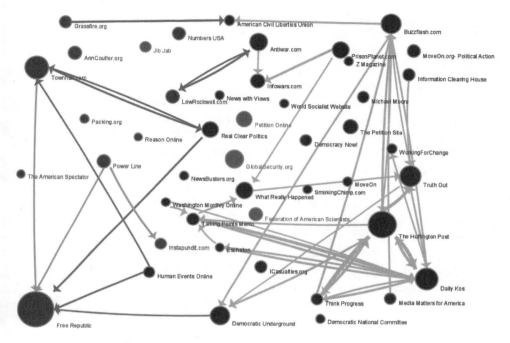

FIG. 1

sionals—hardly a representative cross section of American society. Bloggers were also overwhelmingly white and male and extraordinarily well educated: roughly two-thirds had attended an elite college or university, and 60 percent had graduate education. Perhaps most striking, more than two-thirds of traffic within the sample went to sites of bloggers with a JD, MD, or PhD.

If we compare the thirty op-ed columnists published by the *New York Times*, the *Washington Post*, the *Wall Street Journal*, and the *Los Angeles Times* over the same period to the top thirty bloggers, the results look similarly dramatic. The bloggers are more likely to have attended a top university; while 20 percent of the op-ed columnists have a doctorate, 75 percent of the bloggers do. Moreover, the columnists provide greater substantive representation of women and ethnic minorities.

In part, the elite profile of top bloggers is good news. Nearly all of the most widely read blogs are published by individuals with professional socialization in journalism, law, or academic research. These are all areas with strict professional ethics against factual inaccuracy. Despite persistent claims that bloggers are a bunch of pajama-clad, rumor-mongering amateurs, the bloggers that actually get read are better educated and better credentialed than traditional opinion journalists.

At the same time, these findings certainly contradict the central thrust of Benkler's account. Benkler declares in reference to the mass media, "a society that depends for its public sphere on a relatively small number of actors . . . to provide most of the platform of its public sphere, is setting itself up for, at least, a form of discourse elitism." If the actors are prominent independent bloggers rather than firms, the biases may be different, and commercial pressures may play less of a role. In mainstream media, Benkler asserts, those who are "inside" the media are "able to exert substantially greater influence over the agenda, the shape of the conversation, and through these the outcomes of public discourse, than other individuals or groups in society."[44] Yet as his own examples show, elite bloggers are often able to set the agenda for the blogosphere, and occasionally they are able to set the agenda for mainstream media itself. Benkler's defense of political blogging is a call for egalitarianism. In practice, bloggers are a powerful embodiment of the "discourse elitism" he denounces.

All deliberative theorists emphasize, in different ways, the importance of inclusivity in the public sphere. Yet some theorists have long dissented from the deliberative consensus, arguing that deliberative democracy is really a rebranding of political elitism. As Lynn Sanders puts it, "some citizens are better than others at articulating their views in rational, reasonable terms," and those whose voices are left out are likely to be disproportionately female, ethnic minorities, and poor.[45] Peter Berkowitz states the case even more strongly, arguing that the inclusive rhetoric surrounding deliberative democracy is nonsense.

> Since it shifts power from the people to the best deliberators among them, deliberative democracy . . . appears to be in effect an aristocracy of intellectuals. In practice, power is likely to flow to the deans and directors, the professors and pundits, and all those who, by virtue of advanced education, quickness of thought, and fluency of speech can persuade others of their prowess in the high deliberative arts.[46]

Something very much like Berkowitz's vision has already taken hold online. The online public sphere is already a de facto aristocracy dominated by those skilled in the "high deliberative arts."

The Tail of the Blogosphere: Long, but Not Public

If the political blogosphere has promoted a form of discourse elitism, those not-so-elite sites at the bottom of the pyramid also present problems for Benkler's account. Collectively, these sites may get a substantial fraction of traffic, but any single one of them is insignificant individually. The problem is that the least trafficked sites do not seem to meet Benkler's own definition of what counts as public. And they certainly do not meet the standards of inclusivity or "publicity" endorsed by deliberative theorists.

Conversations about matters of public concern, Benkler emphasizes, are not automatically part of the public sphere. As he puts it, "dinner table conversations, grumblings at a bridge club, or private letters" do not count as part of the public sphere if "they are not later transmitted across the associational boundaries to others who are not part of the family or the bridge club."[47] This standard reminds one of the famous Zen koan about a tree falling in the forest. If someone writes about politics on his blog but nobody reads it, does it count as part of the public sphere? Benkler's answer is an unequivocal no.

The problem with this is that 99 percent of Web content about public issues doesn't qualify as part of the public sphere by this measure. Technorati is one of the most widely used indexes of blog content; as of November 2006, it claimed to track more than thirty million "active" blogs (i.e., blogs that were updated within the past three months).[48] Still, as C. Edwin Baker puts it, "on a typical day . . . over 99 percent [of these blogs] will be lucky to receive a single visit."[49] Similarly, in each of the topical political communities mapped earlier, the large majority of sites only got links in the single digits.

Online discussion is fundamentally different in one respect from conversations over a dinner table or a card table. Most online content is potentially public. As the following examples illustrate, a single link from a widely read outlet can transform an obscure blog posting into front-page news. Yet Benkler's standard suggests that content becomes part of the public sphere only when it is transmitted across associational boundaries—not a moment before. Therefore, those who control the act of transmission have the power in the online public sphere. In other words, audience matters. Not only are most bloggers not public, but they cannot become public without help from their more established colleagues.

Scandal and the Online Public Sphere

Thus far, I have presented evidence that traffic patterns on the Web do not allow for the large corps of moderately read Web sites that Benkler's account requires. I have suggested, too, that the patterns of concentration that do exist have made online discourse less accessible in some ways than traditional media outlets. Online gatekeepers are substantively less representative of the public—in terms of education, gender, and race and ethnicity—than the old media commentators that offer the most direct comparison.

Yet what of instances where the Internet has mattered? Thus far, the Internet's clearest impact on public discourse has been made through the scandals it has either discovered or allowed to unfold more rapidly. These are the sorts of incidents that have been repeated, over and over, in media accounts of why blogging matters. The resignations of Senate majority leader Trent Lott, *New York Times* editor Howell Raines, and Rep. Mark Foley have all been attributed to blog-generated pressure. The specific examples that Benkler cites, too, follow this pattern. Problems with Diebold voting machines and Sinclair Broadcasting's attempts to air an anti-Kerry documentary on the eve of the 2004 election both generated spontaneous Internet-organized campaigns. (The role of prominent liberal blogs in fueling and coordinating these efforts seems to have been crucial.)

Scandals thus seem to be something of an exception to the claims previously made. Scandals may be one area in which ordinary citizens can be heard online. Yet I argue that scandals nonetheless reveal much about the limits of the online public sphere.

Reporting scandals is an important part of the public sphere's function. Some scholars have suggested that democratic citizenship can function effectively even if citizens mostly just respond to "fire alarms" or "burglar alarms"—in other words, if they pay attention to politics only in the event of a scandal. Schudson calls this "monitorial citizenship" and argues that it is an acceptable—and far more realistic—alternative to informed citizenship.[50] Other prominent scholars have offered generally approving accounts of this notion as well.[51]

Still, it is impossible to ignore the fact that monitorial citizenship is a retreat from deliberative principles. The appeal of monitorial citizenship derives from the fact that it doesn't require the time, energy, attentiveness, or thoughtfulness that traditional republican citizenship demands. To paraphrase Oscar Wilde, monitorial citizenship doesn't take up many evenings. If we're going to evaluate the online public sphere by the standards of deliberative democracy, celebrating monitorial citizenship is simply conceding defeat.

Scandals do not constitute the sort of moral discussion that some theorists take to be a central justification for deliberation.[52] For one thing, they do not typically involve areas of tough moral disagreement. There was little debate about whether Rep. Mark Foley should have been sexually propositioning underage House pages. No one thought that CBS should base its reporting on forged documents. Partisans and pundits may have disagreed about the precise meaning of Trent Lott's remarks at Senator Strom Thurmond's birthday party, yet both sides loudly repudiated the segregationist ideals that underpinned Thurmond's 1948 presidential campaign. In short, scandals are powerful political moments because they accuse public figures of doing things that the public already agrees are unacceptable.

Scandals are thus unusual. They represent political information of extremely high value, appeal to widely shared political values, and are usually easy to understand. Most often, scandals also involve information that serves the interests of one set of partisans or another. All of these characteristics make scandals exceptionally transmissible within networks.

The fear is that those at the bottom will only get noticed when what they have to say is congruent with the views and interests of the gatekeepers. In part, it is this fear that pushes Benkler to reject commercial media—which he suggests do a fine job of covering issues that will bring them commercial success. It is only when the interests of the media do not align with the interests of the public that problems ensue. Scandals do not test this proposition.

Moreover, the details of the most prominent blog-driven scandals don't seem to include much of a role for ordinary citizens. Consider the incident that right-leaning bloggers branded as "Rathergate." On September 8, 2004, CBS claimed to have unearthed documents from the Vietnam War era proving that George W. Bush, then a lieutenant in the National Guard, had not completed his service. Late that same night, a posting on the conservative forum FreeRepublic.com claimed that the report was based on forged documents. The apparent forgery was publicized by conservative bloggers and (subsequently) by traditional media. NBC ultimately said that it could not substantiate the documents, firing the report's producer. When Rather retired in March 2005, many suggested that the controversy served to shorten his tenure.[53]

Initial media coverage suggested that this was a clear instance of the Internet empowering the voiceless such that an online "nobody" could take down the biggest of "big media" Goliaths. Yet when the *Los Angeles Times* tracked down the pseudonymous poster who had made the initial claim of forgery, they found that "Buckhead" was the alter ego of Harry MacDougald, a prominent Atlanta lawyer and well-known GOP activist.[54] In the aftermath of the Lewinsky affair, MacDougald had led the national fight to disbar President Clinton over perjury charges.

A remarkably similar story has emerged concerning the Mark Foley scandal. On September 24, 2006, copies of Foley's suggestive e-mails to a male House page of high school age were posted on an obscure blog. These e-mails were linked to by Wonkette (a prominent blog focused on political gossip) on September 27 and broadcast by ABC News's Brian Ross on September 28. Ross had received copies of the e-mails more than a month earlier but did not report on them until after the Wonkette blog highlighted the story. (Subsequent investigations found both more explicitly sexual content and evidence that House Republican leadership had long known about Foley's behavior.) Here, too, the initial narrative suggested that the Internet had allowed an ordinary citizen to take down a congressman. In fact, subsequent coverage revealed that the anonymous blogger who published the e-mails was Lane Hudson, a professional staffer at the Human Rights Campaign, the nation's largest gay and lesbian advocacy group. According to published reports, Hudson initially received copies of the e-mails through his work with the organization but was prevented by his superiors from going to the media with them.[55]

In two of the clearest incidents of blog influence, then, the story was not about empowering ordinary citizens. On the contrary, the moral seems to be that the Internet gives prominent activists, disgruntled professional staffers, and other existing political elites the means to circumvent long-standing institutional constraints. This may be a good thing for democratic practice, at least in some circumstances. But to conclude from such experiences that the Internet is "democratizing" politics is simply to misunderstand the phenomenon.

Conclusion

It is perhaps unfair of me to criticize a few chapters of Benkler's much larger book and ignore the rest—particularly when the project as a whole is so valuable. Collective action is at the heart of politics, and few accounts of collective action in the information age have the depth and richness of Benkler's. If we want to understand what the Internet means for political life—indeed, why the blogosphere is possible in the first place—Benkler provides myriad insights.

It is therefore important not to overstate my disagreements with Benkler. These center on my claim that collective political debate is different from the many other areas of online collective action that Benkler elucidates so well. For example, in discussing the successes of open-source software, Benkler describes the governance structure of these projects as "meritocracy"—hierarchy, but soft hierarchy. Hierarchy works in software programming in part because code can be judged by essentially objective standards: how fast the code runs, how straightforward it is to understand, how resistant is it to those who would try to break it. In this realm, Benkler's arguments about community production are exactly right, because what we care about is the final software product. In open-source software, grossly unequal contributions are perfectly acceptable; it is fine if most development work is done by a small core group while everyone else just finds and fixes bugs.

Benkler's account works well for other forms of political-minded, community-based production, too. If what we want is accurate, well-written entries in Wikipedia, then these hierarchies of online life are a good thing. The top political bloggers are undoubtedly good at what they do. The content on the top political blogs is consistently smart and factually accurate. Few scholars explain why this is so as well as Benkler does.

Yet well-written, credible blog entries are not all that we care about. Deliberative democrats propose that the public sphere is not a product but a process, and this process requires a level of conversational equality that is missing online. From Habermas onward, the goal has been to provide a public sphere where all citizens have a more equal say. Simply put, that has not happened. Talk about "collaborative filtering" or "meritocracy" cannot paper over the enormous online divide whereby a few dozen educational and professional elites get more attention than the rest of the citizenry combined. In a world of thirty million active blogs, most citizens are more likely to win the lottery than to receive a front-page link on DailyKos or Instapundit.

Deliberative theorists argue that the advantages of deliberation are both moral and epistemic—that the conclusions that deliberation comes to are both reliable and fair. Yet thus far, online political discussion seems to provide more of the epistemic advantages than the moral ones. Deliberative democracy asks a lot of those who participate in the public sphere.

Those who run top political outlets are far better trained and equipped to meet deliberative demands than most citizens are. In this sense, the "discourse elitism" that Benkler decries is a partial blessing.

Nonetheless, the central problem with the online public sphere is that it excludes so many citizens. It is bewildering—and darkly humorous—to see white, male bloggers with Ivy League degrees writing about how the Internet is empowering "ordinary citizens." What they really mean by this is that the Internet is empowering people like themselves.

NOTES

1. L. Rainie and J. Horrigan, "Election 2006 Online," January 17, 2007, http://www.pewinternet.org/pdfs/PIP_Politics_2006.pdf.

2. A. Lenhart and S. Fox, "Bloggers: A Portrait of the Internet's New Storytellers" (Washington, DC: Pew Internet and American Life Project, 2006), http://www.pewinternet.org/pdfs/PIP%20Bloggers%20Report%20July%2019%202006.pdf.

3. C. R. Sunstein, *Infotopia* (Oxford: Oxford University Press, 2006).

4. R. Rogers, *Information Politics on the Web* (Cambridge, MA: MIT Press, 2004), 3.

5. A. Chadwick, *Internet Politics* (Oxford: Oxford University Press, 2006).

6. D. Drezner and H. Farrell, "Web of Influence," *Foreign Policy* 145 (2004): 32–40.

7. Y. Benkler, *The Wealth of Networks* (New Haven, CT: Yale University Press, 2006).

8. See also Prior's essay in this volume.

9. G. R. Chaddock, "Their Clout Rising, Blogs Are Courted by Washington's Elite," *Christian Science Monitor*, October 27, 2005; J. Shafer, "Judith Miller's New Excuse," *Slate*, March 16, 2006, http://www.slate.com/id/2138161/.

10. N. M. Levey, "Anti-Foley Blogger Speaks Out," *Los Angeles Times*, November 10, 2006, A13.

11. H. Yeager, "Blogs, Bias, and 24-Hour News," *Financial Times*, September 24, 2006.

12. J. Habermas, *The Structural Transformation of the Public Sphere*, trans. T. Burger (Cambridge, MA: MIT Press, 1989; originally published in French in 1962); J. Habermas, *The Theory of Communicative Action*, Vol. 1 (Boston: Beacon, 1984); J. Habermas, *Between Facts and Norms*, trans. W. Rehg (Cambridge, MA: MIT Press, 1996).

13. J. Rawls, *Political Liberalism* (New York: Columbia University Press, 2005).

14. J. Cohen, "Deliberation and Democratic Legitimacy," in *Deliberative Democracy: Essays on Reason and Politics*, ed. J. Bohman and W. Rehg (Cambridge, MA: MIT Press, 1997), 67–91.

15. C. S. Nino, *The Constitution of Deliberative Democracy* (New Haven, CT: Yale University Press, 1998).

16. A. Gutmann and D. Thompson, *Democracy and Disagreement* (Cambridge, MA: Harvard University Press, 1996).

17. J. S. Dryzek, *Deliberative Democracy and Beyond* (Oxford: Oxford University Press, 2002).

18. B. Ackerman and J. S. Fishkin, *Deliberation Day* (New Haven, CT: Yale University Press, 2004).

19. C. R. Sunstein, *Republic.com* (Princeton, NJ: Princeton University Press, 2001).

20. Benkler, *The Wealth of Networks*, 182.

21. E.g., L. Dahlberg, "The Internet and Democratic Discourse: Exploring the Prospects of Online Deliberative Forums Extending the Public Sphere," *Information, Communication, and Society* 4, no. 4 (2001): 615–33.

22. Chadwick, *Internet Politics*, 102.

23. Benkler, *The Wealth of Networks*, 177.

24. Ibid., 10.

25. Ibid., 239.

26. Ibid., 242.

27. Ibid., 248.

28. Sunstein, *Infotopia*, 185–86.

29. D. Drezner and H. Farrell, "The Power and Politics of Blogs" (paper presented at the annual convention of the American Political Science Association, Chicago, September 2–5, 2004).

30. B. von Sternberg, "From Geek to Chic: Blogs Gain Influence," *Star Tribune* (Minneapolis), September 22, 2004.

31. G. Reynolds, *An Army of Davids: How Markets and Technology Empower Ordinary People to Beat Big Media, Big Government, and Other Goliaths* (Nashville, TN: Nelson Current, 2006).

32. H. Hewitt, *Blog: Understanding the Information Reformation That's Changing Your World* (Nashville, TN: Nelson Business, 2005).

33. J. Armstrong and M. M. Zuniga, *Crashing the Gate. Netroots, Grassroots, and the Rise of People-Powered Politics* (White River Junction, VT: Chelsea Green, 2006).

34. D. M. Pennock and others, "Winners Don't Take All: Characterizing the Competition for Links on the Web," *Proceedings of the National Academy of Sciences* 99, no. 8 (2002): 5207–11.

35. E.g., A.-L. Barabási, *Linked: The New Science of Networks* (Cambridge, MA: Perseus, 2002); B. A. Huberman, *The Laws of the Web: Patterns in the Ecology of Information* (Cambridge, MA: MIT Press, 2001).

36. Drezner and Farrell, "The Power and Politics of Blogs."

37. L. A. Adamic and N. Glance, "The Political Blogosphere and the 2004 U.S. Election: Divided They Blog," *Proceedings of the 3rd International Workshop on Link Discovery* (New York: ACM, 2005), 36–43.

38. M. Hindman, K. Tsioutsiouliklis, and J. A. Johnson, "Googlearchy: How a Few Heavily-Linked Sites Dominate Politics on the Web" (paper presented at the annual meeting of the Midwest Political Science Association, Chicago IL, April 15–18, 2003).

39. M. Hindman, *The Myth of Digital Democracy* (Princeton, NJ: Princeton University Press, forthcoming).

40. C. Paterson, "News Agency Dominance in International News on the Internet," in *Converging Media, Diverging Politics: A Political Economy of the News Media in the United States and Canada*, ed. D. Skinner, J. Compton, and M. Gasher (Lantham, MD: Lexington, 2005), 145–64.

41. Benkler, *The Wealth of Networks*, 204.

42. Hindman, *The Myth of Digital Democracy*.

43. N. Z. Bear, "Blogging Ecosystem Project," data aggregated by Sitemeter.com, http://truthlaidbear.com/TrafficRanking.php (accessed December 2004).

44. Benkler, *The Wealth of Networks*, 204.

45. L. M. Sanders, "Against Deliberation," *Political Theory* 25, no. 3 (1997): 348. See also I. M. Young, *Inclusion and Democracy* (Oxford: Oxford University Press, 2002).

46. P. Berkowitz, "The Debating Society," *New Republic*, November 26, 1996, 36.

47. Benkler, *The Wealth of Networks*, 177.

48. BBC News, "Blogosphere Shows Healthy Growth," November 8, 2006, http://news.bbc.co.uk/2/hi/technology/6129496.stm.

49. C. E. Baker, *Media Concentration and Democracy: Why Ownership Matters* (New York: Cambridge University Press, 2007).

50. M. Schudson, *The Good Citizen: A History of American Civic Life* (New York: Free Press, 1998).

51. J. Zaller, "A New Standard of News Quality: Burglar Alarms for the Monitorial Citizen," *Political Communication* 20, no. 2 (2003): 109–30; D. Graber, "Mediated Politics and Citizenship in the 21st Century," *Annual Review of Psychology* 55 (2004): 545–71. See also Prior's essay in the present volume. But see W. L. Bennett, "The Burglar Alarm That Just Keeps Ringing: A Response to Zaller," *Political Communication* 20, no. 2 (2003): 131–38.

52. E.g., Gutmann and Thompson, *Democracy and Disagreement*.

53. J. Walsh, "Who Killed Dan Rather?" *Slate*, March 9, 2005, http://archive.salon.com/opinion/feature/2005/03/09/rather/index.html.

54. P. Wallsten, "'Buckhead,' Who Said CBS Memos Were Forged, Is a GOP-Linked Attorney," *Seattle Times*, September 18, 2004, http://seattletimes.nwsource.com/html/nationworld/2002039080_buckhead18 .html.

55. Levey, "Anti-Foley Blogger Speaks Out."

Selected Bibliography

Adam, A. K. M. *Faithful Interpretations.* Minneapolis: Fortress, 2006.

Adam, A. K. M. "Integral and Differential Hermeneutics." In *The Meanings We Choose: Hermeneutical Ethics, Indeterminancy, and the Conflict of Interpretations,* ed. Charles Cosgrove, 24–38. Edinburgh: T and T Clark, 2004.

Adamic, L. A. "The Small World Web." Paper presented at the European Conference on Digital Laboratories, Paris, 1999.

Adamic, L. A., and E. Adar. "Friends and Neighbors on the Web." *Social Networks* 25, no. 3 (2003): 211–30.

Adamic, L. A., O. Buyukkokten, and E. Adar. "A Social Network Caught in the Web." *First Monday* 8, no. 6 (2003). http://firstmonday.org/issues/issue8_6/adamic/.

Adamic, L. A., and N. Glance. "The Political Blogosphere and the 2004 U.S. Election: Divided They Blog." In *Proceedings of the 3rd International Workshop on Link Discovery,* 36–43. New York: ACM, 2005.

Adamic, L. A., and B. A. Huberman. "The Web's Hidden Order." *Communications of the ACM* 44, no. 9 (2001): 55–59.

Adar, E. "GUESS: A Language and Interface for Graph Exploration." In *CHI 06: Proceedings of the SIGCHI Conference on Human Factors in Computing Systems,* 791–800. New York: ACM Press, 2006.

Adar, E., L. Zhang, L. A. Adamic, and R. M. Lukose. "Implicit Structure and the Dynamics of Blogspace." Paper presented at the Workshop on the Weblogging Ecosystem, New York, May 18, 2004.

Akerman, J. R. "American Promotional Road Mapping in the Twentieth Century." *Cartography and Geographic Information Science* 29, no. 3 (2002): 175–91.

Ali-Hasan, N., and L. A. Adamic. "Expressing Social Relationships on the Blog through Links and Comments." Paper presented at the International Conference on Weblogs and Social Media, Boulder, CO, March 26–28, 2007.

American Association for the Advancement of Science (AAAS). "Geospatial Technologies and Human Rights." 2007. http://shr.aaas.org/geotech/whatcanGIS do.shtml.

Anderson, B. *Imagined Communities.* Rev. ed. London: Verso, 1991.

Anderson, C. *The Long Tail: Why the Future of Business Is Selling Less of More.* New York: Hyperion, 2006.

Armstrong, J., and M. M. Zuniga. *Crashing the Gate: Netroots, Grassroots, and the Rise of People-Powered Politics.* White River Junction, VT: Chelsea Green, 2006.

Arquilla, J., and D. F. Ronfeldt. *Networks and Netwars: The Future of Terror, Crime, and Militancy.* Santa Monica, CA: Rand Corporation, 2001.

Aufderheide, P. "Competition and Commons: The Public Interest in and after the AOL-Time Warner Merger." *Journal of Broadcasting and Electronic Media* 46, no. 4 (2002): 515–32.

Baker, C. E. *Media Concentration and Democracy: Why Ownership Matters.* New York: Cambridge University Press, 2007.

Balkin, J. M. "Digital Speech and Democratic Culture: A Theory of Freedom of Expression for the Information Society." *New York University Law Review* 79, no. 1 (2006). http://www.law.nyu.edu/journals/lawreview/issues/vol79/no1/ NYU 101.pdf.

Barabási, A.-L. *Linked: The New Science of Networks.* Cambridge, MA: Perseus, 2002.

Barabási, A.-L. "The Physics of the Web." *Physics World*, July 2001. http://physics web.org/articles/world/14/7/9.

Barabási, A.-L., and R. Albert. "Emergence of Scaling in Random Networks." *Science* 286, no. 5439 (1999): 509–12.

Bardini, T. "Bridging the Gulfs: From Hypertext to Cyberspace." *Journal of Computer-Mediated Communication* 3, no. 2 (1997). http://jcmc.indiana.edu/vol3/issue2/bardini.html.

Bar-Ilan, J. "Google Bombing from a Time Perspective." *Journal of Computer-Mediated Communication* 12, no. 3 (2007). http://jcmc.indiana.edu/vol12/issue3/bar-ilan.html.

Barnhurst, K. "News Geography and Monopoly," *Journalism Studies*, 3, no. 4 (November 2002): 477–89, http://www.ksg.harvard.edu/presspol/research_publica tions/papers/working_papers/2002_2.pdf.

Battelle, J. *The Search: How Google and Its Rivals Rewrote the Rules of Business and Transformed Our Culture.* New York: Portfolio, 2005.

Baudrillard, J. "Simulacra and Simulation." In *Jean Baudrillard, Selected Writings*, ed. Mark Poster, 166–84. Stanford: Stanford University Press, 1988.

Baudrillard, J. *Simulations.* New York: Semiotext(e), 1983.

Benkler, Y. *The Wealth of Networks: How Social Production Transforms Markets and Freedom.* New Haven, CT: Yale University Press, 2006.

Bennett, W. L. "The Burglar Alarm That Just Keeps Ringing: A Response to Zaller." *Political Communication* 20, no. 2 (2003): 131–38.

Berkowitz, P. "The Debating Society." *New Republic*, November 26, 1996, 36.

Blood, R. *The Weblog Handbook: Practical Advice on Creating and Maintaining Your Blog.* Cambridge, MA: Perseus, 2002.

Blumer, H. "The Field of Collective Behavior." In *New Outlines of the Principles of Sociology*, ed. A. M. Lee, 167–222. New York: Barnes and Noble, 1946.

Boczkowski, P. J. *Digitizing the News: Innovation in Online Newspapers.* Cambridge, MA: MIT Press, 2004.

Boczkowski, P. J., and M. de Santos. "When More Media Equals Less News: Patterns of Content Homogenization in Argentina's Leading Print and Online Newspapers." *Political Communication* 24 no. 2 (April 2007): 167–80.

Bonfadelli, H. "The Internet and Knowledge Gaps: A Theoretical and Empirical Investigation." *European Journal of Communication* 17, no. 1 (2002): 65–84.

Brin, S., and L. Page. "The Anatomy of a Large-Scale Hypertextual Web Search Engine." *WWW7 / Computer Networks* 30, nos. 1–7 (1998): 107–17.

Brooks, T. A. "Private Acts and Public Objects: An Investigation of Citer Motivations." *Journal of the American Society for Information Science* 36, no. 4 (1985): 223–29.

Buckland, M. K. "Emanuel Goldberg, Electronic Document Retrieval and Vannevar Bush's Memex." *Information Science* 43, no. 4 (May 1992): 284–94.

Buisseret, D. *Monarchs, Ministers, and Maps: The Emergence of Cartography as a Tool of Government in Early Modern Europe.* Chicago: University of Chicago Press, 1992.

Bunge, W. "The First Years of the Detroit Geographical Expedition: A Personal Report." In *Radical Geography*, ed. R. Peet, 31–39. Chicago: Maroufa, 1969.

Bunge, W. *Geography of a Revolution.* Morristown, NJ: Schenkman, 1971.

Bush, V. "As We May Think." *Atlantic Monthly*, July 1945. http://www.theatlantic.com/doc/194507/bush.

Carpini, M. X. D., and S. Keeter. *What Americans Know about Politics and Why It Matters.* New Haven, CT: Yale University Press, 1996.

Casson, H. N. *The History of the Telephone.* Chicago: A. C. McClurg and Company, 1910.

Castells, M. *The Internet Galaxy: Reflections on the Internet, Business, and Society.* Oxford: Oxford University Press, 2001.

Castells, M. *The Rise of the Network Society.* Oxford: Blackwell, 1996.

Chaddock, G. R. "Their Clout Rising, Blogs Are Courted by Washington's Elite." *Christian Science Monitor*, October 27, 2005.

Chadwick, A. *Internet Politics.* Oxford: Oxford University Press, 2006.

Chakraborty, J., and M. M. Bosman. "Measuring the Digital Divide in the United States: Race, Income, and Personal Computer Ownership." *Professional Geographer* 57, no. 3 (2005): 395–410.

Chrisman, N. *Charting the Unknown: How Computer Mapping at Harvard Became GIS.* Redlands, CA: ESRI Press, 2006.

Chwe, M. S. Y. *Rational Ritual: Culture, Coordination, and Common Knowledge.* Princeton, NJ: Princeton University Press, 2001.

Ciszek, T., and X. Fu. "An Annotation Paradigm: The Social Hyperlink." In *Proceedings of the American Society for Information Science and Technology* 42, no. 1 (2005). http://www3.interscience.wiley.com.

Clout, H. "Geographers in Their Ivory Tower: Academic Geography and Popular Geography in Paris 1931." *Geografiska Annaler Series B Human Geography* 87, no. 1 (2005): 15–29.

Cohen, J. "Deliberation and Democratic Legitimacy." In *Deliberative Democracy: Essays on Reason and Politics*, ed. J. Bohman and W. Rehg, 67–91. Cambridge, MA: MIT Press, 1997.

Collingwood, R. G. *The Idea of History.* Rev. ed. Oxford: Oxford University Press, 1994.

Cosgrove, D. E., and V. della Dora. "Mapping Global War: Los Angeles, the Pacific, and Charles Owens's Pictorial Cartography." *Annals of the Association of American Geographers* 95, no. 2 (2005): 373–90.

Cover, R. "Audience inter/active: Interactive Media, Narrative Control, and

Reconceiving Audience History." *New Media and Society* 8, no. 1 (2006): 139–58.

Crang, M., T. Crosbie, and S. Graham. "Variable Geometries of Connection: Urban Digital Divides and the Uses of Information Technology." *Urban Studies* 43, no. 13 (2006): 2551–70.

Curry, M. R. "The Digital Individual and the Private Realm." *Annals of the Association of American Geographers* 87, no. 4 (1997): 681–99.

Dahlberg, L. "The Corporate Colonization of Online Attention and the Marginalization of Critical Communication?" *Journal of Communication Inquiry* 29, no. 2 (2005): 160–80.

Dahlberg, L. "The Internet and Democratic Discourse: Exploring the Prospects of Online Deliberative Forums Extending the Public Sphere." *Information, Communication, and Society* 4, no. 4 (2001): 615–33.

DellaVigna, S., and E. Kaplan. "The Fox News Effect: Media Bias and Voting." (April 2006). NBER Working Paper No. W12169 available at SSRN: http://ssrn.com/abstract=897023.

DeSanctis, G., and M. S. Poole. "Capturing the Complexity in Advanced Technology Use: Adaptive Structuration Theory." *Organization Science* 5, no. 2 (1994): 121–47.

Deutsch, K. *The Nerves of Government.* New York: Free Press, 1966.

Deuze, M. A. "The Web and Its Journalisms: Considering the Consequences of Different Types of Newsmedia Online." *New Media and Society* 5, no. 2 (2003): 203–30.

DiMaggio, P., E. Hargittai, C. Celeste, and S. Shafer. "Digital Inequality: From Unequal Access to Differentiated Use." In *Social Inequality*, ed. K. M. Neckerman, 355–400. New York: Russell Sage Foundation, 2004.

DiMaggio, P., and K. Sato. "Does the Internet Balkanize Political Attention? A Test of the Sunstein Theory." Paper presented to the American Sociological Association, Atlanta, GA, April 16, 2003.

Dimitrova, D. V., C. Connolly-Ahern, A. P. Williams, L. Kaid, and A. Reid. "Hyperlinking as Gatekeeping: Online Newspaper Coverage of the Execution of an American Terrorist." *Journalism Studies* 4, no. 3 (2003): 401–14.

Doland, P. J. "Genius Grant Please, or The NSFW HTML Attribute." *Frosty Mug Revolution*, December 28, 2006. http://pj.doland.org/archives/041571.php.

Downs, A. *An Economic Theory of Democracy.* New York: Harper and Row, 1957.

Downs, R. M., and L. S. Liben. "Through a Map Darkly: Understanding Maps as Representations." *Genetic Epistemologist* 16 (1988): 11–18.

Drezner, D., and H. Farrell. "The Power and Politics of Blogs." Paper presented at the annual convention of the American Political Science Association, September 2–5, 2004.

Dryzek, J. S. *Deliberative Democracy and Beyond.* Oxford: Oxford University Press, 2002.

Dykes, J., A. M. MacEachren, and M. J. Kraak. *Exploring Geovisualization.* Amsterdam: Elsevier, 2005.

Edney, M. H. "The Origins and Development of J. B. Harley's Cartographic Theories." *Cartographica* 40, nos. 1–2 (Spring–Summer 2005).

Edwards, E. *Saving Graces: Finding Solace and Strength from Friends and Strangers.* New York: Broadway, 2006.

Egghe, L. "New Informetric Aspects of the Internet: Some Reflections—Many Problems." *Journal of Information Science* 26, no. 5 (2000): 329–35.

Eisenstein, E. L. *The Printing Press as an Agent of Change: Communications and Cultural Transformations in Early-Modern Europe.* Vol. 1. Cambridge: Cambridge University Press, 1979.

Elberse, A., and F. Oberholzer-Gee. "Superstars and Underdogs: An Examination of the Long Tail Phenomenon in Video Sales." Working paper no. 07–015, Division of Research, Harvard Business School, 2007.

Elwood, S. "Beyond Cooptation or Resistance: Urban Spatial Politics, Community Organizations, and GIS-Based Spatial Narratives." *Annals of the Association of American Geographers* 96, no. 2 (2006): 323–41.

Elwood, S. "Negotiating Knowledge Production: The Everyday Inclusions, Exclusions, and Contradictions of Participatory GIS Research." *Professional Geographer* 58, no. 2 (2006): 197–208.

Engelbart, D. "The Click Heard Round the World." *Wired* 12, no. 1 (2004). http://www.wired.com/wired/archive/12.01/mouse.html.

Entman, R. M. "Framing: Toward Clarification of a Fractured Paradigm." *Journal of Communication* 43, no. 4 (1993): 51–58.

Erikson, E. H. *Identity, Youth, and Crisis.* New York: Norton, 1968.

Erle, S., R. Gibson, and J. Walsh. *Mapping Hacks.* Sebastopol, CA: O'Reilly, 2005.

Ettema, J. S., and D. C. Whitney. "The Money Arrow: An Introduction to Audiencemaking." In *Audiencemaking: How the Media Create the Audience,* 1–18. Thousand Oaks, CA: Sage, 1994.

Fallows, D. *Search Engine Users.* Washington, DC: Pew Internet and American Life Project, 2005.

Ferguson, D. A., and E. M. Perse. "The World Wide Web as a Functional Alternative to Television." *Journal of Broadcasting and Electronic Media* 44, no. 2 (2000): 155–74.

Festinger, L. *A Theory of Cognitive Dissonance.* Stanford, CA: Stanford University Press, 1957.

Fishman, M. *Manufacturing the News.* Austin: University of Texas Press, 1980.

Foucault, M. *Society Must Be Defended: Lectures at the College De France, 1975–1976.* New York: Picador, 2003.

Freeman, L. C. "Centrality in Social Networks: Conceptual Clarification." *Social Networks* 1, no. 3 (1979): 215–39.

Gans, H. J. *Deciding What's News: A Study of "CBS Evening News," "NBC Nightly News," "Newsweek," and "Time."* New York: Pantheon, 1979.

Garfield, E. "Citation Behavior: An Aid or a Hindrance to Information Retrieval?" *Current Contents* 18 (1989): 3–8.

Gerhart, S. L. "Do Web Search Engines Suppress Controversy?" *First Monday* 9, no. 1 (2004). http://firstmonday.org/issues/issue9_1/gerhart/index.html.

Giddens, A. *The Constitution of Society: Outline of the Theory of Structuration.* Berkeley: University of California Press, 1984.

Gilbert, G. N. "Referencing as Persuasion." *Social Studies of Science* 7, no. 1 (1977): 113–22.

Gillmor, D. *We the Media: Grassroots Journalism by the People, for the People.* Sebastopol, CA: O'Reilly, 2006.

Gitlin, T. "Public Sphere or Public Sphericules?" In *Media, Ritual, and Identity*, ed. T. Liebes and J. Curran, 175–202. London: Routledge, 1998.

Gitlin, T. *The Whole World Is Watching: Mass Media in the Making and Unmaking of the New Left.* 2nd ed. Berkeley: University of California Press, 2003.

Giuffo, J. "The Web: Unlock Those Links." *Columbia Journalism Review*, September–October 2002, 9.

Glaser, M. "Open Season: News Sites Add Outside Links, Free Content." *Online Journalism Review*, October 19, 2004. http://www.ojr.org/ojr/glaser/1098225187.php.

Goffman, E. *Frame Analysis: An Essay on the Organization of Experience.* New York: Harper and Row, 1974.

Goffman, E. *Relations in Public: Microstudies of the Public Order.* Harmondsworth: Penguin, 1972.

Graber, D. "Mediated Politics and Citizenship in the 21st Century." *Annual Review of Psychology* 55 (2004): 545–71.

Grafton, A. *The Footnote: A Curious History.* Cambridge, MA: Harvard University Press, 1999.

Granovetter, M. S. "The Strength of Weak Ties." *American Journal of Sociology* 78, no. 6 (1973): 1360–80.

Gutmann, A., and D. Thompson. *Democracy and Disagreement.* Cambridge, MA: Harvard University Press, 1996.

Habermas, J. *Between Facts and Norms.* Trans. W. Rehg. Cambridge, MA: MIT Press, 1996.

Habermas, J. *The Structural Transformation of the Public Sphere.* Trans. T. Burger. Cambridge, MA: MIT Press, 1989. Originally published in French in 1962.

Habermas, J. *The Theory of Communicative Action.* Vol. 1. Boston: Beacon, 1984.

Halavais, A. "Informational City Limits: Cities and the Infostructure of the WWW." Paper presented at the workshop "Cities in the Global Information Society: An International Perspective," Newcastle upon Tyne, November 1999.

Halavais, A. "National Borders on the World Wide Web." *New Media and Society* 2, no. 1 (2000): 7.

Hall, E. *The Hidden Dimension.* New York: Doubleday, 1966.

Hamilton, J. T. *All the News That's Fit to Sell: How the Market Transforms Information into News.* Princeton, NJ: Princeton University Press, 2004.

Hargittai, E. "Classifying and Coding Online Actions." *Social Science Computer Review* 22, no. 2 (2004): 210–27.

Hargittai, E. "A Framework for Studying Differences in People's Digital Media Uses." In *Cyberworld Unlimited? Digital Inequality and New Spaces of Informal Education for Young People*, ed. N. Kutscher and H.-U. Otto. Forthcoming.

Hargittai E. "How Wide a Web? Inequalities in Accessing Information Online." PhD diss., Department of Sociology, Princeton University, 2003.

Hargittai, E. "Hurdles to Information Seeking: Spelling and Typographical Mistakes during Users' Online Behavior." *Journal of the Association for Information*

Systems 7, no. 1 (2006). http://jais.aisnet.org/articles/default.asp?vol=7&art=1.

Hargittai E. "Second-Level Digital Divide: Differences in People's Online Skills." *First Monday* 7, no. 4 (2002): 1–18.

Hargittai E. "Serving Citizen's Needs: Minimizing Online Hurdles to Accessing Government Information." *IT and Society* 3, no. 3 (2003): 27–41.

Hargittai, E. "Survey Measures of Web-Oriented Digital Literacy." *Social Science Computer Review* 23, no. 3 (2005): 371–79.

Hargittai, E., J. Gallo, and M. Y. Kane. "Cross-Ideological Discussions among a Group of Conservative and Liberal Bloggers." Unpublished ms.

Harley, J. B., M. Warhus, and E. Hanlon. *Maps and the Columbian Encounter: An Interpretive Guide to the Traveling Exhibition; American Geographical Society Collection.* Milwaukee: Golda Meir Library, University of Wisconsin, 1990.

Harris, L. M., and H. D. Hazen. "Power of Maps: (Counter)Mapping for Conservation." *ACME* 4, no. 1 (2006): 99–130.

Harrison, R. E. *Look at the World: The Fortune Atlas for World Strategy.* New York: Knopf, 1944.

Hartley, J. "Journalism as a Human Right: A Cultural Approach to Journalism." In *Journalism Research in an Era of Globalization,* ed. M. Loeffelholz and D. Weaver, 39–51. London: Routledge, 2005.

Herman, E. S., and N. Chomsky. *Manufacturing Consent: The Political Economy of the Mass Media.* New York: Pantheon, 2002.

Herring, S. C., I. Kouper, J. C. Paolillo, L. A. Scheidt, M. Tyworth, P. Welsch, E. Wright, and N. Yu. "Conversations in the Blogosphere: An Analysis 'from the Bottom Up.'" In *Proceedings of the 38th Hawaii International Conference on System Sciences,* 107–18. Los Alamitos: IEEE Press, 2005.

Hewitt, H. *Blog: Understanding the Information Reformation That's Changing Your World.* Nashville, TN: Nelson Business, 2005.

Heylighten, F., and J. Bollen. "The World-Wide Web as a Super-Brain: From Metaphor to Model." In *Cybernetics and Systems '96,* ed. R. Trappl, 917–22. Vienna: Austrian Society for Cybernetics, 1996.

Hinckle, W. *If You Have a Lemon, Make Lemonade.* New York: Putnam, 1974.

Hindman, M. "A Mile Wide and an Inch Deep: Measuring Media Diversity Online and Offline." In *Media Diversity and Localism: Meaning and Metrics,* ed. P. Napoli, 327–47. Mahwah, NJ: Erlbaum, 2006.

Hindman, M., K. Tsioutsiouliklis, and J. A. Johnson. "Googlearchy: How a Few Heavily-Linked Sites Dominate Politics on the Web." Paper presented at the annual meeting of the Midwest Political Science Association, Chicago, IL, April 15–18, 2003.

Hine, C. "Web Pages, Authors, and Audiences: The Meaning of a Mouse Click." *Information, Communication, and Society* 4, no. 2 (2001): 182–98.

Holmes, N. "The KWIC and the Dead: A Lesson in Computing History." *Computer* 34, no. 1 (2001): 144.

Horrigan, J., K. Garrett, and P. Resnick. *The Internet and Democratic Debate.* Washington, DC: Pew Internet and American Life Project, 2004.

Howard, P. N., and A. Massanari. "Learning to Search and Searching to Learn: Income, Education, and Experience Online." *Journal of Computer-Mediated Com-*

munication 12, no. 3 (2007). http://www.jcmc.indiana.edu/vol12/issue3/howard
.html.

Hoyt, L., R. Khosla, and C. Canepa. "Leaves, Pebbles, and Chalk: Building a Public Participation GIS in New Delhi, India." *Journal of Urban Technology* 12, no. 1 (2005): 1–19.

Huberman, B. A. *The Laws of the Web: Patterns in the Ecology of Information.* Cambridge, MA: MIT Press, 2001.

Huckfeldt, R. R., P. E. Johnson, and J. D. Sprague. *Political Disagreement: The Survival of Diverse Opinions within Communication Networks.* New York: Cambridge University Press, 2004.

Huffman, M. "'Phishing' Scam Takes New Tack." *Consumer Affairs*, March 2007. http://consumeraffairs.com/news04/2007/03/phishing_tactic.html.

Introna, L. D. "Shaping the Web: Why the Politics of Search Engines Matters." *Information Society* 16, no. 3 (2000): 169–85.

Iyengar, S., K. Hahn, and M. Prior. "Has Technology Made Attention to Political Campaigns More Selective? An Experimental Study of the 2000 Presidential Campaign." Paper presented at a meeting of the American Political Science Association, San Francisco, CA, April 2001.

Jackson, M. H. "Assessing the Structure of Communication on the World Wide Web." *Journal of Computer-Mediated Communication* 3, no. 1 (1997). http://jcmc.indiana.edu/vol3/issue1/jackson.html.

Jacob, C. *The Sovereign Map: Theoretical Approaches in Cartography throughout History.* Chicago: University of Chicago Press, 2006.

Jenkins, H. *Convergence Culture: Where Old and New Media Collide.* New York: New York University Press, 2006.

Johnson, S. *The Ghost Map: The Story of London's Most Terrifying Epidemic—and How It Changed Science, Cities, and the Modern World.* New York: Riverhead, 2006.

Katz, E. "And Deliver Us from Segmentation." *Annals of the American Academy of Political and Social Science* 546, no. 1 (1996): 22–33.

Klaassen, A. "The Short Tail: How the 'Democratized' Medium Ended Up in the Hands of the Few—at Least in Terms of Ad Dollars." *Advertising Age*, November 27, 2007, 1.

Klinenberg, E. "Convergence: News Production in a Digital Age." *Annals of the American Academy of Political and Social Science* 597, no. 1 (2005): 48–64.

Koch, T. "The Map as Intent: Variations on the Theme of John Snow." *Cartographica* 39, no. 4 (2004): 1–14.

Koerner, S. L. "Consumer-Centric Research: Insight from the Inside Out." *Hub* (Association of National Advertisers), May–June 2005, 10–13.

Koopmans, R., and A. Zimmerman. "Visibility and Communication Networks on the Internet: The Role of Search Engines and Hyperlinks." Paper presented at the CONNEX workshop "A European Public Sphere: How Much of It Do We Have and How Much Do We Need?" Amsterdam, November 2–3, 2005.

Kovach, B., and T. Rosenstiel. *The Elements of Journalism: What Newspeople Should Know and the Public Should Expect.* New York: Crown, 2001.

Kuklinski, J. H., P. J. Quirk, J. Jerit, D. Schwieder, and R. F. Rich. "Misinformation and the Currency of Democratic Citizenship." *Journal of Politics* 62, no. 3 (2000): 790–816.

Lanham, R. *The Economics of Attention: Style and Substance in the Age of Information.* Chicago: University of Chicago Press, 2006.

Lasica, J. D. "Blogs and Journalism Need Each Other." *Nieman Reports* 57, no. 3 (2003): 70–74.

Lasica, J. D. "Transparency Begets Trust in the Ever-Expanding Blogosphere." *Online Journalism Review*, August 12, 2004. http://ojr.org/ojr/technology/10922 67863.php.

Lazarsfeld, P. F., and B. Berelson. *The People's Choice: How the Voter Makes Up His Mind in a Presidential Campaign.* 3rd ed. New York: Columbia University Press, 1968.

Lehman-Wilzig, S., and N. Cohen-Avigdor. "The Natural Life Cycle of New Media Evolution: Inter-Media Struggle for Survival in the Internet Age." *New Media and Society* 6, no. 6 (2004): 707–30.

Lenhart, A., and S. Fox. *Bloggers: A Portrait of the Internet's New Storytellers* (Washington, DC: Pew Internet and American Life Project, 2006). http://www.pewinternet.org/pdfs/PIP%20Bloggers%20Report%20July%2019%202006.pdf.

Lessig, L. *Free Culture: How Big Media Uses Technology and the Law to Lock Down Culture and Control Creativity.* New York: Penguin, 2004.

Lewin, K. "Frontiers in Group Dynamics," part 2, "Channels of Group Life; Social Planning and Action Research." *Human Relations* 1, no. 2 (1947): 143–53.

Lin, J., A. Halavais, and B. Zhang. "The Blog Network in America: Blogs as Indicators of Relationships among US Cities." *Connections* 27, no. 2 (2006): 15–23.

Lippmann, W. *Public Opinion.* New York: Free Press, 1922.

Lowrey, W. "Mapping the Journalism-Blogging Relationship." *Journalism* 7, no. 4 (2006): 477–500.

MacKinnon, R. "Blogging, Journalism, and Credibility." *Nation*, March 17, 2005. http://www.thenation.com/doc/20050404/mackinnon.

Marlow, C., M. Naaman, D. Boyd, and M. Davis. "HT06, Tagging Paper, Taxonomy, Flickr, Academic Article, to Read." In *Proceedings of the Seventeenth Conference on Hypertext and Hypermedia* (New York: ACM, 2006), 31–40.

McAdams, M., and S. Berger. "Hypertext." *Journal of Electronic Publishing* 6 (2001). http://www.press.umich.edu:80/jep/06-03/McAdams/pages/.

McGuire, W. J. "The Nature of Attitudes and Attitude Change." In *The Handbook of Social Psychology*, ed. L. Gardner and E. Aronson, 136–314. Reading, MA: Addison-Wesley, 1969.

McQuail, D. *Mcquail's Mass Communication Theory.* Thousand Oaks, CA: Sage, 2000.

Menczer, F., S. Fortunato, A. Flammini, and A. Vespignani. "Googlearchy or Googlocracy?" *IEEE Spectrum* 43, no. 2. http://spectrum.ieee.org/print/2787.

Mindell, D., J. Segal, and S. Gerovitch. "From Communications Engineering to Communications Science." In *Science and Ideology: A Comparative History*, ed. M. Walker, 66–96. London: Routledge, 2003.

Monmonier, M. *How to Lie with Maps.* Chicago: University of Chicago Press, 1996.

Monmonier, M. "Mapping under the Third Reich: Nazi Restrictions on Map Content and Distribution." 2005. http://www.sunysb.edu/libmap/coordinates/seriesb/no2/b2.htm.

Mouzelis, N. "The Subjectivist-Objectivist Divide: Against Transcendence." *Sociology* 34, no. 4 (2000): 741–62.

Mutz, D. C. *Hearing the Other Side: Deliberative versus Participatory Democracy*. New York: Cambridge University Press, 2006.

Mutz, D. C., and P. S. Martin. "Facilitating Communication across Lines of Political Difference: The Role of Mass Media." *American Political Science Review* 95, no. 1 (2001): 97–114.

Napoli, P. M. *Audience Economics: Media Institutions and the Audience Marketplace*. New York: Columbia University Press, 2003.

Napoli, P. M. "Deconstructing the Diversity Principle." *Journal of Communication* 49, no. 4 (1999): 7–34.

Napoli, P. M. "Evolutionary Theories of Media Institutions and Their Responses to New Technologies." In *Communication Theory: A Reader*, ed. L. Lederman, 315–29. Dubuque: IA: Kendall/Hunt, 1998.

Napoli, P. M. "The Internet and the Forces of 'Massification.'" *Electronic Journal of Communication* 8, no. 2 (1998). http://www.cios.org/www/ejc/v8n298.htm.

Negroponte, N. *Being Digital*. New York: Knopf, 1995.

Nelson, T. H. "Complex Information Processing: A File Structure for the Complex, the Changing, and the Indeterminate." In *Proceedings of the 1965 20th National Conference*, ed. Lewis Winner (New York: ACM, 1965), 84–100.

Nelson, T. H. *Remarks on Xanadu*. Maastricht: Internet Research 3.0, 2004.

Neuendorf, K. A., D. J. Atkin, and L. W. Jeffres. "Reconceptualizing Channel Repertoire in the Urban Cable Environment." *Journal of Broadcasting and Electronic Media* 45, no. 3 (2001): 464–82.

Neuman, W. R. *The Future of the Mass Audience*. New York: Cambridge University Press, 1991.

Neuman, W. R. "The Threshold of Public Attention." *Public Opinion Quarterly* 54, no. 2 (1990): 159–76.

Nino, C. S. *The Constitution of Deliberative Democracy*. New Haven, CT: Yale University Press, 1998.

Nyce, J. M., and P. Kahn. *From Memex to Hypertext: Vannevar Bush and the Mind's Machine*. San Diego: Academic Press, 1991.

Orlikowski, W. J. "The Duality of Technology: Rethinking the Concept of Technology in Organizations." *Organization Science* 3, no. 3 (1992): 398–427.

O'Sullivan, D. "Geographical Information Science: Critical GIS." *Progress in Human Geography* 30, no. 6 (2006): 783–91.

Owen, B. M., and S. S. Wildman. *Video Economics*. Cambridge, MA: Harvard University Press, 1992.

Paglen, T., and A. C. Thompson. *Torture Taxi: On the Trail of the CIA's Rendition Flights*. Hoboken, NJ: Melville House, 2006.

Pan, B., H. Hembrooke, T. Joachims, L. Lorigo, G. Gay, and L. Granka. "In Google We Trust: Users' Decisions on Rank, Position, and Relevancy." *Journal of Computer-Mediated Communication* 12, no. 3 (2007). http://www.jcmc.indiana.edu/vol12/issue3/pan.html.

Park, H. W. "Hyperlink Network Analysis: A New Method for the Study of Social Structure on the Web." *Connections* 25, no. 1 (2003): 49–61.

Park, H. W., and M. Thelwall. "Hyperlink Analyses of the World Wide Web: A

Review." *Journal of Computer-Mediated Communication* 8, no. 4 (2003). http://www.jcmc.indiana.edu/vol8/issue4/park.html.

Paterson, C. "News Agency Dominance in International News on the Internet." In *Converging Media, Diverging Politics: A Political Economy of the News Media in the United States and Canada*, ed. D. Skinner, J. Compton, and M. Gasher, 145–64. Lantham, MD: Lexington, 2005.

Pennock, D. M., G. W. Flake, S. Lawrence, E. J. Glover, and C. L. Giles. "Winners Don't Take all: Characterizing the Competition for Links on the Web." *Proceedings of the National Academy of Sciences* 99, no. 8 (2002): 5207–11.

Pew Research Center for the People and the Press. *Online Papers Modestly Boost Newspaper Readership.* 2006. http://people-press.org/reports/display.php3? PageID=1069.

Pickles, J. *Ground Truth: The Social Implications of Geographic Information Systems.* New York: Guilford Press, 1995.

Pickles, J. *A History of Spaces: Cartographic Reason, Mapping, and the Geo-Coded World.* London: Routledge, 2004.

Polanyi, M., and H. Prosch. *Meaning.* Chicago: University of Chicago Press, 1975.

Prior, M. *Post-Broadcast Democracy: How Media Choice Increases Inequality in Political Involvement and Polarizes Elections.* New York: Cambridge University Press, 2007.

Project for Excellence in Journalism. *The State of the News Media 2007.* Washington, DC, 2007.

Putnam, R. D. *Bowling Alone: The Collapse and Revival of American Community.* New York: Simon and Schuster, 2000.

Rainie, L. *Public Awareness of Internet Terms.* Washington, DC: Pew Internet and American Life Project, 2005.

Rainie, L., and J. Horrigan. "Election 2006 Online." Pew Internet and American Life Project. Washington, DC, January 17. http://www.pewinternet.org/pdfs/PIP_Politics_2006.pdf.

Raisz, E. *General Cartography.* New York: McGraw-Hill, 1948.

Ratajski, L. "Commission V of the ICA: The Tasks It Faces." *International Yearbook of Cartography* 14 (1974): 140–44.

Rawls, J. *Political Liberalism.* New York: Columbia University Press, 2005.

Rayward, W. B. "H. G. Wells's Idea of a World Brain: A Critical Reassessment." *Journal of the American Society for Information Science* 50, no. 7 (1999): 557–73.

Reynolds, G. *An Army of Davids: How Markets and Technology Empower Ordinary People to Beat Big Media, Big Government, and Other Goliaths.* Nashville, TN: Nelson Current, 2006.

Robinson, A. H. *The Look of Maps: An Examination of Cartographic Design.* Madison: University of Wisconsin Press, 1952.

Rogers, R. *Information Politics on the Web.* Cambridge, MA: MIT Press, 2004.

Rose, S. "What's Love Got to Do with It? Scholarly Citation Practices as Courtship Rituals." *Language and Learning across the Disciplines* 1, no. 3 (1996): 34–48.

Rust, R. T., W. A. Kamakura, and M. I. Alpert. "Viewer Preference Segmentation and Viewing Choice Models for Network Television." *Journal of Advertising* 21, no. 1 (1992): 1–18.

Safire, W. "Netroots." *New York Times Magazine*, November 19, 2006.

Sanders, L. M. "Against Deliberation." *Political Theory* 25, no. 3 (1997): 347–76.

Scharnhorst, A., and M. Thelwall. "Citation and Hyperlink Networks." *Current Science* 89, no. 9 (2005): 1518–23.

Schiller, Herbert. *Culture, Inc.: The Corporate Takeover of Public Expression.* New York: Oxford University Press, 1989.

Schudson, M. *The Good Citizen: A History of American Civic Life.* New York: Free Press, 1998.

Schudson, M. "Good Citizens and Bad History: Today's Political Ideals in Historical Perspective." *Communication Review* 1, no. 4 (2000): 1–20.

Schulman, S. L. "The Community-Identity Junction." Paper presented to the Interpublic Group of Cos, New York, September 15, 2006.

Schulman, S. L. "Future Thinking." Paper presented at the Family Friendly Programming Forum Conference, Los Angeles, November 28, 2006.

Schulten, S. *The Geographical Imagination in America, 1880–1950.* Chicago: University of Chicago Press, 2001.

Sears, D. O., and J. L. Freedman. "Selective Exposure to Information: A Critical Review." *Public Opinion Quarterly* 31, no. 2 (1967): 194–213.

Shafer, J. "Judith Miller's New Excuse." *Slate*, March 16, 2006. http://www.slate.com/id/2138161/.

Shannon, C. E. "A Mathematical Theory of Communication." *Bell System Technical Journal* 27, no. 3 (1948): 379–423, 623–56.

Shea, K., and J. Wesley. "How Social Networking Sites Affect Employers, Students, and Career Services." *NACE Journal* 66, no. 4 (2006): 26–32. http://www.naceweb.org.

Shi, X., and B. Tseng. "Looking at the Blogosphere Topology through Different Lenses." Paper presented at the International Conference on Weblogs and Social Media, Boulder, CO, March 26–28, 2007.

Shirky, C. "Power Laws, Weblogs, and Inequality." In *Reformatting Politics: Information Technology and Global Civil Society*, ed. J. Anderson, J. Dean, and G. Lovink, 35–42. London: Routledge, 2006.

Shiver, R. "By the Numbers." *American Journalism Review*, June–July 2006. http://www.ajr.org/article_printable.asp?id=4121.

Silverstone, R. "Mediation and Communication," in *The Sage Handbook of Sociology*, ed. C. Calhoun, C. Rojek, and B. Turner, 188–207. Thousand Oaks, CA: Sage, 2005.

Simon, H. A. "Designing Organizations for an Information-Rich World." In *Computers, Communications, and the Public Interest*, ed. M. Greenberger, 38–52. Baltimore: Johns Hopkins University Press, 1971.

Simon, H. A. *Administrative Behavior: A Study of Decision-Making Processes in Administrative Organizations.* New York: Free Press, 1997.

Singer, J. B. "Who Are These Guys? The Online Challenge to the Notion of Journalistic Professionalism." *Journalism* 4, no. 2 (2003): 139–63.

Smith, N. "Real Wars, Theory Wars." *Progress in Human Geography* 16, no. 2 (1992): 257–71.

Sparke, M. "Between Demythologizing and Deconstructing the Map: Shawnadithit's New-Found-Land and the Alienation of Canada." *Cartographica* 32, no. 1 (1995): 1–21.

Sparke, M. "A Map That Roared and an Original Atlas: Canada, Cartography, and the Narration of Nation." *Annals of the Association of American Geographers* 88, no. 3 (1998): 463–95.

Straubhaar, J. "Choosing National TV: Cultural Capital, Language, and Cultural Proximity in Brazil." In *The Impact of International Television: A Paradigm Shift*, ed. M. G. Elasmar, 77–110. Mahwah, NJ: Erlbaum, 2003.

Sunstein, C. R. *Infotopia*. Oxford: Oxford University Press, 2006.

Sunstein, C. R. *Republic.com*. Princeton, NJ: Princeton University Press, 2001.

Surowiecki, J. *The Wisdom of Crowds: Why the Many Are Smarter than the Few and How Collective Wisdom Shapes Business, Economies, Societies, and Nations*. New York: Doubleday, 2004.

Talen, E. "Bottom-up GIS: A New Tool for Individual and Group Expression in Participatory Planning." *Journal of the American Planning Association* 66, no. 3 (2000): 279–94.

Thelwall, M. "What Is This Link Doing Here? Beginning a Fine-Grained Process of Identifying Reasons for Academic Hyperlink Creation." *Information Research* 8, no. 3 (2003). http://informationr.net/ir/8-3/paper151.html.

Thompson, C. "Blogs to Riches: The Haves and Have-Nots of the Blogging Boom." *New York Magazine* 20 (February 2006). http://nymag.com/news/media/15967.

Tremayne, M. "News Websites as Gated Cybercommunities." *Convergence* 11, no. 3 (2005): 28–39.

Tremayne, M. "The Web of Context: Applying Network Theory to the Use of Hyperlinks in Journalism Stories on the Web." *Journalism and Mass Communication Quarterly* 81, no. 2 (2004): 237–53.

Tuchman, G. *Making News*. New York: Free Press, 1978.

Turner, F. J. *The Frontier in American History*. New York: Henry Holt and Company, 1921.

Turow, J. *Americans and Online Privacy: The System Is Broken*. Philadelphia, PA: Annenberg Public Policy Center, 2003. http://www.annenbergpublicpolicycenter.org/AreaDetails.aspx?myId=2.

Turow, J. *Breaking Up America: Advertisers and the New Media World*. Chicago: University of Chicago Press, 1997.

Turow, J. "The Critical Importance of Mass Communication as a Concept." In *Mediation, Information, and Communication: Information and Behavior*, ed. B. D. Ruben and L. Lievrouw, 3:9–20. New Brunswick, NJ: Transaction, 1990.

Turow, J. *Media Systems in Society: Understanding Industries, Strategies, and Power*. White Plains, NY: Longman, 1992.

Turow, J. *Niche Envy: Marketing Discrimination in the Digital Age*. Cambridge, MA: MIT Press, 2006.

Turow, J. *Open to Exploitation: American Shoppers Online and Offline*. Philadelphia, PA: Annenberg Public Policy Center, 2005. http://www.annenbergpublicpolicycenter.org/AreaDetails.aspx?myId=2.

Turow, J., C. Hoofnagle, D. Mulligan, N. Good, and J. Grossklags. "The FTC and Consumer Privacy in the Coming Decade." Paper presented at the Federal

Trade Commission meeting "Protecting Consumers in the Next Tech-ade," Washington, DC, November 8, 2006. http://www.annenbergpublicpolicycen ter.org/AreaDetails.aspx?myId=2.

United Nations Development Program. *Human Development Report 2006: Beyond Scarcity; Power, Poverty, and the Global Water Crisis.* Basingstoke Hampshire and New York: Palgrave Macmillan, 2006.

United States Joint Forces Command. *Geospatial Intelligence Support to Joint Operations.* Washington, DC, 2007.

Van der Veer Martens, B. "Do Citation Systems Represent Theories of Truth." *Information Research* 6, no. 2 (2001). http://informationr.net/ir/6-2/paper92.html.

Verba, S., K. L. Schlozman, and H. E. Brady. *Voice and Equality.* Cambridge, MA: Harvard University Press, 1995.

Verhulst, S. "Mediation, Mediators, and New Intermediaries." In *Media Diversity and Localism: Meaning and Metrics*, ed. P. Napoli, 113–37. Mahwah, NJ: Erlbaum, 2005.

Von Foerster, H. *Understanding Understanding: Essays on Cybernetics and Cognition.* New York: Springer-Verlag, 2006.

Von Sternberg, B. "From Geek to Chic: Blogs Gain Influence." *Star Tribune* (Minneapolis), September 22, 2004.

Walker, F. A. *Statistical Atlas of the United States.* New York: J. Bien, 1874.

Wallsten, P. "'Buckhead,' Who Said CBS Memos Were Forged, Is a GOP-Linked Attorney." *Seattle Times*, September 18, 2004. http://seattletimes.nwsource .com/html/ nationworld/2002039080_buckhead18.html.

Walsh, J. "Who Killed Dan Rather?" *Slate*, March 9, 2005. http://archive.salon .com/opinion/feature/2005/03/09/rather/index.html.

Walther, J. B. "Computer-Mediated Communication: Impersonal, Interpersonal, and Hyperpersonal Interaction." *Communication Research* 23, no. 1 (1996): 3–43.

Wang, Y. M., M. Ma, Y. Niu, and H. Chen. "Spam Double-Funnel: Connecting Web Spammers with Advertisers." Paper presented at the Sixteenth International World Wide Web Conference, Banff, Canada, May 8–12, 2007.

Webster, J. G. "Audience Behavior in the New Media Environment." *Journal of Communication* 36, no. 3 (1986): 77–91.

Webster, J. G. "Beneath the Veneer of Fragmentation: Television Audience Polarization in a Multichannel World." *Journal of Communication* 55, no. 2 (2005): 366–82.

Webster, J. G. "Diversity of Exposure." In *Media Diversity and Localism: Meaning and Metrics*, ed. P. Napoli, 309–25. Mahwah, NJ: Erlbaum, 2006.

Webster, J. G. "The Role of Structure in Media Choice." Forthcoming.

Webster, J. G., and S. F. Lin. "The Internet Audience: Web Use as Mass Behavior." *Journal of Broadcasting and Electronic Media* 46, no. 1 (2002): 1–12.

Webster, J. G., and P. F. Phalen. *The Mass Audience: Rediscovering the Dominant Model.* Mahwah, NJ: Erlbaum, 1997.

Webster, J. G., P. F. Phalen, and L. W. Lichty. *Ratings Analysis: The Theory and Practice of Audience Research.* 3rd ed. Mahwah, NJ: Erlbaum, 2006.

Wellman, B. "The Three Ages of Internet Studies: Ten, Five, and Zero Years Ago." *New Media and Society* 6, no. 1 (2004): 123–29.

Wells, H. G. *World Brain.* London: Methuen, 1938.

White, D. M. "The Gatekeeper: A Case Study in the Selection of News." *Journalism Quarterly* 27, no. 4 (1950): 383–90.

Winston, B. *Media Technology and Society: A History from the Telegraph to the Internet.* New York: Routledge, 1998.

Yeager, H. "Blogs, Bias, and 24-Hour News." *Financial Times*, September 24, 2006.

Yim, J. "Audience Concentration in the Media: Cross-Media Comparisons and the Introduction of the Uncertainty Measure." *Communication Monographs* 70, no. 2 (2003): 114–28.

Young, I. M. *Inclusion and Democracy.* Oxford: Oxford University Press, 2002.

Yuan, E. J., and J. G. Webster. "Channel Repertoires: Using Peoplemeter Data in Beijing." *Journal of Broadcasting and Electronic Media* 50, no. 3 (2006): 524–36.

Zaller, J. "A New Standard of News Quality: Burglar Alarms for the Monitorial Citizen." *Political Communication* 20, no. 2 (2003): 109–30.

Zittrain, J. "A History of Online Gatekeeping." *Harvard Journal of Law and Technology* 19, no. 2 (2006): 253–98.

About the Authors

Lada A. Adamic is an assistant professor at the School of Information and the Center for the Study of Complex Systems at the University of Michigan. Her research interests center on information dynamics in networks: how information diffuses, how it can be found, and how it influences the evolution of a network's structure. This has led her to study human interactions in digital media, including blogs, e-mail, and online social networks.

Jeremy W. Crampton is an associate professor of geography at Georgia State University in Atlanta. His research interests focus on the role of maps and mapping in the production of knowledge and particularly on the politics of space. He maintains two blogs: one on the work of Michel Foucault and the other (written under a pseudonym) on mapping. His book *The Political Mapping of Cyberspace* was published by the University of Chicago Press in 2004. His latest book is *Space, Knowledge, and Power: Foucault and Geography* (London: Ashgate, 2007), coedited with Stuart Elden.

Seth Finkelstein is a professional programmer who has donated his skills and an enormous amount of time to fighting to keep the Internet free. He attended MIT, earning degrees in both physics and mathematics, and learned about the potential of electronic communication during its early development. He was the first person to decrypt censorware ("filter") secret blacklists, and expose what was actually banned. The material he developed first brought these issues to public attention and was the basis for many groundbreaking articles and reports about censorware. This work then generated evidence for an early court case challenging censorware in public libraries. He was a cofounder of an investigatory organization called Censorware Project (though he is no longer associated with it). For his achievements opposing Internet censorship, he was honored with a

Pioneer Award from the Electronic Frontier Foundation. He was primarily responsible for winning one of few Library of Congress exemptions from the Digital Millennium Copyright Act.

Alexander Halavais is an assistant professor of communication at the University at Buffalo's School of Informatics, where he also directs the MA program in informatics. His research looks at "social computing" and its impact on social change, journalism, education, and public policy. The *Online Journalism Review* recently referred to Halavais as one of a number of new "blogologists" who seek to study the social effects of this use of the Internet. Much of this work examines the intersection of geographical location and online content. In particular, he has analyzed the hyperlinked networks among nations, cities, blogs, and political Web sites. He has written a set of tools (the Informicant package) that may be used to facilitate data collection from the Web. In addition to teaching about new information technologies, Halavais teaches communication theory at the undergraduate and graduate levels. He has recently edited a reader called *Cyberporn and Society* and teaches a course on the same topic.

Eszter Hargittai is an assistant professor of communication studies and sociology and a faculty associate of the Institute for Policy Research at Northwestern University, where she heads the Web Use Project. She received her PhD in sociology from Princeton University, where she was a Woodrow Wilson Scholar. She was a fellow at the Center for Advanced Study in the Behavioral Sciences at Stanford in 2006/7. Her work focuses on the social and policy implications of information technologies. She has her own Web site at http://www.eszter.com.

Tom Hespos has been working in online advertising since the commercial explosion of the World Wide Web in 1994. As one of the first professionals in buying online media, Tom has held management-level positions at K2 Design, Blue Marble ACG, Mezzina Brown & Partners, and his own agency, Underscore Marketing. Tom also writes regularly for industry trade publications. Since early 1998, he has published a weekly column on buying online media, in such publications as *ClickZ*, *Media-Post*, and *iMedia Connection*. His writing has also appeared in *Business 2.0*, the *Industry Standard*, *DM News*, and many other business publications. Tom is also the founder of the Old Timers List, a private discussion list for experienced online marketing professionals. He blogs at http://www.hespos.com.

Matthew Hindman is an assistant professor of political science at Arizona State University. He was previously a fellow at Harvard's Kennedy School of Government and holds a doctorate from Princeton University. He is currently completing a book about the Internet's impact on American politics.

Philip M. Napoli is an associate professor in the Graduate School of Business and director of the Donald McGannon Communication Research Center at Fordham University. His research focuses on media institutions and media policy. Professor Napoli's books include *Media Diversity and Localism: Meaning and Metrics* (Mahwah, NJ: Erlbaum, 2007); *Audience Economics: Media Institutions and the Audience Marketplace* (New York: Columbia University Press, 2003); and *Foundations of Communications Policy: Principles and Process in the Regulation of Electronic Media* (Cresskill, NJ: Hampton, 2001). His research has been supported by such organizations as the Ford Foundation, the Social Science Research Council, the Benton Foundation, and the National Association of Broadcasters.

Martin Nisenholtz was named senior vice president of digital operations for the New York Times Company in February 2005. He is responsible for the strategy development, operations, and management of the New York Times Company's digital properties. Martin joined the Times Company in 1995 as the founding leader for the *New York Times* on the Web (NYTimes.com). In 1983, Martin founded the Interactive Marketing Group at Ogilvy & Mather, the first interactive development group at a major U.S. agency. He holds a BA degree from the University of Pennsylvania and an MA from that university's Annenberg School for Communication.

Eric Picard is a senior product planner in the Microsoft Digital Advertising Solutions group. He leads a team focused on business strategies for emerging digital media advertising opportunities, such as digital TV, mobile, video games, and music. Eric is also Microsoft's representative to a variety of Interactive Advertising Board (IAB) committees. Eric has been active in most of the critical industry conversations related to technology, including the IAB's Broadband Committee, Rich Media Task Force, and Measurement Task Force. He writes a monthly column called "Using Ad Technology" for the industry publication *ClickZ* and is a frequent speaker at industry conferences.

Markus Prior is an assistant professor of politics and public affairs in the Woodrow Wilson School and the Department of Politics at Princeton University. He received his PhD from Stanford's Department of Communication in 2004. He is the author of *Post-Broadcast Democracy* (New York: Cambridge University Press, 2007), an early version of which won the American Political Science Association's E. E. Schattschneider Award for the best dissertation in American politics. The book examines how broadcast television, cable television, and the Internet have changed politics in the United States over the last half century. His work has also appeared in the *American Political Science Review*, the *American Journal of Political Science*, the *Journal of Politics*, and *Political Communication*.

Stacey Lynn Schulman is senior vice president of Turner Entertainment Ad Sales Research. Within her role, Schulman works closely with David Levy, president of Turner Entertainment Ad Sales and with the Ad Sales executive management teams for Adult Swim, Cartoon Network, Court TV, TBS, and TNT, as well as Turner Sports. Through January 2007, Ms. Schulman was president of the Consumer Experience Practice of the Interpublic Group Companies, which advised marketers on how to effectively connect with consumers in the evolving media landscape. Widely respected in the industry, she is an award-winning professional who is routinely quoted in trade and consumer media outlets, and has appeared on CNN, CNBC, and FOX News Channel to discuss media trends. In addition to her professional commitments, Ms. Schulman is an adjunct faculty member at the Massachusetts Institute of Technology. She resides in Harlem.

Marc A. Smith is a senior research sociologist at Microsoft Research (MSR) specializing in the social organization of online communities. He leads the Community Technologies Group at MSR. He is the coeditor of *Communities in Cyberspace* (London: Routledge, 1999), a collection of essays exploring the ways identity, interaction, and social order develop in online groups. Smith's research focuses on the ways group dynamics change when they take place in social cyberspaces. Smith is applying this work to the development of a generalized community platform for Microsoft, providing a Web-based system for groups of all sizes to discuss and publish their material to the Web. Smith received a BS in international area studies from Drexel University in Philadelphia in 1988, an MPhil in social theory from Cambridge University in 1990, and a PhD in sociology from the University of California, Los Angeles, in 2001.

Lokman Tsui is a doctoral candidate at the Annenberg School for Communication of the University of Pennsylvania. His dissertation examines how information communication technologies are being mobilized to address imbalances in global news flows. His research has appeared in *Global Dialogue, China Information,* and the newsletter for the International Institute for Asian Studies. He has served as guest editor of *China Information* for a theme issue on the sociopolitical impact of the Internet in China. His research interests also include collaborative and participatory media, filtering and censorship, (regulation of) flows of information and people, diaspora and transnationalism, and global and comparative communication research. He divides his time between Philadelphia, Amsterdam, and Hong Kong.

Joseph Turow is the Robert Lewis Shayon Professor of Communication at the University of Pennsylvania's Annenberg School for Communication. He is the author of more than sixty articles and nine books on mass media industries, including *Niche Envy: Marketing Discrimination in the Digital Age* (Cambridge, MA: MIT Press, 2006). His continuing national surveys of the American public on issues relating to marketing, new media, and society have received much attention in the popular press as well as in the research community. His research has received financial support from the John D. and Catherine T. MacArthur Foundation, the Kaiser Family Foundation, the Robert Wood Johnson Foundation, the Federal Communications Commission, and the National Endowment for the Humanities, among other organizations.

Stefaan G. Verhulst is the chief of research at the Markle Foundation. Prior to his arrival there, Mr. Verhulst was the cofounder and codirector, with Prof. Monroe Price, of the Programme in Comparative Media Law and Policy (PCMLP) at Oxford University, as well as senior research fellow at the Centre for Socio-Legal Studies. In that capacity, he was appointed the sociolegal research fellow at Wolfson College, Oxford. In addition, he was the UNESCO chairholder in communications law and policy for the United Kingdom. Before his move to Oxford in 1996, he had been a lecturer on communications law and policy issues in Belgium and founder and codirector of the International Media and Info-Comms Policy and Law Studies program at the University of Glasgow's School of Law. Mr. Verhulst has served as consultant to various international and national organizations, including the Council of Europe, the European Commission, UNESCO, the United Nations Development Programme, the U.S. Agency for International Development, and the Department for International Development in the United Kingdom.

James G. Webster is a professor of communication studies at Northwestern University. His research interests include audience measurement, communications policy, and understanding audience behavior in the new media environment. He is the author of *Ratings Analysis: The Theory and Practice of Audience Research* (2006), which is now in its third edition, and coauthor of *The Mass Audience: Rediscovering the Dominant Model* (Mahwah, NJ: Erlbaum, 1997). He has been a member of the editorial board of the *Journal of Broadcasting and Electronic Media* since 1985.

David Weinberger is the author of *Everything Is Miscellaneous: The Power of the New Digital Disorder* (New York: Times Books, 2007) and *Small Pieces Loosely Joined* (New York: Basic Books, 2002) and coauthor of *The Cluetrain Manifesto* (New York: Basic Books, 2000). He is currently a fellow at Harvard's Berkman Center for Internet and Society. He has a doctorate in philosophy and has been an assistant professor, a marketing VP, and an advisor to political campaigns. He lives in Boston.

Index